A
SEASON
INSIDE

VILLARD BOOKS
NEW YORK
1988

A
SEASON
INSIDE

One Year in
College Basketball

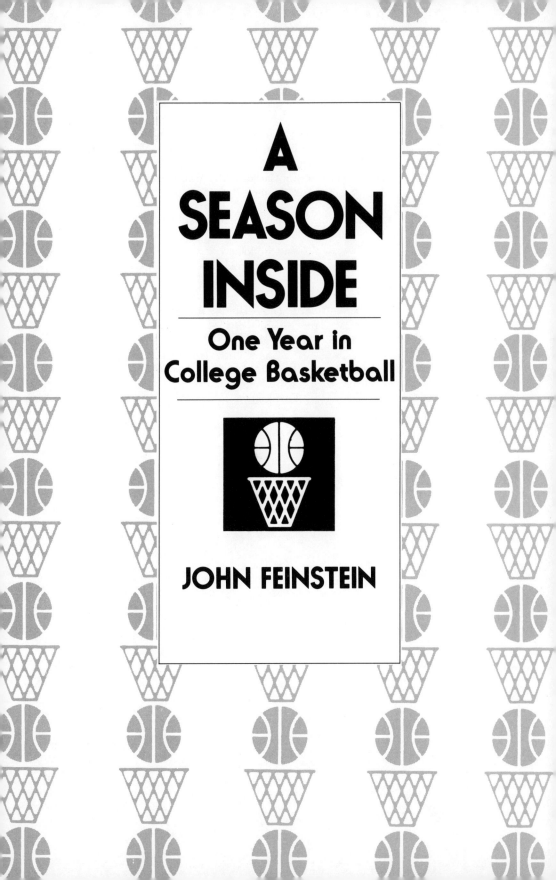

JOHN FEINSTEIN

Library of Congress Cataloging-in-Publication Data

Feinstein, John.
A season inside.

1. Basketball—United States—History. 2. College
sports—United States—History. I. Title.
GV885.7.F45   1988   796.32'363'0973   88-40147
ISBN 0-394-56891-5

Manufactured in the United States of America
9 8 7 6 5 4 3 2
First Edition

For Mary Clare . . .
who made it all worthwhile

INTRODUCTION

The sun was just beginning to appear on the eastern horizon when we walked out the front door of the hotel. It was a few minutes before 7 A.M. on the third day of the NCAA basketball tournament. As I opened the trunk, Hoops looked at me through the slits that passed at the moment for his eyes and asked, "Where are we going?"

I had to think for a moment. "Notre Dame," I finally said, pleased with myself.

Hoops nodded. "Who are we seeing play?"

That one was too much. I was stumped. I reached into my coat pocket for my schedule. As I did, I almost dropped my coffee, which would have been a major catastrophe, and started to lose my footing on the ice. But I hung on to both, with as much grace as possible—which wasn't much—and pulled the schedule out. "Purdue–Memphis State, and DePaul–Kansas State," I announced.

Hoops said nothing. I started the car. We pulled out of the hotel and onto the interstate, heading fifty miles north for the Dayton Airport. "Hey, you know what," Hoops said. "This is going to be fun. I'm really psyched."

I sipped the coffee. Like Hoops, I was beginning to wake up too. "Another day, another plane, another tip-off. What else is there in life?"

Hoops—who in real life is Dick Weiss of the *Philadelphia Daily*

News—had been with me since Thursday. We had seen four NCAA Tournament games that day in Chapel Hill, leaving the Deandome at 1 A.M. Up at 5:30, we had flown to Cincinnati, arrived in the middle of a snowstorm, and seen four more games. Now, the second round was beginning and we were off to South Bend for a mere doubleheader. If all went well, we would drive two hours from South Bend to Chicago that night and fly to Lincoln, Nebraska, Sunday for one more double-header.

Four days, four cities, four planes, four hotels, and twelve games. What the hell, it was March. "We can rest," Hoops said, "on April fifth."

He was right of course. March is for basketball. April is for resting. And the rest of the summer is waiting for basketball to start again. Purdue and Kansas State won that day. We had fun. Of course.

Ed Tapscott, the very articulate basketball coach at American University, once said this about his sport: "Basketball is a culture. If you don't grow up with it or come to understand it completely, you can never really appreciate it. But if you do, no one can ever say anything that will change the way you feel about it."

Everyone who loves a sport makes arguments for why it is the best. I love baseball, always have and always will. But I *live* basketball, specifically college basketball. I can still remember the chills I felt during the first college basketball game I saw in the old Madison Square Garden—the 1965 NIT final—when the St. John's student section filled the old arena up with chants of, "Let's go, Red-Men," and I can still feel the chills I felt on April 4, 1988, when the Kansas band played its fight song while Danny Manning and his teammates jumped all over each other in the middle of Kemper Arena. Twenty-three years have gone by and the feeling never changes.

What I set out to do in this book is to explain the culture. The date October 15 is part of the culture, and so are the war stories of recruiting and the great rivalries and the old gyms and snowy nights in the Midwest and even balmy afternoons in Hawaii when two teams play a great game in front of five hundred people. The culture is full of characters, both good guys and bad guys. Each year there are different stories, new heroes and new villains. Some things never change, others always do.

While I wanted to see as much as I could, I knew I could not see everything. There are many superb stories to be told in Division 2 and Division 3 and on the NAIA and junior college levels. Hersey Hawkins of Bradley had one of the great seasons in 1987–88 that any college guard has had in recent years. I didn't get to see him play except on television and I feel I missed out. I missed the earthquake in Alaska because I got sick—thank goodness it only happened once all season—and I wish I had been there to see Richmond upset Indiana. I couldn't see everything. But I tried.

In all, I saw 104 college basketball games, assorted high school games, a couple of games in an armed forces tournament, and several dozen practices. I selected a group of players and coaches to be the main tellers of this story, to try as best I could to tell the story of one season in this game, and this culture, through their eyes. The book is not exclusively their story, but a large portion of it is.

I have many memories of this season. Some of them are those that millions saw on their TV screens: Danny Manning's extraordinary NCAA performance, Billy King's defense on Mark Macon, the sadness of the Purdue seniors in their final game, and the joy of the Tennessee players the night they upset Kentucky and probably saved their coach's job.

But two of the stories I have told in the book stick with me as I begin my annual countdown to October 15: One is the memory of the Villanova players, less than four hours before they would play Big Bad Kentucky in the NCAA Tournament, staging their game-day sing-along, rolling in the aisles with one another laughing, all of them caught up in the sheer joy of just being there. As I sat with them, I couldn't help remembering my experience in 1986 in Indiana, where Bob Knight didn't allow anyone to talk during the pregame meal, thinking, "My God, these are a bunch of kids who are going to play a *game.*" That was all it was. Not life or death, just a game. And the Villanova kids went out and pounded the oh-so-serious Wildcats, shocking the hell out of all those Kentucky fans who think the game is a religion.

My other vivid memory of this past season is walking into a tiny bar in Clemson, South Carolina, in January, trailing Lefty Driesell and hearing the place literally erupt as he walked through the door. If there has ever been a cult hero, it is Charles G. Driesell. That's what this book is about. A culture and some of the people who make it what it is. College basketball is a game played inside. This is the story of one season inside college basketball. Not all of it, but everything that can be done if you can get from Chapel Hill to Cincinnati to South Bend to Lincoln in four days.

It was fun. Right, Hoops?

—JOHN FEINSTEIN, SHELTER ISLAND, N.Y.
MAY 1988

A
SEASON
INSIDE

1
THE
CHAMPIONS

April 4, 1988 . . . Kansas City

For a split second, he didn't move. The ball was cradled in his hands the way a doctor might hold a newborn; the grip firm, yet soft and clearly full of love, with just a touch of wonder. Danny Manning loved this moment, perhaps more than any other in his entire life. He had fantasized it thousands of times and now, when it was real, he wasn't quite sure whether to believe it.

But his eyes and ears told him it was true. He looked at the Kemper Arena scoreboard and there it was: Kansas–83, Oklahoma–79. And the clock said :00. The questions had all been answered. The basketball was his to keep and so was this feeling. If it had been tangible, Manning would have gripped the feeling so tightly he might have choked it. Instead, he had the ball.

When a full second passed and he still hadn't jolted awake in bed to realize it was just another dream, when he heard the cheers of joy still ringing in his ears and understood that it was 10:09 P.M. on a warm April night in Kansas City and he, Daniel Edward Manning, had become a part of history, he reacted. His face exploded into a look of utter ecstasy and he began searching for people to hug.

He didn't have far to go. Chris Piper was running toward him, arms in the air, his head back, screeching something that was unintelligible to Manning. It didn't matter. Piper had been there all four years at Kansas with Manning. They had suffered together, living through all the near-misses and the key injuries, wondering often if there was such a thing as a happy ending and holding each other as if the other were a life raft when it seemed so often that their epitaph would be, "If Only . . ."

Now, there would be no epitaph, just a legacy—and a happy ending. And so, as was only right, Manning and Piper fell into each other's arms, living a moment so filled with happiness that, later, it hardly seemed real. Then their teammates were climbing on them, clutching and grabbing at them, each player a part of this because no one—not even their coaches—among the thousands in the arena or the millions watching on television could understand how this felt. For that brief moment, before fans and officials and TV types and newspaper people interrupted, it was just the Jayhawks, piling on one another, sharing a feeling that was theirs and theirs alone.

They had won a national championship. They had beaten 290 other teams and they had beaten the odds. They had beaten their own self-doubts and they had beaten a season that seemed to have beaten them on a couple dozen occasions. The coaches had put in the hours too and felt the pain, but for coaches it was different. Ten years from now they would still be coaching. College basketball players have a brief lifespan. They are freshmen one minute; alumni, it seems, only seconds later.

Within minutes of Manning's grabbing that last rebound, the rest of the world would intrude on them. Manning and Coach Larry Brown would be hustled in front of the television cameras. The others would find microphones and cameras and pencils surrounding them. They would all look into the stands for family and for friends to begin to share the joy with them. But those first few seconds belonged to them and to no one else. No one.

One of the most intelligent things the people at CBS do in those initial moments following the last game of the basketball season is shut up. Eventually, millions of words will be written and spoken about this game, this team, this night. Briefly, though, the pictures speak the most eloquent words of all.

No one needed to describe what Danny Manning had just done. No one needed to say anything about the feelings of Stacey King, the wonderful Oklahoma forward who sat on the scorer's table sobbing. And, as the Jayhawks unpiled, there was little doubt about what Manning would do next. He headed straight for his mother. When he was a little boy and his father was away playing ball or coaching ball or driving a truck to keep food on the family table, Danny Manning's best friend was his mother. She had shared his tears and felt his sorrow and, when his father couldn't be there, his loneliness. More than anyone, she had convinced him to stay in college a fourth year, to pass up the mind-boggling NBA money for twelve more months. Now, she shared his joy and a feeling that millions and millions of dollars could never buy.

A few feet away, Ed Manning was being a coach. He had sat on the Kansas bench almost paralyzed during those final seconds, his heart pounding so hard he was afraid his son might hear it. Twice, Danny had gone to the foul line in the last fourteen seconds with the game in the balance. Twice, he had calmly made both free throws. When the buzzer finally went off, Ed Manning wanted to race to his son, embrace him and tell him how proud he was and how much he loved him.

But Ed Manning is an assistant basketball coach, a professional. So he did the professional thing. He went looking for the losers to shake hands, to offer condolences. Two days earlier when Kansas had beaten Duke in the semifinals, he had sought out Billy King, who, as a high school senior, had chosen to play for Duke over Kansas. When they shook hands, King had started to cry and Ed Manning knew this could easily have been his son crying those tears. He had put his arms around the losing player and comforted him.

It was a good three or four minutes into the championship celebration before father and son finally found each other. The embrace was brief, but Ed Manning said what he wanted to say: "I told you so," he whispered, and Danny nodded because his father was one person who had never stopped believing.

On the Kansas bench, Larry Brown sat dry-eyed, surrounded by close friends and family. He had always believed Danny Manning could be this kind of basketball player, that he was good enough to carry a team to the national championship. His job, for four years, had been to convince Danny that he was that good. Brown had screamed and pleaded and cajoled. He had called Danny names and looked him in the eye as if to say, "If you were a man, you would deck me."

Often, Manning just pressed a button inside his head and tuned the little coach out. He was sick of the yelling, to the point where he almost ignored his mother's advice; he had wanted to get away from his last year with the intense little coach. Only at the end did he really understand what Brown had been telling him. "The best player has to be the leader, Danny. It has to be *your* team, not *my* team. You can tell them things I can't. Don't worry about the past or what people say or think. Just play."

Finally, he had just played. Brown knew that for all the x's and o's he had drawn, for all the pep talks he had given, the one thing he had done to bring this about was get through to Manning. Often, he had thought that would never happen. As recently as February he had screamed at Manning for not breaking up a locker-room fight. "You sit there and watch like one of the guys," he told Manning. "Goddamn it, when are you going to realize you're *not* one of the guys!"

Just in time, Manning realized it. And so, this night was his. Within minutes of accepting the national championship trophy, Larry Brown would be asked where he planned to coach next year. "All I want to do," he said, "is say the words, 'We won the national championship.' "

He said them and smiled, totally happy. At least for a minute.

For every bit of elation Kansas felt, Oklahoma felt pain. While the Kansas players piled on one another, the Sooners watched. They didn't see, of course, because each of them was, in a sense, blinded by his own thoughts. Like the Jayhawks, just like every player who has ever put on a college uniform, they had fantasized themselves in that pile. To be so close, only to end up watching, is a feeling so awful that the losers usually can't describe it. It is a little bit like being shot. At first, the shock is so great you don't quite understand how badly you have been hurt.

Thirty-five times, the Sooners had done their victory jig. They were the outlaws, the team so strong no one could kick sand back in their faces, even though everyone was dying to do it. This team was a bully, a big, frightening, lightning-quick bully that beat you to a pulp and then jumped on you with both feet while you lay on the floor bleeding and helpless.

But now, the bully had been transformed into a group of heartbroken kids. Too often, those who merely watch say it is only a game. When you focus your mind on one thing for 173 straight days and come up two or three plays short of achieving that one thing, it is not just a game. When your life has been devoted, first and foremost, to basketball for almost as long as you can remember being alive, there is more than just a game involved.

National championship games become part of forever, especially now when everything is on tape, when the media crush is so overwhelming. If Indiana's Keith Smart had a dollar for every time his shot, the one that beat Syracuse in 1987, had been replayed, he could buy himself a team, an arena, and a couple of cities. Manning's postbuzzer joy and King's tears were now part of tournament history. Neither player would forget this night, could ever forget this night, nor could anyone else who took part.

In the front row of the arena, close enough to feel the game, to almost reach out and touch the game, sat the players from Duke and Arizona. That was as close as they would come, however. The Blue Devils, in coats and ties, and the Wildcats, in shorts and jeans, all wished desperately that they were in uniform that night. Each of them had believed two days earlier that they would be playing in this game, that they were good enough to be the ones cutting down the nets, the final act of any important championship celebration.

Now, like everyone else, they were spectators. They didn't feel the pain the Sooners felt, just a dull ache at what might have been. "All I could think," said Arizona's Steve Kerr, "was that we were *supposed* to be out there."

Ironically, players from the two teams had happened upon one another the previous evening in a bar. They ended up drinking together until dawn, drawn toward each other because of shared suffering. If things had been different, they would have met in front of millions of people and there would have been no room for friendship or camaraderie. Instead, while only several dozen people watched, they drank, told jokes, and clung spiritually to one another, trying to forget.

All four teams had gone through a lot to get to Kansas City. They were the last four among 291 who started. In the end, though, only one team can feel what Kansas felt. Everyone else becomes a spectator.

But in October, when the leaves are turning and the weather is just starting to get brisk, everyone is Danny Manning or Keith Smart. Some know they can't be The One, not really, but they dream about it anyway. Others know they have a chance and they think about it more often. Others believe it to be their destiny. Often, they become obsessed by it.

Unlike any other sport, they all begin at the same time. The same day every year. No other sport is as precise. They all begin together, each of them pointing for the same night. Only two make it there. And, among approximately 3,500 college basketball players, no more than fifteen get to feel the oh-so-pure joy of being The Champion.

Kansas won in 1988, but it was not the only winner. Winning and losing is certainly very much a part of college basketball, as with any other sport. But to those who point each year to October 15 the way little children point to Christmas, the season is a companion, a way of life, a certainty you can cling to. To those who love the sport, the feeling each spring as the national champions celebrate is a mixed one: There is joy for the winners, sadness for the losers, and an empty feeling because the season is over.

But there is also a bright side: While the hopes of last October are six months removed, the fantasies of next October are only six months away.

2
IN THE
BEGINNING . . .

Larry Brown had one of those looks on his face that Danny Manning
didn't like to see. Manning was about to escape Allen Field House,
having gone through the regimen of Kansas's annual Media Day, to
spend a few hours relaxing before coming back late that evening to start
the basketball season. Practice began at *exactly* 12:01 A.M. on October
15. This was a three-year-old tradition at Kansas, something Manning
looked forward to because it was like a giant coming-out party. But
now, the man for whom the occasion was named—"Late Night with
Larry Brown"—was calling his name, and it wasn't to tell a joke.

"When are you guys going to come over tonight?" Brown asked the
best player he had ever coached.

"Don't know, maybe about ten-thirty or so."

Brown stiffened. "Look, Danny, you decide what time and you tell
the other guys. You make sure they're here, okay? You're in charge."

Manning nodded. Practice didn't formally begin for another nine
hours and already Brown was starting again. He wondered again if he
hadn't made a mistake passing up the NBA for his last year of college.
But, looking around the floor, Manning saw the reasons he had stayed.
In one corner, Archie Marshall was answering reporters' questions.
Eighteen months earlier, in a Final Four game against Duke, Marshall

had crashed to the floor of Reunion Arena in Dallas, his knee torn up. He had sat out the entire 1987 season, rehabilitating the knee so he could come back and play with Manning one last season.

During the springtime, when Manning was in the throes of deciding whether to return to Kansas or take the pro money, Archie Marshall had said mournfully to Manning's mother, "Mrs. Manning, Danny's going to turn pro and I'll never get to play with him again."

"Archie, don't you worry," Darnelle Manning had said. "I'll take care of that."

She had done just that. Never once had she told her son he had to stay in school or wailed about him getting his degree. But Danny knew how she felt and he wanted to play with Archie. And, he wanted another year with his dad, who was standing quietly a few feet away while Brown was telling Danny one more time that he was in charge.

Ed Manning is one of those huge men who has never felt the need to be terribly verbal. He played pro basketball for nine years, a power forward at 6–7 ½, a player who made up for a lack of natural talent with desire and hard work. His son, so much more gifted, had yet to acquire his father's toughness. That frustrated Ed Manning at least as much as it frustrated Brown. And, on occasions when Brown and Ed Manning would yell at her son during games, Darnelle Manning would sit in the stands and think, "Why are they always yelling at that child?"

She knew the answer, just as her son knew the answer. Both coaches saw one thing in Danny Manning: greatness. Both felt an obligation to bring out that greatness. It had not been easy for any of them. Now, standing on the brink of their last season together, Brown, Ed Manning, and Danny Manning all knew this was the last time around. October 15, 1987, was an ending as well as a beginning. Once midnight struck that evening, every hour of every day would put Danny Manning closer to the end of a college career that had begun with soaring hopes three years earlier. Many of those hopes had been realized, but there were still doubts, still questions about whether Manning would ever play up to his extraordinary potential.

One thing Manning knew for certain: His coach and his father would be on him nonstop from 12:01 A.M. until whenever. . . .

While Kansas was gathering for its annual party, 290 other basketball teams were doing the same thing, many of them practicing at 12:01 A.M., too. In the last ten years, as the money available to the sixty-four teams that make it to the NCAA Tournament has run amok—each Final Four team received $1.1 million in 1988—more and more schools have joined Division 1 of the NCAA hoping for a piece of that huge cake.

Because it only takes twelve players to field a team and only one or two stars to have a good team, Division 1 schools come in all shapes and sizes. The Big East, considered by many the most powerful basketball conference in America, has six schools so small that they do not field Division 1 football teams. (It takes at least forty players to man a football squad, often fifty or sixty. One star, or two or three, for that matter, cannot bring glory—or a million dollars—to a football school.) Georgetown, the 1984 national basketball champion, plays football in Division 3. So does Villanova, the 1985 national basketball champion. There are Division 1 schools with gyms that can barely hold two thousand people, Division 1 schools that most people don't even know are in Division 1. How about Radford, Akron, and Winthrop, to name a few? Or, for that matter, Baptist, Monmouth, and Florida Southern. No Orange Bowl teams in that group.

That is why, on October 15, everyone has hope. If Cleveland State can beat Indiana in the NCAA Tournament, if Arkansas–Little Rock can beat Notre Dame, if North Carolina–Charlotte can be one shot away from reaching the national title game, then anyone with twelve uniforms, two backboards, and a few basketballs can think themselves next March's David.

At Kansas, there was no talk about David. Only about this being Manning's last shot. "Danny's the best player in the country," Brown said that afternoon. "And I feel good about the way we coach." He paused and said something coaches aren't supposed to say. "Deep down, I'd be disappointed if we didn't win it all. That's the only way I'd really be satisfied: if we won the national championship."

Brown was not the only coach and Kansas not the only school with those kinds of thoughts on that Wednesday afternoon. At Arizona, Lute Olson looked at the team that took the floor for the first day of practice and thought back four years, to his first practice in Tucson, and couldn't help but smile. "I remembered walking off the floor after that practice and looking at my assistants and saying, 'What have we done? What have we gotten ourselves into?' "

Olson had left a Top Twenty program at Iowa to take over a 4–24 Arizona team; he opted for the sun over security. The only player who had been at that first practice in 1983 who was on the floor now was Steve Kerr. Olson offered Kerr his last available scholarship that first year, largely out of desperation. He had seen Kerr playing in the Los Angeles summer league. Kerr was too slow and couldn't jump, but he could shoot. If Olson had still been at Iowa, he wouldn't have given Kerr a second glance. But, starting from square one, he was willing to take a chance. Even though when his wife Bobbi saw Kerr play, her reaction was, "Lute, you've got to be *kidding.*"

Lute wasn't kidding, he was desperate. And so Steve Kerr landed at Arizona. No one, not Kerr, not Olson, could imagine the extraordinary story Kerr would write there. Midway through his freshman year, Kerr's father was assassinated in Beirut, shot twice in the head as he stepped off an elevator on his way to work. Two nights later, because he thought that was what his father would have wanted, Kerr played against Arizona State.

He broke down during a pregame moment of silence, but when he came into the game he hit his first shot—and ended up scoring 12 points during an easy Wildcat victory. From that day forward, Kerr was Tucson's adopted son. He became a starter as a sophomore, an all-Pacific 10 player as a junior, and made the World Championship team coached by Olson during the summer of 1986. Late in the Americans' semifinal game against Brazil, Kerr went up to pass, came down wrong, and landed writhing in pain, his knee torn up.

The initial diagnosis was simple: torn ligaments, a probable career-ending injury. Kerr cried that night, but he never gave up. He went through reconstructive surgery, spent the winter rehabilitating the knee and the summer getting back into playing shape. Now, as practice began, the knee felt fine and Kerr was eager, though nervous since it had been fifteen months since he had played in a real game.

In West Lafayette, Indiana, the trepidation on opening day had nothing to do with injuries, although Troy Lewis, Purdue's leading scorer in 1987, had broken his foot in early September. Lewis would be fine long before the season began.

But Lewis knew, as did fellow seniors Todd Mitchell and Everette Stephens, that this was going to be a difficult season. During their first three years at Purdue, the Boilermakers had won sixty-seven games. They had played in three NCAA Tournaments. They had been Big Ten cochampions in 1987 along with Indiana, the Bob Knight-coached team that had gone on to win the national championship.

Each March, however, Purdue had come up shy: a first-round loss to Auburn in 1985, a first-round loss to Louisiana State in 1986, a second-round loss to Florida in 1987. In '85, they had been freshmen, a young team just learning. Okay. In '86, they had been sent to play at LSU, an unfair draw since they were seeded higher than the Tigers. They lost in overtime. Okay. But in '87 they played Florida in Syracuse, a perfectly reasonable place against a beatable team. They lost by 20.

No excuses were left. And Coach Gene Keady had made it clear all summer that he was miserable about the way the '87 season had ended—a 36-point loss to Michigan in the regular-season finale, ending their chance to win the Big Ten outright, didn't help Keady's mood— and that the three seniors had better show from day one that they were going to be the leaders of this team. Keady wanted to make damn sure they weren't going to accept any more March failures. He wasn't.

"We know," Todd Mitchell said, "that nothing we do before March really matters. We've done everything else. We're going to be judged on one thing this season, the NCAA Tournament. That's fine with us. That's the way it should be."

But already, even before the first practice began, there were tensions. There were two other seniors on the team, Jeff Arnold and Dave Stack, who were academically ineligible to play. When Keady had called the senior trio that August to ask them how they felt about the situation, their answer had been unanimous and blunt: Get rid of them. Arnold and Stack, in their minds, had been in trouble almost from day one at Purdue. They really didn't deserve another chance.

Keady thought the team needed Arnold, who was 6–10 and could rebound coming off the bench. "One more chance," he told the seniors.

Okay, they thought, one more chance. Arnold and Stack were at practice that first day. It was the beginning of their last chance.

The tension that existed as practice began at Villanova was very different from Purdue. Rollie Massimino, the little coach who had become a megastar almost overnight in his championship season of 1985, had been through the worst season of his coaching life in 1987.

His team wasn't very good. The final record had been 15–16. But that was only a small part of the problem. In December, Massimino had learned that Gary McLain, the starting point guard on that miraculous 1985 team, was in the process of selling a story to *Sports Illustrated* in which he confessed, at length, to having used and sold cocaine while at Villanova. Even worse, McLain claimed in the story that Massimino had been aware of the problem but had never done anything beyond warning him to stop. The implication was that Massimino didn't want to deal with McLain's addiction just so long as McLain continued to play well.

Given a choice between being accused of that kind of exploitation or of having both his hands cut off, Massimino would have willingly given up his hands. Always, he had prided himself on the family atmosphere he had created at Villanova, not just because his players graduated but because even after they left, they were still part of Villanova and Villanova basketball. This was a coach who got his players up at 5:30 in the morning during preseason to work out, and then gave them milk and cookies after the workout.

Now, for a price, Gary McLain was going to tell the world Rollie Massimino *didn't* care, that he was just another coach who cared only about winning. It would be March before the story appeared. But Massimino knew in December. He told no one. "We noticed something was wrong with him," said Mark Plansky, a junior on that team. "He wasn't himself. The emotion just wasn't there. But we had no idea what it was."

Massimino is known as the Danny DeVito of coaches. It doesn't matter how many thousands of dollars he spends on clothes, he always ends up looking like an unmade bed at the end of a game. "He starts the game looking great," his son R. C. once said, "but by halftime he's sort of unraveled."

Not in 1987. Massimino might as well have been Tom Landry on the bench. "I was," he remembered, "a mannequin."

When the story broke, his players and friends understood why he had been so distracted all season. Just before publication, Massimino talked to McLain. "He told me, 'Coach, I'm doing this to help kids. Nothing will happen to you or the program because you are too big.'"

That was a little hard for Massimino to swallow since McLain had only told his story in return for a lot of money—about $20,000. But he had to live with it and deal with it.

"The whole thing was scary," Massimino said. "Honest to God, I swear on my five children, if I had known, I would have tried to help him. I always tell our guys that if they have a problem and they come to me, I'll help them. But if I catch them, they're history.

"I always thought I knew my people and my kids. This time I didn't. I take responsibility for that but it hurt me to think anyone could believe I would know what was going on and not do anything about it."

A press conference was called to respond to the McLain story. For an hour beforehand, Massimino sat in his office with university lawyers poring through a carefully worded statement, rehearsing what to say and what not to say. Finally, it all kicked in.

"I got up, ran out of the office and said I couldn't do this," he remembered. "I went into [Assistant Coach] Steve Lappas's office and I sat down and I cried. It all just got to me at once. Then I walked back in and I said, 'Forget the speech, I'm just gonna go out there like I always have and say what I think. I've been Rollie for thirty-two years in this business and that's who I still am.' "

So he went out and talked about how much it hurt. And, when he was finished, he said he only wished Gary McLain well. Later, that summer, he helped get him a tryout with a team in Holland. A lot of Massimino's friends were furious with him for helping McLain. "He's still one of my kids," Massimino said in reply.

But now it was October. The 15–16 team was back, minus leading scorer Harold Jensen. Recruiting had been a disaster: One player reneged on a verbal commitment and had gone to Pittsburgh and one decided at the last minute to play baseball.

A few people picked Villanova as high as fifth in the Big East. A few more picked the Wildcats as low as ninth. The consensus: sixth or seventh. "The thought of being mediocre scares me," Massimino admitted. "But I've always said the real guy comes out under adversity. Maybe I needed a shock like last year. Maybe it had all gotten a little too easy.

"I've told this team our job this season is simple: Find a way. I told them they *better* find a way. Because if we finish seventh in the league, they'll find me in the Schuylkill River."

• • •

One person who would not have minded seeing Villanova finish seventh—or lower—in the Big East was Paul Evans. Across the state from
Philadelphia, Evans was assembling a very talented team at Pittsburgh.
In his first season at Pitt, 1987, after moving there from Navy, Evans
had put together a 24–9 record, tying for first place in the Big East.

This was no small accomplishment for what was largely the same
team that had been 15–14 the previous year. Evans had come in vowing
that the talented, undisciplined team would become a disciplined one
or heads would roll. On the very first day he ran a practice at Pittsburgh,
Evans threw Jerome Lane out of practice. The two fought most of that
year, but when it was over Lane had become the first player under 6–7
to lead the nation in rebounding since Elgin Baylor, thirty years earlier.

But as he was earning respect for his coaching abilities, Evans was
doing very little to win friends or influence people around the Big East.
Evans is, to put it mildly, outspoken. What he thinks he says and if
people don't like it, tough. When Bobby Martin, a talented 6–10 high
school center, changed his mind about his verbal commitment to
Villanova and signed with Pitt, Massimino was angry and unhappy.
When he made that unhappiness public, Evans lashed back at him,
accusing him of doing a lousy recruiting job.

That began a war of words that would continue through the summer
and only get worse during 1988.

Evans didn't want a running feud with Massimino any more than
Massimino wanted one with him. But neither man was about to back
down from the other. The troubles with Massimino did not affect
Evans's coaching. But they didn't make life any simpler for him. And
this promised to be a difficult year. He had been a successful Division
2 coach at St. Lawrence, a highly lauded coach for six years at Navy,
and surprisingly successful during his first year at Pitt.

Now, Pitt was being picked first by many in the Big East. It was in
most top fives around the nation. With Lane, Charles Smith, Demetrius Gore, and Rod Brookin back, along with a very strong freshman
class, the Panthers' potential seemed unlimited.

But it was not that simple. Even before practice began, Evans had
lost his starting point guard from the previous year, Michael Goodson,
to academic troubles. Goodson was one of those kids plenty smart
enough to do the work, but too cool to take the time. That left Evans
with a choice between a former walk-on, Mike Cavanaugh, or a freshman, Sean Miller, at point guard. He would eventually choose Miller,

but starting a season with Final Four dreams with a freshman running your team was not exactly ideal.

"People are picking us too high," Evans insisted, sounding like any coach dealing with high expectations. "We're experienced in some areas but too inexperienced in others. If we had Goodson, it would be different. But we don't."

For much of his coaching career, Evans had been the underdog. Now, he was the favorite. It would be a new experience for him. It would not be an easy or a pleasant one either.

If Evans needed lessons in how to deal with attention, he might have picked up a phone and called Jim Valvano. In 1983, Valvano had become as big a name as there was in basketball when he took a North Carolina State team that had finished third in the Atlantic Coast Conference all the way to the national championship. It was a feat similar to the one that Massimino would perform two years later, but Valvano did it first.

And he did it with remarkable flair. The night before his team played in the national semifinals against Georgia, Valvano, pouring sweat from a fever, won a dance contest in Albuquerque. Then, in the final, the Wolfpack, given no chance against a great Houston team led by Akeem Olajuwon, not only won the game 54–52 but did it on a miracle shot at the buzzer, Lorenzo Charles snatching Dereck Whittenburg's woefully short desperation shot out of the air and dunking it, to end the game.

That shot and the aftermath, Valvano running from corner to corner of the court trying to find people to hug, was rerun more times than all the episodes of *I Love Lucy* combined. If Valvano had been boring, those few moments would have made him a star.

And Valvano was not boring. He was funny, hilariously funny. He loved to talk—especially when he was being paid a lot of money for talking. He marketed himself and his championship into a business worth $750,000 a year. Huge money for speaking and clinics; radio and TV shows out the wazoo. Shoe and clothing contracts, outside businesses. Want a statue commemorating the accomplishment of a great athlete? Call JTV Enterprises.

What's more, Valvano, even though he was criticized at times for not focusing enough on coaching, continued to win games. His teams reached the final eight in 1985 and 1986 and after a bad regular season in 1987, won the ACC Tournament, shocking a vastly superior North Carolina team in the final in an upset faintly reminiscent of 1983.

Valvano was rich. He was a winner. He even did a stint on the *CBS Morning News* for a while, jokingly claiming to his friends—and his wife, of course—that Phyllis George, then the show's anchor, was madly in love with him.

But inside Valvano's head, the old Peggy Lee song kept playing: "Is That All There Is?" He had accomplished everything he had wanted to accomplish in life by the age of forty: He had married his childhood sweetheart and produced three beautiful daughters. He was a millionaire. He had won a national championship. He was a hero where he lived and his own boss since 1986 when he had become N.C. State's athletic director in addition to everything else he was doing.

It was all very simple. What's more, Valvano knew his 1987–88 team could be pretty good. With a little luck, very good. The key was junior center Charles Shackleford, an immensely talented but just as inconsistent 6–10 specimen who could shoot the ball with either hand but often seemed willing to take the worst shot he could find. If Valvano could get Shackleford to concentrate every game for forty minutes, the Wolfpack would be terrific. All the other pieces were in place. There were four good guards—two seniors and two freshmen—and an excellent power forward in Chucky Brown. The only question mark was at small forward.

And yet, as he began his eighth season coaching State, Valvano wondered how much longer he wanted to go on doing it. There had been plenty of chances to get out. If he wanted to be a TV commentator, he could do that. If he wanted to be a full-time athletic director and not coach, he could do that. If he wanted an NBA job—the New York Knicks had approached him during the summer—he could undoubtedly do that. Hollywood was even a possibility. During the summer, Valvano had taped a TV variety show pilot.

But he was still coaching—at State. There were reasons for this. First and foremost, there was his family. Even though he and his wife Pam had grown up in New York, they were comfortable in Raleigh and their children considered it home. Their oldest daughter, Nicole, was a State freshman who would finish her first semester with a 4.0 grade point average. "All that proves," Valvano cracked, "is that she is the first child in history to take after neither one of her parents."

Once, Valvano had called a family meeting to discuss his giving up coaching to be a full-time athletic director. "It would mean more time at home," he told his daughters. They liked that. "It would mean less pressure," he added. They liked that too. "It would mean more family weekends together." They were loving it by now.

"And it would mean less money. Nicole, you might have to give up your car."

Nicole and Jamie, the middle daughter, looked at one another. "New information has just come in," Nicole said. "We vote you coach."

So he coached. Often, he wondered why.

While Valvano wrestled with his choices, Don DeVoe had no doubt in his mind about where he wanted to be and what he wanted to do. He was starting his tenth season as the coach at the University of Tennessee and his fondest wish was to start his eleventh season there on October 15, 1988.

But that was no sure thing. DeVoe had two years left on his contract. If the University did not extend that contract at the end of the season, it would leave him a lame duck coach, something neither the school nor he could tolerate. Already, recruiting had become extremely difficult because the whispers were everywhere that DeVoe would not be back the next season.

DeVoe was human and he was aware of the whispers. He couldn't avoid them. After seven solid seasons at Tennessee—five NCAA bids, five twenty-victory seasons—DeVoe had suffered through two straight losing seasons. There had been injuries and problems, but most of all there had been losses. The University was about to open a brand-new $37 million, twenty-five-thousand-seat basketball arena and a losing record would mean rows and rows of empty seats. Another losing season and DeVoe would definitely be gone. He knew that. What he didn't know was how many wins he needed to survive. When he asked athletic director Doug Dickey the question, Dickey was direct, but not specific: "Show me improvement, Don," he said. "I need to see improvement."

The record the previous season had been 14–15, 7–11 in Southeast Conference play. That was the starting point for DeVoe.

Improving on that record might not be that easy. Already, on October 15, there were headaches. The previous spring, feeling he needed help in recruiting, DeVoe had hired Bill Brown as an assistant coach from California State at Sacramento. Brown had gone back to California before moving to Knoxville and while he was there had been arrested along with several others during a drug bust. DeVoe had no choice: Brown resigned immediately.

Then, the night before practice started, the Volunteers' best player, Dyron Nix, had been in a car accident. Nix lost control of his car and hit a telephone pole. His passenger, a member of the Tennessee women's basketball team, was injured so seriously that she didn't play all season. Nix, after a scary night in intensive care, came through without any serious injuries. He would be back practicing after two weeks.

But as practice started, DeVoe couldn't help but think, "What else can happen to us?"

If ever a coach and a program had reason to feel jinxed, it was DeVoe and Tennessee. The new arena, two years late already, had been plagued from the day it got off the planning board. A construction worker had died on the project, one construction company had been fired, and two law suits were still pending. As if that wasn't enough, the man who had contributed the first $5 million to get the project started, B. Ray Thompson, a man whose fondest wish had been to see Tennessee play in the new building, was dying of cancer. Everyone at Tennessee hoped he would live to see the inaugural game, scheduled for December 3 against Marquette.

B. Ray Thompson died on October 22. The season was still six weeks away. DeVoe knew it might be a long one.

For Rick Barnes, October 15 was the Christmas morning he had dreamed of all his life. And, like any little kid, he just couldn't wait to open his presents. That is why his George Mason basketball team was on the floor that day at 6 A.M. There was no midnight practice only because George Mason isn't the kind of school where thousands of people will show up to celebrate the opening day of basketball practice.

But Barnes didn't care. All he knew was that he was a head basketball coach. He knew that outside the Washington, D.C., area very few people had heard of George Mason, a commuter school in Fairfax, Virginia, twenty-five miles from downtown Washington. But he also believed that with a two-year-old, ten-thousand-seat arena, an ever-growing student body, and a spot in a very respectable conference—the

Colonial Athletic Association—GMU had the potential to get noticed in the near future. If it had the right coach.

Barnes believed that it did.

Rick Barnes was thirty-two but looked twenty-two. Ten years ago, when he had been twenty-two and no doubt looked twelve, he had managed to get an interview with Eddie Biedenbach, then the coach at Davidson, for a graduate assistant's job. Barnes had grown up in North Carolina and played at Lenoir Rhyne, a decent player in a decent small college program. When he graduated he knew his playing days were over. He also knew exactly what he wanted to do: coach.

Through a friend he managed to arrange an interview with Biedenbach. It was scheduled for nine in the morning. Not wanting to take any chances on being late, Barnes left his house at 6 A.M. and was at Davidson by eight. He sat down in the bleachers to wait for Biedenbach. An hour went by. Then two. Barnes asked the assistant coaches if they knew where Biedenbach was. On the road recruiting. He would be in, but they weren't sure when.

Barnes kept waiting. At noon, he thought about going to get something to eat but decided against it. What if Biedenbach came in briefly and he missed him? He waited. His suit, the only one he owned, was beginning to stick to him, the weather in North Carolina being warm in the springtime. The assistants kept saying they knew Biedenbach was coming in. Barnes nodded, famished and exhausted, but stubborn.

At six o'clock, the assistants went home. They were sorry they had made a mistake about Biedenbach coming in. He must have gotten tied up because he hadn't called in either. Barnes decided to wait just a little longer. Finally, at 7 P.M., he gave up. Eleven hours was enough. He walked to the gym door, opened it, and in walked Eddie Biedenbach.

Barnes had never met him, but he knew him from pictures. "Excuse me," he said, "but you are Coach Biedenbach, aren't you?"

A look of horror crossed Biedenbach's face. "Oh my God," he said, "you're Rick Barnes!"

Biedenbach had forgotten the appointment. He felt so guilty he offered Barnes the job—for $2,500 a year—on the spot. That was all Barnes wanted. The wait had been worth it. From Davidson, he went to George Mason as Joe Harrington's assistant coach and then to Alabama and Ohio State for one year each. When Harrington resigned in the spring of '87 to take the job at Long Beach State, athletic director Jack Kvancz knew exactly who he wanted to hire.

"When Rick was here as an assistant, I always thought he would be a great head coach," Kvancz said. "When Joe left, I talked to some other people, but I knew I wanted Rick."

Harrington knew that too. The day he took the Long Beach job he called Barnes on the phone. "Pack your bags, Barney," he said. "You're gonna be a head coach."

He had held the title for six months by the time October 15 rolled around. He had already made it clear to his players that if they missed class, missed a meeting, missed anything, they would be in trouble. But the first practice was different. This made it real. The first game was five weeks away. For the moment though, Barnes was a rarity: a head basketball coach who had never once been second-guessed.

There were, of course, many schools where October 15, while significant as the first day of practice, was not that big a deal. No midnight practices, no first years or last years, just another season with high expectations.

One of those places was Duke. After struggling his first three years, Coach Mike Krzyzewski had put together one of the top programs in the country. In the four previous seasons, the Blue Devils had gone 108–30. They had played for the national championship in 1986; and in 1987, a so-called rebuilding year after the graduation of four seniors off the '86 team, they went 24–9 and made it back to the round of sixteen.

Now, with four starters back from that surprising team, there was Final Four talk around Duke again even though nationally, few people ranked Duke in the top ten. Top Twenty yes, top ten, no.

But Duke was a confident team and no one on the team was more confident than Billy King. He had come to Duke three years earlier as a good-field, no-hit freshman. In other words, he could guard people, but he couldn't shoot. That reputation had grown—in both directions. King was, to put it kindly, an awful shooter. He had hit less than 50 percent of his free throws in his career and anything other than a layup was an adventure for him.

But oh could he play defense! He guarded point guards and power forwards and everyone in between. King was 6–6, quick enough to handle a little guy, big enough to handle people up to 6–8. He and Kevin Strickland, his roommate from day one at Duke, were the two seniors on this team. Realistically, King knew that a player who can't score in college isn't too likely to play in the NBA. He would get his degree in political science in May and hoped for a career in television. With his good looks, easy smile, and quick, sharp wit, King was a natural for that profession. Or almost any other. One of his nicknames was "Senator," because a lot of people who knew him expected him to talk his way into politics someday.

"If there's one thing Billy can do better than anybody," Strickland said, "it's talk."

But politics and television and anything else would come later.

Right now there was only basketball. King was the youngest of four children. His father had died when he was four and Billy had started playing basketball when he was six. It had been, outside of his mother, the most important thing in his life since then. He was 5–2 in the second grade and 6–2 by the seventh grade. He had gotten his first recruiting letter—from the University of Maryland—at the age of ten after he had attended summer camp there. Yes, age ten. He was now twenty-one. He had never even dabbled with any seriousness in other sports. "Once, I played soccer and in the first game I played in, I tripped over the ball, took a bad spill and twisted an ankle," he said. "I decided it was an omen and that someone was telling me to stick to basketball." He now had one more year of his life to devote to basketball. He wanted to be certain that it was a special one.

"A lot of seniors just want to get through their last year and get their shot at the money in the pros," he said. "I know the odds are that I won't get that money and that a year from now I won't be playing basketball anymore. In a way, that's scary—because for as long as I can remember I've played basketball. There's nothing I love doing more than playing basketball.

"But this is probably it for me. I don't want to look back next year at this season and say, 'What if I had done a little more?' I want to walk away from it knowing I did everything I could do. And that means making sure everyone on the team does that. Kevin and I are the captains now. This should be *our* team. If it messes up, it's our fault."

While King felt responsible for the rise or fall of his team at Duke, Walker Lambiotte knew very well, as practice began at Northwestern, that he would have nothing at all to do with the success or failure of the Wildcats.

Lambiotte was a transfer. He had left N.C. State after two frustrating years and, after a confusing summer, had landed at Northwestern playing, ironically, for Jim Valvano's college coach, Bill Foster. The choice was not an easy one for Lambiotte. He had left a team that had won forty-five games during his two seasons there for a team that had won fifteen during that same time.

Foster was another in a long line of coaches hired to try to get Northwestern out of the Big Ten cellar. His track record said he had a chance. A coaching nomad, he had turned losers into winners at Bloomsburg, Rutgers (where he coached Valvano), Utah, and Duke. Only in his last job, South Carolina, had he failed. There, he had been fired after six years, three years after a heart attack had almost driven him out of the business.

Foster was fifty-five when South Carolina fired him. His family and friends would have been delighted had he taken his 407 victories and retired to an easier job in administration or scouting or promotions, a side of the business that had always interested him anyway. But Foster didn't want to go out a loser and so, when Northwestern offered him a chance to rebuild a program that had been a consistent loser, he grabbed it.

"The good news is, I can get the job," he told friends jokingly. "The bad news is, I'm going to take it."

The first-year record was 8–20, the same as his predecessor Rich Falk. Foster had to get some players, that was clear. Suddenly, in the spring of 1987, Walker Lambiotte was available. Lambiotte had been one of those can't-miss high school seniors in 1985. He starred at the summer camps, made every All-America team, and was recruited by every big-time program around.

He was from Virginia and the Cavaliers recruited him, but his older brother Kenny had gone there, transferring away after only two years, even switching sports—basketball to football—at the University of Richmond. Maryland wanted him. So did Duke. And so did N.C. State.

Valvano went after Walker Lambiotte hard. He was the kind of player his program really needed—Lambiotte could play and he was a good student. Valvano had been criticized for having a high transfer rate and a low graduation rate. Lambiotte was appealing because he was someone with a 3.4 gpa who, it just so happened, could run and jump.

"Walker was a V job all the way," Tom Abatemarco, then Valvano's top assistant, remembered. "The father loved him right away and Jim knew it. We just stayed out of the way and let Jim do it all."

Jim did it. Walker Lambiotte chose State, a decision that hurt Mike Krzyzewski and thrilled Valvano. Lambiotte started often and played a lot his first year. He still started as a sophomore but his minutes dwindled and then dwindled further. He began to worry what his junior year would be like. He asked Valvano. "You've had two years of learning here," Valvano responded. "You should play a lot."

But Lambiotte wasn't sure. He wasn't sure if the way State played suited his own style. Lambiotte is a shooter, a lefty with a deadly touch. He is also a very good athlete. But he is not a ballhandler. He does not create his own shots. Most of State's players do create their own shots, inside or outside. A guard who fit exactly that description, Rodney Monroe, had been signed. Lambiotte went home for spring break and talked it over with his parents. He had trepidations about transferring: the stigmas attached, sitting out a year from basketball—which all transfer student-athletes must do—and starting all over again. But transferring had worked out well for brother Kenny.

"In the end, I just thought to myself, 'Am I getting better the way I want to?' " he said. "The answer was no. I talked it over with my dad and he agreed. He was the one who called Coach Valvano and told him. I didn't want to do it. It would have been hard for me because it was never anything personal. I still like the guy."

And Valvano liked Walter Lambiotte. But as practice began, the shooter was preparing to play—or in the case of this sit-out season, *not* play—for Bill Foster.

Nowhere in the country do they enjoy October 15 more than in Lawrence. There are a number of reasons for this, not the least of which is the absolutely horrific record of the Kansas football team. In 1987, the record was 1–10 and the victory was 13–12 over Southern Illinois. By October, everyone is more than ready for hoops to begin.

It goes beyond that, though. This is one of the great traditional basketball programs in the country. Phog Allen Field House, named for the legendary Kansas coach, is one of the great old arenas in the country, a place that reeks with memories and rocks every time the doors open.

In 1985, Mark Friedinger, then a Kansas assistant, suggested to

Larry Brown the notion of opening the season with a 12:01 A.M. practice. The idea was hardly original. Kentucky has done it for years and many others also do it now. But Friedinger and Brown came up with a twist of their own. They decided to call the event, "Late Night with Larry Brown." On a college campus filled with David Letterman watchers, this was bound to get some attention.

The first "Late Night" was that October and more than eight thousand people showed up. The Jayhawks were coming off a 26–8 season and with Manning just a sophomore, expectations were high. It was also a novelty. People wondered how the second year would go. It went even better. This time twelve thousand people showed up. The Kansas Athletic Department was so excited that it wanted to charge admission for the third year. Brown wouldn't allow it. But there were "Late Night" T-shirts ($10) and pizza for sale.

Allen Field House was packed. All 15,800 seats were filled, most of them by 10 P.M., an hour before the prepractice festivities were to begin. While the players were gathering, Brown sat in his office with a friend watching game seven of the Cardinals–Giants playoff series. Already, the annual rumors that he would leave Kansas at the end of the season had started—especially with Manning graduating.

Brown had thought about leaving the previous spring to coach the New York Knicks. At the same time, Manning had thought about leaving to turn pro. Both were still in Lawrence, however, for reasons of their own. Maybe that was why the T-shirts said "Still Late Night, still Larry Brown."

The party began at 11 P.M. with a look-alike contest. The guy doing Larry Brown walked with a noticeable limp, a tribute to the hip surgery Brown had undergone the previous spring. "I thought I got rid of that thing," Brown said, watching. "Pee Wee Herman" beat out "Letterman" to win the contest and got booed. All seemed right with the world.

Then came a search for the missing Jayhawk, the KU mascot for seventy-seven years. A contest was held to replace the Jayhawk. Just as the girl in the white hot pants and black high heels was about to be declared the winner, the Jayhawk showed up. Can't win 'em all.

Finally, just before midnight, the players showed up dressed in sunglasses and raincoats. The seniors were the last to arrive. Only one of them—Manning—wasn't in sunglasses. To thunderous cheers, he led his teammates in a truly atrocious version of "My Girl." That Manning was willing to lead the song was a tribute to how far he had come since he had been an almost painfully shy freshman.

That his voice was lousy didn't matter. Brown shrugged. "I'd rather be his agent as a basketball player than as a singer," he said, laughing.

Finally, with all the lights turned out, the clock struck midnight, the Jayhawks took off their raincoats and practice, in the form of a scrimmage, began. Kevin Pritchard scored the first basket of the season, Manning gave him the first high-five, and everyone partied well into the night.

As the Jayhawks left the floor an hour later, the band played—what else?—"Kansas City." One hundred and seventy-three days later, they would be in that city. But no one in the building could even begin to imagine the journey that would take them there.

3
RECRUITING

More than any other sport, college basketball starts in stages. The games begin in November; practice in October. And recruiting begins full-blast in September.

In one sense this is a misnomer because for college basketball coaches recruiting is a never-ending process. Even while you are wrapping up the recruitment of high school seniors, you are already going after juniors, looking at sophomores, and wondering about freshmen. There may even be an occasional eighth grader who is worth checking out.

The recruiting game is a chameleon, constantly changing because the NCAA comes up with new rules on an almost annual basis. Once, not all that long ago, recruiting was simple. When the season was over, coaches went to some high school state tournaments, took in several all-star games, and made their pitches to that year's graduating seniors.

There was no such thing as a letter of intent. That is why a player like Tom McMillen could change his mind on the day he was supposed to register for classes at North Carolina in 1970 and instead register at Maryland.

Now, because recruiting has become so intense and extreme, there are restrictions. There are rules. There are binding letters of intent. Once, a basketball player could not sign such a letter before April. But because so many players were being hounded even *after* they had made verbal commitments, there is now an eight-day signing period in November which allows players who have made a decision to sign with a college before their senior season begins.

The raison d'être of this rule makes absolute sense: If a player makes his decision and signs early, he may then play his senior season free of recruiting burdens. It cuts down on circus productions like the one that surrounded Ralph Sampson in 1979.

Sampson was so confused that when he walked to the microphone at a packed press conference in May to announce his decision, he still didn't know where he was going. He opened his mouth and said, "I have chosen, Ken . . . Virginia." The three live TV crews in the room from Kentucky almost had cardiac arrests on the spot. It was that close—and that confused.

Now, in 1987, Alonzo Mourning, this year's Ralph Sampson, would make his choice—Georgetown—in November. It was still a circus—with a shoe company representative playing a role—but it was a shorter circus.

The downside of the rule is that it has pushed recruiting up so that much of it is being done during a player's junior year and the ensuing summer. The letters and phone calls that followed a player as a senior in the past are now just as intensely there as soon as his junior year begins.

This is not to imply that the life-and-death pursuit of players or cheating in recruiting is a new thing. It isn't. Gene Corrigan, who has been athletic director at Virginia and Notre Dame and is now the commissioner of the Atlantic Coast Conference, probably explained it best: "Recruiting hasn't changed very much at all in the last thirty years. It's just that now everyone notices the cheating. It has always been there."

Because everyone notices now and because recruiting became a twelve-month-a-year affair during the 1970s, the NCAA changes the rules more often than Elizabeth Taylor and Mickey Rooney change spouses. Once, there were no restrictions on how often you could visit a recruit, on how often you could see him play, on how many visits he could make, on how much time coaches could spend on the road.

Now, everything is regulated. Each school may pay for a maximum of eighteen official visits for athletes to its campus. Each athlete may officially visit only five schools. There are lengthy "dead" periods when coaches are not allowed off campus to recruit or to see games. And, the period when colleges may officially visit homes has been cut back to twenty-one days. In 1987 that meant home visits began on September 17 and ended on October 7.

Naturally, coaches hate anything that limits their recruiting time. But the rules make sense. They have brought a tiny semblance of sanity to an insane pursuit.

Once, when there were no limits on coaches, Dave Pritchett, then an assistant coach at Maryland, rented seven cars in seven cities in two days. Pritchett was so intense about recruiting that when he left town on a recruiting trip he would always park in a tow-away zone. Why? "Because I could never remember where I had parked my car but I always knew where it would be towed to."

Makes perfect sense. There is one problem—and it is a very real one—with the limits. They hurt the smaller schools. Now, the player who was willing to visit a small school in the past might pass it up; able to make only five visits, he doesn't want to "waste" one. With the shorter visitation period, a player may limit the list of schools invited into his home and lop off the smaller school that just wants a chance to make a pitch.

"The rich get richer is what it is," said Rick Barnes, who saw the rules work in his favor while at Alabama and Ohio State but was now being hurt by them at George Mason. "If a kid has only five visits and he has a chance to go to a school and see a football game on that last visit, what's he going to do? It's frustrating."

But that is the nature of recruiting. It is always going to be frustrating and agonizing, no matter what the rules. When coaches leave the profession, they all say, to a man, that their greatest relief is not having to recruit anymore.

"It is demeaning," Valvano said. "I have to go in and sell myself and my university. Why should I have to do that to a seventeen-year-old kid? Why should I answer his questions, many of which are totally ridiculous? When I think about coaching in the pros, the thing I think about most is that I would never have to recruit again."

Sometimes, coaches snap and say what they're really thinking. American University Coach Ed Tapscott, winding down the nonstop three weeks of home visits, found himself in the house of an excellent athlete who was, to be polite, a shaky student.

"In the middle of our talk, the kid said to me, 'Hey Coach, how many seats are there in your new arena and how many times will you be on television next year?' I just snapped. It was too many visits and too many questions like that. I said to him, 'Look, you can't even read and write and you're asking me how many times you're going to be on television? You've got some nerve.'

"I thought there was an outside chance that maybe the family would like it, you know, the tough, honest approach. But my reaction was just instinctive and they didn't go for the tough, honest approach."

Honesty is often not the best policy in recruiting. Jim Boeheim, the Syracuse coach, went into the home of Jerrod Mustaf, the highly sought 6–10 DeMatha High School senior, knowing that Mustaf thought of himself as a small forward. Boeheim hadn't seen Mustaf play much but his assistants had.

"When he asked me where I thought he would play, I said, 'Inside.' He said, 'Have you seen me play?' I said, 'No, not really, not yet, but I'd be very surprised if you aren't better off playing inside.' I could tell by looking at him that we were done."

Mustaf, who is a Maryland freshman, confirms the story and Boeheim's notion. "When he said that, I knew for sure I wouldn't be going to Syracuse."

What makes coaches truly crazy are the often wacky reasons that players use to choose a school. Rarely does a player choose a school simply because he believes it will be the best place for him athletically and academically. Sometimes the weather on a particular visit decides. Sometimes a pretty date on that visit decides. Sometimes nice uniforms decide. Sometimes, it is even sillier than that.

Tapscott, who needs all the breaks he can get coaching at a small school like American, lost a player last spring because of Kermit Washington, the best player in AU history.

"We were recruiting a kid from Florida named Deron Hayes," he explained. "The kid was about six-five, not a great player but a good one, the kind who could help us. He had a great visit to campus. He even told me when he was here that he'd like to settle in the Washington, D.C., area after college. Then, a few days later he calls me up and says he's going to Penn State."

Tapscott said his question to Hayes was direct: "Why the hell are you going there?" From there, the conversation went like this:

Hayes: "Well, coach, they have a lot of tradition."

Tapscott: "That's in football, not basketball."

Hayes: "Well, coach, I think a degree from Penn State would mean more than a degree from American."

Tapscott: "Come on, Deron, that's not it, you know our board scores are higher on the average than theirs are."

Hayes: "Well, coach, a lot of my friends from home are going to school up there."

Tapscott: "Deron, you told me you were ready to leave high school behind and move on to college. That's not it either. Now come on, why Penn State?"

Hayes (softly): "Coach, I can wear number twenty-four there."

Tapscott knew he had hit the real reason. Kermit Washington had worn No. 24 and American had retired it after his graduation. Hayes wore No. 24 in high school. He could not have worn it at American.

"If I had been smart, I would have told him I could arrange for him to wear it and then after he signed, explain that I couldn't work it out," Tapscott said. "But I'm not that smart."

Or that dishonest. In recruiting, that is a weakness.

One of the more unusual recruiting stories in the country was that of Jerrod Mustaf. In many ways, Mustaf was every college coach's dream. He was 6–10, a gifted, graceful athlete who could run, shoot, and pass. He could play inside when he had to although, as he made clear to Jim Boeheim, he preferred to be outside. He came from one of the great high school programs in America, DeMatha High School in Hyattsville, Maryland, where he played for the legendary coach Morgan Wootten. He was a good student, a bright youngster who would do well academically anywhere he decided to go.

What made Mustaf different was the involvement of his father in the recruiting process. Parental involvement—to the point of being interfering and domineering—was certainly nothing new in recruiting. It is something coaches deal with all the time. Often, in their recruiting folders coaches write notes that say things like: "The father is the key here." Or, "Johnny will go to college where his mother wants him to go." Thus the phrase, "recruit the parents."

That was the case with Jerrod Mustaf. Although Sharr Mustaf insisted, as all parents do, that the decision on where to attend college was Jerrod's and Jerrod's alone, that was clearly not so. In fact, Sharr Mustaf readily admitted that he had gone to his son before his senior season and said, "Son, please let me use you."

At least, unlike many parents, Sharr Mustaf wanted to use his son for a good cause. Born and raised in North Carolina, a former Grey-hound sales officer who had retired on disability, Sharr Mustaf was a handsome man of forty-six who felt deeply about the exploitation of blacks in athletics. That was where Jerrod came in. His son's ability gave Sharr a chance to do something. That was why he had convinced his son to leave his mother in Whiteville, North Carolina, and move in with him and his second wife in order to play at DeMatha.

"I can remember when Jerrod was a freshman, Sharr saying to me, 'Coach, this boy has a chance to do something for his race,' " Morgan Wootten said. "It was something that I think was in his mind when he brought Jerrod to DeMatha."

As a DeMatha freshman, Jerrod Mustaf had played with Danny Ferry, then a senior. He was comfortable with Ferry and liked him but was pleased as a sophomore when Ferry had gone on to Duke and he became the focal point of the DeMatha offense. Ferry's last team had lost the city championship game, the big game every year for DeMatha, and the Stags lost again in Mustaf's sophomore and junior years. "I don't want to leave here without having won a city championship," he said at the outset of his senior year. "That's the most important thing to me this season."

That and choosing a college. In late August, Sharr Mustaf sent Morgan Wootten a copy of a letter he was sending to the eight coaches who were being invited to make home visits to the Mustaf home. The eight schools on the Mustaf visit list were Maryland, Howard, Georgia Tech, North Carolina, Duke, Syracuse, Villanova, and Notre Dame. The coach at each of those schools received the following letter, dated August 29, 1987:

Dear Coach,

Thank you for the interest you have shown in our son's academic and athletic future. Your institution has a rich tradition of scholarship and athletic achievement which recommends it highly to us. The decision that Jerrod has to make, relative to which university to attend, is a critical one that our family must take very seriously. We have given it considerable attention and have decided that there is some specific information that we require to make an informed decision. We have outlined the components of this information below. We would like for you to address these points and be in position to discuss them with us when you visit our home.

We are concerned to know the following:

—What percentage of your university's faculty positions is held by Blacks?

—What percentage of your university's tenured faculty positions is held by Blacks?

—What is the nature of the academic and social support services available to Black students designed to address the unique circumstances many of them bring to the higher education environment?

—What percentage of Black students who enroll at your university actually graduate?

—What percentage of Black members of your basketball team have graduated during the last ten years?

—What has been the academic major distribution of your basketball players during the last five years?

—What percentage of your athletics department's procurement budget is awarded annually to Black-owned businesses?

—Is there an academic advisor, full or part-time, attached to your basketball team?

—What percentage of your university's top administration positions is held by Blacks?

—What positions do Blacks occupy on your athletic department staff?

As you can see, these inquiries are designed to get a fuller picture of life at your university. Jerrod has indicated a desire to attend a university that has an excellent academic program, a positive athletic tradition, and a demonstrated awareness obligation to provide access to all segments of our society. We are sure that there are many things about your program that you would like to bring to our attention. We are eager to consider them along with the information we have requested.

We would like for you to join us on [fill in a different date for each coach] from 6 P.M. to 7:30 P.M. to discuss Jerrod's academic and athletic future. We would be happy to clarify any aspect of this request. Please feel free to contact us. You may contact us through DeMatha High School. We look forward to welcoming you into our home.

Sincerely,

Mr. and Mrs. Sharr Mustaf

The intent of the letter was clear. Each school recruiting Jerrod was to be graded on its response to the letter. Of course, there was no doubt that Howard, a black school, would easily grade the highest. And, in fact, Howard would be one of the three "finalists" eventually chosen.

But Howard was just a smoke screen. At no point was there any chance that Jerrod would end up there.

When he read the letter, Wootten was thrown at first. He knew this letter would cause controversy, but he also thought many of the questions quite legitimate. "The only thing I suggested to Sharr was that he not pin each coach down to such a specific time because the recruiting period (three weeks) was so tight," Wootten said. "He understood that."

The letter, though completely different in nature, brought back memories of the infamous "Ewing letter" of 1980 in which "the committee" helping Patrick Ewing choose his college had informed the schools recruiting him that, among other things, Ewing would need untimed testing while in college. Some of the schools that lost out on Ewing—all of whom would have accepted him in a second—used that letter to try to prove that Georgetown was admitting someone who was academically unqualified.

This was different. But it was still controversial. When word leaked out, as was inevitable, that the Mustafs had written a letter to the coaches demanding statistics on black involvement in their school, a lot of people were quick to judge Sharr Mustaf as some kind of racist.

Sharr Mustaf is no racist. Talk to him for five minutes and that will become apparent. But he is extremely race conscious. He believes that blacks have an obligation to do for other blacks because more often than not, whites won't do for them. This, he felt, was his chance.

Exactly how Jerrod felt about this is tough to say. He was quick to explain that he agreed with everything his father was doing and that these were questions that were important to him too. "I went along with it and I was behind what my father was doing," he said. "I would like to be an example to other blacks in the future."

All well and good. The problem, according to those who became familiar with the situation, was that Sharr Mustaf had made up his mind where Jerrod would go to college before any coach set foot inside his house. Almost everyone agrees that Jerrod Mustaf was destined to play for a black coach because of his father's beliefs. John Thompson, the most successful and visible black coach in the country, was out; the Georgetown coach did not recruit DeMatha players because of his long-standing twenty-year feud with Wootten. Quite correctly, Sharr Mustaf saw this as foolish: "Even if John doesn't end up taking the kid at Georgetown or the kid doesn't want to go there, why should any of them be denied the chance to be recruited by Georgetown because of something that happened between John and Morgan before any of these kids were even born?" he asked.

Good question. But Georgetown was still out. So was Howard, even though A. B. Williamson was a proven winner and his school would easily score the best on the letter test. Jerrod Mustaf wanted to play for a school that could legitimately contend for a national championship. Howard did not meet that requirement. That left Maryland. There, Bob Wade was black, the chancellor was black. Sharr Mustaf felt comfortable with them and with the school. By the time the eight coaches had finished their visits, the word was out on the coaching grapevine: Mustaf is a lock for Maryland; the father has decided.

Father and son deny this vehemently. "My favorite team from the time I was in the ninth grade on was North Carolina," Jerrod said. "I always thought back then that I would end up playing there. But I also liked Duke a lot. I liked Coach [Mike] K's [Krzyzewski] motion offense and I liked the idea of playing with Danny [Ferry] again. Also, Coach [Mike] Brey had gone down there from here [DeMatha] and I liked that. The coach I think I liked best of all as a person was [Georgia Tech's] Bobby Cremins. I thought he was a great guy. Any of those schools had a good chance."

Villanova, Syracuse, and Notre Dame had been invited in more out of curiosity than anything else. When Syracuse Coach Jim Boeheim told Mustaf that even though he hadn't seen him play, he believed he was an inside player, that eliminated the Orangemen from contention. "I was shocked that the man would come into my home without having seen Jerrod play," Sharr Mustaf said.

The Villanova and Notre Dame visits were without incident but neither school did anything to really move itself up on the list. "Coach Massimino was a lot of fun, though," Jerrod remembered. "There was no doubt in my mind I could be comfortable playing for him."

The most rancorous visit was the one made by Krzyzewski and Brey. Sharr Mustaf asked Krzyzewski at one point why he didn't have any black assistant coaches. Krzyzewski had been prepared to hire Stu Jackson the previous summer before Jackson decided to follow Rick Pitino from Providence to the New York Knicks. At that point he had hired Brey. Krzyzewski didn't feel the need to tell Sharr Mustaf this. Instead, he just said, "I hire coaches, not blacks or whites."

According to everyone present, one could feel the icicles in the room from that moment on. "My father didn't like that answer at all," Jerrod Mustaf said. "I didn't think Coach K. did a very good job with the visit. It's probably fair to say they were eliminated after that."

Sharr Mustaf goes further. "If the man hadn't come to my house, he might have gotten my son."

Krzyzewski, who liked Jerrod Mustaf very much as a player and a person, is philosophical. "I told them the truth, which is more than a lot of guys do. I think if Jerrod had visited and spent time with our players, black and white, all his questions would have been answered. But I don't believe we were ever going to get that chance."

Dean Smith's visit didn't go much better, at least from the Mustaf point of view. Smith told the Mustafs that if Jerrod really wanted to do something for blacks, he would go and play for John Thompson at Georgetown. Sharr Mustaf found this silly. "If there's one thing John Thompson doesn't need it's more black faces on his bench," he said. "He's already got plenty."

What Smith was doing was fairly obvious. Sensing that he had no chance to get Mustaf, he was trying to deflect him to Thompson who was a good friend and, just as important, not in the ACC. The strategy failed. "There was a time when I was almost sure I would play for North Carolina," Jerrod Mustaf said. "But to tell you the truth, the system there is almost exactly like DeMatha. I had four years at DeMatha. I felt like it was enough. I was ready for something new."

Five schools were out, three were left. Except Howard really never had a chance and Georgia Tech was a long ways off. Sharr Mustaf had told Wootten he wanted his son close to home. During Wade's visit, Chancellor John Slaughter took part in a conference telephone call, telling the Mustafs all the things he was doing for blacks at Maryland. Slaughter would resign as chancellor before the school year was out, but the Mustafs had no way of knowing this.

After the home visits, Jerrod Mustaf made two of his five official visits: to Maryland and to Howard. He briefly saw the Georgia Tech campus during a clinic in November but he never officially visited there or anywhere else. In December, he announced he had narrowed his list to Maryland, Howard, and Georgia Tech. No one in college basketball had any doubt about who would win that battle.

"We're not even working the kid," Georgia Tech assistant Perry Clark said. "The decision's been made." And no one in college basketball, fairly or unfairly, believed that Jerrod Mustaf had made that decision. It would be March before an announcement, though. In the meantime, Jerrod Mustaf would lead DeMatha to the city title and his father would go to work as an employee of the state of Maryland, working as a bailiff in the Prince George's County courthouse.

The 1987 recruiting season, while important to every coach in the country, was absolutely essential to Gary Williams. Entering his second season at Ohio State, Williams had earned a reputation as a coach who could get the most out of his talent. The question was, could he recruit big-time talent to get the most out of?

In four years at American and four at Boston College, he had been one of those coaches who won more games per season than he was supposed to. He had done the same thing in the 1987 season at Ohio State: He took a 14–14 (regular season) team in 1986 that then lost its leading scorer to the NBA, and coached them to a 19–12 record. That mark earned an NCAA bid, and the Buckeyes had beaten Kentucky in the first round before narrowly missing what would have been a stunning upset against Georgetown.

The 1987–88 Ohio State team would not be as good. Dennis Hopson, who had emerged as a star in his senior season under Williams, was gone, the first-round draft pick of the New Jersey Nets. Three impressive freshmen had been signed, but two of them were victims of Proposition 48, the two-year-old NCAA rule that required minimum academic standards for a player to be eligible. They could not play until they were sophomores.

That meant Williams had one good recruiting class—with an asterisk. Because he had taken two Prop 48s his first year, he could not afford to take any more in his second. It was impractical and it wasn't good for the school's image to start loading up on academic question marks.

Put simply, Williams had to prove himself as a recruiter this fall. There were four excellent seniors in Ohio. More than anything, Williams's predecessor, Eldon Miller, had been hurt by his inability to keep top Ohio players in the state. Williams had to reverse that trend and prove he could bring in at least one key player a year from out of state.

Ohio State is not an easy coaching job. It is a school that once was one of the dominant powers in the game, reaching three straight NCAA championship games from 1960 to 1962 (winning the title in 1960) with players like Jerry Lucas, John Havlicek, Mel Noell, Larry Siegfried, and a foul-prone bench warmer named Bob Knight.

But the Buckeyes have not won a Big Ten championship since 1970. Miller had some excellent teams, reaching five straight NCAA Tournaments at one point. But he never won the league and never got past the round of sixteen. One bad year and he was gone, fired at midseason.

Williams knew as he began his second season that 20–13 the first year was okay, especially because it exceeded expectations. He knew that a less-than-great second year could be survived too. But after that, the honeymoon was over. He had to have a top recruiting class to go with the first one. One good class is never enough.

There were four Ohio players Williams was focusing on: Bill Robinson, a seven-foot center from the Akron area, whose height and excellent grades made him a must; Eric Riley, a 6–11 forward from Cleveland who came from the same high school as Treg Lee, one of the two Prop 48s sitting out; Mark Baker, a 6–1 jet from Dayton, the kind of point guard Williams craved; and Jeff Hall, a 6–6 country kid who could shoot the ball. The key out-of-state recruit was Chris Jent, a 6–7 shooter from Sparta, New Jersey. Jent was a kamikaze-type player. His attitude reminded Williams a little bit of Larry Bird.

For Williams this would be a difficult fall. He is a man who has lived and breathed basketball for as long as he can remember. He was a good player at Maryland in the 1960s, a coach-on-the-floor type who still brags about holding the school record for most consecutive field goals—eight.

He began coaching straight out of college and quickly worked his way up the coaching ladder from high school to college assistant to head coach at American at the age of thirty-two. For years he has been hailed as one of the bright young coaches in the country. Now, he knew, it was time to take the next step.

"It's nice when people say we do a good job getting the most out of our talent," he said. "But I want to get to the point where if we do that, we win all the time. I want to attack people and not worry about it."

Williams's coaching style is an attacking one, pressing all over the floor, fast-breaking at every opportunity. It fits his personality. He is as intense as anyone in the sport. He coaches every possession as if it is his last one. Fortunately, he has the kind of sense of humor where he can laugh at himself when the game is over—though not always right away. He is the same way about recruiting.

Williams's two full-time assistants—his recruiters—are about as different as two men can be—which is ideal. Randy Ayers played at Ohio

State. He is 6–5, black, and has the dignified air of a judge. He is quiet, but articulate, someone who makes an excellent first impression and then builds on it.

Fran Fraschilla is a compact bundle of energy, a talker, someone who leaves few thoughts unspoken. He came to Ohio State in 1987 from Ohio University and he knows every nook and cranny of the state.

On September 23, Williams, Ayers, and Fraschilla visited Eric Riley. The basics of a recruiting visit in this day and age are almost always the same: set up a date and time. Try to know who will be there. If the parents are divorced or separated, find out if the parent the player doesn't live with will be there. Get good directions to the house so as not to get lost. Leave early in case you do get lost.

The three Ohio State coaches left Columbus at 3:30 P.M. for the two-hour drive to Cleveland. The visit was scheduled for 7:30. One of the advantages Ohio State has is being smack in the middle of the state. Almost every place in-state can be reached in two hours.

Williams's mood was good. He felt the school was in very good position with Robinson and Baker. Riley could go either way. The presence of Treg Lee would seem to be an advantage but Williams was concerned that, having played in Lee's shadow in high school, Riley might be worried about doing that again in college.

Still, he felt they had a shot at Riley. Both he and Ayers felt the mother, Beulah Riley, liked them; and they felt that she would play a major role in Eric's decision.

More often than not, a recruiting visit is the culmination of more than a year of work. Initial contact with a player starts early in the junior year—at the latest—and by the time a player is in his senior year the schools that are serious about recruiting him have written and phoned on several dozen occasions. In Riley's case, he and his mother had received thirty-one letters and three telegrams from Ohio State dating back to the summer of 1986. Between the time of the visit in September and the day he made his decision in November, there would be nineteen more letters and one more telegram. Those figures are about average for a good, but not great player.

In the car, the coaches reviewed the points they wanted to make: the education Riley would get—they knew that was very important to his mother. Playing time—it was there for him. And, how important it would be to have gone to Ohio State if he settled in Ohio after graduation.

Williams made one other point to the coaches: "Let's stay off the subject of Treg (Lee) unless they bring it up."

Once in Cleveland, the coaches went straight to the Riley house. They found it by 5:45, well before the scheduled visit. This is part of the recruiting manual: find the house first, then go look for something to eat. Almost always, dinner is the first fast food place that shows up. This night, it was McDonald's.

At 7:25, five minutes early, the coaches were back at the Rileys'. Eric and his mother lived in a middle class neighborhood which, on a warm early fall evening, was full of children playing in the street. Eric Riley was a slender youngster with a baby face and an easy smile. He looked Williams in the eye as they shook hands. Williams liked that.

Once everyone was seated, Fraschilla took out the tape that had been made especially for this visit. This is a new thing in recruiting, a creation of the age of VCRs. Almost every coach in the country brings a tape with him into a recruit's home. Some even bring portable VCRs in case the family doesn't have one. Rarely is the portable needed.

Most of the tapes are similar. They recount the virtues of the school, the coach, the players, the conference. There are prominent former players talking about how lucky they were to attend the good old alma mater.

The Ohio State twist is the start of the tape. In this case, the tape began with a shot of St. John Arena, Ohio State's home court. It is empty. Into it walks the narrator who is saying, "St. John Arena. Many of the greatest names in basketball began their careers here. Players like Jerry Lucas, John Havlicek, Clark Kellogg, and Eric Riley."

There is a pause to give the recruit and his family a chance to drink in the last name. And then: "Well, maybe not yet, Eric, but you could very easily join those great names *if* you choose Ohio State."

This is a fairly simple thing to do and Ohio State certainly isn't unique in using this tactic. At N.C. State, Valvano plays recruits a dummy radio tape in which they score the winning basket in a crucial game.

Even so, people notice. It shows them that extra time was taken. Just as important, it is a good ice-breaker at the start of a visit when everyone is a little nervous. As the tape finishes, Fraschilla says, "I'm ready to sign."

Everyone laughs. Beulah Riley has a number of questions for the coaches. She is a tall, dignified woman who has an older son, Jerome, playing at Kentucky State. Ayers, who has known the family longest, calls her Beulah. Williams and Fraschilla call her "Mrs. Riley."

Ohio State has been in the news recently because of the controversy over football player Cris Carter, who had signed illegally with an agent and lost his eligibility. Beulah Riley is concerned about this. Could Eric lose his scholarship while at Ohio State?

"If he signed with an agent, yes," Williams answers. "Or if he cheated in school or flunked out."

Eric Riley is confused. "Coach," he asks, "do I have to get an agent?"

For a moment, Williams is stunned. Coaches often forget in recruiting they are dealing with teenagers. Some are street-smart beyond their years. Others, like Riley, are just kids.

"Eric, you can't have an agent under any circumstances while you're in college," Williams says. "It doesn't matter where you go. If you ever take anything from an agent, you'll never play in college again and you'll lose your scholarship."

Beulah Riley is nodding. "We understand, right, Eric?"

Her son nods. "Now I do."

That hurdle cleared, things begin to loosen up. Suddenly, there is a knock on the back door. Eric answers it. A middle-aged man walks into the room with him. Beulah Riley looks up, sees him, then stares at the floor without saying a word.

"This is my father," Eric Riley says softly.

The coaches jump to their feet. There are handshakes all around. Beulah Riley never moves. Benny Riley sits down on the couch next to his son. The mood has gone from relaxed to awkward. Williams speaks first.

"We were just sort of answering any questions that you all might have about Ohio State, Mr. Riley. If you've got anything you want to add or ask, please go ahead because that's what we're here for."

Benny Riley nods. "Wherever he goes, I want him to get a degree," he says. Everyone agrees that is of paramount importance. The rest of the visit goes by without any problems, though Beulah Riley is very quiet. She and her husband never exchange a look or a word.

Finally, shortly after nine, the coaches leave. "We'll see you at school October thirtieth," Williams says, a reference to Riley's official visit.

Once in the car, all of them—even Ayers—are talking at once. The back-door arrival of Benny Riley, both literally and figuratively, is just the kind of thing recruiters hate. What does it mean? What is his role? They have been dealing with Beulah Riley all along. Has someone else gotten to the father? Dark thoughts cross a recruiter's mind late at night.

"For the moment," Williams says, "let's pretend it didn't happen. Keep dealing with Beulah because we don't want to upset her. She and the father obviously don't get along. But you guys keep your ears open and see if you can find out anything about Benny."

Williams leans back in his seat. "I hate surprises," he says, knowing he is smack in the middle of a game that is full of them. Tonight is just another example.

The key out-of-state recruit for Williams was Chris Jent, who is from Williams's home state—New Jersey. Jent was exactly the kind of player Williams felt he had to get—in addition to the Ohio players—because there was such impressive competition to get him.

Georgia Tech had been involved with Jent early and, during the summer, had been considered the favorite to land him. Pittsburgh was heavily involved, aided by the fact that Assistant Coach John Calipari had roomed with Jent's high school coach, Dennis Tobin, at North Carolina–Wilmington. "I won't bring up the fact that we kicked their ass while I was at American," Williams said, "unless we lose the kid."

And then there was Louisiana State, a late entry in the Jent sweepstakes. Jent had caught Dale Brown's eye during the Nike summer camp at Princeton, New Jersey. The Nike camp is a late but powerful arrival on the summer camp scene. During the last twenty years, summer camps have become an important part of the recruiting process. They give college coaches a chance to see top players going up against other top players on a daily basis, sometimes two or three times a day.

Because they have become such showcases, the three major camp operators—Nike, Howard Garfinkel, and Bill Cronauer—have become almost as cutthroat in recruiting players to their camps as colleges are in recruiting them to their schools.

Nike was started in 1978 under the name "Athletes for a Better Education." The players were required to attend classes in the morning that purportedly helped prepare them for dealing with the academic pressures of college.

Now, that name has been dropped, and what you see is what you get at Nike. It is a basketball meat market—coaches watching players while players watch coaches to see who is watching them most carefully. Coaches who have contracts with Nike can use their influence to get players invited to the camp, and they let recruits know that.

Nike puts a lot of money into college basketball. It pays a lot of coaches a lot of money (unlike the pros, Nike can't pay the athletes to wear their shoes—that's against NCAA rules—so it pays the coaches, often more than $100,000, to provide shoes); it sponsors the annual coaches' all-star game at the Final Four and it runs the summer camp. No one wants to mess with Nike.

It was in Princeton that Dale Brown noticed Jent. In some ways Jent did not have, as the scouts put it, a good camp. A shooter, he did not shoot very well. The consensus, and no one is ever sure what creates a consensus, was that his stock dropped during the camp.

But Brown loved him. He liked the way he played, diving for balls, willingly giving up his body. "I can coach him," he told his new assistant Craig Carse. "Let's try to get involved, even though it's late."

Brown wrote Jent and his parents a long letter telling them how impressed he had been with Chris and asking if they would consider adding LSU to the list of schools that would visit Jent's home. "The letter was so flattering," said Arnie Jent, Chris's father, "I really couldn't say no."

Once Brown decides he wants something—or someone—he will do almost anything to get it or him. Brown is one of college basketball's true characters. Some hate him and ridicule him. Others see him as a twentieth-century Don Quixote, always tilting at a windmill somewhere. Brown has done battle with the NCAA, "as crooked an organization as there is in this country"; with Bob Knight, "a truly evil, cunning, and sick person"; and the recruiting process itself—"What we really are, all of us, is a bunch of white slavers going into Africa to bring back the biggest, best studs we can find."

He is a nonstop talker who will tell you about his poor, fatherless boyhood at any hour, day or night. He loves to recite sayings. "I can still remember sitting on the fire escape of our building when I was ten years old, and my mother coming out and telling me, 'Be different than me. Be yourself. Don't be frightened.' I'm not frightened of anything."

Probably, that is true. Brown took over the LSU program in 1972 when it was one of the worst basketball schools in the country in a league, the Southeast Conference, that had traditionally been Kentucky and the nine dwarfs. He had turned LSU into a power, reaching the Final Four in 1981 and 1986 and the Final Eight in 1987.

The '87 loss rankled, though, because it had been to Indiana and Knight, a game in which LSU had a big lead only to lose by a point at the buzzer. The game had been controversial, Knight drawing a technical foul in the first half and then slamming a phone in anger while the officials watched and didn't react.

"He should have been out of the game, gone," Brown said. "He stole that game from us. He intimidated the officials. Everyone in the country knows it but no one will say it. Well, I'll say it. I want that son of a bitch to know there's one guy who isn't afraid of him. I want to play him, anywhere, anytime, but he won't do it. And before the game, I'd like the two of us to be locked in a wrestling room naked by ourselves and let's see which one of us comes out."

As Brown talked about Knight this cool Friday September afternoon, his assistant, Carse, was driving toward the Jent home. Pittsburgh had already visited Jent, Georgia Tech would be in on Sunday, and Ohio State would visit the following Wednesday. Brown was wound up.

He was under fire again, but didn't care. He was about to receive a verbal commitment from Stanley Roberts, a 6–10 center from South Carolina. In August, Brown had made a commitment to hire Roberts's high school coach the following season. One month later, without ever visiting LSU, Roberts committed to the school.

There is nothing in the rules against what Brown had done. What's more, the move was hardly unique. In fact, it was the fifth time Brown had done it during his LSU career. But because Roberts was so highly regarded, this had attracted a lot of attention.

"The NCAA called me and said they were looking into it," Brown said, "I said to the guy, 'What are you looking into? Where's the violation? You guys have been after me so long, you think there's one rule out there I don't know?' "

One of the schools that had been after Roberts, and lost him to Brown, was Georgia Tech. Two days later when Tech Coach Bobby Cremins and his assistant Kevin Cantwell visited the Jents, Arnie Jent would comment on how charming he had found Brown. "I was afraid," Cantwell said later, "that Bobby was going to throw up all over their rug."

Brown knew he had only an outside shot at Jent. His mission on this visit was to convince Jent to visit LSU. If he could do that he believed Jent might make a last-minute switch in his thinking.

Sparta is a comfortable, upper-crust suburb in northern New Jersey. Chris Jent is the third of Arnie and Trish Jent's four children. His two older brothers, Tim and Eric, were athletes too. Arnie Jent was a basketball player at the University of Detroit and is now an account executive at the Atlantic Design Company.

Brown and Carse arrive shortly after 6 P.M. and are welcomed by Chris, his parents, and Megan, Jent's four-year-old sister. There is nothing subtle in Brown's pitch. He is selling from the minute he sits down in the comfortable Jent living room.

"Craig," he says to Carse, "when Nike was over, who did I tell you was my favorite player in the camp, my absolute number-one favorite player, the guy I wanted more than anyone?"

"Honest to God, Mr. and Mrs. Jent, it was Chris," Carse says, answering his boss. "I knew it, too. I knew the way Chris played that was what he was going to say."

Brown is rolling. "You remember when I called you this summer just to say hi and see how you all were doing?" The Jents nod. "You know where I was? The Amazon. I went down there to spend some time in the jungle and when I got to a phone I called you from there. Cost me $112. It was worth it, though."

The Jents are wide-eyed. Brown goes on. "You know, coming over in the car, I was thinking about this whole recruiting thing that all we coaches do. Let's be honest about it. The whole thing is a giant hypocrisy. I'm sitting here with you tonight telling you why it would be great for Chris to come to LSU, how easy it is for all of you to fly from Newark to New Orleans and for him to get home when he wants to, how the travel isn't a problem. Tomorrow, I'll be home telling a bunch of in-state recruits how much it will help them to stay home and go to LSU.

"We all do that. But, let's be honest, it's a business. We'll all sit here and tell you how we want to do what's right and we want to make the world a better place. Hell, if any of us were serious we'd drop all this, drop all the money we make, and go work with Mother Teresa. What are the chances of that happening?

"But I will say this to you, Chris, and to you, too, Mom and Dad. I try to recruit leaders and I think that's what Chris will be when he's through playing basketball. We've got two kids ready to sign with us who play Chris's position but I've told them I won't offer them a scholarship until you tell us no because you are our number-one priority.

"And I'll tell you something, Chris, and I've said this very few times in my coaching career: You come to LSU and in four years you will be a number-one draft choice. I guarantee that. I'm certain of it. Our style of play is perfect for you."

There is more: Brown talks about the summer jobs program at LSU, telling Jent he'll make $12 to $15 an hour. He talks about Ricky Blanton, his best player, saying, "You two would be like Siamese Twins. You both play like Attila the Hun." When Megan wanders by, Brown grabs her and bounces her on his knee. Finally, he brings out not one but two tapes.

The first one is a highlight tape of the '87 season put together by Brown's daughter. The second is a tape of Brown's television show during the last weekend of the '87 regular season. Brown always brings his seniors' parents on the show, and in this case, the mother of Anthony Wilson had read him a lengthy poem, thanking him for taking care of her son the previous four years.

By the time the second tape has been shown, Brown and Carse have been in the house more than two hours. Brown goes through his litany one more time and then Arnie Jent walks down the driveway to the car with the two coaches. By the time Brown gets in the car, he is flying.

"Now I really want that kid," he says, breathlessly. "I think we'll get a visit from him, and if we do, we'll get him. That kid should play for me."

The Jents were impressed by Brown. But not impressed enough to change the recruiting process they had started so long ago. Jent's decision would come down to two schools: Ohio State and Pittsburgh. Brown and LSU had lost.

Williams and his coaches had felt all along that Pittsburgh was their big competition for Jent. They were concerned about Calipari's friendship with Dennis Tobin and about the lure of the Big East to a player who had grown up in Big East territory during the league's remarkable recent rise to prominence.

Their advantage, they felt, was that Jent had relatives in Columbus and, coming from a close family, would feel comfortable going to school in a place where he had family nearby. Jent had made an unofficial visit to Ohio State during the summer, driving to Columbus and staying with his relatives.

By the time Williams and Fraschilla visited Jent on October 1, most of America's coaches were near exhaustion. They had been on the road almost nonstop for fifteen days and still had six days left. "This is like a long sprint," Williams said. "You have to go all out from start to finish but by the end, you're running out of gas."

Before leaving his hotel for the Jents' house, Williams calls home. His daughter, Kristen, has an important test that day. Like many coaching fathers, Williams feels guilty about the time he spends away from home.

As he and Fraschilla leave the hotel, they run into the Rutgers coaching staff. Craig Littlepage, the Rutgers coach, starting his third season, is under fire after two twenty-loss years in a row. Not keeping New Jersey players at home has been Rutgers's problem. The fact that Rutgers isn't even involved with a player like Jent is symptomatic of the problems there.

Littlepage greets Williams warmly. "What are you guys doing in New Jersey?" he asks. "Didn't you know we've already bought all the players?"

The coaches chat briefly, bemoaning the intensity of the twenty-one-day visitation period. Williams gets in the car and shakes his head. "I feel bad for Craig. I think he's gonna get fired at the end of the year if they don't turn it around. He may just be too nice a guy for this business."

Williams is right. Rutgers will lose twenty games and Littlepage will be fired. The new coach will be a Rutgers alumnus, Bob Wenzel. His first pledge as the new coach will be to keep New Jersey players—like Chris Jent—at home.

Williams's visit with the Jents is completely different from Brown's. The Jents, while somewhat overwhelmed by Brown, are clearly comfortable with Williams. Chris, almost silent during Brown's visit, talks up a storm with Williams. Surprisingly, for a family that would seemingly have seen every recruiting trick there is, the personalized tape goes over big.

"Hey, that's really something," Chris Jent says when the narrator mentions his name.

Williams stays two hours, more to socialize than to sell. There isn't much new to say. Fraschilla does give Jent four typed pages listing the benefits of Ohio State. It lists all of Williams's assets and fourteen reasons why Jent should go to Ohio State. It ends with a list of OSU's great players: "Jerry Lucas . . . John Havlicek . . . Kelvin Ransey . . . Clark Kellogg . . . Herb Williams . . . Brad Sellers . . . Dennis Hopson . . . Chris Jent . . . The tradition continues!"

Williams doesn't "negative recruit." He won't put down another program. But Fraschilla does make this point: "Chris, the reason you should come to Ohio State is Gary Williams. He's signed on for the long haul. I hope *I'll* be there a long time, but with assistants you never know. We come and go more. You should never pick your school because of an assistant coach."

Fraschilla isn't talking about himself when he says this. He's talking about Calipari.

When the visit is over, Williams feels confident. "I really think I have a good thing going with him," he says. "If he has a good visit to school and feels comfortable with our kids, I think we'll get him."

Jent will visit October 30, the same weekend that Eric Riley and Mark Baker will visit. That weekend will be as important—if not more important—to Williams than any he will face all season.

That is the nature of college basketball. No one wins without players. That is why the games on the court are so much simpler than the ones off the court. In recruiting, everyone has an angle, a pitch. Those are the good guys. The bad ones are the cheaters, the ones who pay players and get away with it because the NCAA enforcement staff is so undermanned that it can only catch the amateur cheaters like Marist and Cleveland State. The experts, the ones who have been doing it for years, never get caught. They are too smart and/or too powerful.

Valvano says it best: "If you are a decent human being on any level you must hate what we do in recruiting."

And no one is a better recruiter than Jim Valvano.

4
YOU'RE IN THE
ARMY, (OR NAVY)
NOW

The first player chosen in the 1987 NBA draft rounded the corner, car keys in hand, and started for the door.

"And just where do you think you're going?" The woman's voice was stern, though she was fighting a grin.

"Lunch," he answered. "If that's okay with you, that is."

"Okay then," the woman said. "But you still have work to do when you come back."

Ensign David Robinson nodded, smiled, and ducked his head going through the door of the trailer. It was a warm November day in south Georgia. Ten days earlier he had signed a contract to play basketball for the San Antonio Spurs that had made him rich, extremely rich. Over an eight-year period, the Spurs would pay him about $26 million. "It's the kind of money," he said, "that doesn't even seem real to me."

This, though, was very real. This was King's Bay, Georgia, the offices of the Resident Officer in Charge of Construction on what would become, during the next three years, a giant submarine base. Robinson, six months removed from the Naval Academy, worked for the ROICC negotiating with contractors. For this, he was paid considerably less than $26 million. About $1,500 a month was more like it.

"I live a double life," he said, sitting in the tiny town of St. Mary's fanciest restaurant, a Pizza Hut. "In one world, I rule. Everything I could possibly want is there on a silver platter for me. I'm rich and famous and because of that I have power.

"In the other world I'm at the bottom of the totem pole. I have to ask permission to go to lunch. I fetch coffee for people. It helps me keep things in perspective. The best thing about the Navy is the worst thing about the Navy: Everyone gets treated the same."

David Robinson is seven-foot-one. He can run, jump, and shoot. To most of the world that makes him a superstar, a basketball player with unlimited potential. To the Navy, it just makes him a headache. He's too tall, too rich, and too famous. But he spent four years at the Naval Academy and graduated with a degree in engineering.

No one, not Robinson, not the Navy, ever imagined when he enrolled as a 6–7 freshman with some interest—but not a lot—in basketball, that he would end up as the college player of the year. The Navy is not entirely unreasonable. It is willing to let Robinson out in two years, three years less than the five-year commitment usually required of Academy graduates. It wants him to play in the Olympics as Ensign David Robinson. After that, after he has been the Navy's top recruiter for two years, he can play all the basketball he wants and make all the money he wants.

In the meantime, he asks permission to go to lunch. "I never dreamed that playing basketball would ever become so important to me," he said. "I understand the Navy's point of view completely. But it's hard for me. When I watch the Spurs play, I know I could help, I know they could win more games if I was playing. But right now, all I can do is wait."

He smiled. "It isn't so bad, though. I've got a lot to look forward to."

The same could not be said for Kevin Houston, at least in basketball. It was a remarkable coincidence that both Houston and Robinson had been college seniors in 1987. While Robinson had been the third leading scorer in the country at Navy, Houston had been two spots ahead of him—at No. 1—while playing for Army.

It was rare enough that Army or Navy would produce a genuine star. For each school to produce one at exactly the same time was extraordinary. But although they each had military academy backgrounds, the differences between Robinson and Houston were far more striking than the similarities.

"He's seven-one and he can run and he can jump," Houston said. "I'm five-eleven and I don't run or jump very well. About the only thing we have in common is that we can both play pretty well."

Robinson was a fluke of nature. He had never cared that much for basketball and had chosen the Naval Academy for a specific reason. His father, Ambrose Robinson, had spent twenty years in the Navy and David wanted to follow in his footsteps. But then he grew six inches in two years and become a great player. That changed his plans.

Houston always wanted to play basketball. His father, Jerry, had played for Joe Lapchick at St. John's in the 1960s. In fact, it was Jerry Houston who made the last two free throws in Lapchick's farewell to coaching, a 55–51 victory over Villanova in the 1965 NIT Final.

Jerry Houston coached basketball after he was through playing. He coached high school ball, boy's club ball, and for one year was an assistant coach at Fordham. Although Kevin grew up in suburban Pearl River, New York, he was shaped as a basketball player in New York City, where his father took him to play against the best players.

Houston certainly didn't look like a schoolyard ballplayer. With his reddish hair and freckles he looked a lot more like Tom Sawyer than a basketball player. "When I first started playing in the city a lot of guys looked at me and thought I was some kind of white, suburban, faggot jump-shooter," Houston said, laughing at the memory. "But I sort of enjoy proving to people that I can do what they don't think I can do."

That was the story of Houston's college career, too. Only Army recruited him with any real zeal and his decision to go to West Point was based on one thing: a chance to play. He got it right away and, just as quickly, became a key player. "One thing about Kevin is that he's never been awed by anyone he's played against," Army Coach Les Wohtke said. "That has a lot to do with his playing background."

If Houston had played almost anywhere in the country other than a military academy he would have been the best-known person on campus. But at Army, football is still the only sport that truly matters and, because he didn't *look* like a player, Houston went unnoticed most of the time.

"I'd come down to the gym in the spring to play pickup ball and I couldn't get chosen," he said. "I'd have to wait around and call winners to get a chance to play. No one knew who I was and when they looked at me no one figured I could play.

"The summer before my senior year I was stationed at Fort Knox. One weekend, Ron Steptoe [a teammate from Army] and I went over to a gym to play. We walked in and there were nine guys in the place.

With us, that made eleven. I said to Ron, 'When we choose up, watch, I won't be picked.' I was hoping we would shoot free throws to see who played or something. But no. They chose up and guess who ended up watching?"

Houston can tell these stories and laugh because he knows he can play. He proved it beyond any doubt his senior season when he averaged 32.9 points per game, including a 38-point game at Navy. "I've never seen a guy light it up like that in my life," Robinson said. "He never changed expression. He just kept pouring it on."

Houston plays with the same deadpan expression whether he hits ten straight shots or misses ten straight. Nothing seems to bother him. But in the spring of '87, when the invitations went out to the Pan American Games trials, Houston didn't get one. That bothered him.

"My first thought was, 'Damn, how could they leave me out?' " he said. "I'm not even saying I would have made the team but I thought I deserved the chance to try out. It really pissed me off. I still don't understand it."

Houston was not alone. Wohtke was baffled. Ironically, Robinson, who really didn't care whether he played in the Pan Ams, had a virtually automatic spot on the team. Houston, who would have committed to an extra five years in the Army just for a trials invitation, never got a phone call.

That is the difference between being 7–1 and 5–11. The gap is much wider than fourteen inches. Robinson, in addition to his $26 million contract, has a life filled with endorsements and a very probable spot on the Olympic team to look forward to. Houston knows that most of his basketball is behind him. "Anything I do from here on will be my last hurrah," he said. "But that's all I want is that last shot, one more chance to really prove I can play."

As he spoke, Houston was sitting in a small restaurant less than a mile from West Point, where he was temporarily assigned as a graduate assistant coach. This was in November, two days after Robinson had signed his contract. Houston was happy for Robinson but he was a lot happier about news he had just received: His application to try out for the All-Army basketball team had been approved. This meant that instead of shipping out to Fort Sill, Oklahoma, for officer's basic training in field artillery, he would be going to San Francisco in January to try out for the Army team, a group of all-stars that would barnstorm the country.

To Houston, this was the one last chance he had been hoping for. The All-Army team would finish its tour in March at an armed forces tournament in North Carolina. At that tournament, an all-Armed Forces team would be chosen. They would play together through April. That would mean that *if* Houston could get an invitation to the Olympic Trials he would be in playing shape when they began on May 18.

"When I heard I was going to San Francisco, it was like new life," he said. "I really thought maybe it was over for me, but now I've got this shot. Ever since I got the news, I've been working out every night after the team practices to get the feel back."

Houston was not alone when he practiced. His wife of five months, Elizabeth, rebounded for him. He shot, she rebounded and passed. This was where Kevin Houston's last go-round began.

"If Kevin had to put the basketball down and walk away, I think he could do it without any regrets," Wohtke said. "He's given the game everything he has. But I think the people in the game owe him more than that. He deserves the chance to find out, one way or the other."

It would be April before Houston would find out if he would have that chance. In the meantime, he kept shooting and Elizabeth kept rebounding.

When he had time to play, Robinson had no trouble finding rebounders. He was working out with Jacksonville University which was located less than thirty miles from King's Bay. But even this setup was complicated. In order to be allowed to practice with Jacksonville, Robinson had to be listed as a volunteer coach for the team. The NCAA, ever vigilant, was on top of that. If something is irrelevant, you can be sure the NCAA will be on the scene.

Intellectually, Robinson understood that he was a very lucky person. But emotionally, not playing bothered him. Those who had known him a long time thought this was funny, since Robinson had never really cared about basketball until he had become very good at it. Robinson understood the irony involved, too. He is an inordinately bright young man who, even with all the attention he has received, has remained unaffected. His newfound financial status amused him as much as anything.

"A couple weeks ago I was in a Burger King," he said. "The guy behind the counter recognized me and he said, 'Hey Robinson, when you sign your contract for all that money come back here and I'll give you some free food.' I looked at him and said, 'Why would you give me free food *after* I'm rich? Why not give it to me now when I need it?'

"But that's the way the world is. If you've got things, people want to give you more. If you haven't got anything, no one wants to give you a thing.

"The night I signed my contract in San Antonio I went into a bar with some people. I was amazed. All of a sudden, I had gotten much better looking. I was a lot funnier. And everyone wanted to buy me a drink. I thought it was remarkable how I had suddenly been transformed at the age of twenty-two. It couldn't have been the money, right?"

Robinson was laughing. His two-year commitment to the Navy is not the only thing that makes him different from most NBA top draft choices.

When he first emerged as a star during his sophomore year at Navy, there was a lot of pressure on Robinson to transfer. If he had left the Academy before his junior year, he would have been free from his five-year service commitment. But after a good deal of agonizing, Robinson decided to stay.

He often wondered during his junior year if he had made a mistake. He wanted to play pro basketball when he graduated. The Navy held the cards, though. It could release him from his commitment because he was too tall ever to go to sea. It could compromise, ask him to stick around for a couple years as a recruiter while playing in the Olympics. Or it could be hard-nosed and demand he stay in the service for five years. It was the last possibility that scared Robinson.

"I really didn't have any idea what they were going to do," he said. "But the five years was possible, I knew that. Once, I had looked forward to it. Now, I was scared of it."

In February of his senior season he got the word: two years. The Navy had compromised. The night before he learned what his fate was, knowing the decision was coming, Robinson played the worst game of his career in a loss to Richmond. "It was the only time the whole thing got to me," he said. "I didn't even care that much when we lost. I was really bad."

The two years meant Robinson would be expected to play for the

U.S. in the Pan American Games and the Olympics. Having played against the Soviets the previous summer in the World Championships, Robinson would have preferred the NBA. But the choice wasn't his.

Robinson ended his college career by scoring 50 points in Navy's first-round NCAA Tournament loss to Michigan. At game's end, as the Navy band played the alma mater, Robinson felt frightened for the first time in memory. "It was like a moment of silence for my college career," he said. "I realized it was over and I thought, 'What happens next?' It was scary."

He was stunned when the agents who started hounding him from that night forward told him he could be worth $2 million a year. Robinson had been thinking that $100,000 to play basketball was an awful lot of money. Now he was being told his *shoe contract* would be worth a lot more than that.

Still, there was the Navy side of his life. Graduation came in May and Robinson was assigned to King's Bay. "South Georgia?" he thought. "A great place for a seven-one black guy to be hanging out." Then he got lost driving down there, and then the Americans lost the Pan American final to Brazil and everyone wanted to know what happened. The summer couldn't end soon enough for Robinson.

In the meantime, he had hired an agency, Advantage International, and negotiations with the San Antonio Spurs were going forward. When he finally signed, Robinson thought it all quite wonderful.

"Except for this: Here I am being given all this money. I've worked four years to get here. Now I'm a pro and what am I doing? Sitting behind a desk. It doesn't make a whole lot of sense."

But then neither story, Houston's nor Robinson's, made much sense as their first year out of college began. The nation's leading scorer had his wife rebounding for him. And the highest-paid basketball player in the world had to ask permission to go to lunch.

5
YOU DON'T HAVE
TO BE JEWISH TO
BE A SCHMUCK

Rollie Massimino is a man of sayings and slogans. Some are eloquent: "Complacency is the foundation of failure." Others are more Rollie-like: "In the face of adversity, the true guy comes out."

But as he sat in the middle of a second-floor ballroom at the Grand Hyatt Hotel three weeks before Villanova's opening game, Massimino's favorite slogan passed through his mind more than once: "You don't have to be Jewish to be a schmuck."

"Schmuck" is a Massimino word, along with "straphanger" and "jag." Everyone in his life, with the exception of his wife Mary Jane, is at some point a schmuck, a straphanger—strap for short—or a jag. More often than not, they are terms of endearment, because if Massimino doesn't like someone, there are other words he uses to describe them. There is no explaining why he uses these terms and there is no making sense of them, just as there is no making sense of why Massimino calls his sophomore forward Rodney Taylor "Duke."

Ask him why Taylor is Duke and he will say: "I don't know. It's just what I call him."

Schmuck had been a Massimino word since boyhood. The son of a shoemaker, he grew up in a Jewish neighborhood in northern New Jersey. He likes to joke that "some of my best friends are Italian," because many of his close friends were Jewish. The Italians were his relatives.

He was a good small-college guard at the University of Vermont and has coached ever since he graduated, first in high school, then in college. He was an assistant at Pennsylvania when the job that would make him a star came open at Villanova.

November 5 was the annual Big East Media Day at the Grand Hyatt. All nine league coaches attend along with two of their players. The setup is simple. First, the coaches go into the room where all the TV crews set up and answer TV questions while the players sit in the next room with the print media and answer their questions. Then, after an hour, everyone switches.

The only exception to this is Georgetown Coach John Thompson. When Thompson is with the print media, so are his players. When he goes to do TV, they go with him. No one from the Big East has ever asked Thompson to follow the same system everyone else uses. They are just thankful that he shows up at all.

Once upon a time, when Villanova was the defending national champion—that was all of two years ago—trying to get near Massimino or his players on Media Day was a little bit like trying to get Springsteen tickets. But in 1987, Massimino, Mark Plansky, and Doug West would have had a tough time finding a fourth for bridge if they had been together during the interviewing period.

As the press moved around the room, studiously avoiding Villanova, Plansky nudged West. "The 'Neers are out in force today," he said. "We'll bring them back, though."

'Neers is a Villanova expression, short for "Wagoneers." Wagoneers as in Bandwagon, as in people who jump from bandwagon to bandwagon. The Villanova bandwagon was empty in November and everyone at the school was aware of it.

In May, Massimino had called his players together after the networks had finalized their television schedules for the following winter and told them that Villanova hadn't been selected for one network TV game for the first time in years.

"That's where we are," he told them. They were a little angry and very embarrassed. That was what Massimino wanted.

All summer he suspected he had a team that would surprise people. Because of the recruiting disasters and because of the previous season, the Wildcats would be picked to do very little in 1988. That was fine with Massimino.

But he knew he had a rebuilding project to do and he knew it had to start at the top. The McLain drug debacle had left him drained the previous season. He had internalized his anger so much that friends had worried he was driving himself to a heart attack. He had to get Rollie back to being Rollie.

So, he started to eat again. His weight had dropped to 210 during 1987, not exactly thin for someone who is barely 5–8, but thinner than in the past. "I coach better," he said, "when I'm fat." He ate his way back up to 225.

He abandoned the pretense of being an elder statesman. He couldn't be Dean Smith on the bench. He had to be Rollie. That meant controlled hysteria. Even in expensive clothes, Rollie had always looked disheveled during games. That was where the Danny DeVito image came from. It worked for him too. Rollie was Everyman, screaming at injustice until his hair stood on end.

There was more. He and his coaches had to work harder than they had in the past. "If we had a letter in 1987 it was 'S,' " he said. "S as in *soft* and *sucks*. We were soft and we sucked. That started with all of us coaches."

It would be the same for the players. Tom Greis, who had been unable to run up and down the floor as a freshman, was ordered to lose thirty pounds. "Lose it or don't bother showing up on October fifteenth," was the word from Rollie, Greis lost it. Kenny Wilson, the tiny jet of a point guard, had to be more disciplined. West had to be more consistent. Plansky, the only senior starter, had to be more confident. Taylor had to be healthy after playing only five games as a freshman.

"We had good players," Massimino said. "What we didn't have was confidence. That had always been our trademark. On the road, in close games, we always found a way. Somewhere the year before we had lost that. We were losing the close ones. I told them whatever we did this season we were going to do it aggressively. If we lost, we lost, but we were going to go down swinging."

When the team came together on October 15, Massimino gave them not one, but two mottoes. One was "Find a way." The other was "The Wildcats are back." The latter was a throwback to 1973, Massimino's first year on the job. It made sense because this team was starting all over again.

The perception, though, was that Villanova was in trouble. That was why the 'Neers stayed away in New York. Villanova was a nonstory.

They were picked sixth or seventh in the league, depending on which poll you looked at. Some people thought they might finish ninth.

The season would begin in Hawaii, in a tough tournament that included teams like Kansas, Iowa, Illinois, Baylor, Stanford, and Nebraska. The opener was against a decent Nebraska team and, if that game produced a victory, the next opponent would probably be Illinois. The third game in three days would in all likelihood be against Kansas or Iowa.

Massimino would know quickly whether his team was as good as he thought or as bad as the world thought. For now, though, he sat in the solitude of the crowded room, puffing on a cigar, looking every minute of his fifty-three years, watching the 'Neers do their work.

Across the room from Massimino sat Paul Evans. He was as much in demand as Massimino was not. Along with Syracuse, which had been picked No. 1 nationally in many polls, Evans's Pittsburgh team was seen as a dominant factor in the Big East.

This was a new role for Evans—playing the favorite. He had always coached underdog teams in the past, first at St. Lawrence, then at Navy. But one of the reasons he had left Navy for Pittsburgh was that he wanted to be at a school where the Final Four—and the national championship—were not unreasonable goals.

For this Pitt team, even with the loss of point guard Goodson, those did not seem to be unreasonable goals. Lane, the leading rebounder in the country, was back, along with silky-smooth center Charles Smith, standout sophomore Rod Brookin and three-year starter Demetrius Gore. What's more, Evans had recruited four excellent freshmen to go with the veterans returning from a team that had won twenty-four games the preceding season.

One of those freshmen was 6–10 Bobby Martin. It was Martin's decision to go to Pitt, after initially committing verbally to Villanova, that had put Evans and Massimino at odds.

But the story wasn't that simple. Evans and Massimino were bound to be at odds because of their personalities. Both were competitive men and good coaches. The similarities ended there. Massimino never made a move without his wife. Where he went, she went. They had been married for thirty years. Their five children were as much a part of the Villanova team as the Villanova team was part of the family.

Evans was completely different. It wasn't so much that he had been married and divorced three times, because he was as devoted in his own way to his two children (one by each of his first two marriages) as Massimino was devoted to his children. It was more of an approach problem. Evans was a maverick, an ask-no-quarter, give-no-quarter guy. He had come into a league with a very definite pecking order—Commissioner Dave (Mr. Television) Gavitt was at the top along with Massimino, Thompson, and St. John's Coach Lou Carnesecca—and said screw the pecking order. He had spoken his mind in a league where speaking your mind was frowned upon.

The older coaches didn't think he had paid his dues. Evans thought dues-paying was for unions. And so, when Massimino accused Pittsburgh of cheating to get Bobby Martin, Evans told the press what Massimino had said. When Gavitt told Evans to be quiet, Evans told the press that Gavitt had told him to be quiet.

His bluntness was not going to win him any popularity contests. But Evans didn't really care. The only contests he cared about were the ones on the basketball court.

Evans had always wanted to be a coach. He was born in Pennsylvania but had grown up in upstate New York with his parents, who adopted him after his natural parents died while he was an infant.

He was a good athlete, a three-sport star in football, basketball, and track. By the time he was a junior in high school, Evans knew he wanted to coach. "I had one of those career meetings with the guidance counselor at the end of my junior year and I said, 'I want to be a coach.' She looked at me and said, 'But what do you want to do for a living?' "

He went to Ithaca College and became a dean's list student when an ankle injury forced him to give up all sports but track. After graduation, he married his high school sweetheart and became a successful high school coach. During his second year as a coach, late in the season, he was called up to active duty by the National Guard.

His team was undefeated. Only six games were left to play. Evans didn't mind being called up but not *now*. There was only one solution—or so he thought. He and a friend went into the weight room and, while Evans closed his eyes, his friend brought the full force of one of the weights down on Evans's arm. They raced to the hospital for X rays. The nurse came out with a smile on her face. "Good news, Mr. Evans," she said. "There's no sign of a break. You should be all right in a few days."

Evans didn't bother trying to break the arm again. The unbroken one hurt too much.

He moved into college coaching as a freshman coach at Geneseo before getting the job at St. Lawrence, as much because he had coached some football and taught some math as anything. He was a big winner at St. Lawrence on the Division 2 level but wondered when he would get a shot at a Division 1 job. In 1979, he interviewed for the Dartmouth job but lost out to Tim Cohane. That annoyed him since he had beaten Cohane in the Division 2 playoffs two years in a row.

The following year, the Cornell job became available. The athletic director was Dick Schultz, now the executive director of the NCAA. Schultz interviewed Evans at length and told him he would be in touch. Evans finished a 22–5 season that Saturday with an easy victory over his alma mater, Ithaca, but was disappointed that Schultz wasn't at the game.

The next day Schultz called. He was sorry but because of public relations he had decided to hire a Bob Knight assistant, Tom Miller. Evans was crushed. "I was thirty-four and I had decided a few years earlier that if I didn't have a Division One job by the time I was thirty-five I was going to get out," he said. "I just didn't want to spend the rest of my life driving a bus."

Four days after telling him he couldn't hire him at Cornell, Schultz called Evans back. Would he be interested in the Navy job? Navy Athletic Director J. O. (Bo) Coppedge had called Schultz looking for names. Schultz had mentioned Evans.

Evans was thrilled. He never stopped to think about Navy's complete lack of basketball tradition; about the height restrictions; about the five-year service commitment required of all graduates. "I was too stupid to know I couldn't do it there," he said, smiling. "I figured Knight had gotten it done at Army, why couldn't I do it at Navy?"

It wasn't easy. Evans's first two teams were 9–17 and 12–14. He was criticized for trying to play an up-tempo game at a school clearly not fit to play up-tempo basketball. But Evans was putting the pieces together. His third team set an Academy record for victories by going 18–8. Evans was shocked when the NIT never noticed his team and no other schools noticed his victory total.

The next year the record was 24–8 with a freshman named Robinson averaging six points a game. Still no NIT bid and no job offers. The next year, when Robinson blossomed, the Midshipmen were 26–6. They reached the NCAA Tournament, stunned LSU in the first round, and had Maryland down 11 before losing in the second round. Now people noticed Navy—and Evans. California called. So did Old Dominion. And Rutgers. He was even interviewed for the prestigious Kentucky job.

None of those jobs felt right, though, so Evans stayed where he was. The next year the record was 30–5. Robinson was a superstar. The Midshipmen beat Tulsa, Syracuse (at Syracuse), and Cleveland State in the NCAA Tournament before losing to Duke in the regional final. Evans couldn't keep track of the job offers: Southern California, Houston, Northwestern, Pittsburgh.

He knew his time was up at Navy even though Robinson had one more year. He wanted his top assistant, Pete Herrmann, to succeed him, but he didn't want to leave Herrmann with a bad team. And, he didn't want to leave at the same time as Robinson and be perceived as riding Robinson's coattails. Pittsburgh was the best job. There were good, though undisciplined players there and it was in the Big East.

There were also rumors that Pitt was about to get nailed by the NCAA. That was alleged to be part of the reason why Roy Chipman had resigned early in the season. But Pitt's people told Evans they were clean. Evans took them at their word, and it turned out to be the right decision—the NCAA posse never did come to town.

Evans made it clear from day one to the experienced Pitt players that their lives would be simple: my way or the highway. When Lane talked back to him, he got tossed from practice. When someone messed up, everyone ran. The players responded to what Evans was telling them.

"It really wasn't that hard to get their attention," he said. "The year before they had done it their way and they stunk. They had to be willing to give my way a chance."

Not that all was bliss. Evans's hard-nosed manner angered the players at times. They thought he was unfair. He thought they were too wild. He told them to avoid parties, they went to parties. He responded by lengthening practice. In all, though, the marriage worked—to the tune of twenty-four victories. And yet, Evans finished the season less than happy with his team.

"Once we won twenty games and clinched a share of the Big East title we didn't have another good practice the whole season," Evans said. "That's the problem with the older guys on this team. They're satisfied too easily. We have to get away from that this year if we're going to be any good."

Evans had told his team in no uncertain terms it was too easily satisfied. Bluntness is a policy with him. It was that bluntness that had gotten him into a shouting match with Massimino at the Big East meetings that spring.

The league had wanted to pass an unwritten rule that it believed would prevent repeats of the Bobby Martin incident. The rule would hold that if one league school had a verbal commitment from a player the other league schools would stop recruiting him. Massimino balked.

"I've been the nice guy too many years," he said in the meeting. "I'm tired of being pushed around by people because I try to do things the right way and they don't."

Evans, knowing Massimino was referring to him, shot back, "Rollie, don't blame me because you screwed up your recruiting."

After that, it got unpleasant. Now, the season was about to start. Evans had a team with high expectations and Massimino had a team with low expectations. Before the year was over, they would meet—and clash—again.

Six days after the Big East Media Day, most of the top high school seniors in America began signing national letters of intent. Villanova signed two good players that day and received a verbal commitment from a third. Pittsburgh, in the running for three top players, struck out: zero for three. Ohio State signed four—the four it wanted.

Chris Jent opted for the Buckeyes over Pittsburgh. Bill Robinson signed as did Mark Baker and Jeff Hall. Eric Riley, with seven days left during the signing period, was still undecided. Williams was ecstatic. He had gotten three Ohio players and a top player from out of state. He had also gotten a center, two mid-size players, and a point guard. Riley would be a bonus since he could play power forward, but he would have to compete with his high school teammate Treg Lee at that spot.

The last crucial period for Williams during the fall had been Halloween weekend, when Jent, Baker, and Riley made their visits to Columbus. Williams had already gotten the good news that Robinson was going to sign, although he didn't want to announce it until the signing date.

Having three recruits visit the campus on the same weekend would make things hectic. Before they arrived, a careful itinerary had been prepared for each one, including meetings with teachers and counselors and one-to-one sessions for each player with Williams. Jent, who was interested in communications, would be introduced to some local TV people. Riley and Baker, who were black, would meet with two-time Heisman Trophy winner Archie Griffin to talk about what life on campus was like for blacks at Ohio State. All three would be introduced to Gov. Dick Celeste before the kickoff of the football game on Saturday.

Driving to the airport Friday morning to pick up Jent, Williams was tight, as tight as he might be on the day of a big game. Fraschilla was with him. Ayers had driven to Dayton to pick up Baker. Riley was driving from Cleveland with his father. Beulah Riley wasn't coming—a fact that made Williams nervous.

As he drove, Williams sipped his third cup of coffee. "I never drank it until three years ago," he said. "I started so I would cut down on Coca-Cola. Now, I'm hooked on this stuff."

Since the home visits, Williams and his staff had kept up a steady stream of mail and phone calls to the recruits. This weekend was the key though and they knew it. The weather had turned up sunny. Williams was thankful. "Sometimes, if it rains, that sets a whole mood and there's nothing you can do to overcome it. This is a good start, anyway."

With each assistant assigned to a player—Fraschilla/Jent, Ayers/Baker, and part-timer Paul Brazeau/Riley—Williams would have to run practice alone that afternoon. He had been uptight earlier that week in practice and didn't want to be that way today. It wasn't so much being on best behavior as being careful not to be on worst behavior. "I can't get on a profanity roll today. Even if the guys mess up."

The afternoon will be full of routine meetings for the recruits. The evening will be more important.

Dinner is very carefully planned. Two current players will join the recruits and the coaches. One is Jerry Francis, a junior, who was Jent's counselor at a summer camp. The two became friends there and Williams wants someone Jent feels comfortable with to come along. What's more, Francis is exactly the kind of person Williams wants representing Ohio State: articulate, funny, and not caught up in the notion of being a basketball player.

The second player invited to dinner is freshman Perry Carter, who knows both Riley and Baker from the Nike camp. After dinner, the recruits will be turned over to the players for a night on the town.

According to Williams's schedule, dinner is set for 7:30. He shows up on time, along with Carter and Francis. The coaches and the recruits are nowhere in sight. They wait. At 7:45, Williams is getting antsy. He paces for a while, then sits down and shakes his head.

"You know, I'm really not sure I want to be doing this when I'm fifty," he says. "As I get older, I wonder about it more and more. This is all I've ever done but maybe I'd be happy doing something else. It's all so consuming. Look at me now. It's Friday night and I'm spending it with a bunch of teenagers. Nothing against them but if I'm going to be with a teenager, I'd like it to be my daughter. Sometimes it seems like I never see her."

He stops at that thought. "You know, I have a picture of her in my mind that's so vivid. She's nine years old, just a little girl going to school. Now, she's seventeen, driving a car and getting ready for college. What happened? How can she not be nine anymore? Where did all that time go? Tomorrow, it will be the same thing, I'll be working with these guys all day. That's been my life for twenty years."

Williams looks at his watch. It's almost eight. The softness in his voice disappears. "Where the hell are those guys?"

They arrive at eight. As the group is being seated, Williams takes Fraschilla aside, not wanting to demand an explanation for their tardiness in front of the players. "Gary, the reservation was for eight."

Williams shakes his head. "My schedule says seven-thirty." It was a minor issue, but in the middle of a vital weekend, the kind of annoyance Williams could have lived without.

The dinner came off without a hitch. No one drank any alcohol. This is an interesting side of recruiting. The coaches would have loved a drink but weren't about to have one in front of the players. The players would love a drink but wouldn't dare order one in front of the coaches. So everyone drinks iced tea.

Dinner over, it is time for Francis and Carter to take over. As the five players drove off, Williams stood with his coaches in the restaurant's parking lot. "All you can do now is hope everyone shows up in one piece in the morning," he said, echoing every coach's lament. He turned to his coaches. "I need a beer."

Undoubtedly, so did the players.

Everyone turned up in one piece the next day. The weekend was a success. Ten days later, Jent and Baker both signed with Ohio State. Robinson formalized what he had told Williams, and Hall also signed. Riley was still undecided. Then, four days after the signing period began, Ohio State fired football coach Earle Bruce, a move that brought national outrage.

Bruce had the best record in the Big Ten during his eight years as coach but that wasn't good enough for many powerful OSU alumni. So, ignoring the recommendation of Athletic Director Rick Bay, University President Edward Jennings fired Bruce. Bay was so upset by Jennings's decision that he resigned.

This turn of events stunned Williams. Bay was the man who had hired him, someone he liked and respected. The firing wasn't just unfair, it was an embarrassment to the entire school. Two days later, Riley announced that he was going to Michigan. Williams was convinced that any chance to get him went out the window after the Bruce firing. His suspicions were confirmed when Riley's coach told him that everyone had felt the firing was a sign of instability in the leadership at Ohio State. Williams couldn't really argue. He just felt lucky that the other four players had signed before the firing.

Still, he felt they needed reassurance. He called all four to tell them the basketball program would not be affected by what had happened. He still had a long-term contract and wasn't going anywhere.

It was a disturbing turn of events, though. Just when Williams should have been basking in a smashing series of recruiting victories, he was caught in the middle of a major controversy. The new athletic director was a quickly-moved-up assistant named James Jones. Williams didn't know him well. He would shortly.

While Williams was focusing a lot of his attention on the future at Ohio State, no one at Purdue was looking past the upcoming season. The Boilermakers' attitude was perhaps best summed up by Coach

Gene Keady's annual list of ten goals that was posted in the locker room. At the top of the list were two words: "FINAL FOUR!"

The other goals didn't really matter because all of them could be reached—but if the first one wasn't, the other nine would be meaningless. No one was more aware of this than the senior trio of Troy Lewis, Todd Mitchell, and Everette Stephens.

But already, ten days before the season began, there were problems. On October 23, Jeff Arnold and Dave Stack, the two seniors who were academically ineligible for the first semester, were arrested during an on-campus party. The cops had been clearing the place out when Arnold went back for a coat he had forgotten. Apparently, Arnold had not moved quickly enough in leaving to satisfy the police. When they told him to get moving, he didn't. Words were exchanged and Arnold ended up in handcuffs. When Stack tried to go to his aid, he ended up in handcuffs too.

The story was in the student newspaper that Monday. Lewis, Mitchell, and Stephens were reading it at lunch when the assistant coaches wandered by. "They're gone, aren't they?" Lewis asked, pointing to the story.

The coaches nodded glumly. Like the seniors, they remembered Keady's "one more chance" edict of the summer. That chance had been used up.

Arnold was really the issue here. Stack was a little-used player who had never really fit in at Purdue. If he was a good guy and sat on the end of the bench, that was fine. If he was a bad guy, there was no room for him.

But Arnold could be a key player. He was 6–10 and a pretty good athlete who had improved steadily since migrating to Purdue from California four years earlier. Arnold was a flake and everyone knew it. Mitchell, Lewis, and Stephens all liked him and knew that he could help this team, perhaps even as a starter.

But they also felt his continuing escapades could hurt the team. Arnold liked to party, have a good time. That didn't make him unusual. But he seemed incapable of drawing the line between fun and trouble. When he had first become ineligible Lewis had told him bluntly: "You fucked up again, Jeff, just like you've been doing for four years."

Arnold hadn't argued. Now, Arnold and Stack were certainly gone. The three seniors had mixed emotions about it. They felt empathy for them, especially Arnold, but they also felt that if Keady didn't show who was boss, things could get out of hand on the team.

"We walked into practice that day," Lewis said later, remembering that Monday in October, "and Jeff and Dave were there. Well, there was a recruit in, so we figured maybe Coach Keady was waiting to tell them. But that night, we had a meeting. Coach said that Arnold and Stack were going to run after practice every night and that if anyone screwed up they were going to be in trouble. I was sitting in the back of the room thinking, This is wrong. These two guys don't deserve to be on this team.' What I should have done was stand up and say, 'Coach, I don't want to play with these guys anymore.' "

Mitchell and Stephens agreed with Lewis. But they didn't say anything either. That night, back in their apartment, Mitchell and Lewis found themselves talking about Bob Knight. Both had been recruited by Knight, though not terribly hard. Lewis had dropped Indiana from consideration when Knight had cursed in front of his mother. Mitchell kept remembering then-Assistant Coach Jim Crews saying, "It takes a special person to play at Indiana."

"I decided right then," Mitchell said, "that I just wasn't that special."

Mitchell and Lewis had become friends during a recruiting visit to UCLA. Lewis was one of those players everyone wanted. Mitchell attracted less attention because many people thought he would play football in college, rather than basketball.

The two stayed in touch after the UCLA visit and when Mitchell decided to go to Purdue, he called Lewis to tell him. Lewis had been hounded so badly by recruiters that he was hiding out at his father's house to stay away from the constant phone calls at his mother's. When Mitchell called to tell him he was going to Purdue, Lewis said, "You know, I think I'll go there too."

They had been roommates and best friends from day one. Stephens, who had come to Purdue from Evanston, Illinois, joined their circle as a freshman but didn't get as much attention as "TNT" (Todd 'n Troy) until he became a key player his junior year. Now, the three often seemed inseparable, although Stephens tended to go off with his own set of nonbasketball friends more often than TNT did.

None of them had ever regretted choosing Purdue, except perhaps during the snowstorms that buffeted West Lafayette during the winter, when they thought about the warm-weather schools that had recruited them. But now, they thought Keady could use a shot of Bob Knight's toughness. "If this had happened with Knight," Lewis said, "he would have called the two guys in and said, 'You fucked up one time too many, you're gone.' But Coach just isn't that way. He wants everything to be right this season, exactly right."

There was more. Although Keady is known as "the bulldog," as much for appearance as approach, he is, underneath the tough veneer, a softie. Throwing a player off his team was a very difficult thing for him to do, regardless of whether the player was a star or a scrub.

These problems were exactly what Keady had hoped to avoid during the preseason. During his first seven years at Purdue, he had carefully built one of the strongest programs in the country. But because of the repeated March failures, the Boilermakers still weren't getting the recognition they felt they deserved.

No one was more aware of this than Keady. A week before practice began, he had been asked to appear on Roy Firestone's ESPN talk show. Great, Keady thought, some national exposure. He had flown to Los Angeles and then squirmed for twenty minutes while Ted Green, subbing for Firestone, asked him a series of questions about Bob Knight, Digger Phelps, and his former boss, Eddie Sutton.

Keady knew that he could win twenty games for the next one hundred years in a row and no one was going to notice Purdue until it got to the Final Four. This team should be a Final Four team. It had a superb point guard in Stephens, a deadly shooter in Lewis, an outstanding inside-outside player in Mitchell, a solid center in Melvin McCants, and good, young depth.

"This team should have a better chance in March than any we've had," Keady said. "We're bigger and stronger and we've got the experience. The way we're playing right now [November 10] we don't belong in the Top Twenty. But if we had Arnold and Stack in there, I wouldn't be uncomfortable being ranked Number One."

And Keady fully expected to have Arnold and Stack back in January, when they would become academically eligible. In the meantime, though, there were nagging worries: Lewis had broken his foot in September and Mitchell had undergone arthroscopic knee surgery on October 28. Both were now back practicing but weren't yet 100 percent.

And the memories of '87 nagged, the blowout loss at Michigan that gave Indiana a share of the Big Ten title, followed by the Hoosiers' success and the Boilermakers' failure in postseason.

"I think Indiana doing as well as it did blew our *not* doing well out of proportion for all of us, starting with me," Keady said. "I think the

Florida game was my fault. We played as if we were afraid to fail.
That's not any good. This year, I just want us to go out and play every
game."

The games would begin on November 20. Already, it had been a
tough season at Purdue. And March was still a long way off.

6
TIP-OFFS

The college basketball season formally began on Friday night, November 20, when the third annual preseason National Invitation Tournament opened up with seven first-round games—the eighth would be played Saturday—at various sites around the country.

Once, college basketball began everywhere on December 1, never earlier. But in recent years, with the proliferation of holiday tournaments, the first games have been staged earlier and earlier. Now, in addition to the sixteen-team NIT, there is the annual tip-off game held at the birthplace of basketball, Springfield, Massachusetts. There is the Great Alaska Shootout on Thanksgiving weekend, not to mention the Maui Classic and dozens of other classics and nonclassics held, quite literally, around the world. Clemson and Oregon State began their seasons in Taiwan. Truly, a neutral court.

No one was more ready for the start of the season than Rick Barnes. He had intentionally made life difficult for his team almost from his first day at George Mason. He honestly believed that discipline—a *lot* of discipline—was the only thing that would allow the Patriots to improve on the 17–14 record they had compiled the previous year.

What's more, the team was filled with academic question marks and Barnes wanted to avoid that kind of trouble. He had devised something he called the "Pride Sheet." Each Friday, the players had to come into Barnes's office and sign the sheet.

The sheet read as follows:

> I have attended and have been on time for all my classes, met with all my tutors, met all study hall requirements, taken care of all meetings with the academic coordinator and professors and I am up to date on all my current assignments. I have also left a copy of my next week's schedule on Coach Barnes's desk.
>
> I understand the academic office will send a weekly report to Coach Barnes concerning my progress and attendance to my academic commitments. These reports will be supplemented by information from my professors. The reports will go on record without question.
>
> I understand by signing this statement, I am giving my word that I have fulfilled all of my stated commitments. If for any reason I was unable to meet a certain commitment, I had made prior contact with the coaching staff and receive permission. IF I SIGN THIS AND HAVE NOT BEEN TRUTHFUL, I UNDERSTAND THAT I WILL BE PENALIZED A GAME. If I have failed my responsibility, I will meet with Coach Barnes and explain my reason. I am aware that my failures could result in disciplinary actions against myself and teammates at Coach Barnes's discretion.

Heavy stuff. If anyone could not sign the sheet on a given Friday, the whole team got up at 6 A.M. to run. If a player signed the sheet when he should not have, he was automatically suspended one game. Punishments became more serious for second and third offenses.

"If these guys don't have the discipline to go to class, they aren't going to have the discipline to be any good," Barnes said. "I know this isn't going to be easy and we may lose some guys. But the ones who stay will be better off."

Even with the Pride Sheet, it was not an easy fall. There were a lot of early mornings for the players and coaches. If Barnes didn't like practice in the afternoon, he brought the players back at night. If he didn't like it at night, they came in early the next morning.

Everyone was pointing for November 20, the date of the NIT opener against Seton Hall. But three days before the opener, disaster struck. No one had worked harder during the offseason than senior point guard Amp Davis. Barnes had told him that he wouldn't play if he didn't lose weight and Davis had lost thirty pounds. At 5–10, he had gone from 195 down to 165.

Davis, Barnes felt, would be a key to how the team played. Then, three days before the season began, Davis came to see him. He had been accused of cheating on a test—for a second time. The first time, Davis had admitted he was guilty. This time he insisted he was innocent.

It didn't matter. Guilty once, Davis was considered guilty until proven innocent this time. He wouldn't make the trip. Barnes made Davis tell his teammates what had happened. When Davis began to cry during his confession, star forward Kenny Sanders grabbed him and hugged him. If nothing else, Barnes thought, the tough preseason had produced a close team.

But he was going to New Jersey without his point guard to play a Seton Hall team that would be very tough to beat under any circumstances. Additionally, Barnes had suspended freshman reserve forward Harold Westbrook for one game for missing a class.

Playing in the NIT, even in the role of sparring partner for Seton Hall, was a big thing for George Mason. The school had only been playing in Division 1 for nine years; this was a major opportunity to get people to notice a school few even knew existed.

Barnes was tense on game day, a frigid, gray day. The game would be played at Rutgers because the NIT insisted that all its games be played in gyms with at least 8,000 seats. So instead of playing before a sellout crowd of 3,000 at Seton Hall, the teams played before 1,200 people in the 9,000-seat Rutgers Athletic Center.

At 11 A.M., the Patriots went to the gym for their pregame shootaround. The players were so tight they couldn't make a shot. Barnes was worried. Back in the hotel, he called his old boss, Gary Williams, looking for advice and encouragement.

"You've waited so long for this you think it's the only game you're ever going to coach," Williams told him. "It's a very long season. Win or lose, you've got a hell of a lot left to do."

And what about Davis, how should he deal with that? "You let the kid dictate your actions by his," Williams said. "See how he responds to all this."

Barnes felt better after talking to Williams. He had learned a lot from him, including how to curse. "I swear, I never used any of those words until I worked for Gary," he said. "Now, I use them all the time."

Everyone seemed looser at the pregame meal. Later in the season,

Barnes would start skipping pregame meals because he felt his presence made the players nervous. Today, though, he was there, watching them eat pretty much whatever they wanted. This was one decision Barnes had made when he became a head coach. Most coaches spend a lot of time worrying about what to feed their players at pregame meal. Not Barnes.

"The best these guys play is in summer league," he said. "And all they eat then is McDonald's. So why worry about it?"

The team arrived at the gym two hours before tip-off so Barnes could take them through videotape of Seton Hall one more time. As the players warmed up, Barnes talked calmly with Seton Hall Coach P. J. Carlesimo.

In truth, Carlesimo had a lot more to be concerned about than Barnes. He was entering his fifth year at Seton Hall, the last year of his contract. The administration had essentially given Carlesimo a "make the NCAAs or walk" edict. And yet, Carlesimo seemed unbothered by the extra pressure. He had grown a beard during the offseason and had taken a "so what" approach to his ultimatum.

"If the ship sinks," he said, "I think there'll be a lot of people around to throw me a life raft."

All true. Carlesimo was one of the best-liked people in the sport. In the Big East, a league full of jealousies and antagonism, everyone liked P. J. Carlesimo. But he wanted to keep this job. If he was going to survive, Seton Hall could not afford to lose to anyone like George Mason.

Barnes knew his team was supposed to lose. He knew no one was going to judge him on one game, or for that matter, one season. But logic wasn't at work here. He was a wreck. "How much time?" he kept asking his coaches while the players were on the floor warming up. "God," he finally said, standing up, "it seems like we've waited *forever* to play this game."

The locker rooms at Rutgers are tiny, so narrow that if two players are trying to dress at the same time on opposite sides of the room, they can't do it. The players crowded together—because they had no choice—as Barnes gave them final instructions.

"Remember what we've said all week," he began softly. "Make them prove to us they can hit the outside shot. Take the ball to them every chance you get. Head-hunt out there, put your bodies on them. And rebound. We have to have all five guys on the boards to have a chance against this team."

He paused. They had heard all of that before. "Only you guys know how hard you've worked to get here tonight. The NIT has put us here for one reason—so Seton Hall can advance. That's fine. This is our opportunity to prove a lot of things.

"One more thing. I've waited ten years for this night. Sometimes, when I was out recruiting, I wondered if this was what I really wanted. But working with you guys these last six months, I know it is. You've done a great job preparing for this . . ."

Barnes stopped. He was getting choked up. You aren't supposed to break down *before* your first game. "Okay," he said, gathering himself. "Get out and work for forty minutes and you'll come back in here a happy team."

Out they went. Barnes shook hands with his assistants and walked onto the floor. It was not exactly the scene he had envisioned for his first game. The gym was practically empty and, if not for the Seton Hall pep band, would have been virtually silent. But Barnes was exactly where he wanted to be.

Or so he thought. It took Seton Hall seven seconds to score. It took Mason's Steve Smith fifteen seconds to toss an air ball. In seventy-seven seconds, Seton Hall jumped to a 7–0 lead. The Patriots looked frightened. Before his team had scored a point for him, Barnes had to call the first time-out of his coaching career.

"We're all right," he said. "Just do what we do every day in practice. Don't try to do anything special."

They calmed down. Smith scored the first basket on a pretty feed from Brian Miller. Steadily, the Patriots came back. When Earl Moore hit two free throws with 4:32 left in the half, they had the lead 26–25. "They can't guard us," Barnes screamed during a radio time-out. "Just keep taking the ball at them."

On the other bench, Carlesimo, who might have had reason to panic, didn't. "Basketball is a game of runs," he said later. "They were bound to come back on us."

It was 28–28 with four minutes left before the half, but the Patriots couldn't keep pace. Seton Hall put together a 13–2 run, capped by a Nick Katsikis jumper at the buzzer.

Barnes was calm at the half. "That was their twenty minutes," he said. "This will be ours. Take good shots, take it to them, and you'll be the most talked-about team in college basketball tomorrow."

The Patriots tried. But the Pirates were just better than they were. George Mason got within 56–50 with twelve minutes left but Katsikis hit two straight three-pointers and it was 62–50. From there it was a coast, Seton Hall winning 85–63.

Barnes was resolute in the aftermath. "Stay together," he said. "We need to learn from this and not bicker about who messed up. We all did. We've got a lot of work to do but it's a long way from here to March."

He walked out of the locker room. One game into his coaching career, Barnes couldn't avoid the oldest coaches' lament in the book: "Men," he said, looking at his assistants, "we've got to get some players."

November 21 . . . Springfield, Massachusetts

Although the NIT gets a twenty-four-hour jump, the official start of the basketball season is the annual tip-off game played in Springfield. This is "The Peach Basket Classic," named of course for the famous peach basket that Dr. James Naismith put up in 1890 at the very beginnings of basketball.

This game was born in 1979, the idea being to promote the Basketball Hall of Fame by bringing two big-name college teams to Springfield to start each season. Duke and Kentucky played that first game, a rematch of the 1978 national championship, and Duke came from behind to win in overtime. Since then, the game has grown. It is now an automatic sellout each year and it comes at the end of a full week of events.

This year's matchup is an intriguing one. Syracuse and North Carolina had played in the Eastern Regional final in March. Syracuse had won the game by killing Carolina on the boards. Dean Smith had been so upset by his team's performance that it was August before he could look at the tape.

In the interim, Syracuse had come up one point shy of the national title, losing to Indiana 74–73 in the final, while Smith's best player, J. R. Reid, had been charged with assault during a preseason fight in a Raleigh nightclub. Reid and teammate Steve Bucknall had gotten into an altercation with an N.C. State student, and it had ended with Reid spitting at their antagonist.

As a result, even though neither player had been convicted of anything yet, Smith had suspended them for this game. "When children make a mistake," Smith said, "you discipline them immediately."

The suspensions pleased no one. The game's organizers were less than thrilled that Reid wouldn't be playing. ESPN, which would televise the game, wasn't too pleased that it couldn't push the Reid-Rony Seikaly matchup during pregame hype.

And of course there was Syracuse Coach Jim Boeheim, the most put-upon man in college basketball. In truth, Boeheim is one of the nicer guys in the game. He has a sharp wit, is charmingly blunt—"That story you wrote really sucked," is one way he greets reporters he knows—and is a very underrated coach.

But Boeheim is the victim of his appearance and of his voice. Always, he looks unhappy. He can't help it. And he does whine. Shortly after the Orangemen had beaten North Carolina in March, Boeheim launched into a diatribe about how difficult it was to get Seikaly to play hard. Seikaly, sitting next to Boeheim, looked at him and said, "Hey, Coach, cool it. We won."

"Oh yeah," Boeheim said, remembering.

Even when he isn't whining, Boeheim *sounds* like he's whining. His voice is high-pitched and shrill. It was best described by a reporter listening to Boeheim during a press conference who shook his head and said, "You know, if a hemorrhoid could talk, it would sound just like Jim Boeheim."

Now, Boeheim was in a no-win, yes-whine situation. If his team beat Carolina without Reid, everyone would shrug and say, "Big deal, Reid didn't play." If his team should lose to the Tar Heels, people would say, "Can you believe Dean found a way to win that game?"

Smith, naturally, relished this role. Rarely was his team a legitimate underdog, although Smith always tried somehow to make it one. He was always claiming that his opponent had a psychological advantage. Always. In 1981, before playing Virginia in the Final Four, Smith insisted the Cavaliers had a psychological advantage because they had already beaten UNC twice that season. "They'll be very confident because they know they can beat us," he said.

Carolina beat Virginia. Then, getting ready to face Indiana in the final, Smith said, "You know Indiana will have a psychological advantage because we've beaten them and they'll want revenge."

Makes perfect sense.

Now, Carolina really did have a psychological advantage. Smith couldn't avoid it. There was revenge. There was the underdog role. There was Reid's absence. Another Smith saying: "You can always play one great game without a key player."

So what was Smith's comment before the game? "I just hope we don't get blown out."

Of course.

Carolina didn't get blown out. Even without Reid, the Tar Heels still had a very talented club. Rick Fox was a freshman with a pro's body. Pete Chilcutt, a redshirt freshman, played superbly. Combined, they scored 29 points and had 20 rebounds. It would have been tough for Reid and Bucknall, the two players they replaced in the lineup, to match those numbers.

Still, in the early going, it looked like Syracuse might turn the game into a rout. The Orangemen built a 50–39 lead at the half, finishing with a 13–5 spurt that was keyed by Sherman Douglas, the brilliant point guard. By intermission, he had 17 points. Seikaly had 14. Only Fox, playing in his first college game, had kept the game even that close, scoring 12 points.

But Carolina came back. It kept creeping closer and closer, finally tying the score at 81–81 with 1:18 left on a Kevin Madden lay-up. The Tar Heels took the lead at 83–81 on a Jeff Lebo steal that led to a Ranzino Smith lay-up. But Seikaly tied the game with eleven seconds left with two free throws, and Derrick Coleman made it 85–83 by making two more free throws after stealing the inbounds pass.

When Lebo couldn't get open with time running down, it looked like Syracuse would survive. But Lebo shoveled the ball to Chilcutt, who spun in the lane, tossed up a fourteen-foot jumper and watched it bounce off the side of the rim, off the backboard and *in*—as the buzzer sounded.

Overtime. When a shot like that drops, destiny has taken over. Syracuse led briefly in the overtime, but Madden put Carolina ahead for good with two free throws and Fox ended the game with a thunderous dunk for a 96–93 win.

Syracuse, the top-ranked team in the country, was 0–1. Smith was a genius . . . again. Boeheim was a goat . . . already. Rick Fox and Pete Chilcutt were tabbed as stars. Smith was thrilled. "Gee, I hope J.R. can get his spot back in the lineup," he joked.

All was right with the world in Chapel Hill. And in Syracuse, too. Boeheim was unhappy. That meant basketball season was officially under way.

With its victory over George Mason, Seton Hall was one of eight teams to advance to the second round of the NIT. The other winners were Purdue, Iowa State, New Mexico, UCLA, Florida, Georgia Tech, and Middle Tennessee State.

For the second round, the NIT came up with these matchups: Georgia Tech at Florida, UCLA at New Mexico, Iowa State at Purdue, and Middle Tennessee State at Seton Hall. This was part of the problem with the NIT, both the three-year-old preseason version and the fifty-year-old postseason version. Ever since the postseason tournament fell on hard times in the 1970s, every move the NIT makes is based on dollars.

Once, the NIT was as glamorous a tournament as the NCAA. Madison Square Garden was the mecca for college basketball and winning the NIT was just as prestigious as winning the NCAAs. Even after that changed during the 1950s, the NIT was still a very successful tournament. But in the 1970s, when the NCAA began expanding its field, first from twenty-five to thirty-two teams in 1975 and then to forty, forty-eight, fifty-three and, ultimately, sixty-four teams, the NIT fields became weaker.

As the fields got weaker, attendance dropped steadily. By 1977, the tournament was in serious trouble. The games weren't drawing, CBS had canceled its TV contract, and there was talk of folding the tournament. That was when Pete Carlesimo came up with the idea of holding the early rounds at campus sites.

Carlesimo had just been named the executive director of the tournament and his move probably saved his new job, as well as the old tournament. The semifinals and final stayed in New York. The first three rounds—the tournament expanded from sixteen to twenty-four to thirty-two teams—were played on campus. The money made from those games wiped out any potential deficit in New York.

At the same time that it moved the tournament out of New York, the NIT committee began "reseeding" after each round. What that really meant was that it could create any matchups it wanted. In 1985, when Carlesimo came up with the idea for a preseason NIT, the same "reseeding" formula was used.

Often that means fairness gets left out of the picture. The committee wants certain teams in New York to sell tickets and boost cable TV
ratings. Those teams usually get to play at home and play weaker teams
whenever possible.

Why then would UCLA, clearly a more attractive team than New
Mexico, be sent to play at New Mexico? Easy: The Bruins had drawn
an embarrassing 2,100 fans for their opening game in Pauley Pavilion
against Oral Roberts. New Mexico had drawn 17,000 for Weber State
and would draw 17,000 again. That was a lot of revenue.

The pairings that raised eyebrows, though, were Georgia Tech–
Florida and Middle Tennessee–Seton Hall. The consensus was that
Tech, Florida, and Purdue were the three strongest teams in the tour-
nament. What's more, Seton Hall had drawn poorly playing George
Mason at Rutgers. Why hadn't Middle Tennessee been sent to Florida
and Seton Hall to Georgia Tech?

The answer was simple. The committee wanted Seton Hall in Madison Square Garden. They were semilocal, they were Big East, and they
were coached by Peter John Carlesimo, who just happened to be the
oldest of Peter A. Carlesimo's ten children. The father was retiring at
the end of the season as the NIT's executive director. The son was
trying to save his job at Seton Hall. If the Pirates made it to New York,
it was a good story. If the committee gave Seton Hall a little extra
shove, well, it certainly wasn't the first time they had greased the skids
to get a team to the Garden.

Given a second home game and a beatable opponent, the Pirates
kept their end of the bargain, easily beating Middle Tennessee before
another tiny crowd at Rutgers. The other winners were New Mexico,
Florida, and Iowa State. The surprise of the group was Iowa State,
which went into Mackey Arena, shot the lights out, and upset Purdue.
It was a loss that created a good deal of anxiety at Purdue. For the
Cyclones, it meant a chance to get some media attention in the East.

Coming to New York is still a big deal for a college basketball team.
The Garden is still, after all, the Garden. John Condon, who has done
the PA for forty years, is still doing the PA. Feets Brodie, who has sat
by his side running the clock for the last thirty-one years, is still there
running the clock. "I've done over two thousand games," Brodie said.
"One of my stopwatches is in the Hall of Fame."

If there was a way to put his voice in the Hall of Fame, Condon's
would be there. Anyone who grew up in New York can recite all his
little sayings: "Score the goal, score the goal, credit the goal to

_____. _That_ was goaltending." And: "New York has ten seconds to attempt a goal. Ten seconds New York." Condon often wears sunglasses while working to protect his eyes from the bright lights. It gives him an air of mystery.

Of course, New York isn't just bright lights and glamor. It's dangerous too. Stuart Greenberg, a manager for New Mexico, found that out the hard way when he was sent back to the hotel before the opening game Friday night to retrieve the contact lenses that Lobo Kurt Miller had left in his room.

As he walked out of the Garden, three young men approached Greenberg, stuck something hard in his ribs, and demanded his wallet. Greenberg had $240 in meal money stolen. Shaken, he still got to the hotel to get Miller's contacts. They didn't help. Miller was zero-for-three and New Mexico got blown out by Seton Hall, 88–67.

This was no committee setup. New Mexico had a solid team but the Pirates blew them out from the first minute, leading 50–28 at halftime and never looking back.

No one enjoyed the victory more than Pete Carlesimo. He sat in the stands with his wife, almost motionless the whole game, arms folded, face never changing expression. It was only afterward that he cried like a proud father.

"I've been in sports fifty years," he said softly, "and I can't remember ever feeling like this. When P.J. took over the program at Seton Hall he had to start from zero. He's had tough times there but look how far he's brought them."

Pete Carlesimo, who is seventy-two, looks like a cross between former Chicago Mayor Richard Daley and Jabba the Hutt, the _Star Wars_ character. He is known as a tough guy, a hard bargainer who gets his way more often than not. There was no toughness in him now, though. Only pride. "A lot of people asked us to explain the draw the first two rounds," he said. "Look, we take a lot of factors into account and attendance is one of them. But P.J.'s team proved it belonged."

True. But the attendance was disappointing, only 7,311. Carlesimo didn't make excuses. "It breaks my heart," he said. "Fortunately, we've done so well with the early-round games outside New York that we'll still make money.

"If you go to New Mexico, Florida, Iowa, you see headlines about the NIT. Here, though, New York, it isn't that big a deal. New York fans only respond to the big names. It hurts me to see crowds like this.

Carlesimo's immediate reaction was to grab Morton, put his arm around him, and say, "It's all right, it's all right."

A few minutes later, when Carlesimo went out to receive the runner-up trophy, the man presenting it was his father. Their hug was long, lingering, and emotional. "I wanted to win because of what it would have meant for the program," Carlesimo said later. "But I wanted to win for my dad, too. I'm prejudiced, but I think he saved the NIT."

In 1987, it was the son—and his team—more than the father that saved the NIT.

The atmosphere the next afternoon at the Joe Lapchick Tournament final was decidedly different from the one in downtown Manhattan the night before.

St. John's has staged this tournament to open the season for thirteen years now. It is named for the legendary St. John's coach who retired in 1965. His replacement back then was a diminutive assistant coach named Lou Carnesecca. He has coached the Redmen ever since, except for a three-year break when he tried his hand at the pros, coaching the New York Nets in the old ABA.

To everyone in Queens, Carnesecca is just Looey. In his favorite Italian restaurants, he is Looey. On the street corners and in the schoolyards, he is Looey. And in Alumni Hall, he is Looey.

The Lapchick is a Thanksgiving weekend tradition. Looey usually invites three turkeys to Alumni Hall and the Redmen carve them up while 6,006 pack the old building to get an early look at what Looey has this season.

Always, it seems Looey has something. He has never coached a losing team in twenty years at St. John's and never failed to make postseason play. And, he has never lost a game in the Lapchick Tournament.

"Why shouldn't we win?" he will say defensively. "If you come to my house for dinner, don't you want me to enjoy the evening?"

This is typical Carnesecca logic. He is, in his own words, a master at *ignoratio elenghi*—Latin for "circumventing the issue." Looey can circumvent the issue in several languages. It is part of his charm.

This year, though, Looey may have miscalculated. Loyola–Marymount, Westhead's team, fit the profile of a good Lapchick team when it was scheduled: last in its conference and going nowhere. Harvard and Tennessee Tech, the other two teams, certainly cooperated, losing easily on Saturday. But Loyola is another case. With transfers like

Corey Gaines and Hank Gathers and a solid player in Mike Yoest, the Lions are good. Very good, in fact.

What's more, they like to take about ninety to a hundred shots a game. Carnesecca is much more comfortable when there are about a hundred shots in the game *total*. This final will not be your typical Lapchick blowout.

The fans wander in shortly before tip-off on a rainy Sunday afternoon. This is a family crowd. They go to church, get in their cars and drive to Alumni Hall, one of the few places in New York City where parking is both easy and free.

Looey has a brand-new backcourt this season, a pair of jets imported from San Jacinto Junior College—Greg (Boo) Harvey and Michael Porter. Harvey and Porter would probably fit in better with Loyola's run-and-gun style. That is apparent early in the game when Looey jumps off the bench as Harvey races past him and screams, "Boo, slow down!"

This is a fascinating game from start to finish. Loyola keeps sprinting while St. John's filibusters. The fans are confused: The game is close, something is wrong, and yet they sense that their team is playing pretty well.

Carnesecca doesn't want the Lapchick streak to end during his reign. When his Italian center, Marco Baldi, makes two horrendous plays in a row, Looey curses him out—in Italian. Still, the Redmen lead 44–40 at halftime.

The game seesaws the whole second half. The difference is Shelton Jones, this year's designated senior star for St. John's. He finishes with 25 points and 16 rebounds, showing the kind of spark he never had his first three years.

But Gathers, who wears white tassles on his sneakers to emulate his hero, Muhammad Ali, keeps the Lions close. When Jeff Fryer hits a jumper with thirty-eight seconds left, an 11-point St. John's lead is down to 85–84.

The Redmen spread out, trying to kill the clock. Loyola lets it run to fifteen seconds before fouling Porter. Calmly, Porter makes the first free throw. But he misses the second. Gathers rebounds and tosses an outlet pass toward Gaines. Remarkably, Porter flashes between them, steals the pass and lays the ball in with six seconds left to make it 88–84. Ball game.

But no. As the ball comes through the net, St. John's Matt Brust

grabs it. Technical foul. All game long, the Redmen have been touch-
ing the ball coming through the basket to try to slow the Loyola fast
break. Westhead's complaints have been heard and this is the fourth
technical called for delay of game.

Looey is so exorcised he leaps in the air and one of his hearing aids
pops out. "I've seen a thousand games," he will say later, "and I've
never seen the rule interpreted like that in my life." Where is Steve
Honzo when you need him?

Yoest makes only one of the technicals, making it 88–85. A three-
pointer can still tie, but Fryer comes up way short and time runs out.
The Lapchick record is intact: 26–0 and thirteen first-place trophies.
Everyone goes home happy.

"That's a heck of a club," Looey says. "They're an NCAA team."
He's right. Loyola will win twenty-three straight games and finish 26–4,
but Looey doesn't know that in November. He once called U.S. International a heck of a club after beating them and added, "They're going
to beat a lot of people." U.S. International was 1–17 at the time.

But Looey is happy . . . sort of. "We made enough mistakes to put
Goodyear out of business," he says. *What????* And: "Running was their
idea, not ours." And: "I don't understand the technical fouls. We're
just poor Ascensions. Someone else will have to explain what happened."

Someone asks if playing a tough game this early in the season might
help the Redmen in the long run. Looey laughs. "You ever hear a coach
say to his team, 'Let's go out and have a tough one tonight?' Who needs
it? It's like when you hear a kid say, 'I wasn't up for the game.' What
does that mean? Does a kid sit there and say, 'I'm going to stink
tonight?'

"It's a funny game. We won. It's nice. If we lost, would the school
close tomorrow? It isn't that important. Nobody remembers who won
this tournament five years ago, six years ago, seven years ago."

Wrong, Looey. Everyone remembers who won five years ago, six
years ago, seven years ago. It was St. John's, St. John's, and St. John's.

Looey smiles. "Oh yeah," he says, "I forgot."

By the time Thanksgiving weekend is over, almost every college basketball team in America has opened its season. Some like to start with
walkovers—Georgetown begins every year in Hawaii playing a team

called Hawaii–Loa—while others seek out the tough holiday tournaments to get extra games against top competition.

One team that coveted an early challenge was Arizona. The Wildcats had wiped out the Soviet Union in their preseason exhibition game and were wound up for the Great Alaska Shootout, knowing that Syracuse and Michigan, both ranked in most top fives, were waiting for them there.

For Steve Kerr, this would be a weekend when he would find out a lot about himself and his knee's progress, since he would be facing Michigan's Gary Grant and Syracuse's Sherman Douglas, two of the top point guards in the country.

Even if he never scored another basket, Kerr's story was already extraordinary. It is a story that reads like a movie script, except that if you sent it to Hollywood you'd be laughed right off the lot. "It has to be believable to sell," they would tell you. "This one will never fly."

It wouldn't fly as fiction. Too corny. Think about it: Bright, articulate kid comes out of California recruited by no one and lands, thanks in large measure to his father, in a rebuilding program at Arizona. Four months after he enrolls, his father is assassinated by terrorists in Lebanon. Two nights later, the kid comes off the bench and leads his team to a dramatic victory. He becomes a star and a hero. Then, he tears up his knee playing for the U.S. and is told his career might be over. He comes back and becomes the leader of a top ten team.

Never happen, right? But that's the catch: The story's true. The only person who doesn't see anything terribly remarkable in it is Steve Kerr. "To me, it doesn't seem like that big a deal," he said. "I guess that's because I lived it. For a long time, people looked at me as a victim. I think now, they see me as a person. I prefer it that way. I really don't think of myself as being all that different than other guys."

But Kerr is different. Every time life has knocked him down he has gotten up. It isn't that nothing bothers him, it's just that nothing is going to defeat him.

He was born in Beirut, the third child of Malcolm and Ann Kerr. Malcolm Kerr had also been born in Beirut and it was there that he met his wife. He had just graduated from Princeton and was doing postgraduate work. She was on her junior year abroad from Occidental College. They were married in 1957 and eventually had four children: Susan, John, Steven, and Andrew.

The Kerrs lived all over the world while their children were growing up: Beirut, Cairo, Oxford, the south of France, Tunisia, and Los Angeles. Steve was always the family jock. "My first memories are of wanting to play ball," he said. "I learned to read by reading the sports pages of the newspaper. Whenever we were in L.A. my dad would take me to Dodger games and UCLA basketball games all the time. He loved it almost as much as I did."

Malcolm Kerr was on the UCLA faculty for twenty years, even when teaching abroad. For a couple of years, Steve Kerr was a UCLA ballboy. His first close-up heroes were college basketball players. He played all sports when he was young, although his quick temper as a baseball pitcher unnerved his parents.

"He just didn't handle losing very well at all," Ann Kerr said. "It was especially bad when he was pitching. Malcolm and I were actually sort of relieved when he started playing basketball all the time. You can't afford to lose your temper every time something goes wrong in that sport. We were much more comfortable with that."

By ninth grade, basketball was Kerr's sport. The family was living in Cairo and Kerr played for the American school team. They mostly played adult club teams, often on outdoor courts that had rocks in them. The games were rather crude, but Kerr was happy.

"People don't understand what Cairo is really like," he said. "They think of Egypt and they think of pyramids and camels. Actually, for an American teenager, Cairo is a great place. There are Americans all over and there aren't very many rules you have to follow. I had a great time over there."

He returned to Los Angeles for his sophomore year at Pacific Palisades High School, largely to play on a more competitive level. By his junior season, his parents had come back to the U.S. and Kerr was starting to attract notice from college scouts because of his range as a shooter.

With Malcolm Kerr back in the Middle East, Ann Kerr stayed behind in Los Angeles during Steve's senior season to help him deal with the recruiting process. There wasn't very much to deal with. The scouting services had labeled him too slow. No one called. Finally, Gonzaga asked him to fly up for a visit.

"I flew up there and what they did was try me out," Kerr remembered. "I had to play against John Stockton [now a star with the Utah Jazz] for two hours. I didn't do very well. When it was over, the coach, Jay Hillock, said to me, 'It wouldn't be a problem if you were a step slow, but you're two steps slow.'"

Kerr was crushed. When he graduated from high school that spring he still had no idea where he would be going to college.

In the meantime, Malcolm Kerr's lifelong dream had come true: He had been offered the job as president of the American University in Beirut. Being an expert on the Middle East, this was what he had always wanted. But he also knew there was danger associated with the job. Beirut was very different from what it had been in the 1950s, when it was known as "The Paris of the Middle East."

Now it was caught in the middle of an ugly war. The man Malcolm Kerr would succeed, David Dodge, had been kidnapped in 1982 and held hostage for a year. Malcolm Kerr called a family meeting to talk about the job.

"We all knew the risks involved," Ann Kerr said. "But this was the job Malcolm had always dreamed about. There was never really any doubt about going."

Steve was seventeen at the time. He remembers that family meeting. "I didn't say much," he said. "I never really considered what was happening. Obviously, I was kind of naïve but it's the kind of thing where you think, 'This can't happen to me.' This was just my dad's job. I never thought about it any differently."

His older brother John did think about it differently. Hauntingly, Steve can still remember John saying to his father, "I just don't want Mom to end up a widow."

Steve looks back now and knows that hindsight is useless. "When I think about it," he said softly, "I don't feel any bitterness. Just sadness. My dad is the reason I'm at Arizona, he's the reason I'm the basketball player that I am. Sometimes, when I think of the success I've had I think about how much he would have enjoyed it all. I just wish he was here for all of this."

It was Malcolm Kerr who brought Arizona and Steve Kerr together. During the summer of 1983, after graduating from high school, Steve played summer league basketball in Los Angeles. His father was home for the summer and they spent a good deal of time together. Often, when Steve played, Malcolm watched. Malcolm Kerr once said that his greatest joy, next to being president of AU–Beirut, was watching Steve play basketball.

Kerr's play in the summer league attracted attention. Colorado was interested but didn't have a scholarship to offer. Kerr was welcome to come there and walk on if he liked. Cal State Fullerton was not only interested but was willing to offer Kerr a scholarship. A first. And then there was Arizona.

Lute Olson had taken the Arizona job that spring, knowing he had a major rebuilding job ahead of him. He was scouring the California summer leagues in search of underclassmen with potential when he spotted Kerr. He was surprised—and intrigued—when he learned that Kerr was a high school graduate without a college.

"We had a scholarship left, we weren't very good to say the least, and this kid could shoot," Olson remembered. "I thought he was worth looking at again."

Olson sent Assistant Coach Kenny Burmeister to look at Kerr. Burmeister wasn't sold. Olson went back again, this time taking his wife Bobbi with him. Bobbi Olson had seen a lot of basketball. When she saw Kerr she turned to her husband and said, "Lute, are you kidding?"

Olson was hesitant. In the meantime, Fullerton was pressing Kerr for a decision. He wanted to go to Arizona—sight unseen—but suspected Olson was delaying in the hope that someone better might come along.

"I spent three days trying to get the Arizona coaches on the phone to find out whether they wanted me or not," Kerr said. "They were all out on the road. Finally, I just gave up, figured they were ducking me and called Fullerton and told them I would come. They were really nice and back then they had a better team than Arizona did. But to tell you the truth I wasn't that thrilled about going to college just off the freeway next to Disneyland."

Two days after Kerr had committed to Fullerton, Olson finally called back. Kerr told him he was going to Fullerton. Olson wished him luck and said he was sorry Arizona had lost him. Kerr was baffled. Arizona had never offered him a scholarship.

"Somewhere, our communication broke down," Olson said. "I had the impression we had simply lost Steve to Fullerton. I didn't realize he wanted to play for us."

Malcolm Kerr did. He noticed his son moping around the house, clearly unhappy about the way things had turned out. So, he sat him down and said, "Where do you want to go to college?"

"Arizona."

"Fine, then. Let's call Coach Olson and tell him that."

Olson remembers the phone call vividly. "Malcolm asked me if we wanted Steve at Arizona. I told him we did. Then he said to me, 'This is a very important question. Steve is torn up about having made a commitment to Fullerton. He doesn't want to renege. But he really wants to go to Arizona.'

"I told Malcolm that it might sound self-serving but if a kid wanted to go to another school after committing to mine, I wouldn't want him to come because no one wants someone in their program who is going to be unhappy."

Malcolm Kerr talked with his son again. He pointed out that nothing had been signed and that four years was a long time. The decision was made. Steve would enroll at Arizona.

That done, he went off on vacation with his family to Beirut. Malcolm Kerr was taking up residence there as the president of AU–Beirut. On the day Steve was supposed to leave Beirut to fly home and start school, his mother took him to the airport.

"While we were in the terminal, they started shelling the airport," Steve said. "They were trying to get planes as they sat on the runway. The driver who had taken us to the airport told us to get away from all the windows. Then, he decided to get us out of there and back to the embassy."

Two days later the same driver took Kerr on a terrifying ride through Syria to Amman, Jordan. They were stopped a number of times but the driver, who knew the route and the games, talked them through. Kerr flew home from there. Several months later he learned that his driver had been killed by a sniper shortly after that ride.

Kerr fit in quickly at school and with the basketball team. He was the third guard, the shooting specialist off the bench on a lousy team. But he was happy.

Then, on January 18, 1984, Kerr was awakened shortly after midnight by a telephone call in his dorm room. His brother's nightmare had become reality: Malcolm Kerr had been shot and killed by two assassins outside his office in Beirut.

The first member of the Arizona coaching staff to hear the news was Assistant Coach Scott Thompson. He raced over to Kerr's dorm and found Kerr sitting motionless on his bed, paralyzed by what he had been told. When Thompson sat down, the first thing Kerr said to him was, "I've got to talk to my mother."

It took several hours, but Kerr finally got his mother on the phone. She and his brother Andrew were both okay. The next two days are a blur in Kerr's memory. What he does remember is that the only escape from his grief came when he was on the basketball court. Arizona State was coming to Tucson to play two days after the murder. Olson asked Kerr if he wanted to play. Kerr said absolutely.

"It was the only thing to do," he said. "My dad would have been very disappointed in me if I hadn't played. What's more, there was nothing I could do at that point. I knew my family was safe. I was going to the memorial service the next day. It just wouldn't have made sense not to play."

A moment of silence for Malcolm Kerr was planned before the tip-off. Initially, Olson intended to keep the team off the floor until it was over. But Kerr came to him and said he felt he needed to be there. Olson then decided the whole team should be there with him.

It is difficult to imagine the emotion of that evening. Even with Arizona's arch-rival in the building, few people in the McKale Center that night were really focused on basketball. The violence of the shooting that had taken place thousands of miles away was tangible as everyone stood in silence. Kerr broke down. So did many in the crowd.

Eight minutes into the game, Olson sent Kerr in as part of his normal rotation. The first time he touched the ball—eighteen seconds after coming in—Kerr was open. Instinct took over. He shot from twenty feet. Swish. It is unlikely that a shot to win a national championship was as electrifying as that one.

"I'm not sure I can describe the feeling in the building that night," Olson said. "All I know is, I cried and I certainly wasn't alone."

The legend of Steve Kerr was born that night. He scored 12 points—shooting five-of-seven from the field—and the inspired Wildcats destroyed a superior Arizona State team 71–49 for their first Pacific 10 victory under Olson. From that night forward, Kerr became Tucson's adopted son. Whenever he scored a field goal and the PA announcer screeched, "Steeeeeve Kerrrrrrrrr!" Thirteen thousand people screeched it right back. Everyone in town wanted to invite Kerr to dinner. Every school wanted him to speak to its students.

Almost always, Kerr accepted. At times, being such a hero was embarrassing to him. He had never thought of himself as special, and that attitude is exactly what made him special. Also, he kept his self-deprecating sense of humor even amid the constant adulation.

He became a starter as a sophomore, then, as a junior moved to point guard. There he became a star, the leader of a very young team, picked in preseason to finish eighth, that shocked people by winning the Pac–10 title. When people asked Kerr about his emergence as the team's leader, he laughed.

"You want to know why I'm the leader," he said. "It's simple. Last summer we went to France. I speak French. The other guys don't. Every time they wanted to hit on a girl, they needed me to interpret. That's when I became the leader."

Olson, who was continually amazed by Kerr's improvement as a player, didn't buy that line. "He's the best leader I've ever seen," he said. "If he told this team that green was orange, they would all believe him."

During the summer after Kerr's junior year, Olson coached the U.S. team in the World Championships in Spain. Kerr made the team and was a key player. Then, during the semifinal game against Brazil, he drove the lane looking to create a play against Oscar, the Brazilian shooting specialist who would torture the U.S. a year later in the Pan American Games final.

"I remember going by Oscar easily because he couldn't guard anyone," Kerr said. "I saw Charles Smith open and I jumped in the air to pass him the ball. But someone stepped in front of him so I sort of twisted in the air to get a shot off. When I came down my whole body was off-balance. I felt my knee just blow out when I landed. The pain was unbelievable."

David Robinson, the center on that team, was sitting on the bench when Kerr fell. He can still see the play in his mind's eye: "When Steve came down it was one of the most horrifying sounds I've ever heard. You knew it was bad right away."

It was torn ligaments, bad enough that team doctor Tim Taft felt he should immediately tell Kerr that this was often a career-ending injury. When that diagnosis reached Tucson, hysteria broke out. The word was that Kerr was through as a player. Kerr never believed that for a minute, although when someone asked him what he would do if he couldn't play again he grinned and said, "I'll just have them fire Coach Olson and take his job."

There was no need. Kerr went through reconstructive surgery, worked all through the '87 season on rehabilitation, and began playing again in the spring. Slowly, his confidence was coming back. But as the Wildcats flew into Anchorage the day before Thanksgiving, Kerr had misgivings. In the cold weather, the knee felt stiff. He wondered if he could compete with Grant and Douglas.

The answer to that question was an emphatic yes. In the semifinals, he completely outplayed Grant. Kerr was so excited that when Grant started talking to him during the game, he talked back to him. And when he buried a key three-pointer late in the game, Kerr pointed right at Grant as if to say, "Take that."

Two days later, after enduring an earthquake in the morning—"A nice way to start the day," Kerr said—the Wildcats upset Syracuse. Suddenly, people were taking notice of them. Dick Vitale was screaming on ESPN that Sean Elliott was an All-America. Kerr, people noticed, wasn't just a good story, he was a good player.

"I finally feel as if people have completely accepted me as a person, not just as a victim," he said. "This is a great feeling to be on a team with this kind of potential. I hope we can keep it going all year."

They were certainly started in the right direction.

7
"IT'S STILL
EARLY BUT . . ."

One of the last teams in the country to open the season was the University of Tennessee. There was something correct about this delay, because the arena that the Volunteers were scheduled to open their season in was already two years late.

When the Thompson–Boling Arena had first been conceived in the early 1980s, Tennessee was battling Kentucky for supremacy in the Southeast Conference. Building an arena that would have more seats than Kentucky's 23,000-seat Rupp Arena seemed a logical step.

But almost since the day that B. Ray Thompson anonymously put up the first $5 million of the $37 million it would take to build the arena, Tennessee basketball had seemed jinxed. Not only had the construction of the building been a disaster—one death, two construction firms, and two pending lawsuits—but the basketball program had slipped steadily.

The story that may best sum up what had happened to Tennessee basketball was Doug Roth. In high school, Roth was coveted by everyone. He was 6–11, a good athlete, a good student, and his statistics were superb. He could shoot with both hands and, best of all as far as Don DeVoe was concerned, he was from Knoxville.

"When I first saw Doug Roth play as a junior in high school, I thought he was a breakthrough player for our program," DeVoe said, looking back. "We were averaging about twenty wins a year at the time. I thought he was the kind of player who could take us to twenty-three or twenty-four wins a year."

DeVoe worked diligently to make sure Roth stayed home when it came time to choose a college, and when Roth announced in 1985 that he was going to Tennessee, DeVoe was elated. Roth had been named to virtually every high school All-America team there was. DeVoe, often accused of not being a good recruiter, had pulled off a major recruiting coup.

But that summer, DeVoe went to see Roth play in the annual Olympic Festival. Suddenly, playing against players who were much bigger and quicker than the ones he had played against in high school, Roth looked human. Very human. DeVoe also noticed that Roth had trouble at times doing simple things like catching the ball. There was a reason: Roth was legally blind in his right eye.

During Roth's first two seasons at Tennessee, the Volunteers won a *total* of twenty-six games, a far cry from the average of twenty-three or twenty-four a season DeVoe had anticipated. There were many other reasons for the team's troubles, but Roth, who averaged 3 points a game as a freshman and 9.7 as a sophomore, became a symbol of all those problems.

No one was more frustrated by those problems than DeVoe. This was a coach who had only had one losing season during his first fourteen at three different schools. Suddenly, at the age of forty-five he had rolled back-to-back losing seasons: 12–16 and 14–15.

"A lot of things went wrong those two years," he said. "Our best player, Fred Jenkins, missed eighteen of our thirty-six conference games with injuries. Roth didn't pan out the way we thought he would. We had other injuries. But the bottom line, to be honest, was that I hadn't recruited well enough. If we had more depth, we could have overcome the injuries.

"Instead, we only won one conference road game [out of eighteen] in two years. We lost games that Mary Poppins would have won. Last year we were up 12 on Kentucky with 1:10 left and found a way to lose. We just have to find a way to be more consistent this year and, more than anything, to play better defense."

Defense has always been the cornerstone of DeVoe's coaching approach, not surprising considering his background. He was born and raised on his parents' 179-acre farm in Clinton County, Ohio, and to a large extent still looks and sounds like the farmer's son that he is: He is tall and clean-cut-looking with a quick, eager laugh and a sincerity and intensity that carries over into his coaching.

DeVoe went to Ohio State on a partial scholarship during Fred Taylor's glory years there. He fully intended to get his degree in animal sciences, go back to the farm and breed livestock. But after one semester under Taylor and a coaching class taught by Woody Hayes, DeVoe wanted to coach.

He graduated in 1964 with a degree in education and began looking for a coaching job. A year later, one of his former teammates, Bob Knight, was named the head coach at Army. He hired DeVoe as his assistant. Five intense years later, DeVoe left Knight to go back to Ohio State as a graduate assistant.

"Those were tough years working for Bob," he said. "But I learned a lot from him. I figured I was destined for small college coaching somewhere and I would need a graduate degree. So, I decided to go back to Ohio State and work for Fred [Taylor] again while I got my master's."

DeVoe not only got his master's, he got an offer to be the head coach at Virginia Tech—and took it. One year later, the Hokies wrote one of the more remarkable stories in the history of the NIT when they won four games by a total of five points and won the tournament on a desperation buzzer-beater by Bobby Stephens, stunning Notre Dame 94–93 in overtime.

DeVoe can remember most of the details of that tournament, including riding the subway with his team to the Garden for each game. "It's funny how hard it becomes to top something like that," he said. "That was an amazing experience for me as a coach. I've had success since then, but nothing that felt quite as exhilarating as that."

DeVoe continued to win at Virginia Tech and when Taylor, under pressure, resigned at Ohio State midway through the '76 season, DeVoe's name was immediately linked with the job. He was on his way to a 21–7 record at Virginia Tech and, being an Ohio State alumnus, most people thought DeVoe would be hired.

DeVoe was on the last year of his contract at Tech. He didn't want to sign a new contract. Ohio State was a possibility, although he told the school he would not talk to them until his season was over. The season ended, shockingly, with a first-round loss to Western Michigan in the NCAA Tournament, a game DeVoe still shakes his head about. The next day DeVoe interviewed at Ohio State. But he came away sensing he was not going to get the job.

"It was just a gut feeling," he said. "The next day I was driving from Blacksburg to Philadelphia and I heard on the radio that Eldon Miller had gotten the job. It didn't shock me. But then when I got home, I found out that Virginia Tech had hired a new coach, thinking I was going to Ohio State. All of a sudden, I didn't have any job at all. It was pretty depressing."

DeVoe landed at Wyoming for two years before Tennessee came after him. Ironically, he got the Tennessee job in large part because of the recommendation of then UCLA Athletic Director J. D. Morgan. When Morgan was looking for a coach to replace Gene Bartow in 1977, he had called DeVoe. Eventually, Morgan hired longtime UCLA assistant Gary Cunningham, but when Tennessee Athletic Director Bob Woodruff called the next year looking for names, Morgan mentioned DeVoe.

During his first season at Tennessee, DeVoe won twenty-one games and beat Kentucky three times. His first five Tennessee teams reached the NCAA Tournament. The next two settled for the NIT but won twenty games each. It was the last two teams that had been failures.

Tennessee is not a school that deals well with failure. And DeVoe is not the kind of coach who can lose and remain popular. He has always been private, but became even more so when he went through a divorce in 1983. He has since remarried and has two young children with his second wife, Ana. But he is not comfortable out on the town or palling around with the alumni. To be popular, he must win. For two years, he had not won.

Now, with the new arena finally opening, DeVoe is feeling heat. Losing teams mean empty seats, especially in a huge arena. Tennessee, with Jenkins and leading scorer Tony White gone, is going to have to show improvement for DeVoe to keep his job. He knows that. His players know that.

DeVoe has a good enough reputation in the coaching profession that he knows he will find work somewhere if he loses his job. But he has no desire to leave Knoxville. His wife is from there, he honestly believes that the new arena will be a major recruiting tool, and he is comfortable there after ten years.

Knoxville is, in many ways, a typical southern college town. It is neither big nor small. On the ride in from the airport one passes, among other things, a flea market, Madame Rene's palm readings, the Baptist Exercise Center; a strip joint, and a sign that says: "HAVING AN AFFAIR? . . . Rodeway Inn Convention Center."

Once across the Tennessee River one turns right, and there on the banks of the river loom both the Thompson–Boling Arena and Neyland Stadium, which has been expanded over the years to now seat 103,000. Both the stadium and the arena are completely orange inside. There is no doubt that this is Big Orange Country.

And, while they love their football here first and foremost, they take their basketball quite seriously. Ray Mears, DeVoe's predecessor, brought in players like Bernard King and Ernie Grunfeld and challenged Kentucky for SEC supremacy. DeVoe, even with his recent troubles, has a record of 10–9 against Kentucky. That goes a long way toward keeping your job at Tennessee. But a third straight losing season will finish DeVoe and he knows it.

On opening night though, the past is forgotten . . . at least for one evening. The opponent is Marquette. Once, this would have been a very tough opener, especially back in the days when Al McGuire was coach. But Marquette has fallen on even harder times than Tennessee. It is a perfect opening night foil.

And so, all goes well. Well, almost all. The bathrooms in the new arena back up when suddenly confronted with 25,272 people and the two locker rooms are flooded. There is also some leakage from the roof. Only a little, though. And when the band plays "The Tennessee Waltz" just before tip-off, the new place is rocking.

Tennessee struggles for a half, leading just 33–30 at intermission. But a 13–4 run at the start of the second half breaks the game open, and the Vols cruise to an 82–56 victory before what will be the only sellout crowd in the new building all season.

"It's as big a win as I can remember since I've been at Tennessee," DeVoe says when it is over. "To open the new place like this in front of all these people is terrific. We've had some fun wins, some wins we didn't deserve, but I can't remember one that was bigger."

DeVoe is genuinely excited. His team played good defense and his three new players—junior college transfer Clarence Swearengen and freshmen Greg Bell and Rickey Clark—played well. The kind of spark he has been looking for was evident.

Bell may have a distinction that no other player in America can claim: He is playing in a building he helped build. A year ago, Bell enrolled at Tennessee as a Proposition 48 freshman. At the time, the rule (since changed) said that a player could retain all four years of his eligibility if he paid his own way to school during the year he was forced to sit out. Bell paid his way by working on the construction crew that built the Thompson–Boling Arena. Having helped build the place, Bell would now be asked to help fill it. Against Marquette, he shoots three-for-four in his college debut.

It is a big night for Tennessee and a big night for DeVoe. But it is only one night and one game. No one knows that better than DeVoe.

December 5. . . Indianapolis

This was the joke they were telling in the Hoosier Dome today: Question: What is the one thing about the first annual Big Four Double-header that isn't like the Final Four?

Answer: Notre Dame is playing.

Well, that may be just a bit unfair but there is little doubt that this is a gala event. They will sell 43,000 tickets to these two games and it could have been a lot more. When you put Indiana, Kentucky, Louis-ville, and Notre Dame in the same building in a central location for one afternoon, there is virtually no limit to the number of tickets that could be sold.

In the twelve years since John Wooden retired, Indiana (3), Louis-ville (2), and Kentucky (1) have won exactly half of the twelve national championships. Even Notre Dame has made a Final Four appearance during that period (1978), although Digger Phelps still hasn't won a Final Four game.

This extravaganza was a long time in the making. It was originally discussed in the early 1980s when the Hoosier Dome was first opened. Since all four schools are within a couple hours' drive of the Dome, the notion was to put the four of them there at the same time and rake in the money. Not to mention playing some pretty good basketball in the process.

Naturally, there were holdups during negotiations. The Kentucky schools didn't like the idea of going into Indiana every year. They wanted to rotate the site. But neither Louisville nor Lexington had a building comparable in size to the Hoosier Dome and neither city was nearly as centrally located.

Then there was the question of format. Bob Knight wanted a two-day tournament. Eddie Sutton wanted a one-day doubleheader. What about matchups? It was finally resolved this way: a four-year contract and a one-day doubleheader, Kentucky schools playing Indiana schools with the opponent switched every year. In other words, Big Four Classic 1 would match Notre Dame–Louisville and Indiana–Kentucky. Big Four Classic 2 would be Indiana–Louisville and Notre Dame–Kentucky, and No. 3 would have the same matchups as No. 1.

Each school would get 25 percent of the ticket allotment and the TV revenue would be split four ways. It was a can't-miss deal. All four schools were perennially good to excellent, all four coaches were national names, and all four had truly fanatical fans.

The whole weekend had all the trappings of a Final Four. The coaches closed their practices on Friday and the city began filling up that evening. By noon on Saturday, two hours before tip-off, I-65 was jammed with cars coming up from Kentucky.

Notre Dame was the only one of the four teams not in the Top Twenty. Kentucky was sitting second behind North Carolina. Indiana was fifth and Louisville, even though it had yet to play a game, was fourteenth.

Indiana was 2–0, including an impressive victory earlier in the week over Notre Dame.

But it had already been a tough season for Bob Knight. Perhaps in the future he should consider sitting out the next season after a major victory in his life. In 1977, following Indiana's 1976 national title, he had thrown three players off the team after an incident in Alaska and gone 14–13, his worst record ever at Indiana. In 1982, after his 1981 national championship, Knight thought about giving up coaching, was distracted all season, and watched his team struggle to win nineteen games. In 1985, the year after the Olympic gold medal, he threw the infamous chair.

Now came 1987. In March, the Hoosiers had won the national title. In November, they opened their season with an exhibition game against the Soviet Union. Knight had complained publicly that American colleges shouldn't play the Soviets because all they were doing was helping prepare them—the enemy—for the Olympics. But he then scheduled them himself, largely because he thought he could beat them.

He was wrong. The Soviets played perhaps their best game of the tour in Bloomington and were up 60–43 early in the second half when

Knight began ranting at referee Jim Burr about one of the Soviets' taking a place on the foul lane illegally during a free throw. Burr gave Knight one technical. He raged on. Two technicals. Still, he continued. Finally, three technicals. Knight was ejected. Burr told him he had to leave. Knight refused.

"If you don't leave," Burr said, "then the game is forfeited."

"I'm not leaving," Knight said.

"Is that final?" Burr asked. Knight nodded. Burr marched to the scorer's table to make the forfeit official. In the meantime, Knight was screaming at Bill Wall, the executive director of ABA-USA and the sponsor of the tour and the game, to do something—intervene. Wall was not going to intervene during a game. Burr signed the forfeit. Knight took his team off the floor.

It was an awful and humiliating moment for Knight, for Indiana, and for the United States. The Soviets were completely bewildered, as were the Indiana fans. The next day Knight "apologized," as only he can, blaming his past relationship with Burr for the incident and saying he was sorry Indiana's fans didn't get to see the last fifteen minutes of the game.

Two days later, Indiana President Thomas Ehrlich, undoubtedly delighted that Knight would pull such a stunt during his first year as IU's president, issued a "strong reprimand" to Knight for his actions. Exactly what a "strong reprimand" was no one knew for sure, but one thing was fairly certain: Ehrlich had no desire to begin his tenure at Indiana by having a confrontation with the most popular man in the state.

Knight's apology was meaningless. During the next few days he told friends that the incident was Burr's fault and that it was unfair that he had been accused of pulling his team off the floor since he had only told his players to leave after the game had been forfeited. The fact that his actions caused the forfeit didn't affect Knight's semantical game at all.

Perhaps most amazing was Knight's reaction to Wall's refusal to step into the debacle. Wall had been a Knight loyalist throughout his tenure as Olympic coach, a good friend who let Knight do exactly what he wanted even if it angered others. Even in the aftermath of this incident—which had made a mockery of an international game—Wall refused to be critical of Knight.

And yet, Knight was furious with Wall because he hadn't intervened during the game. The incident, in Knight's mind, was Burr's fault and also Wall's fault. He, of course, was not at fault in any way. He cut off all communication with Wall, who accepted his fate like any good soldier would, never once suggesting that perhaps Knight's behavior might make him a less-than-appropriate cochairman of the 1988 Olympic selection committee.

Indiana had other problems that would become public during the season. Knight was unhappy with Rick Calloway, the two-year starter at small forward who was being asked to play inside more this season. Knight considered benching him for the Kentucky game but decided against it. That would come later.

And then there was Keith Smart. The hero of New Orleans after making the jump shot that beat Syracuse in the national championship game, Smart had spent most of the preseason in the doghouse. One day in practice, Knight had told Smart that he was "the worst player in America."

This was hardly unusual. Knight likes to keep his stars from getting big heads, and with Smart's New Orleans success he had reason for extra concern. But unlike the seniors of 1987, Steve Alford, Daryl Thomas, and Steve Eyl, Smart had not had three years of preparation to deal with the constant mental pounding Knight's seniors are expected to take. Because he was a junior college transfer he had only been in the program for one year, and much of that year he had been sheltered by the presence of those three seniors.

Now he was getting blasted and having a tough time with it. His early play reflected that. One day in practice, Knight got so angry with Smart that he took the entire team into the locker room and made the players tell Smart how bad he was. Insiders insisted this was not merely "BK Theater," the tag the players put on Knight's infamous mind games. Smart really was playing poorly.

And yet the Indiana team that came into the Hoosier Dome appeared capable of defending its national title. Smart was bound to come around, and two precocious freshmen, Jay Edwards and Lyndon Jones, had been added to an already deep team.

The other teams were question marks. Kentucky had the 1988 version of Steve Alford in Rex Chapman, the sophomore guard so beloved in Kentucky that he was tagged "The Boy King" by the media. To think that race is not a factor in these things is naïve. Most of the fans who get in to see Indiana and Kentucky play are white. Most of the players they watch are black. When a truly gifted white player comes along, he quickly becomes a hero to the white fans. Alford had been through this at Indiana, now Chapman had that status at Kentucky.

Indiana–Kentucky was clearly the feature game, so much so that ABC–TV, which was televising the doubleheader, asked that it be made the second game, a reversal of the original schedule. Louisville had won the national title in 1986 but hadn't even made the NCAA Tournament in 1987. Notre Dame had reached the round of sixteen in 1987, but that was the first time it had made any noise at all in postseason play since Danny Ainge had gone ninety-four feet through five players in five seconds to beat the Irish in the 1981 round of sixteen.

Since then, Digger Phelps had been a well-dressed coach who spent a lot of time winning games against Yale and Pennsylvania. Notre Dame's schedule contained so many walkover games that the joke around the Midwest was that the Irish were going after a fourth straight Ivy League championship.

They did have one very special player, though, in David Rivers. Beyond being a superb guard, Rivers was a profile in courage. He had almost died in a serious automobile accident in August of 1986, but had come back to play the entire season. Phelps sang Rivers's praises so often and so highly that, as good as he was, Rivers could not possibly live up to his billing.

Except in the Hoosier Dome, he did. From the start, it was apparent that Louisville wasn't ready to play. Perhaps the Dome background affected the Cardinals' shooting, but their zero-for-fourteen from three-point range was pathetic any way you looked at it. And Rivers was giving LaBradford Smith, Louisville's talented freshman, a lesson in college basketball.

Rivers did everything but freshen up Phelps's flower. He penetrated over and over for easy baskets. When the Cardinals tried to lay back, he bombed from outside. Rivers is small at six feet and perhaps 160 pounds, but he can take a pounding. He has a knack for bouncing off people like a pinball running back and never losing his balance. He scored 32 points and had 7 rebounds. Smith, who would become a very good player during the season, fouled out with 5 points on 1-of-5 shooting and 5 turnovers. He had a cut lip to boot. Welcome to the big time, kid.

Notre Dame won 69–54 and it really wasn't that close. The Cardinals shot 37 percent for the game and weren't totally embarrassed only because center Pervis Ellison, missing in action for much of his sophomore year, started his junior season with 23 points and 9 rebounds. That was an encouraging sign for Denny Crum, who had gone through a strange three seasons: 19–18, 30–7 (national championship), and 18–14.

But that game was only the warmup act. Rivers had been a man among boys, but now it was time to bring the men in blue and the men in red out.

This is not your average rivalry between two programs that always produce good teams. There is genuine animosity between the two schools. Knight and Sutton are on-again, off-again friends. Publicly, each tries to be complimentary of the other, but privately there is no love lost.

Beyond that, Kentucky fans greatly resent the aspersions Knight has cast on their program over the years. Once, during an interview on the Kentucky radio network, Knight said the Kentucky–Indiana rivalry didn't mean very much to him, "because of all the crap that's gone on down here [Kentucky] in recruiting over the years."

That sort of "crap" would rear its head again in the spring when a Kentucky assistant was accused of putting $1,000 in $50 bills in a package containing a tape that he had sent to the father of Kentucky recruit Chris Mills.

Knight had even told friends as recently as 1986 that he wanted to discontinue the series with Kentucky. But since Sutton was only in his third year at Kentucky, Knight had decided, at least for the moment, to take him at his word when he said the program was now clean. The money involved in the doubleheader might have had a little to do with that liberal stance on Knight's part.

If Kentucky–Indiana occasionally got ugly *off* the court, it was never anything less than fabulous *on* the court. From the start, this was a game worthy of all the hoopla surrounding it. Calloway, whose Indiana career would end unhappily in March, was superb, scoring 26 points and pulling down 11 rebounds. He kept the game close because Smart and Dean Garrett were cold most of the day, shooting two-for-nine and eight-for-twenty-four respectively.

Their performances mirrored those of Chapman and UK forward Winston Bennett, who were six-for-eighteen and three-of-eight, respectively. The Kentucky heroes on this day were Ed Davender (22 points) and previously little-used senior big men Rob Lock (14 points, 8 rebounds) and Cedric Jenkins (14 points, 10 rebounds). Jenkins would become a forgotten man after New Year's but on this day he was formidable.

No one ever really had command of the game. Kentucky took a 22–17 lead, helped by an intentional foul call that almost made Knight crazy. *"Jesus Christ!"* he shrieked at the referee, kicking (fortunately) the air in disgust. The Hoosiers came back to lead 27–24 and led 38–36 at the half on a rebound basket by Edwards, the gifted freshman.

Indiana pushed the lead to 46–40 early in the second half, forcing Sutton to call time. Just as the teams broke their huddles, a huge cheer went up from the Notre Dame section. Their fans, listening to various Walkmans throughout the stands, had just heard football player Tim Brown announced as the Heisman Trophy winner in New York. David Rivers never got a cheer that loud.

Kentucky came right back to lead 50–49 on a Jenkins ten-footer, then got a six-point lead of its own at 57–51 with 8:03 left. Indiana came back, tying the score at 59. Back and forth they went, the defensive intensity at both ends remarkable. Truly, this was a March atmosphere in December. During one possession, Garrett blocked three different Kentucky players' shots.

They finally came to the last minute even at 67–67. Kentucky went inside to Lock, who was fouled with forty-seven seconds to go. He made both free throws for a 69–67 lead. Indiana wanted to go to Garrett. Steve Eyl got it to him, but he bobbled the ball and Lock grabbed it. He quickly passed it to Chapman, who was fouled with twenty-five seconds left.

The Boy King doesn't miss free throws. He made both and Kentucky had control at 71–67. Smart missed another shot, but this time Garrett rebounded and hit the follow with nine seconds left, making it 71–69. IU called time.

During the time-out, Sutton set up an inbounds play to get the ball to Lock, who had made all sixteen free throws he had taken during the season. The ball went to Lock and he was fouled immediately. Naturally, he missed. Indiana raced down, out of time-outs. Calloway drove from the right, where he was cut off by Jenkins and Lock. His shot was way short. But Edwards grabbed it in midair and in one motion tossed it through the hoop just before the buzzer sounded.

Overtime.

"I couldn't believe it," Lock said later. "I felt like I had given away the game."

He hadn't. Kentucky kept its cool in overtime and Garrett and Smart kept missing. Chapman, however, did not. With the Hoosiers leading 76–75, he calmly tossed in a three-pointer with 1:48 left to put the Wildcats up by two. IU had three chances to tie: Garrett missed from the field, Smart missed the front end of a one-and-one, and Smart turned the ball over. Chapman grabbed the loose ball when Smart lost it and threw a long pass to Richard Madison, who dunked with thirty-three seconds left. This time, the Hoosiers couldn't rally and Kentucky had the victory.

Kentucky celebrated as if it had won the national championship. Most amazing perhaps was the reaction of the Louisville fans: They celebrated along with their hated in-state rivals. Knight left the building a few minutes after the buzzer with a copy of *The Hunt for Red October* tucked under his arm.

So far, it had been a pretty blue season for him. And there was more to come.

December 8 . . . Washington, D.C.

If he coaches for twenty-five years, Rick Barnes will remember the first month of his career as a head coach in striking detail.

He had started with a 22-point loss, missing his starting point guard who had been suspended because of cheating allegations. He had followed that with career victory number one, a romp over North Carolina–Greensboro. That had been followed by a stunning upset of Wichita State, an NCAA team in 1987 (and, as it turned out, 1988) in a wild game that ended 95–94 with Wichita State Coach Eddie Fogler furious at the officials.

In the meantime, Amp Davis had been cleared to play because his trial on cheating charges had been delayed until the next semester. Barnes had decidedly mixed emotions about this. On the one hand, he desperately needed Davis. On the other, he was trying to build a program that would have integrity and players who went to class. An accused cheater hardly fit that mold.

"Amp swears he didn't do it," Barnes said. "He admitted to it the first time so I'm inclined to believe him. But who knows? (Athletic

Director) Jack (Kvancz) says we go by innocent until proven guilty. If I find out he is guilty, though, he's gone, I don't care what happens in the damn trial."

As he talked, Barnes was sitting in the empty stands of George Washington University's Smith Center. It was about two hours before George Mason would play George Washington and Barnes was trying to keep himself relaxed.

For him, this was a big game. In a city where Maryland and George-town dominate the fans and the news, the mid-sized schools like GW, Mason, American, Navy, and Howard spend a lot of time scuffling for attention. George Mason had never beaten GW (0–5), and Barnes thought a victory over the Colonials would be a major breakthrough for his program.

What's more, both teams were coming off major upset victories: Mason over Wichita State and GW at Michigan State. The winner of this game would make some serious headlines in Washington. Barnes felt his team—and his school—needed that.

But he was concerned. Exams were coming up. Even though it was early in the season, he thought his players were a little tired. He had worked them very hard in preseason and demanded a lot from them. "It's a big gamble," he said. "As hard as I've been on them, I could lose them. But I think this is the only way to get it done."

The need to beat GW and end the 0–5 skein was what Barnes emphasized to the team before tip-off. "Whether you know it or not, GW looks down on us," he told the players. "They think they're in a better league [Atlantic 10] than we are and they have a better program than we do. Well, why shouldn't they feel that way? We've never beaten them. Tonight is the time to change that and the only way to do that is kick their tails."

Barnes used this approach for two reasons: It made sense, and his assistants had told him that the players really disliked GW. "It's amazing," Barnes said with a grin, "what a motivator hate is in competition."

He was much more relaxed before this game than before Seton Hall. Two victories, especially the one over Wichita State, had helped his self-confidence. But he was concerned about how his team would come back three days after a major victory. "I'm worried," he said, "that they're going to start thinking they're good."

His misgivings were well placed. GW was going to fade badly later in the season but in December it was playing solid basketball. And the Patriots seemed to think they could race the ball up the floor without running any semblance of an offense and control the game. After nine minutes, it was 15–14, GW. Then, it got ugly. The Colonials went on an 11–1 run to make it 26–15. Nothing went right for GMU. Kenny Sanders missed two free throws and two lay-ups. Davis and Steve Smith kept turning the ball over. Barnes tried a time-out to calm them down. It didn't work. After Sanders finally made a lay-up to make it 26–17, GW finished the half with a 14–1 binge for a 40–18 lead. The last ten minutes, the margin had been 25–4—Mason had only one field goal.

It was, to put it mildly, humiliating.

Barnes was wild—genuinely wild—at halftime. Fury is not really in his nature. He is a mild-mannered southerner with an easy-going drawl and a quick smile. All of that was gone now.

"You win one fucking game and think you're good! One game and that was a fluke! You let them just go out and kick your ass completely and totally! You don't care that you were horrible! That's what bothers me!"

Barnes turned as if to write something on the blackboard, stopped and slammed his hand full-force into the blackboard. It fell over with a crash.

No one moved. Barnes went on. "You guys think you want it, you think you know how to win, but you don't. All I ask out of you is forty hard minutes every night. Well, you've gotten your ass kicked for twenty minutes now and I'm telling you right now you better go out and kick theirs in the next twenty. *Goddamn IT!* Do you know they're sitting over there right now *laughing* at you? I don't know about y'all but that makes me want to get sick!"

He stormed into the hallway, his coaches behind him. Once the door had shut, Barnes turned quickly to his trainer, Frank Novakoski, and said, "Get me some ice, I think I broke my hand." It wasn't broken, but Barnes was feeling plenty of pain. He wasn't about to show it in front of the players, though.

The second half was a little better. For fourteen minutes, the Patriots made little dent in the lead, still trailing 61–43 with 6:30 left. Finally, they put on a desperate rally, pulling to within 69–63 with 1:11 to go. But a chance to get within four was missed. After GW's Joe Dooley had missed the front end of a one-and-one, his teammate Mike Jones somehow slipped inside to tip the ball in. That made it 71–63 with 1:05 left and killed the rally. The final was 76–69.

"At least you didn't die," Barnes told his players. "But don't be satisfied with that comeback. You stunk. You shouldn't sleep tonight. I know I won't. This should show you with our style we can come back on anyone. But it should also show you that you can get your ass kicked by anyone if you aren't ready to play."

He walked out of the locker room. Assistant Coach Mark Davis said softly, "We played six good minutes."

Barnes nodded. "I know that. It's my fault."

He would be up all night looking at tape. It was three weeks into his coaching career.

December 11 . . . Chicago

It seemed as if he scored every time he touched the ball. Walker Lambiotte was loose, his self-confidence flowing. It was a cold Friday afternoon and Northwestern was going through its final workout before a Saturday game against Rollins.

"He gives us another level, talent-wise," Coach Bill Foster said, watching Lambiotte. "We haven't exactly had a lot of guys here the last few years who could shoot like he does and were good athletes, too."

Unfortunately for Foster, Lambiotte would not be any help the next day, or for that matter, during the entire season. Because he was a transfer, Lambiotte had to sit out the season. He could practice with his new team but on game day he sat on the end of the bench in street clothes, twitching with pent-up nervous energy.

"I never thought the day would come in my career where I was jealous of guys for running sprints," Lambiotte said, laughing. "Part of playing basketball is bitching about having to run. The first time the other guys had to run and I didn't, it about killed me. Playing games is something I've taken for granted all my life. Now, I just watch."

In some ways, Lambiotte's is a common story in college basketball: Kid picks a school, finds out he isn't going to play as much as he thought, and transfers in order to play more. In an era where many coaches employ roughly the same tactics as a used-car salesman to sell their schools, players find themselves disappointed with shocking regularity.

Lambiotte had left N.C. State for the usual reason: playing time. But the road that led him to that decision was anything but usual. Coming out of high school, Lambiotte was tagged as a can't-miss player. In his junior year, he had proven himself in the All-Star camps against the best players, and had been the subject of an intensive recruiting fight that involved N.C. State, Virginia, Duke, Virginia Tech, and Maryland—among others.

Lambiotte was a coach's dream. Although he was from a rural area, Poquoson, Virginia, he came from a family that certainly knew college was more than just sports. His father, who had been an outstanding player in his own right at Richmond, was a lawyer. His older brother, Kenny, had played basketball at Virginia for two years before pulling one of the more unusual transfers ever, moving from Virginia to Richmond and from basketball to football. He had done so well playing quarterback at Richmond that he ended up making it with the Philadelphia Eagles as a backup pro quarterback.

In a family of athletes (his sister is also a basketball player) Walker was the best athlete. He had learned basketball from his father and brother; his rivalry with his brother was such that the two often didn't talk after playing one-on-one. By his senior year, Walker was 6–6. He could run, jump-shoot—and read and write.

His decision to attend N.C. State had a lot to do with the charm of Jim Valvano. Lambiotte liked Valvano, his father loved Valvano. The recruitment of Lambiotte by State was what coaches call "a living room job." Valvano had won the recruiting fight sitting in the Lambiottes' living room.

At the end of his last high school season, Lambiotte played in all the big-time all-star games. Once again, it was apparent that he could hold his own against the best. He was voted MVP in one of the games and played well in all of them. He went to State thinking he had a chance to start as a freshman.

His thinking was correct. Lambiotte was a starter or the first sub off the bench at the beginning of the season. But, as the year progressed, his playing time started to dwindle. Sometimes Valvano would start him, take him out after a few minutes, and leave him on the bench the rest of the evening.

This was a very good State team led by Chris Washburn, Charles Shackleford, and senior guards Nate McMillan and Ernie Myers; they reached the NCAA Final Eight. Lambiotte wasn't thrilled about his spotty playing time but felt that was part of being a freshman.

"Coach V was always wild with playing time," Lambiotte said.

"There were games where I would play most of the first half, then not play at all the second half. But I understood. We had a lot of talent and I was a freshman so I figured that was part of the learning process. But then when it kept happening my sophomore year, I started to get worried about it."

The Wolfpack was not nearly as good in 1987 as it had been in 1986. Washburn had opted to turn pro, Shackleford was struggling with inconsistency, and Kenny Drummond, the junior-college point guard, dropped off the team and out of school at midseason.

Once again, Lambiotte was often a starter. But once again he would start, come out, and often not return. Then late in the season, when Valvano changed the team's tempo, deciding to walk the ball up, and began playing Quentin Jackson and Vinny Del Negro extensively, Lambiotte's playing time went to almost zero. He was confused and hurt.

"What was really bothering me was that I didn't feel like I was getting any better," he said. "I think coming out of high school I had a pretty good understanding of my strengths and weaknesses. My shot wasn't really a good shot technically. I could get it to fall, but it needed work. I wasn't becoming a better player. That worried me."

By midseason, Lambiotte and his family were talking transfer. This was somewhat traumatic for the family because they had already lived through one transfer and never dreamed they would find themselves going through it again with Walker. Unlike a lot of players who get benched, Lambiotte didn't feel anger. He still liked Valvano, but felt his first concern had to be what was best for him. And staying at State might not be what was best.

Lambiotte was genuinely torn. He talked to his brother about what the year without playing would be like. "He told me that if I took the right approach and used the year, it would be okay," he said. "There are advantages to having a fifth year. You can get ahead academically, focus more on your game, and you've just got more time. The hard part would be not playing for a year after a year in which I hadn't played very much."

Lambiotte changed his mind on several occasions. He wanted to go, then he wanted to stay. He liked it at State as a student. Was transferring just for playing time a mistake? Finally, he decided to talk to Valvano about it.

Valvano hadn't lost faith in Lambiotte. As a coach, he knew that some players were ready as freshmen, others bloomed later. Del Negro, who had become a star late in his junior year, was a perfect example. "I think next year should be your year," Valvano told Lambiotte. "You've spent the last two years learning. Next year you will have completed most of the learning process and you should really be ready."

Valvano's comments confused Lambiotte further. True, he could see he'd have more playing time at small forward the next year, since Bennie Bolton would be gone. But he had *had* playing time and lost it. What if that happened again?

Lambiotte decided he had to get away from State for a few days to make up his mind. He went home and sat on the beach. This was a tough time. He was, in essence, deciding whether to repudiate the most important decision of his life. He had to decide whether to go somewhere and *start all over:* new school, new teachers, new friends, new coaches, new teammates. And Lambiotte knew that transfers generally were not treated with a lot of sympathy by the public.

"It just seemed to me that whenever you hear someone talk about a guy who transferred, they never say 'transfer,' " he said. "They always say, 'He quit.' I didn't like the idea of being labeled a quitter."

But at the same time, Lambiotte could hear his mother's words in the back of his mind: "Maybe quitting is just staying in the same place and sitting."

Lambiotte knew he didn't want to sit. There were no guarantees at State. The extra year might help. He decided: "I'm leaving," he told his father.

It was his father who gave Valvano the news. Valvano was disappointed; he liked Lambiotte and he honestly felt he would get to play in the future. But he understood, too. Lambiotte was not the first player to leave State because of lack of playing time. When you recruit a lot of athletes there are going to be some who don't get to play.

One decision made, another one was necessary: where to transfer to? "It isn't like there's a guidebook on how to do it," Lambiotte said. "I wasn't even sure where to start."

He didn't have to start. Once the word got out that he was leaving, coaches began courting him. In some ways, it was like being recruited all over again. Lambiotte wasn't very comfortable with that. He wanted to make a decision and get it over with. He was playing summer ball—and playing well—and that was causing a lot of action on the Lambiotte telephone. Kentucky called. So did Michigan. And Syracuse.

Lambiotte wanted a program that played against top-caliber teams. But obviously, he didn't want to repeat his mistake—he wanted to go where he was going to have a good chance to play. He visited California. He liked the school and he liked the coaches. He was tempted. But it was a long way from home.

And then there was Northwestern. Foster had just completed his first season and, having gone 8–20, knew he had a major rebuilding project on his hands. Foster had recruited Lambiotte when he was at South Carolina, so he knew the family and they knew him. And, since Foster had coached Valvano in college, he could pick up a phone and ask Valvano what kind of kid Lambiotte was.

Northwestern needed players. It was in the Big Ten so the competition would certainly be there. Then, at the last minute, Lambiotte almost canceled his visit there. "I'd been on the road so much I just didn't want to go to the airport and get on another plane. I went back in the house and said, 'Dad, let's just skip this. I'll go to Cal.' He told me to make the visit, then I could rest all I wanted."

Lambiotte made the trip. He liked the school and the coaches. It was a lot closer to home than Cal and he liked the idea that he would still be playing in one of the best leagues in the country. "In the end, the decision was easy: good school, very good league, a good chance to play and a good coach. The only thing that worried me was how cold they said it gets here. The first time I felt this wind [they call it "The Hawk"] it cut right through me."

The wind wasn't the only thing that made things tough for Lambiotte. There were days in practice when Foster had to ignore him to get the team ready to play a game. "Standing and watching, knowing you aren't going to get a shot for the rest of the day is tough," he said. "I understand it, but it's hard."

And the Wildcats truly were bad. They won their first two games, against Washington–St. Louis and Rutgers, but then Duke, Foster's old team, came to town and blew them away in the last fifteen minutes. "I had played against those guys last year," Lambiotte said. "I tried to talk to our guys on the bench about what they could do, but really, I can't do much except keep working and wait for next year."

In a sense, that summed up the situation at Northwestern.

One day, watching TV, Lambiotte saw *The Jim Valvano Show* suddenly pop onto his screen. The show's opening was full of spectacular plays by the Wolfpack. And there, skying for a dunk, was a familiar figure: Walker Lambiotte.

Sitting in his dormitory at Northwestern, Lambiotte smiled. "I guess the dunk was so awesome," he said, "that they couldn't part with it even though they've parted with me."

He smiled for a moment, thinking about the past, even knowing it was just that—past. The future, even in the middle of a cold Chicago December, looked pretty good.

December 12. . . Iowa City, Iowa

George Bush was in Iowa today. Not many people outside of his entourage really cared. Lute Olson was also here. *Everyone* cared about that.

This was the return of the prodigal son. For nine years, Olson was an icon in this state, the man who rebuilt Iowa basketball, taking the Hawkeyes to five straight NCAA Tournaments and, in 1980, the Final Four.

But in 1983, feeling as if he wasn't appreciated by *everyone* and lured by the warm weather, Olson migrated west to Arizona. There, he had done the same kind of rebuilding job. In the meantime, after three uncomfortable years under Olson's successor, George Raveling, when Raveling also went west (to Southern California) Iowa had hired Tom Davis. Davis had gone 30–5 in 1987 and become an immediate hero.

Now, Olson and Arizona were coming to town and the two heroes, the old and the new, would meet in Carver–Hawkeye Arena, the five-year-old jewel that had been built for Olson. It was The House That Lute Built, but now it was The House That Tom Owned.

Six hours before tip-off, Steve Kerr sat in the coffee shop of the Highlander Motel sipping a soda, a grin playing at his features. "Coach really wants this one *bad,*" he said. "I can't remember ever seeing him quite this tight for a game. He wants to come in and show these people he knew exactly what he was doing when he left here."

Kerr shivered slightly. "The weather alone would make me want to get out of here," he said. "This cold [25 degrees] is bad for my knee. When we were up in Alaska it really got stiff. The same thing here. It makes me worry about what it will feel like in twenty or thirty years if it hurts now."

For the moment, Kerr was more concerned with Iowa's press than with his knee. Like the Wildcats, the Hawkeyes were 6–0. While Arizona had been winning the Great Alaska Shootout, Iowa had been in Hawaii (Kerr was jealous) beating Illinois and Villanova impressively to win the Maui Classic.

To say that there was huge anticipation surrounding this game would not do it justice. Even though the game was being televised locally, scalpers were getting $100 a ticket outside the arena. Lute's return was about as big as it gets in Iowa City; the fact that both teams were ranked in the top five only added to the drama.

Olson is not a man who likes to admit to a lot of emotion. He has classic Scandinavian looks, topped off by silver hair that never—ever—moves. It looks as if someone painted it on. Kerr, because he is Kerr, can joke that it is a toupee. No one else would dare kid about the Olson locks.

But this will be an emotional night for Olson. He will enter the arena uncertain about how he will be received. When Olson left here for Arizona, many Iowa fans felt jilted. They felt that after the school had built an arena that was a monument to him, he had, more or less, done a pigeon routine on it and flown off.

But Iowans are not grudge-holders. They remembered the jilting a little, but they remembered all the wins a lot. Olson, proving that he has a flair for the dramatic, waited until everyone else was in place—players, coaches, fans—before he made his entrance. Everyone in the place knew he was coming because several TV crews and a horde of photographers came backing into view just ahead of him.

As he walked out of the tunnel and into the bright lights, the reaction was a bit hesitant. A few fans hollered, *"Loot, Loot,"* the cry they used to stand and scream in unison when he made his entrance. But then, after he had walked about five steps, they all just stood up together and cheered.

Olson would not have been human if he hadn't reacted. His face broke into a huge grin and he waved in all directions to acknowledge the cheers. "They could have been a lot less kind than that," he said later. "I was really touched."

Of course once the game began the cheers were all for Davis and Iowa. That this was a big game emotionally for both teams was evident right away. It took 2:45 before anyone scored. At the first TV time-out, with 15:33 left in the half, Arizona led 2–0, Tom Tolbert's jumper being the only points. Iowa didn't score until its tenth possession, when Ed Horton hit a free throw with 14:17 left. At the second TV time-out, with 9:48 left, it was 9–3 Arizona.

"For a while there I thought we might have a scoreless first half," Olson joked.

Kerr, who was handling Iowa's press just fine, couldn't believe how tight everyone's shooting was. These teams had both played in big games already this season, but this one seemed to have grabbed everyone by the collar.

"I was just hoping that we'd snap out of it first," he said.

They didn't. Iowa did, thanks to a couple of three-pointers by point guard B. J. Armstrong, and built a 22–16 lead with 3:38 left. Carver-Hawkeye Arena was shaking with noise. But Kerr, who had missed his first two shots, shook loose for a three-pointer of his own and then, at the first-half buzzer, he hit another one to give Arizona a 26–24 lead.

Kerr was so fired up that he shook his fist right in Armstrong's face. To most, that was a very un-Kerrlike move. To Kerr, it was very Kerrlike. "He's a hell of a player," he said later of Armstrong. "It had been a tough half. When I hit that shot, I just wanted to say, 'Yeah!' so I did. The fans got all over me about it in the second half but that was fine. They were entitled."

Kerr is not easily intimidated. Neither are his teammates. This was the kind of game that seemed destined to come down to a last shot. But in the last seven minutes—shortly after the Iowa band had played "Hava Nagila," a crowd favorite here, during a time-out—the Wildcats took command.

Tolbert took a pretty pass from Kerr and hit to make it 50–47. Then, after a careless Armstrong pass, Tolbert scored on the break to make it 52–47. Roy Marble missed at the other end, then Sean Elliott, quiet most of the evening, hit for a 54–47 lead with 4:42 left. The Hawkeyes never got closer than three after that and Olson walked off with a 66–59 victory that he readily admitted was special.

"I think the players sensed that this one was kind of big for the old coach," he said. "I tried to downplay the whole thing but I don't think I fooled 'em for a second. They knew. You don't spend nine years of your life in a place without coming back and having special feelings."

Kerr had played superbly, scoring 15 points, handing off for 6 assists and, most remarkably, only turning the ball over once in forty minutes against the Iowa press. "Without Kerr we don't win this game," Olson said. "He's the difference between us being a good team and being a special team."

Kerr was thrilled with the win and with his play. He was also thrilled the next day when the team headed home. It was 50 degrees warmer in Tucson than in Iowa City. After a week in Alaska and three days in Iowa, Kerr had seen all the winter he wanted to see, at least for a while.

December 15. . . Arlington, Virginia

College basketball is played in many different settings. There is the hugeness of the domes, the elegance of the Dean E. Smith Center (Deandome for short) in Chapel Hill and the rowdiness of Cameron Indoor Stadium just down the road at Duke. There is the tradition of the Palestra and Madison Square Garden and the sheer noise of The Pit in Albuquerque.

But nothing is quite like The Fort. For more than thirty years, college basketball has been played in the Fort Myer Ceremonial Hall, a four thousand-seat relic of a gym with dim lights, sporadic heat, and blacked-out windows. For a long time both George Washington and American played their home games here. When GW built its own gym in the early 1970s, it moved out. But AU stayed. Now, finally, in 1988, the Eagles will move into their own on-campus arena. But the season will start at The Fort because the new place isn't ready yet.

Poetically, one of the last games to be played in the old place will be against George Washington. "Be it ever so humble," AU Coach Ed Tapscott says with a grin, "I just hope the Fort Myer jinx is at work tonight."

GW is 5–1 and on a roll. American is 2–3 and struggling.

Often, just getting a game started at The Fort is an adventure. The last time these two schools played here was two years ago, just two days after the Beirut bombings that had killed many American Marines. Normally, to get on the base one just drives to the main gate and is waved through by a saluting officer. But in the aftermath of the bombings, every car was being stopped and checked and everyone was being asked for ID, including all the players on both team buses.

The game began in a virtually empty building with no PA announcer, a missing referee, and one statistician. Tonight, that isn't a problem. Driving through the gate, one is struck by the contrasting sights: There is barbed wire on the left side of the road but if you look beyond it you can see a breathtaking panorama of the nation's capitol all lit up with Christmas lights.

Parking is in the lot across the street from the Officer's Club and the main entrance is across from the movie theater. The movie tonight is *Revenge of the Nerds II.*

There are, according to the official attendance figures, 1,284 people in the Ceremonial Hall, many of them GW fans. It is just as easy for GW people to hike across the river as it is for AU people. But things are looking up for the Eagles: Their band has actually found the place for the first year in memory and three of their cheerleaders are cute. Very cute in fact. This is a major upset in itself.

Fortunately for everyone involved, it is not that cold out. There have been nights in The Fort where one could see one's breath at tip-off. One year, back when Georgetown still deigned to play American, John Thompson took his team into the locker room and refused to come out until the gym warmed up. Another year, a sliding door got stuck— open—before a game while concessions were being brought in and the game was played with a windchill factor well below freezing. AU won the toss that night and elected to kick and take the wind.

Tonight, the only real problem is with the forty-five-second clock. The four is a nine on the clock so the officials have to explain that ninety-five seconds actually means forty-five seconds.

Everyone agrees that's just fine. At The Fort this is a very minor problem. The Jinx is evident early. AU falls behind 4–0 but then thirteen minutes into the game, roars back to lead 22–10. GW Coach John Kuester is beside himself, not sure who to rage at, his team, the officials, or The Jinx. The Colonials rally to within 32–24 at halftime and come back ready to make a run after the intermission.

There's one problem, though. Both forty-five-second clocks have gone out completely. The man in charge of fixing the problem is Dick Myers, AU's assistant athletic director. Once, Dick Myers was the assistant general manager of the Washington Redskins. That is a long way from fixing a forty-five-second clock in an Army base not named after you. It takes twenty-five minutes to get one clock functioning.

"Just another night at The Fort," says AU Sports Information Director Terry Cornwall.

It is a bad night for Kuester and his team. They tie the game at 38–38, but with the score 48–45, the Eagles go on a binge, outscoring GW 12–4 for a 60–49 lead with 5:30 left. At one point, three GW students become so frustrated that when referee Tom Fraim makes a call against their team, they jump off the bleachers and surround Fraim, waving their arms and yelling. Fraim isn't pleased. One of them is escorted out.

This isn't even close to a tough night for security, though. Two years ago, a fight broke out during an American–Westchester game. As the players rolled on the floor, armed MPs and dogs came roaring through the doors and onto the floor to break up the fight. That won't be necessary tonight.

GW goes quietly, losing 78–63. It is never close the last five minutes. The Jinx has worked again. "Tough place to play," Kuester says. "Of course, they have to play under the same conditions. We have nothing to complain about."

Tapscott, with only one game left to play here, is getting nostalgic. "I've coached in here nine years. It's home. Look, so what if we change in a weight room. Tom Scherer [senior center] knows that he hangs his clothes on the bench press machine. That's where he changes. We know which bench is our bench. We're comfortable here."

Make no mistake though, Tapscott is looking forward to his new gym. "We have to have it," he says. "But you know, this place is like a throwback. It's like this is the last bastion of fifties basketball. You expect to walk in here and see a bunch of white kids with crew cuts and black high tops and maybe one black guy on the team.

"But times change. Now we've got a black guy coaching the team." Tapscott smiled. "Of course I do have two white guys with crew cuts."

They are inside throwing their uniforms on the bench press machine. Soon, they will have a real locker room. But, like everyone else who ever set foot inside the place, they'll all remember The Fort.

December 19. . . Raleigh, North Carolina

When top teams get together to play each other in December basketball games it is usually for one reason: television. It was not so many years ago that the best teams put together December schedules that their JV teams would be able to handle, looking to load up on wins to impress the NCAA Tournament Committee in March.

But, thankfully, times have changed. The tournament committee looks at strength of schedule first in selecting teams and, just as important, TV has become an important scheduler. If one of the networks wants Kansas and North Carolina State to play in December, you can bet Kansas and North Carolina State will play.

The two schools have played the last three years in a row, largely because the networks (first CBS, now ABC) thought that bringing Danny Manning back to North Carolina would be a good story. They couldn't match Kansas with North Carolina because Larry Brown played for Dean Smith and Smith doesn't believe in playing his friends during the regular season. The fact that Smith's assistants publicly ripped Brown after he signed Manning doesn't change any of this.

The Brown–Smith–N.C. State–Manning family quadrangle is one of the more interesting to come along in recent years. It began, really, when Danny was still a little boy and his father, Ed Manning, was still playing in the old ABA for the Carolina Cougars. The coach was Larry Brown.

Ed Manning used to bring Danny with him to practice in those days and Danny can remember Larry Brown helping to teach him how to hold a basketball. He can also remember him shouting a lot. Danny's first impressions of Larry Brown? "A little man with a big mouth," he says, smiling but not joking.

In all, Ed Manning played pro ball for nine years. He was, by his own description, "a garbage man," a player not blessed with great gifts but a hard worker who came in every night and played tough defense, rebounded, and hustled. "Ever since he was little I've always told Danny that no matter how bad you're playing, you can always hustle," Ed Manning said. "Hustle isn't a talent, it's just something you have to want to do."

When Ed Manning retired he went into coaching, working at North Carolina A&T. But in 1978, he got caught in the middle of a coaching shake-up and found himself out of work. With two young children to support he found work driving a truck. This meant he was on the road constantly, just as he had been as a player and then a coach.

The travel was hard on father and son. Danny, just beginning to blossom as an athlete, couldn't really understand why his father was away all the time. Often, he would ask his mother why his dad never came to his Little League games or his basketball games when all the other fathers, or so it seemed to Danny, were there.

"I always tried to explain to Danny that his dad was out doing what he had to do for him and for the family," Darnelle Manning said. "He knew that his dad loved him, but it was hard for him because he felt deprived."

By the time he was a freshman at Page High School in Greensboro, Danny was emerging as a star on the basketball court. He was already 6–6, not that surprising since his father was almost 6–8 and his mother just under six feet. But he wasn't just tall. He was agile, quick, and seemed to have an instinct for the game. When he did get to see his son play, Ed Manning recognized this quickly.

"A lot of players have to work very hard to develop offensive moves," he said. "Danny never did. He just had a knack for it. He could do more with a basketball instinctively when he was fifteen or sixteen than I ever could."

Although the Mannings were hardly wealthy when Danny was growing up, both mother and father worried about their son becoming spoiled by the adulation he was receiving because of his athletic ability. When Danny tried to quit the baseball team in junior high school to concentrate on basketball, Ed wouldn't let him. "You start something," he told his son, "you finish it."

"They fought about things like that," Darnelle Manning said. "Danny never understood how easy he had it compared to Ed when he was a boy. Ed used to drive the school bus every day to and from school, pick up all the kids, drop them all off and then go to school in between. He worked on his daddy's farm [in Summit, Mississippi] from the time he was little. He went to a segregated school and never had any idea what a summer camp was. The toughest thing Danny ever had to do was cut the grass."

And yet, Darnelle Manning understood her son's frustration when his father went back on the road again and again. "I know it bothered him when I was the only mother at father-son dinners," she said. "But it couldn't be helped."

During Danny's junior year, he was targeted as one of *the* players in the country. He was 6–10 and he could run, pass, and shoot. It was also during that year that his father began to have heart problems.

The doctors tried to treat him with medication, but it didn't work. The doctors told the Mannings there was really no choice: Ed needed bypass surgery. It was dangerous, but necessary. The night before the operation, driving home from the hospital, Darnelle Manning explained to her son exactly what was involved in the surgery. "I didn't want to hold anything back," she said. "Danny had to understand that his daddy was sick and there were risks involved. I called a spade a spade."

When Darnelle Manning was finished, her son was silent for a moment. Then he began crying uncontrollably. "He was crying so bad I had to pull the car over. He was just frightened. I didn't blame him."

Ed Manning came through the surgery. And, as often happens when a father and son have not been close, they became closer afterward. "Danny didn't say a whole lot while I was in the hospital," Ed Manning remembered. "But he was always there. I knew how much he cared."

That winter, as a junior, Danny led Page High School to the state championship. He was being courted heavily by both North Carolina and N.C. State. Both felt they had a great chance to sign him the following fall. They were right. Almost certainly, Danny Manning would have played for Carolina or State *if* Larry Brown had not become the coach at Kansas.

Brown was coaching the New Jersey Nets in the NBA when Ted Owens, the longtime coach at Kansas, was forced to resign. One of the first people Kansas called during the search for a new coach was Dean Smith—Kansas, Class of '53. Smith, knowing that Brown was unsure about whether he wanted to stay in the pro game, suggested the school contact him.

If Brown was certain about one thing it was that he wasn't certain about staying in the NBA. He had been successful everywhere he had coached—Carolina in the ABA, Denver in the NBA, UCLA in the NCAA, and New Jersey back in the NBA. But even though he won, Brown was never really happy. That had as much to do with the nature of the man as with the nature of the jobs. When he was in the pros, he wanted a college atmosphere. When he was in the colleges, he wanted the money of the pros.

Kansas called Brown. Brown thought about it and decided he wanted to go back to college. He took the job with almost a month left in the Nets season. That created a tremendous amount of bitterness in New Jersey—but by that time Brown was in Lawrence putting together a coaching staff.

One of the first people Brown called was Ed Manning. Did the fact that Ed had a son who was a junior in high school and perhaps the best player in the country influence him?

"Certainly," he said. "I never said it didn't influence me. But what really makes me mad is when people say I hired a truck driver. They act like Ed never played or coached. He did both. They act like I never heard of Ed Manning before I came to Kansas. He played for me. He was a friend. I knew if I hired him, even if we didn't get Danny, that he'd be my friend and work hard for me."

The ironic thing about Brown, who has been accused of disloyalty in so many places, is that he treasures loyalty. He knew Ed Manning would be loyal to him and he knew there was a damn good chance Danny would be loyal to his father.

Hiring Ed was not all that easy. First, on the Kansas side there was the job description. It said "college graduate." Ed Manning had left Jackson State three credits shy of a degree. Brown changed the job description. When that got out, the howling in North Carolina could be clearly heard in Kansas.

Back in North Carolina, the Manning family was meeting to talk about the job. Darnelle Manning didn't want her husband driving a truck all night after his heart surgery. Ed Manning wanted badly to get back in coaching. But then there was Danny, who was being asked to leave his home, his friends, and his teammates with one year left in high school.

"Danny wanted to stay behind and finish up at Page," Darnelle Manning said. "I told Ed I would stay behind with him and then move out in a year. Ed said no. If his family couldn't go with him, then he didn't want to go. We talked some more and finally decided this was best for Ed and for the family."

This was a major move, though, and Darnelle Manning wanted to be sure it was not going to be a brief one. "When we went out to see Larry," she said, "I told him if he didn't stay at Kansas at least five years, I'd kill him."

As soon as Ed Manning's hiring and Danny Manning's transfer from Page High School to Lawrence High School became official, the screaming intensified. Larry Brown was not, by any stretch of the imagination, the first coach to hire an assistant with the recruitment of a star player in mind, but he had done it to the detriment of Dean Smith and Jim Valvano, who in addition to being big stars back home, had just won the last two national championships.

Neither was thrilled. Valvano didn't even bother to continue recruiting Manning. Smith went through with his home visit, telling Danny Manning, "Don't go to school to make your father happy or to make Larry Brown happy. Go where you think you'll be happy."

That was exactly the advice Darnelle Manning gave her son. When Danny worried about how it might affect his father if he didn't go to Kansas, his mother told him, "You worry about you and no one else."

Darnelle Manning wasn't certain Kansas was the best place for her son. She knew how much Ed expected from Danny and how demanding he would be coaching him.

"You have to be sure you can deal with your daddy's mouth for four years," she told him.

Danny nodded. "Mom, if I go too far away you'll never see me play and you've been coming to my games since fifth grade."

"Danny, if you go play in West Hell I'll see you play."

He thought about it some more and finally told his parents: "I want to play at Kansas."

The decision surprised no one. The circumstances that led to it meant that Manning would be under the microscope before he ever played a college game. He would be joining a veteran team, one that had reached the NCAA Tournament in Brown's first season. They compared him to Magic before he ever scored a college point and predicted great things for the Jayhawks.

"My freshman year, I worried too much about people's expectations of me," he said. "I kept hearing about how great I was supposed to be and when I didn't play that way I let it bother me. It took me a while to figure out that if you try to live up to other people's expectations of you, you're bound to fail."

His team didn't fail that year, going 26–8. Manning was the only freshman starter and tried hard to let the older players be the stars. He is not, contrary to what has been written about him, shy or quiet, but he is uncomfortable with the trappings of stardom.

"My friends always laugh when they read about how shy and quiet I am," he said. "When I'm comfortable, I'm not either one of those things. But when I go out in public, I'm never sure how to handle all the attention. People come up and want autographs or to talk about the game. It's nice that they care but sometimes I just want to say, 'You know, I didn't come out tonight to sit around and analyze the game with you.' But that's rude and if I do it, people will think I'm an asshole."

Manning didn't want anyone to think ill of him, so he rarely asserted himself, on or off the court. Almost from the first day he was at Kansas until the last, Brown was on him about that. Each year, he turned up the volume of his criticism, trying to make Manning understand that the best player has to be the leader whether he's a freshman or a senior. Manning really didn't want that role. He just wanted to play.

"I think Danny would be happiest if he could just be the best player and have all the other players know it," Brown said. "He would rather not deal with all the other things that are part of being a star. He's got to learn that the world's just not that way."

As a sophomore, Manning started to become the star everyone had thought he would become. Playing with a strong senior group led by Ron Kellogg and Calvin Thompson, he led the Jayhawks to a 35–4 record and the Final Four. Ironically, his best and worst games of the year came against schools from North Carolina.

In December, because TV dictated it, Kansas went to Greensboro to play N.C. State. Kansas won the game, but Manning, booed unmercifully by the crowd which saw him as a traitor, had a terrible game. "He just couldn't handle it," Brown remembered. "He was so hurt by the booing that was all he could think about."

Manning got even with the Wolfpack in March. During the last ten minutes of the Midwest Regional Final, with KU trailing State by six points, he took over the game. He scored 26 points, was voted MVP of the regional, and got his team to the Final Four.

But a week later, against Duke, Mark Alarie, a smart, experienced senior, kept pushing Manning away from his favorite shooting spots. He held Manning to 4 points and Duke beat the Jayhawks, 71–67, in a brutal, draining game. It was during that game that Archie Marshall, flying in for a lay-up, went down with the knee injury that would require surgery, keeping him out for the entire '87 season.

Manning was devastated by the loss. "He blamed himself," his mother remembered. "I was concerned during that time because Larry and Ed were so tough on him. It seemed like all they could see was the negative. I kept telling Ed he needed to pat the boy on his butt more often. He would say he was just being a coach and I would say, 'That's our child, first, last and always. Tell him how proud you are of him.' "

Ed Manning was proud of his son, but he also knew there were ways he could get better. "Mothers never see any need for improvement in their sons," he said smiling. "Coaches do."

So do players. Danny understood his father's criticisms and knew his father was proud of him without being told. "My dad just isn't a verbal person," he said. "That's not his way. But I knew how much he cared and I knew he was always there to talk to if I needed him. I've just always talked to my mother more because she's always been around. I've only been around Dad a lot during the last couple of years."

With the senior class of '86 gone the next year, Manning had to step forward and be the team's leader. Still, his way of leading was by example. Brown kept pushing him to do more, Manning just kept playing. Finally, after the Jayhawks had been blown out by a mediocre Arkansas team, Brown asked Manning to come out to his house for a talk.

"We really got some things out in the open there," Manning said. "I was just more comfortable because we weren't in the office and I finally told him what I was thinking. I was sick and tired of all the yelling and I thought the other guys were too.

"Coach Brown is always going to yell, that's just his way, he can't coach any differently. But I thought he needed to lighten up. He told me he wanted me to yell more and I said, 'Why? You do enough yelling for all of us.' "

The exchange was good for both men. Brown wanted Manning to be more open about his frustrations and he wanted him to be able to feel that he could come to him and tell him when he thought he was doing something wrong. Manning left happy to have blown off some steam and with a thought that he never let go of the next two years: "If the team loses, it's the best player's fault. He has the most to do with winning, so he must have the most to do with losing."

The Jayhawks finished strong that year, reaching the NCAA round of sixteen, winning twenty-five games, and losing a tough game to a good Georgetown team. When Brown signed two good junior-college guards—Otis Livingston and Lincoln Minor—and added another juco, Marvin Bradshaw, to Marshall's return, it looked like the Jayhawks would be a Final Four contender again—*if* Manning stayed for his senior year and *if* Brown didn't jump ship again, this time to the New York Knicks.

As it turned out, Manning came much closer to leaving than Brown did. "I had delusions of grandeur," he said. "The thought of making all that money just to play ball and not worry about school or anything was very tempting. I figured I could always come back and get my degree, so why not?"

Darnelle Manning knew how her son was thinking. She wanted him to stay in school, not just for the degree but because she wasn't sure he was mature enough yet to deal with the emotional rigors of the NBA. But she knew that to play the wailing, "don't leave" mother would be a mistake.

And so, when Danny said to her one afternoon in the kitchen that he thought he wanted to turn pro, she calmly answered, "Go ahead. Take the money and run."

Danny was shocked. "This is too easy," he thought. He asked his mother what she really thought.

"If you go, you'll have the money, no doubt about it," she said. "You'll have money, money, and money. Now, what can you have if you stay? A degree. A championship ring, maybe. The Olympics. And the money, I suspect, will still be there."

Danny Manning laughed when his mother was finished. "I think I see your point," he said. The decision was made. Darnelle Manning was relieved.

"His father never went back for his degree and I'm sure Danny never would have either," she said. "But more than that, I thought he had his whole life to be an adult but only one last year to enjoy being a child. I'm glad he decided to stay."

So was Brown, who had rejected an offer from the New York Knicks. He started the season with high hopes. Even after two losses in Hawaii, one to Iowa and one to Illinois, he wasn't that concerned. "This time of year is for learning," he said.

But N.C. State, even if it was a learning game, was a big one. It was Manning's first trip back to North Carolina to play since the booing experience of his sophomore season. And State was a very good team— one that Valvano was still tinkering with, but a very good team nonetheless.

The game was scheduled during Christmas break. But the State students wanted to see the game, so many hung around an extra couple of days, others came back for it. This created a problem for State officials. They had sold the downstairs student seats to the public, figuring the students would be away. When the students began lining up to get in to their regular seats three hours before tip-off, it was apparent there was going to be a problem.

The students wanted in. They were being told to stay out. Finally, Valvano, in his role as athletic director, was called out of the locker room to deal with the situation. Brown, sitting in the arena relaxing, saw him coming and asked what was going on. Valvano explained.

"Let's go talk to them," Brown said.

The two men walked to the door where the students were being held back by security. Valvano explained the seats had been sold. "But they're our seats, we're your best fans," the students answered.

"Hey, Jimmy, I agree with them, I think you should let them in," Brown said.

"Yeah, I probably should," Valvano said.

Before he could think about that for another moment, the rope was down and the students were racing into the building toward their seating section. Valvano and Brown just stood to the side watching, Brown laughing hysterically. That was enough for Valvano. He shrugged his shoulders, turned to his assistants and said, "You deal with it." Then he headed back for his locker room.

The assistant athletic directors tried. They pleaded with the students, now taking up the whole downstairs section behind the benches, to leave. They asked Dick Vitale, who was broadcasting the game on ABC, to make a PA announcement asking them to leave. "No way," Vitale said. "The only person who can do that is Jim Valvano."

Jim Valvano wasn't coming out of the locker room again until just before game time. The students weren't going to leave. Finally, the State people gave up. They began racing around to find folding chairs and benches and began sticking them in aisles and anyplace else they could find. Anywhere there was an inch, a seat was set up. A riot was averted, but if a fire marshal had walked in, Reynolds Coliseum might have been shut down forever.

The game began with Manning scoring 6 of the Jayhawks' first 8 points. State dominated most of the first half, though, leading 35–26 with five minutes to play. Freshman point guard Chris Corchiani, who Valvano had started over senior Quentin Jackson, gave the Wolfpack more quickness and penetrating ability than it had had the year before. State looked tough.

Kansas chipped back to within 41–36 at halftime, but State pushed the lead back up to 9 in the second half. Then it was as if Manning decided he was not going to be denied in this game. He went backdoor for a dunk. He posted up for a jumper, he tapped in a Kevin Pritchard miss. Finally, he made a steal and fed a gorgeous look-away pass to Marshall to tie the game at 56–56 with 9:40 left.

It seesawed from there. Manning put Kansas ahead with two free throws, 66–65. Corchiani got overexcited and threw the ball away. Manning hit a hook for a 68–65 lead.

It was 70–67 when State called time with 1:58 left. In the huddle, Brown called "bump-back-40," a play that calls for the ball to go inside to Manning. Assistant Coach Alvin Gentry looked at Manning as Brown explained the play. Manning looked right back. "Just throw me the fucking ball," he said.

Gentry was shocked. Such talk was very un-Manninglike. First there was the matter of stopping State. Valvano wanted to get the ball inside as much as Brown did. But when the pass went to Shackleford, Manning stepped around him and intercepted. Kansas ran bump-back-40. Manning caught the pass, turned, and shot an eight-footer. It swished with 1:43 left, giving him 32 points and KU a 72–67 lead.

That was the ball game. Manning had come a long way in the two years since he had cringed at the boos in Greensboro. "Now I look at it as sort of funny," he said. "If I had played for State or North Carolina, I would have been cheered in this state. But, that's the way life goes."

He paused. "I'm a senior now. When we were down at halftime, coach got on me. I understand that. At the end, I want the ball because I think I can make something happen."

He wanted the ball. He dealt with the boos. He handled getting yelled at. Danny Manning had come a long way. But he still had a long way to go.

8
THE WEST COAST ...
AND BEYOND

December 21. . . Berkeley, California

The memorable moments have been few and far between for the basketball program at the University of California during the past twenty-eight years. In 1959, the Golden Bears won the national championship. In 1960, they reached the championship game again before losing to Ohio State.

Then Pete Newell retired. And Cal basketball seemed to retire right along with him. During the next twenty-five years, Cal had seven winning seasons. Newell had won his last eight games against UCLA. The year after he stepped down, Cal split with the Bruins. After that, it took twenty-five years—fifty-two games—before they won again.

Newell, who was only forty-four when he got out of coaching, stayed on as athletic director for eight years before moving on to the NBA, first as a general manager, then as a superscout. But his legacy lived on at Cal, where they never quite figured out why he gave up doing something he did so well.

"I had *done* coaching," he said simply. "Plus, my doctor said I needed to give up cigarettes and coffee because they were messing up my lungs. I couldn't coach without cigarettes and coffee."

Almost twenty-eight years later, looking back at what Cal basketball was before Newell and what it became after Newell, Cal decided to name its basketball floor for the man who did the most winning on it. On December 21, 1987, the floor of venerable old Harmon Gym became, officially, "Newell Court."

Exactly what people would call the 6,450-seat place where Cal plays its home games in the future was uncertain. Once, it had just been the men's gym. Twenty-six years after it opened, in 1959, it was renamed Harmon Gym in honor of the man who had given the funds to build the original Cal gym in 1878. When Lou Campanelli became the coach in 1985, he insisted that college teams didn't play in gyms and demanded it be called Harmon Arena. Ray Ratto of the *San Francisco Chronicle* began referring to it as Harmon Gym/Arena/Stop 'N Shop and Drive-Thru Bank.

Whatever it was called, Harmon/Newell is a wonderful anachronism. There are no chair backs, just bleachers, and to get 6,450 in, everyone has to squeeze together real tight. Only here does the pep band have the best seats in the place, right at center court across from the scorer's table.

But this is no ordinary band. It is "the Straw Hat Band," so named for the very obvious reason that its members all wear straw hats. Steve Kerr would get in trouble later in the season for commenting in a guest column in the Cal student newspaper that the band looked like a bunch of Shakey's Pizza countermen.

The Straw Hat Band makes its entrance by marching onto the court—usually right through the visitors' warmup—and across the floor to its seats. It is joined there at game time by Oski the Bear, a truly homely and fantastic mascot. When the Straw Hat Band plays "Fight On Golden Bears," and Oski leads the crowd in finishing the song by yelling, "GRRRRAAAH," Harmon/Newell/Stop 'N Shop is about as much fun as it gets.

The night of the dedication will be a special one. Newell, looking tan and fit at seventy-two, has just flown back from Japan. There, he received the Japanese Sacred Order of the Treasury, as thanks for the work he has done with basketball in Japan during the last twenty-eight years. After Newell had led the U.S. Olympic team to the 1960 gold medal in Rome in his last game as a coach, the Japanese approached him about working with their team to prepare for the Tokyo Olympics.

As the host country, the Japanese were concerned about embarrassing themselves in basketball. Newell worked with the coaches and the team and in 1964, Japan finished fifth—the highest finish for the country in Olympic basketball—losing to the Soviet Union by 4 points. Since then, Newell has gone back every year. He has spent so much time in Japan that Tommy, the second of his four sons, calls him "Papa-san."

For Papa-san, this will be an emotional night. All four of his sons, Pete, Tom, Roger, and Greg, are here. The opponent for Cal is—who else?—UCLA. In 1986, during Campanelli's first season, Cal broke the fifty-two-game losing streak. The record since Newell retired is now 2–56. But the Bruins are not exactly the Bruins of old.

It is a rainy night four days before Christmas but the old place is packed nonetheless. Many of Newell's former players have come for this and the joint is jumping when the teams are introduced. This will be a night for Cal people to remember—and for UCLA people to try to forget.

Three minutes into the game, Matt Beeuwsaert, a transfer from Notre Dame, gives Cal the lead at 7–4 with a three-point play. Amazingly, UCLA will not get even again for the rest of the night.

Cal quickly builds the lead to 15–5 and with the place rocking, UCLA falls apart. To a neutral observer, watching a UCLA team unravel so completely is a shocking sight. Even though John Wooden has been retired thirteen years, it is remarkable, and a bit unsettling, that UCLA has fallen so far. Even in a league as weak as the Pacific 10 they are not a very good team.

A three-point shot by freshman Ryan Drew makes it 18–6, and it keeps getting worse for UCLA. When Beeuwsaert hits a nineteen-footer with 4:10 left, Cal is up 38–16. It is tough to believe that score can be correct. At halftime it is 45–26, putting the crowd in a perfect mood for the dedication ceremony.

The ceremony is, as all ceremonies should be, a simple one. Athletic Director Dave Maggard introduces the luminaries from the Newell era and hands the microphone to one of Newell's former captains, Earl Robinson.

"We all have a lot of memories of this place," Robinson says. "And most of them start with Coach Newell. We know tonight that his four sons are here in the stands and we also know that his number one assistant coach [Mrs. Newell, who passed away in 1985] is up above looking down on us tonight and smiling at what she sees."

Newell speaks briefly, fighting not to be overcome thinking about his wife and looking at his sons. When he is finished, he is handed a straw hat. Then he walks over and leads the band in "Sons of California." Everyone is standing and singing and all four sons are pushing tears back from their eyes. They aren't alone.

When the game is over—Cal wins it 83–70—Newell goes down to the locker room to thank the players for winning the game on this night. "All I know about him," says Ryan Drew, "is that he's a legend here. He won."

Greg Newell, who lives five minutes away from Harmon/Newell/ Drive-Thru, throws a little postgame party to celebrate. "It's funny to have a place named for you," Pete Newell says after pausing to give Greg a hard time about the length of his hair. "When I coached, I almost burned the place down a couple times. I used to smoke during practice and every once in a while I'd drop the butts in the pipes they had on the side of the court for the volleyball nets. I never noticed until we'd smell something burning."

Papa-san laughs. "It was nice to see the old place rocking again," he says. "It was just like the old days."

For one night at least, Pete Newell was part of Cal basketball again. And, just as he had done twenty-eight years ago, he left an admirable legacy behind. The court with his name on it has plenty of reason to be proud.

December 22–31. . . Honolulu

Quick quiz: Name the state that, year in and year out, plays host to more top college basketball teams than any other.

North Carolina? Indiana? Kentucky? California? Wrong, wrong, wrong, and wrong. The answer is Hawaii and it isn't even close.

If you want to lay claim to having a top-flight program, you have to find a way to get your team to Hawaii at least once every three years, if not more. In 1987, no fewer than 35 Division 1 teams played in Hawaii and the only reason the number wasn't higher were the various NCAA restrictions on travel to Hawaii, many of them recently passed to cut down on the excursions.

About the only top coach who doesn't bring his team here on a regular basis is Bob Knight, who last brought Indiana in 1980, lost two games, never let his team see the beach, and flew out right after his last game vowing never to return.

Steve Green, who played for Knight in the 1970s, didn't think it was any loss for the players not to go back to Hawaii. "What difference does it make where you are," he said with a laugh. "Whether you're in Madison, Wisconsin, or Hawaii all you're going to see is the airport, the hotel, and the gym."

That's not true for most other coaches. To them, Hawaii presents many different opportunities.

It can be a recruiting tool: "Come play for us and go to Hawaii." It is a chance to pick up some extra games. Under NCAA rules, games played in Alaska, Hawaii, and Puerto Rico do not count against a team's twenty-eight-game regular season limit. In recent years, some teams have played in Alaska and Hawaii in the same season, picking up an additional six games. It can be a break from the drudgery of staying on campus over Christmas break and going home cold night after cold night to empty dorms or apartment buildings. And, on some occasions, it can even be fun.

"We tell our players they can only spend an hour on the beach," said Louisville Coach Denny Crum, who seems to find a way to play here every year. "They follow our orders. They're on one hour, off one hour."

For the coaches, deciding how much freedom to give the players is often difficult. They don't want to be Scrooge and tell the players just to focus on basketball. On the other hand, they don't want the players to forget the games because, more often than not, they are playing good teams here.

"It's a balancing act," Virginia Coach Terry Holland said. "On the one hand, you want the trip to be something of a reward to the kids for working hard and you want them to have fun. Who knows if any of them will ever come back here again. But the reason you're here is basketball. I just try to say to them, 'Look, you could be practicing here or in Charlottesville, which would you prefer?' "

Holland had the misfortune to coach in the most significant game ever played here. In 1982 he brought his team, ranked No. 1 in the country with senior All-American Ralph Sampson, to Honolulu on what was really a stopover en route home from Japan. The Cavaliers had already done their job for the month, beating Georgetown and Patrick Ewing, then beating Houston (without Sampson, who was ill with the flu) in Japan. Hawaii was a chance to relax for a few days. A game with tiny Chaminade University was scheduled as an excuse for the trip.

Chaminade was—and is—a tiny Catholic school in Honolulu with 900 students and no gym. The game was played, as are all the important games here, in the Neal S. Blaisdell Arena. Because of Sampson's presence, close to 3,000 of the 8,800 seats were filled that night, December 23, 1982.

Chaminade won the game. Sampson was outscored by a 6–7 forward named Tony Randolph, a player he had faced in high school. Randolph, from Alexandria, Virginia, scored 19 points and Sampson only had 12. Chaminade was a smart, well-drilled NAIA team that would finish the season 33–5, but the notion that the Silverswords could beat Virginia was preposterous.

After the game, when someone asked Holland if this was perhaps the biggest upset in the history of college basketball, he nodded his head. It had to be. From that day forth all upsets were measured against Chaminade over Virginia. Nothing yet has equaled it. In Hawaii, it is still referred to simply as "The Upset."

The victory made an instant island celebrity of Coach Merv Lopes, a taskmaster who, along with Athletic Director Mike Vasconceles, had built Chaminade's program by mixing a few local players with a player here and a player there who couldn't make it on the mainland.

Until Chaminade's victory, the only tournament in Hawaii that really mattered was the Rainbow Classic, which started in 1964 and annually brought seven teams in from the mainland to play the University of Hawaii. It was, along with New York's Holiday Festival, *the* Christmas tournament. Back then, Hawaii had a very competitive team. In the early 1980s, just when Hawaii's competitiveness was fading, Chaminade burst onto the scene. After The Upset, Chaminade suddenly found corporate sponsors for its own Christmas tournament. Then, NBC got into the act, deciding to televise a Christmas Day game from Hawaii. Since the Rainbow Classic always started after Christmas, NBC tied in with what was now the Western Airlines–Chaminade Christmas Classic.

Amazingly, Lopes and Chaminade proved that The Upset was not a once-in-a-lifetime fluke. One year later, the Silverswords stunned a Louisville team that ended up in the Final Four that season. And then, a year later, they beat both Louisville and Southern Methodist in back-to-back games.

In a way, the SMU victory was as remarkable as the Virginia victory. SMU came to Hawaii that year ranked No. 3 in the country. The team was undefeated and led by Olympian John Koncak. In the opening round of the tournament, while the Silverswords were doing their number on Louisville, SMU easily beat a very good, Wayman Tisdale-led Oklahoma team.

Because of NBC's involvement, the second-round Christmas Day games were prescheduled: Oklahoma would play Louisville on national TV and then Chaminade would play SMU. Having seen Chaminade beat Louisville, SMU should have known the game would not be a walkover.

"Yeah, we should have known but we didn't," Dave Bliss, then coach of SMU, said. "We went over there to play Oklahoma. We just couldn't believe Chaminade was that good. We still should have won anyway."

SMU actually appeared to have the game won when Koncak blocked a shot out of bounds with the Mustangs leading 70–69 and the clock at :00. But the officials ruled that the buzzer hadn't sounded, meaning there was still a fraction of a second remaining.

Occurrences such as this are not unusual in Hawaii. The local officials have become legendary over the years for their home jobs. In 1981 during the Rainbow Classic, then Bradley Coach Dick Versace became so enraged about the officiating that he walked onto the floor, tore the whistle from around the neck of a referee named Larry Yamashita, and hurled it into the stands.

Valvano, whose team was playing in the next game, raced to courtside immediately. Pointing at Yamashita, he told tournament officials, "I want that guy working my game." Before anyone could ask why, Valvano added, "As long as he doesn't get his whistle back."

Bliss might have had similar thoughts on Christmas Day 1984. After a time-out and a wasted tirade by Bliss, who was convinced the game should be over, Chaminade was allowed to inbound under the basket.

Keith Whitney caught the ball in the corner, spun it in his hands for a proper grip, aimed, and shot. There was no way the shot could have been launched before the buzzer. No matter. The ball hit the side of the rim, bounded into the air and—naturally—fell through the net. The officials emphatically signaled that the shot counted and Chaminade had pulled Upset IV, 71–70.

"We got jobbed," Bliss said, looking back. "But it was our fault for putting ourselves in position to get jobbed." Ironically, Whitney had first heard of Chaminade the day after The Upset, just like millions of others.

But SMU was the last miracle. Teams started coming to Hawaii looking for a tough game from Chaminade. And, even with their newfound notoriety, Lopes and Vasconceles couldn't get a bigger budget or better facilities. In 1986, NBC, cutting back on December college basketball, stopped doing Christmas in Hawaii. That same year, Western merged with Delta. For one year, Delta maintained sponsorship, but then, in 1987, decided to drop out.

Chaminade was still in business, however. In November, Hawaiian Airlines had sponsored the first annual Maui Classic and ESPN televised it. Teams were already lining up to play in 1988. Even without commercial sponsorship, the Chaminade Christmas Classic lived—though just barely.

"We're definitely struggling right now," Vasconceles said on the opening day of the Chaminade Classic, as a crowd of no more than four hundred people drifted around the Blaisdell Arena. "Basketball is down in Hawaii right now. We aren't winning and neither is UH. Plus, this close to Christmas [December 23] you need something special to get people to leave their families or come off the beach. Right now, we haven't got it."

Hard times had truly hit Chaminade. The Silverswords entered the tournament with an 0–7 record. Some of the losses were more than respectable for an NAIA/NCAA Division 2 team: Kansas, Stanford, and Nebraska in the Maui Classic, and San Jose State and Long Beach State on the mainland. But there were also losses to Western Washington and Whitworth.

There were a number of reasons for these troubles: injuries, academic losses, recruiting not panning out. But Vasconceles believed that part of it had to do with Lopes, the fiery coach who had built the program. In 1985, several months after The Upset, Hawaii had fired Larry Little as coach. Lopes was interviewed for the job but eventually it went to Frank Arnold. In two seasons, Arnold won eleven games. He quit in 1987 to become an assistant coach at Arizona State. This time Lopes didn't even get a phone call before Riley Wallace, a former UH assistant, got the job.

"Merv will never admit it but not getting the Hawaii job devastated him," Vasconceles said. "He never stopped working hard but it cost him in enthusiasm and intensity. It's a little bit like scar tissue after a major operation. You're never quite the same.

"He felt slighted. I felt slighted too. We all did. Look at what he had done with almost nothing to work with. They have a million-dollar budget over there. We have a $50,000 budget. Merv was beating teams they couldn't beat and we were drawing as well as they were. Even now, they aren't drawing much better than us and we aren't drawing *anything.*"

Lopes is fifty-three but looks younger. He is a sharp dresser with a sharp, quick tongue. Hurt creeps into his voice when he talks about the Hawaii job. "I'm a here-and-now guy," he said. "It's past, it's over. But you would have thought they would look at what I had done. It was certainly disappointing. Maybe I did something to upset them, I don't know."

Lopes laughed. "Maybe they knew something. Before, I used to walk on water. Now, I'm sinking, sinking, sinking . . ."

Stan Sherriff, the Hawaii athletic director who hired both Arnold and Wallace, insists Lopes has done nothing to offend anyone at his school. "I just think coaching a Chaminade and coaching a Hawaii are two very different things," he said. "I might be wrong. Merv might do a great job. But Frank Arnold was a proven winner [at Brigham Young] in our league [the Western Athletic Conference] when we hired him. His problem is he never understood what the hell Hawaii is all about. Riley Wallace does understand because he was an assistant here for eight years."

All well and good. And Riley Wallace may get the job done at Hawaii. But if you judge a coach by how hard his team plays, it is hard to find any fault with Merv Lopes, regardless of record. On opening night of the Chaminade Classic, the Silverswords, backed by that screaming throng of maybe four hundred people, play Dayton to the wire.

Chaminade is still leading 66–64 with eight minutes left before the Flyers finally wear them down and win, 84–75. Considering the fact that Lopes is down to eight able bodies, this is a more than respectable performance. Chaminade's best player is a slender sophomore forward named Arthur King. In the box score he appears as King Arthur.

Dayton–Chaminade is the final game of a first-day tripleheader. There are six teams in the tournament: Dayton, Chaminade, Virginia, Oklahoma, LaSalle, and Georgia. Because the mainland teams wanted to play three games here, Vasconceles set up a round-robin that isn't really a round-robin because each school only plays three of the other five schools. But it doesn't matter. The teams just want the games.

Virginia, returning to the scene of The Upset for the first time, has an opening-day experience about as miserable as The Upset. The Cavaliers, struggling at 4–4 coming in, run into Oklahoma to start the tournament.

The Sooners have been destroying people by embarrassing scores during December, which isn't unusual. Coach Billy Tubbs is famous for running up the score on the Georgia States and Centenarys of the world. As always, the Sooners have a lot of athletes, but they are the kind of team that, historically, Virginia has been able to slow down and often beat.

For almost sixteen minutes, this is the case once again. A lay-up by freshman Kenny Turner brings the Cavaliers to within 31–27 with a little more than four minutes left in the first half. An Oklahoma mini-run ups the margin to 45–36 at halftime. Still, nothing to be panicked about.

And then came the second half. "The longest twenty minutes of my career," Holland will say when it is finally over. For the first 8:08, Virginia does not score. The Cavaliers can't get the ball across mid-court against the Oklahoma press, much less to the basket. In the meantime, Oklahoma is scoring easy basket after easy basket. By the time the Cavaliers score, the Sooners have ripped off 25 straight points. They lead, 70–36. "The only good thing about it," Holland said, "is that almost no one in the world saw it."

Oklahoma never lets up. The final is 109–61, easily the worst defeat in Holland's fourteen years at Virginia and easily the worst loss any player in a Virginia uniform has ever suffered. "Totally humiliating," point guard John Johnson said. "I don't think any of us has ever been through something like that before."

Outside, it is 85 degrees and the sun is shining brightly. Inside the Blaisdell Arena, Virginia and Holland are wondering why everyone thinks Hawaii is such a great place.

The Chaminade Tournament ends up drawing about one thousand paying customers (at $3 a ticket) for three days. During the Chaminade–LaSalle game on Christmas Eve, a halftime head count produces ninety-seven people in the stands, including the five security guards. If there had been a fire, everyone in the building would have had his own exit.

"We have to get a sponsor for next year," Vasconceles admitted. "I think we will. As long as we can keep the program above water the rest of the year we'll be all right. Merv will find a way."

Lopes isn't that sure. "I'd like to rebuild and I truly believe we will," he said, "if I stay."

Lopes does have one more brush with glory before the tournament is over. On Christmas Day, the last-round matchups are Dayton–LaSalle (Dayton having been beaten 151–99 by Oklahoma on the second day), Oklahoma–Georgia, and Virginia–Chaminade.

Oklahoma–Georgia is easily the best game of the tournament. Oklahoma, as it will prove over and over again throughout the season, is not just a run-and-shoot bandit squad that beats up on bad teams. In Harvey Grant and Stacey King it has as overwhelming a low-post twosome as there is in the country. And with Mookie Blaylock and Ricky Grace making life miserable for opposing guards, the OU press can dismantle people—as Virginia can testify.

But Georgia, which had been routed by an embarrassed Virginia team on Christmas Eve, handles the press and stays with the Sooners right to the finish. Oklahoma has to make its foul shots down the stretch to win, 93–90.

Tubbs is a man known for his braggadocio, which will shortly go into full gear back home as his team begins to get more attention. But for now, he is trying very hard to be low-key.

"We've still got a long way to go to be a real good team," he said. "Our defense still makes us vulnerable on the boards. We don't shoot foul shots that well. We aren't that big."

He smiled. "But you know, if we get a little better in those areas we've got a chance to be pretty good. Even pretty damn good."

Someone asked Tubbs if he was surprised to be undefeated at this stage, since he has three new starters. The real Tubbs surfaced for just a moment. In his best Jack Nicholson-soundalike voice, he answered: "I'm never surprised to be undefeated. When we're 37–0 ask me if I'm surprised to be undefeated and I'll still tell you no."

The final game of the tournament, appropriately, matches Virginia and Chaminade. Both schools have fallen a long way since the night of The Upset. Virginia, which will finish sixth in the ACC, is 5–5 after coming back to beat Georgia. Chaminade is 0–9.

For a while it looks as if history may repeat itself in some small way. Virginia is tired. Maybe the Cavaliers, all of whom are sporting deep tans, have had too much beach time. Maybe they look around at the empty building and see an 0–9 team and think the game is a walkover.

Whatever the reason, Chaminade is leading 33–32 at halftime. Holland knows his team isn't playing very well but he isn't thrilled by the officiating either. Walking off the floor he directs most of his anger in the direction of one Phil Ravitsky, who is an absolute double of Officer Toody, the moon-faced cop in the old *Car 54* series.

Things don't get any better at the start of the second half. Toody keeps making calls that no one among the hundreds in the building can figure out. Finally, with Virginia leading 37–35 and still struggling, Toody calls a phantom charge on John Johnson.

Something kicks in on Holland. "That's it," he says to Assistant Coach Dave Odom, "we're out of here. I'm not taking this anymore. It isn't fair to the kids."

With that, Holland starts toward the scorer's table, fully intending to pull a Bob Knight and take his team off the floor. But Odom is heroic. Almost literally, he throws his five-foot-nine-inch body between the 6–7 Holland and the scorer's table.

"Don't do it, Terry," he pleads. "You'll regret it if you do."

"But they're screwing our kids. I owe it to them to do something."

"Fine, let's do something about winning the damn game."

Holland's fury has been stemmed just long enough. He turns and sits down. "I really don't know what I would have done if Dave hadn't stopped me," he said later. "Maybe I just would have torn the scorer's book up or something."

One disaster averted, the Cavaliers avert the other. Like Dayton, they wear stubborn Chaminade down and finally win the game 66–58. It isn't pretty but it is a darn sight better than 1982.

"Hell yes I was thinking about last time," Holland says. "I was beginning to think this building was haunted."

In a sense, it is, haunted by The Ghosts of Upsets Past. Lopes remembers. "For a while tonight I had the old feeling," he says, sitting in his empty locker room. "I thought maybe for one night the Chaminade mystique might still be there. But it isn't the same around here anymore."

The door opens and a manager comes in. "Coach," he says, "we're missing three basketballs."

"Damn it," says Lopes. "Not again."

It is Christmas Night in a haunted gym. Chaminade and Merv Lopes are 0–10, out three basketballs, and a long, long way from The Upset.

For Jim Valvano, this trip to Hawaii will be strictly business. He has been here often before, three times with his team, once to coach a postseason all-star game and on several other vacation trips.

He has always enjoyed combining work with pleasure here and he has brought his entire family along on the trip. But his mind is on his basketball team.

The Wolfpack is 3–2, having lost to Manning and Kansas and then, surprisingly, by 18 points to an underrated California–Santa Barbara team. Valvano knows he has plenty of talent. But he is concerned about whether it will jell. He is juggling four guards—two seniors and two freshmen—and he is struggling with Charles Shackleford.

Valvano knows that, regardless of how the guard situation plays itself out, Shackleford is the key to this team. The 6–10 junior center is one of those players people look at and say: "He should be unstoppable."

At times, Shackleford *is* unstoppable. He can shoot with both hands, although that ability often produces some shots that are, to be polite, reckless. He has huge hands and feet, meaning he can rebound well but can't run or cut that well. Still, when Shackleford is on and interested, he is a truly great inside player.

Getting Shackleford to concentrate is Valvano's No. 1 priority this year. He is not happy with the center right now. Too many one-handed rebounds, too many missed box-outs, too many silly shots. State will play three straight nights in Hawaii. Valvano's goal is to get Shackleford pointed in the right direction by the end of game three.

It is ironic to Valvano that the key to his team's success this year is getting someone to concentrate. Because for Valvano, staying focused on coaching is perhaps the toughest thing he has to do in his life right now.

James Thomas Valvano grew up in Queens, the oldest son of Rocco and Angelina Valvano. He was a star athlete at Seaford High School, earning ten letters in three sports. He met the girl he would marry, Pamela Susan Levine, in eighth grade and courted her through high school and college.

He went to Rutgers on an academic scholarship and wound up a starter in a superb backcourt, playing next to Bobby Lloyd, an All-American. In 1967, Valvano's senior year, Rutgers finished third in the NIT, losing in the semifinals to Southern Illinois, even though Valvano scored 21 points in the first half.

"I was nine-for-ten at halftime," he said. "They kept moving out on me and I kept moving back until I drilled one from twenty-seven feet. Didn't do much the second half, though. It was tough shooting with my left hand wrapped around my neck. What a choke-ola that was. They were good, but hell, we should have beaten them."

The summer after he graduated from Rutgers, he married Pam and started his career in coaching. His first job as a head coach was at Johns Hopkins. He spent one year there, then moved on to Bucknell and Iona. At Iona, he became a star, wowing the New York media with his one-liners, signing Jeff Ruland, and putting together a superb team that won twenty-nine games in 1980.

"That may have been the best team I ever coached," he will say, no disrespect meant to the 1983 NCAA championship team. "No one respected us because who the hell respects Iona. Our best player was a big slow white guy [Ruland] and who the hell respects big slow white guys. But we were a hell of a team. We went into the Garden and beat Louisville by 17. Louisville didn't lose again, they won the whole thing."

Iona lost at the buzzer in the second round to Georgetown and Valvano left for N.C. State. Simple story, right? Wrong.

"I wasn't going. I went down to do the interview because I figured I ought to go through the process. I checked into the hotel, turned on the television, and there's my old coach, Bill Foster, coaching Duke against Kentucky in the NCAA Tournament. They're playing at Kentucky and they're beating them. I'm screaming at the TV. Finally, they win it by one. I said, 'That's it, this is what the business is about, winning that goddamn national championship. If they offer me the job, I'm taking it.' "

They offered, he took, leaving behind screaming headlines in New York about Ruland having an agent (he did) and an impending betting scandal that the newspapers said would implicate Valvano (they were wrong).

State went 14–13 Valvano's first year and 22–10 the second, losing in the first round of the NCAA Tournament to Tennessee–Chattanooga. People liked Valvano in North Carolina. He was different with his New York accent and his one-liners and wisecracks, but they liked him. He made them laugh. Still, Valvano learned very early at State that you must win, you must win often, and even when you win often you are still compared to Dean—as in Smith.

"True story," he says, the first two words in many of his stories because he knows people often think them apocryphal. "My first week at State, I need a haircut. So, I go over to the campus barber shop and I sit down and the barber who has been here maybe a hundred years says to me, 'So, you're the new basketball coach, aren't you?'

"I say that I am and he says to me, 'Well, I sure do hope you have more luck than old Norman did.'

"This kind of gets to me. So, I say to the guy, 'Wait a minute, correct me if I'm wrong, but didn't Norm Sloan win a national championship while he was here?' And the guy says, 'Oh yeah, he did. But he was no Dean Smith.'

"So, I think about that for a minute. Remember, Dean hadn't won a national championship at this point, but that doesn't seem to impress the guy. So, finally I say, 'You know, if I'm not mistaken, Norm Sloan went 27–0, undefeated one season while he was here, isn't that right?'

"And the guy looks at me and he says, 'Yup, he sure did. But just think what old Dean would have done with that team.' "

Valvano dealt with the Dean phenomenon by being very respectful to the great man in public. No sense riling anybody up, he figured, especially in an area where people thought you could improve on a 27–0 record.

In his third season, Valvano thought he finally had a team that could compete with Dean—and the rest of the ACC. He had three outstanding seniors—left behind for him by old Norman—in Dereck Whittenburg, Sidney Lowe, and Thurl Bailey. But in January, Whittenburg broke a foot and it looked as if State would be lucky just to get into the NCAA Tournament.

Whittenburg came back the last week of the regular season. In the ACC Tournament, playing each game as if their NCAA bid was at stake—which it certainly was in the first two rounds—the Wolfpack beat Wake Forest by one, shocked North Carolina in overtime, and stunned Virginia and Sampson in the final. They had won the ACC Tournament and reached the NCAAs. Nice season, Coach.

It would have ended exactly that way if Pepperdine had made its free throws in the first round of the NCAA Tournament. State, down six with a minute left, won in double overtime. Then, in the second round, heavily favored Nevada–Las Vegas missed *its* free throws and State won by one. A routine win over Utah and another miracle victory over Virginia—with Sampson somehow *not* taking the last shot with his team down one and his career on the line—and State was in the Final Four.

Great season, Coach.

But Valvano wasn't done. The Wolfpack beat Georgia in the semifinals, setting up a final against a Houston team that had looked unbeatable—and had not been beaten—since December. "Have you got a chance, Jim?" they asked him the day before the game.

"We've got a better chance than all the teams that aren't here," he answered.

State jumped to an 8–0 lead. Houston came back and led by six late in the game. But Houston Coach Guy Lewis, who should be on top of Valvano's Christmas list every year, held the ball, waiting for his players to be fouled, even though his team couldn't shoot free throws. The Cougars missed and missed from the free throw line, State tied and finally had the last shot. Whittenburg's forty-foot bomb was so short that only teammate Lorenzo Charles could touch it, leaping over everyone to dunk at the buzzer for a 54–52 victory.

Valvano raced around like a mad dervish, hugged everyone jammed into The Pit, and became a superstar. He made money so fast he didn't have time to count it. Everyone wanted Jimmy V. to speak. Everyone wanted to hear him tell the story about Charles's dunk. Everyone wanted a piece of him and Jimmy V. gave—for a price.

Even though State stayed good, reaching the final eight two of the next three years, the critics said he wasn't spending enough time coaching. He flew off one weekend after a loss in Louisville to do the color on an NBC game in Champaign, Illinois. "He doesn't care enough," they howled.

Then he became athletic director, too. When the Knicks job opened up, some of his friends figured he would take the job, keep coaching at State, be the athletic director, continue all his TV and radio shows, do all his speeches, and perhaps, just to fill time, run for governor of North Carolina.

What the critics could not understand was that Valvano needs almost every minute of every day filled. He does not waste a lot of time sleeping and he is in constant need of a challenge—especially mental.

He is a voracious reader. On this trip to Hawaii he had brought along Mikhail Gorbachev's *Perestroika*.

"I'm convinced that if we got into a war with them, they'd kick our butts," he said one night. "They're smarter than we are."

Valvano loves coaching. And he hates coaching. He loves the games—on court. And he hates the games—off court. He really enjoys his players. And he hates going through the recruitment that gets them to State. He loves attention and being in the limelight. He hates not being able to spend time alone with his family for eight months of the year.

Jimmy V. will be forty-two in March. He knows, he says, he won't be coaching at fifty. But what will he do? TV commentary doesn't challenge him. He might like to work in Hollywood full-time, but wouldn't that become shallow in a hurry?

He knows he is a very good coach. But he also knows he could be better if he was more driven. But if he was more driven would he be happy? He looks around at the driven coaches at the top of his sport and has no desire to follow in their footsteps.

For now, though, he is in Hawaii for a week he considers very important to his team. The first game is against Creighton. "The way we're playing right now," he says, "we could lose to anyone."

Spoken like a true coach.

Although the Rainbow Classic has lost some luster because of the springing up in recent years of one tournament after another in Hawaii—UH will host three other tournaments itself this season—it is still *the* basketball event in Hawaii.

The tournament begins each year with a dinner at the luxurious Kahala Hilton Hotel, which is on the far side of Diamond Head away from the sprawl of hotels on Waikiki.

Because Hawaii basketball has fallen on hard times (the Rainbows are 1–7 entering the tournament), the hope for the host team going into the tournament is that it can win a game. The last time Hawaii won a tournament game was in 1984, and that was against Cornell. This year, the first-round opponent is Mississippi State, hand-picked because of a 7–21 record a year ago. But Mississippi State has a young, aggressive team and is 7–0, although Coach Richard Williams is quick to point out that the Bulldogs haven't played anybody.

It still sounds like a tough game for Hawaii. "All we're hoping," says Jim Leahey, the master of ceremonies at the dinner, "is that Hawaii gets to play at night after the first round this year."

The tournament's consolation games are played in the afternoon.

Each coach is allotted three minutes to talk about his team. Valvano talks for ten. He introduces the crowd to a Mr. Fujita, who is the director of the three-team tournament held in Japan every December. "Please stand up, Mr. Fujita," Valvano says, waving his arms at him to stand. Fujita stands. "Mr. Fujita is here looking for teams for next year's tournament. He speaks no English. Right now, he thinks I am Dean Smith and we're in. I have instructed all my players to only answer to the name J.R."

Denny Crum from Louisville and Dave Bliss from SMU, both victims of Chaminade three years ago, say the same thing. "It's great to be here, especially since we don't have to play Chaminade."

The Hawaii people, who won't even schedule Chaminade, don't laugh. Everyone else does. When you are 1–7, nothing seems that funny.

When the dinner is over, Valvano and his entourage head for a bar, where a group called The Love Notes is playing sixties music. They sit at a table right at the foot of the stage, a group of twelve that includes Pam Valvano, the assistant coaches and Valvano's "host" for the tournament, Jeff Portnoy.

There are few things in life that Valvano enjoys more than oldies. He knows the words to every song and is singing along with the band—loudly. Pam, who is a good deal more decorous than her husband, thinks he should stop singing so noisily.

"Come on Pam," Valvano says, "this is our past. You should sing too."

Pam isn't going to sing. But Jim is, late into the night. When the band plays "At the Hop," Valvano jumps to his feet. "I used to have them play that song when my team came on the floor at Johns Hopkins," he yells.

The band takes a break. The band members, five of them from New York, come over and Portnoy introduces them to Valvano. Valvano is nostalgic. "When I was dating Pam in college I used to spend all my money calling her on weekends," he says. "The rest, anything I had left, I was saving for a ring. I never really asked her to marry me. When we were seniors, I just gave her the money, six hundred dollars, and her uncle got us a ring. He worked in the diamond district. Can that really be twenty-one years ago?"

It can. The band starts again and Valvano is singing again. The music goes on until 1 A.M., but Valvano is still going when the bar is closing. "I'm really a good dancer, you know," he says—Pam is rolling her eyes again.

He turns to Portnoy. "Do you know how to do the stroll? Here, let me show you." He grabs Portnoy by the arm and, while tourists walk by giving them funny looks, he stands in the doorway leading out of the bar demonstrating the dance.

"I think I've got it," Portnoy says.

"Nah, no way," Valvano says.

He grabs Pam by the arm. "Come on, honey, let's go to bed. These guys will keep us out all night if we don't."

Pam just nods. She has heard all of this before. She thinks her husband is quite silly—but also quite adorable. And she knows by morning he will have forgotten the dancing lessons and be worrying once again about Shackleford.

The Rainbow Classic opened on a Sunday night with a surprisingly large crowd of 2,703 in Blaisdell Arena.

Blaisdell is a story in itself. It rises out of downtown Honolulu like the humpback of a white whale, very out of place among the tourist stops, especially since it is barely a mile from Waikiki. It was built in 1964, one year after Red Rocha became the coach at Hawaii. Then it was a showplace with its 8,800 seats. Rocha built a powerful program at Hawaii, peaking in 1971 and 1972 when his team won twenty-three and twenty-four games. They called that team "The Fabulous Five," and Blaisdell was almost always packed when the Rainbows played.

The arena has aged now, decaying, it seems, along with Hawaii basketball. But it still has its charms. To enter, one must cross a stream that runs around the building like a moat. On one side, one can see the mountains that cut through the middle of Oahu. On another side, one can see Diamond Head.

But what really makes Blaisdell unique is the kind of basketball played inside. All year, top college basketball teams play in packed arenas, usually on frigid evenings. In Blaisdell, they play in front of small, often tiny crowds while most people on the island bask on the beach.

As the host team Hawaii had chosen to play a team, Mississippi State, it figured to beat. There was a problem though. Although Richard Williams was starting four freshmen, the Bulldogs were not without talent. What's more, Williams, who was in his second year coaching at the school, had managed to convince his young team that it could win. For a half, Hawaii played excellent basketball, leading 30–21 at the intermission. But Mississippi State shook its jitters in the second half, held Hawaii to 22 percent shooting, and pulled away to win the game, 68–55.

For Hawaii, this was just the kind of loss that kept attendance and interest dwindling. Once, the Rainbows had a TV contract. It was gone. The only reason they still had a radio contract was that they tied their football deal to basketball. Riley Wallace, who had been hired because he "understood" Hawaii basketball, had a lot of work to do.

"Television is killing us," he said. "Kids want to go where they're going to be on TV. In the old days we could recruit on the East Coast, convince kids to come here and get out of the cold weather. Now, they all want to play in the Big East. They all want to visit, but very few of them want to come."

Image had hurt Hawaii too. During Larry Little's tenure—he had been the last coach with a winning record when he won seventeen games in 1983—it had come out that very few Hawaii basketball players were getting anywhere close to a degree. "It was exaggerated," Little said. "Out of the kids who completed four years, we had close to 60 percent graduation."

Note the words "completed four years." Most players at UH weren't lasting four years. They would come in, play a year or two, enjoy the sun, and move on. "We run into a lot in recruiting," Wallace said. "It isn't just the long trip or lack of attention. We actually lose kids because people tell them about demons and volcanoes exploding. It's rough."

Certainly it couldn't be much rougher for Riley Wallace than it was for Richard Williams, whose job was to convince players that they wanted to spend four years in Starkville, Mississippi. Williams was different from a lot of previous coaches at the school, though. He had played at Mississippi State and he didn't see the job as just a stopping-off point on his way somewhere else.

"I've got the job I want," he said. "Now all I have to do is convince people they want to play for us." He laughed. "I know it isn't easy. [Alabama Coach] Wimp Sanderson told me that the most exciting thing that goes on in Starkville is when they unload the Kroger trucks at midnight. It's all right though, we'll find a way."

Beating Hawaii is no small victory for Mississippi State. It gives Williams's team eight victories—one more than the year before. Still, his team is picked tenth in the Southeast Conference. "Once we leave here, there isn't a game on the schedule I can look at and say we can definitely win it," Williams said. "Ever since we got here, everyone's been telling me to enjoy myself, spend time on the beach and all. I can't do it. Yesterday, I walked down to the beach, looked at the water and said, 'The hell with this.' I went back to the room and looked at some more tape."

The work has paid off with one victory. The trip, for Williams and Mississippi State, is already a success.

While the tournament was opening, Valvano and his team, given the first night off, were at Sea Life Park for the evening. Valvano was fighting the flu and still worrying about Shackleford. During the show, one of the acts was a Hawaiian woman who picked people out of the audience to teach them the hula. Naturally, confronted with the 6–10 Shackleford and 6–8 Avie Lester, she couldn't resist grabbing them and pulling them onto the stage.

Within five minutes, she had Lester doing a respectable hula. Shackleford struggled, drawing hoots from his teammates. "See that," Valvano said. "He just doesn't concentrate. I ought to go tell that woman that now she knows what I put up with every day."

Twenty-four hours later, when State played Creighton, Shackleford wasn't in the starting lineup. He had been five minutes late for a team meeting. Lester, who had been offering people hula lessons all day, started in his place. Shackleford came in and played 28 minutes, scoring 14 points and getting 12 rebounds. Valvano was pleased—slightly. The Wolfpack won easily, 86–55. It would play Louisville the next night. That was the game Valvano wanted to win.

The Cardinals, coming off the disastrous 18–14 season and their awful opener against Notre Dame, were starting to come on. Pervis Ellison was playing hard again and LaBradford Smith was truly a gifted freshman. Louisville has such a fanatic following that in addition to several hundred fans with them in Hawaii, all their games were being televised back home, even though the time difference meant they started at close to midnight. The two Louisville TV men did the telecasts in red-and-white aloha shirts. Jim Leahey, doing the local telecast of the final in Hawaii, worked in a jacket and tie.

Valvano was confident Shackleford would come to play against Louisville. But now he had a different problem. Against Creighton, he had started Quentin Jackson at point guard. Jackson, a senior, had been a key player during State's late rush to the ACC Tournament title the year before. In the five pre-Hawaii games, Valvano had started freshman Chris Corchiani, who was quicker and a better penetrator than Jackson.

After the losses to Kansas and Cal–Santa Barbara, Valvano decided that Jackson needed some playing time. Corchiani only played nine minutes against Creighton; Jackson played twenty-eight. Corchiani had never been benched in his life and he did not take it well. Late that evening, Valvano found him sitting alone in the hotel lobby, sulking. The coach desperately wanted to go to bed because he felt terrible. But clearly, this had to be dealt with.

"I told him the story about Sidney Lowe when he was a senior," Valvano said later. "We were playing West Virginia and running our delay where Sidney passes, catches, passes, catches. He came by me and said, 'Coach, I need a blow.' I said, 'Sidney, your next blow will come when your eligibility is used up.'

"That's the way it will be someday with Chris. I told him that Vinny [Del Negro] and Quentin both thought he was nuts because he thought he should play every minute, every game. They both waited almost three years to play. Someday when he's a senior some hotshot freshman is going to come in and Chris will look at him and say, 'Did I act like that asshole when I was a freshman?' And I'll tell him, yes, he did. And we'll both laugh about it.

"But right now, the problem is very real to him. I understand that. It's like the difference between my nineteen-year-old daughter and my seven-year-old. My nineteen-year-old sees college as a four-year experience, something you get better at as you go along. My seven-year-old wants a new bike *today*. Not tomorrow or Tuesday, today. That's the way freshmen are. You have to be patient with them until they learn to be patient with you."

State and Louisville will play at 6 P.M. At noon, Hawaii and Texas A&M played in the first consolation game. Hawaii had the game won, leading 67–64 with the ball and twenty seconds left. The Aggies fouled

Reggie Cross. He missed the one-and-one. Hawaii extended its defense to deny any three-point shots. Finally, with two seconds left, Darryl McDonald stepped back to twenty-four feet and fired. Naturally, it swished.

Texas A&M won in overtime and Riley Wallace and 994 fans went home muttering, no doubt, about demons and volcanoes.

Thanks to the Louisville and N.C. State entourages, the crowd that evening was 3,275. Jackson started at point guard again but Corchiani played 22 minutes—7 more than Jackson. And, when the game was on the line, Shackleford and Chucky Brown dominated. Shackleford had 18 points and 8 rebounds. Just as important, he held Ellison to 13 points and his presence in the low post opened things up for Brown, who scored 25 points. State pulled away late to win, 80–75.

When Shackleford played well, State had three excellent players: Shackleford, Brown, and Del Negro. The latter two were as consistent as Shackleford was not. Even on a bad shooting night from the field— three of seven—Del Negro had 15 points, 6 assists, 6 rebounds, and zero turnovers.

"When Shack plays like tonight, we're a very good club," Valvano said. "He knows it, we know it, everyone knows it. Tonight, against Pervis, he came to play. We'll see about tomorrow. If the past is any guide, he'll suck."

State's opponent in the final would be Arizona State. The Sun Devils beat Mississippi State, 70–69, when Williams's one veteran starter, Greg Lockhart, took the ball all the way to the basket with his team down three and time running out. The lay-up did the Bulldogs no good. Williams just stood with his arms folded, pointed to his head and said, "What were you thinking?"

A few minutes later, still a bit shocked, Williams was able to joke. "I told the kids that if they thought we were going to go undefeated, they were wrong. We've still got a lot of lessons to learn. I'm sure Louisville will teach us another one tomorrow."

Louisville did just that with an 86–65 victory. But Williams and his young team will win six games in the Southeast Conference and finish 14–15. There is a future in Starkville even if you skip watching those Kroger trucks unload.

The final was closer than Valvano would have liked. Shackleford was just as lackadaisical in the first half as he had been fired up the evening before. State led 37–36 at the half but Valvano was furious. He stormed into the tiny locker room and tore into Shackleford, questioning his desire, his intelligence, his manhood. He roared out the door, thought of a couple more things he wanted to say and turned to go back in, throwing the door open just as team doctor Jim Manley was about to open it on the other side.

Manley, considerably older and thinner than Valvano, went flying. "Jeez, I thought I killed him," Valvano said later. Manley survived. So did Shackleford, who responded to Valvano's tirade by taking over the game when it was on the line. He scored 9 points during an 11–3 burst that put the Wolfpack up 61–53 with 7:50 to go. From there, State cruised to an 83–71 victory. The Most Valuable Player? Charles Shackleford.

Valvano was delighted. He had gotten everything he wanted out of Hawaii: progress from Shackleford, good play from both Corchiani and Jackson, a victory over a very good team, and some consistency. The winner's trophy was a bonus.

As the arena emptied—which didn't take long—the PA announcer was telling the crowd the names of the visiting teams for the 25th Rainbow Classic in December 1988. Yale was on the list. No doubt the Eli would be Hawaii's first opponent. That afternoon, Creighton had beaten the Rainbows for seventh place, Hawaii's ninth straight Rainbow Classic loss.

If Yale isn't the answer maybe Hawaii could try a new strategy in 1989. Invite Chaminade.

January 2, 1988. . . Los Angeles

They sold out Pauley Pavilion today. Sadly, that was news. What was once the proudest college basketball program in America has become an embarrassment. UCLA isn't very good and everyone in Los Angeles knows it.

The sellout today was created by the presence of North Carolina. The fans came to see Dean Smith and J. R. Reid the way they once came to see John Wooden and Lew Alcindor. Or Sidney Wicks. Or Bill Walton. Or Richard Washington. Wooden has been retired thirteen years now and during games he sits in the second row, directly across from the UCLA bench, looking just as impassive as he did when he coached.

In his place sits Walt Hazzard, the fifth coach to try to fill Wooden's unfillable shoes. Hazzard played for Wooden. He was the captain of his first national championship team in 1964. He has tried to inject Wooden's magic back into the program since taking over four years ago, walking across the floor to shake the great man's hand before tip-off, even going back there sometimes at halftime.

Hazzard has had some success. His first team, after a horrendous start, came back to win the NIT. His third team won the Pacific 10, got back into the NCAA Tournament for the first time since 1981, and won twenty-five games. But the best player on that 1987 team, Reggie Miller, a recruit of Hazzard's predecessor Larry Farmer, has gone on to the pros. UCLA still has some talent but it is not a team that plays very hard or very smart. The debacle two weeks earlier at California was a perfect example.

To add to Hazzard's troubles, seven-foot sophomore Greg Foster, a prize recruit two years ago, has disappeared, angry at being benched. He will announce later in the week that he is transferring to Texas–El Paso.

The Bruins are talented enough to compete with North Carolina, especially since the Tar Heels have been all over the map in two weeks, bouncing from home to Champaign, Illinois, to London (yes, England) to Reno, Nevada, to here. They won't take UCLA that seriously and that will keep the game close.

Walking into Pauley on a gorgeous Saturday afternoon, one can still sense the history in the place. There are championship banners hanging from the rafters all the way around the building. Hazzard likes to boast that UCLA doesn't even bother to hang banners for Pacific 10 championships, though they did hang one for the 1985 NIT championship.

But there is something missing: the 1964 banner, the first one. "We sent it out to the laundry," Sports Information Director Mark Dellins jokes. Actually, neither Dellins nor anyone else knows where the banner is. It has been stolen, just like UCLA's greatness.

In truth, although it is less than twenty-five years old, Pauley is an antiquated facility. Once one walks inside, the hallways are about as wide as a basepath, the bathrooms are too small, and the locker rooms are tiny. Yet the place reeks of so much tradition it doesn't really matter.

Tradition, however, isn't going to beat Carolina. The Tar Heels lead early, but as will become a pattern with them, they cannot put the weaker team away. Center Scott Williams is trying too hard, which is understandable. Williams grew up as a UCLA fan, dreaming of playing in Pauley Pavilion. When it came time to choose a college though, the disarray at UCLA frightened him and he opted for the sure winner, three thousand miles away in Chapel Hill.

In October, just after practice began, Williams's father had gone to see his mother, apparently hoping to renew their marriage. When she refused, Scott Williams's father shot her. Then he turned the gun on himself. In a moment, both were dead. Dean Smith had flown to Los Angeles with Williams for the funeral and the two of them had decided it would be better for Scott to keep playing in order to keep his mind off the tragedy. This is Williams's first trip home since the funeral. He has friends and relatives at the game and he is trying to do too much.

Carolina leads from the start, but UCLA hangs close, cutting a nine-point lead to 41–37 at halftime. When Hazzard comes over to Wooden during the intermission, the photographers scramble to take the picture, demanding that passersby clear out of their way. Dellins shrugs: "We've got to hang on to the few traditions we have left."

UCLA hangs on to the game until the end. It is tied at 69–69 after Williams misses a layup and fouls the Bruins' Jerome (Pooh) Richardson going for the ball. Williams has fouled out after shooting three-for-eleven in twenty-three minutes. With 3:27 left, the score is tied and the crowd is into the game.

But Carolina is too good to lose to this team. Ranzino Smith hits a three-pointer, UCLA's Charles Rochelin tosses a brick at the other end, and Jeff Lebo feeds Smith for a lay-up to make it 74–69. Kelvin Butler scores for UCLA, but Reid overpowers everyone going to the basket and is fouled as he hits a falling-down, off-balance shot. The free throw makes it 77–71 with 1:53 left and it is over. The final is 80–73.

UCLA is 4–7 and has lost five games at home. Wooden didn't lose five games at home in ten years. Hazzard has now done it in seven weeks. Things are so bad that staying *close* to Carolina is considered a victory.

Dean Smith, searching for a way to be polite, says of the victory: "I thought we beat what was a very good team *today*." Even El Deano isn't going to try to claim that this UCLA team is very good.

In a narrow hallway, Richardson, whose recruitment out of Philadelphia three years ago was supposed to signal a rebirth at UCLA, is shaking his head in disgust. "I knew it would never be like it used to be when I came here because no one will ever do that again. But I never thought it would be this bad."

Hazzard is resolute. He has blamed his troubles on the press, on tough admissions standards, on the past, even on Dick Vitale. "We're just going through a bad place right now," he insists. "I'm just waiting for things to click around here."

He is not alone.

9
NEW YEAR, NEW SEASON

January 6. . . Landover, Maryland

Paul Evans was uptight. Twenty minutes before his Pittsburgh team was to begin Big East Conference play against defending league champion Georgetown, he sat on his bench watching warmups, chewing intently on a piece of gum.

For a coach with a 9–0 record and a team that was ranked second in the nation, Evans had been through a very tough first semester.

First came the loss of point guard Michael Goodson to academic ineligibility. Then, on a recruiting trip to Los Angeles, Evans and Assistant Coach John Calipari had been caught in the middle of an earthquake. They were asleep in their hotel room when everything began to shake. Panicked, Calipari had raced to the door, thrown it open, and stood there in his underwear, because he had heard you were safer standing in a doorway during a quake. Evans was just as frightened, but the sight of Calipari standing in the doorway sent him into hysterics.

"I was never so glad to leave a place," he said later. "We got out on a red-eye and both went to sleep. Then, about an hour out of Los Angeles I heard this noise, like a thud. It was loud. I woke up and thought, 'That was an engine.' Then I saw the stewardesses all scrambling into the cockpit. I turned to John and I said, 'We just blew an engine.' He gets up, walks straight to the back of the plane and sits down next to a nun. We're over the mountains, it's the middle of the night and we've lost an engine. I didn't think the nun was going to help that much.

"Then the pilot comes on and in that calm pilot voice says we're going to land in Vegas just as a precautionary measure, no big deal or anything. Yeah, sure, no big deal. Fortunately, we did land and we got the hell off and finally got on a TWA flight that got us to New York. We didn't have any sleep but after the earthquake and the engine, I didn't much care."

Then there was the saga of Keith Tower. Although he was not the most highly publicized player Evans was recruiting that fall, he might have been the one he wanted most. Tower was 6–11 and had improved tremendously over the summer. He lived in Corapolis, just outside of Pittsburgh. And he had a 3.7 grade point average. In a program that had developed a reputation for suspect students in recent years, Evans desperately wanted some classroom stars.

Because he was 6–11, a pretty good player and a good student, Tower was being recruited by most of the big-name schools. Evans thought his main competitor was Notre Dame. As it turned out, he was correct.

Evans does not like Digger Phelps. While Evans was at Navy, the two had clashed over scheduling. Notre Dame wanted to continue playing Navy, but only at Notre Dame. Evans wanted to play home-and-home. The series ended up being canceled.

Phelps visited the Towers before Evans did. After the visit, Evans heard from Tower's coach, William Sacco, that during the visit the Towers had asked Phelps if he would schedule any games in Pittsburgh if Keith ended up at Notre Dame. According to Sacco, Phelps had said, "Absolutely. We'll play anyone but Pitt. I'd like to play them but Paul Evans has said some negative things about our players and so I won't play Pitt as long as he's the coach."

Evans was enraged when he heard this. When it was his turn to visit, he asked Jula to bring the subject up to give him a chance to rebut what Phelps had said. Jula did just that, saying, "I was really kind of surprised to hear Digger say that. I can't remember hearing you say anything bad about any of his kids over the years."

"I never have," Evans answered, on cue. "That's just typical Digger. He doesn't want to play us so he makes an excuse like that. Then he'll schedule Robert Morris when he comes to Pittsburgh rather than play us. Look at his schedule now. He plays half the ECC (East Coast Conference) and half the Ivy League."

Tower's mother, Sandra, who was the family spokesperson during most of Evans's visit, said, "I take it you aren't crazy about Digger."

"No, I'm not," Evans said. "I just think he's very arrogant."

Driving away after the lengthy (two-hour) visit was over, Evans shook his head. "I hope we get the kid. But if we don't get him I just hope like hell we don't lose him to Notre Dame."

Five weeks later, Tower signed . . . with Notre Dame.

In all, it was not a good recruiting fall for Evans. Pitt, which had done superbly in recruiting the year before, signing four excellent freshmen, lost out on all the top players it wanted. The only blue-chip recruit left was Don McLean, the center from California. But Evans knew the only way Pitt would have a shot at McLean was if Hazzard kept the UCLA job—and as the season wore on it became more and more apparent that probably wasn't going to happen.

Still, the Panthers were winning. They survived terrible foul trouble to win a tough game at West Virginia and came from 11 points down to avoid a shocking upset at Akron. The freshmen were holding up well under a lot of early pressure, especially point guard Sean Miller, thrown into the breach because of Goodson's absence.

The record was 8–0 when Evans got more bad news: Sophomore Rod Brookin, the team's second-leading scorer, had joined Goodson as an academic casualty. Evans had been on him for three semesters to go to class but he hadn't listened. Now he was gone. "This is why we have to recruit good students," Evans said. "You can't build a program around kids who are going to flunk out."

Nonetheless, in their first game without Brookin, the Panthers blew out Florida, 80–68 on national TV. It was a good victory but Evans knew the No. 2 ranking would not last long once Big East play began. He came to Georgetown desperately wanting a victory. The Hoyas had beaten Pitt twice the previous season, and even though they weren't nearly as strong without Reggie Williams, they were still dangerous. Evans knew that.

"I think we're ready to play," he said, smacking the gum. "The officiating worries me, though. John [Thompson] intimidates them."

It is not the officials who cost Pitt this game, however. It is a brawl almost from the start. Less than nine minutes into the game, Pitt's Nathan Bailey and Georgetown's Mark Tillmon tie each other up

going for a rebound. As they come apart, Tillmon throws an elbow at
Bailey's back. Jerome Lane sees this and comes flying at Tillmon. The
benches empty.

Miraculously, the officials keep a total riot from ensuing. The only
player ejected is Tillmon. But the tone is set. The game will become
a wrestling match with forty-four fouls called. Pitt's freshman guards
can't deal with the Georgetown pressure during several key junctures.

With one minute to go, Georgetown leads 58–56. The Hoyas'
Charles Smith misses a shot as the forty-five-second clock runs out, but
Jaren Jackson rebounds and throws the ball out to center court to
Bobby Winston. Evans sees a walk. Referee Jim Burr does not. Evans
goes nuts. He draws a technical from Burr. Then he gets one from Jody
Silvester. He is about to get No. 3 from Larry Lembo when Lane
intervenes, grabbing Lembo's hands just as he is about to make the "T"
signal and pleading for mercy. Lembo decides two is enough. It is the
first intercepted technical in modern basketball history.

Pitt still loses, 62–57. Evans is outraged. He rips the officials:
"They're getting paid $650 a night [including expenses]. For that much
you'd think the guy could see a travel when a guy takes four steps. He
told me he was looking at the [halfcourt] line for a backcourt call. If
he can't do more than that, he shouldn't officiate in the league."

He also rips Georgetown: "They let John Thompson run everything
at the school. He's more powerful than the athletic director and the
president. The athletic director says he wants to play Maryland and
Thompson says no, so they don't play. It's unbelievable."

In the meantime, Thompson is trying to downplay the fight. "I
didn't really see what happened," he says. "It's not a big deal, though.
I've never seen anybody hurt in a basketball fight. If those kids saw each
other on the street tomorrow they'd stop and talk like nothing happened."

Apparently Thompson has never heard of Rudy Tomjanovich, who
almost lost his face in a basketball fight once. But that is his way: Insist
that others are making too big a deal out of the fights his team gets
into and challenge anyone to challenge him on it. Certainly Big East
Commissioner Dave Gavitt isn't going to challenge the biggest star in
his league.

"It's just good, hard-nosed basketball," Gavitt insists two days later.
"We probably won't have another fight in the league for two years."

Gavitt is close. Georgetown's next fight doesn't come until ten days later. And the Hoyas' next fight with Pitt doesn't come until the next time the teams play.

Evans has only played one league game. He is 0–1 and has lost two starters, survived an earthquake and a lost airplane engine. He has taken on John Thompson, the referees in his league, and Digger Phelps. What he doesn't know is this: The season is just beginning to warm up for him.

January 7. . . West Lafayette, Indiana

The month of December had not been a sanguine one at Purdue either. After opening the season with an easy first-round NIT victory over Arkansas–Little Rock, the Boilermakers had been upset in the quarter-finals by Iowa State.

This had not pleased Gene Keady—to say the least. He had sent the team home for Thanksgiving but not without telling the three seniors one more time that they weren't doing much of a job as leaders.

Mitchell, Lewis, and Stephens were baffled. Also angry. They felt that Keady had given Jeff Arnold and Dave Stack much too much rope, especially after their arrests in October. "Coach's problem is that he's just a softie underneath it all," Stephens said. "He said Arnold and Stack were going to run every day for the rest of the season and he didn't even keep them running for two weeks."

The first two games after Thanksgiving would be on the road against Illinois State and Wichita State. Neither was a great team but both were capable of winning at home. Keady had the team practicing twice a day after Thanksgiving. He was honestly beginning to wonder if this team was going to jell.

"I was so frustrated I started thinking about next year," he said later. "I just didn't know if this team had the toughness you need to be great."

The tension between Keady and the seniors almost went past the breaking point on the day of the Illinois State game. First, Stephens was two minutes late for the team bus. His car battery had gone dead en route to campus and he had hitched, in the snow, to get there.

Keady was tired of excuses. "Everette," he said, "you aren't start-ing." The trip was off to a bad start.

Then, Lewis was late for pregame meal. The clock in his hotel room was five minutes slow and he showed up five minutes late. Keady went with him to his room to confirm the slow clock story, but even when he did, he felt he had no choice. Lewis didn't start either.

"Now, he's decided to make examples of Everette and me," Lewis said. "Neither one of us has been in any trouble for four years and we get benched for stuff like this. Where's the fairness in it? If we had lost that game, things might have gotten really bad."

Purdue didn't lose. Stephens and Lewis both came off the bench to play well and the Boilermakers came from behind to win, 68–61. The next day, Lewis went in to talk to Keady. If it had been the day after a loss, who knows what might have happened. Instead, the two talked out their frustrations and a truce was called. But the three seniors still felt as if they were dealing with a very uptight coaching staff.

Keady was doing his best not to be tight. He felt he had been too tight the year before and that had been reflected in the team's postseason play. But Keady's nature just isn't laid-back. He is as capable of being low-key as he is of not caring about how his team plays.

Purdue survived another scare at Wichita State, going into overtime to win 80–78, and then came home to play five straight games. All were easy victories, including a 101–72 romp over Kansas State. The only tense moment during this period came when Keady told Stephens at halftime of the Kansas State game that he was playing poorly because his mind was on his girlfriend and not on basketball.

Mitchell, the most sensitive of the three seniors, took offense to the comment. "First of all, the way he was playing had nothing to do with his girlfriend. Second, if it did, where does he come off talking about it in the locker room in front of the whole team?"

This was not the first time Mitchell had taken offense to something Keady had said in a heated moment. It would not be the last time either. Throughout the season, Keady kept telling the seniors to focus on this season and not worry about their possible pro careers. He felt their minds wandered sometimes. Mitchell did not. "Goddamn, what does he think, we're stupid? We know what we've got to do right here and now. Next year is next year."

December ended with Christmas tournament victories over Wake Forest and Miami. That made the record going into Big Ten play 10–1. The opener was at Illinois. If Keady had any doubts about his team's desire to do well in 1988, they were wiped out that evening. The Boilermakers took command early in the second half and beat a very good team playing on its home floor, 81–68.

That victory brought Ohio State into Mackey Arena. For the Buckeyes, this was the conference opener. They had gone 7–3 in preseason
and Gary Williams was genuinely worried about their ability to compete in the Big Ten. He was so concerned about the talent gap that
he considered dropping his trademark press against Purdue to avoid a
run-it-up game.

"I wish this was next year," he said the afternoon of the Purdue
game. "Then, I would feel completely different. I would feel like I had
eight or nine guys and I could really go out and attack. That's the way
I like to play. Now, I feel like I'm on the defensive in every game. If
this team finishes the season over .500 it just might be my best coaching
job."

Williams decides to stay with his press but in order to show Purdue
something different, he puts in a triangle-and-two halfcourt defense,
guarding Lewis and Mitchell man-to-man. The defense confuses Purdue so much that at one point in the first half Stephens calls out a zone
offense just as Mitchell is calling out a man-to-man offense. Angry, the
two of them yell at each other. "That's the first time in four years that
we've ever done that," Stephens says later.

Williams keeps his team in the game. It isn't easy, though. Early in
the first half he gets nailed for a technical by referee Jim Bain while
arguing a call that Bain has clearly botched. This is a Bain tradition.
When he blows a call and a coach argues, he often reinforces his error
by calling a technical. No one in basketball is quite sure how Bain keeps
getting top assignments, but he does. He will work a regional final in
the NCAA Tournament in March.

Through everything, Ohio State stays in the game all night. Down
11, the Buckeyes fight back to within 3 at 77–74. But Tony White
misses a short jumper with 2:23 left and a minute later, down 78–74,
Curtis Wilson makes only one of two free throws. That makes it 78–75.
Lewis hits a baseline jumper with just five seconds on the shot clock
and, after Wilson walks, Melvin McCants hits two foul shots to wrap
it up. The final is 84–77.

"If we were any good we would have won the game," Williams said.
"The effort was there. And they were ripe to be picked."

Indeed. With the students still on break, Mackey Arena did not have
its usual electricity. A high school band just wasn't the same as the
Purdue band. And the Boiler Babes had been nowhere in sight. The
crowd, usually the most vocal in the Big Ten, had been quiet almost
the entire night. Purdue was lucky to escape with a victory.

Keady knew this and told his team so. Angrily, he accused Mitchell—who had been just three-of-nine from the floor—of taking bad shots from the outside because his father had been telling him to shoot more.

"That is bullshit," Mitchell said later that evening. "And anyway, what goes on between my dad and me is none of his business."

They hadn't played well, but they had won. They were 2–0 in the Big Ten. Iowa was coming in for an important game Saturday and Arnold was due to rejoin the team on Monday. He had made it through the first semester. Stack had not. He was off the team. Arnold had shown up for the game that night in a tuxedo, complete with red bow tie and cummerbund, living up to his flaky California image.

Later that evening Arnold called Mitchell to make sure he wasn't too upset about what Keady had said about his father. "Jeff's a flake, but he's really a pretty good guy," Mitchell said. "Getting him back should really help us."

Arnold never made it back though. Two days before he was supposed to return, Keady announced that he had not met all the requisites attached to his reinstatement and had been permanently dropped from the team. He was vague and evasive when pressed on why Arnold was gone.

According to some of Arnold's teammates, he was dropped because a drug test had showed traces of marijuana in his system. Later in the year, Arnold insisted that was not the case, that he had been dropped because he had started going back into bars and liquor stores again during the semester break. He did admit that he had tested positive for marijuana as a freshman but denied that was his problem this time.

The three seniors felt sorry for Arnold. None of them thought he was a bad person in any way. But at least now there were no questions lingering. Keady had complained to them since the summer about the troubles that had been caused because of Arnold and Stack. Now, Arnold and Stack were gone. Two days after the Ohio State game, in spite of a missed Mitchell dunk down the stretch, the Boilermakers beat Iowa, 80–79. They were 3–0 in the Big Ten, 13–1 overall, and back in the top five in the polls.

It had been a rough ride but so far the three seniors were hanging on for dear life. They had survived December. They had survived Arnold and Stack. Now, the schedule eased up for a couple of weeks. It was a respite that was much needed and well deserved.

January 9. . . Lawrence, Kansas

This should be a day for celebration here. On a cold, sunny afternoon, Kansas and Missouri are renewing one of college basketball's oldest rivalries, each beginning Big Eight Conference play.

Missouri is the defending conference champion, having beaten Kansas at the buzzer in last year's Big Eight Tournament. In Derrick Chievous, the Tigers have one of the game's best—and most enigmatic—players, one of the few people in the country whose name is even mentioned in the same sentence with Danny Manning.

Then there are the coaches. To say that Norm Stewart and Larry Brown don't like each other is a little bit like saying Muhammad Ali and Joe Frazier didn't get along. Each thinks the other remarkably arrogant. Neither one tries to hide his feelings either.

This is the time of year when college basketball starts to become fun. The warm-up games are over and traditional, longtime rivals begin home-and-home conference play. The players know each other well, the fans know the players and coaches and even the officials. There are memories galore—and new ones being made.

No place is better suited for this kind of game than Allen Field House. This is one of college basketball's ancient gems, a true field house with bleachers on all sides, the smell of popcorn and the aroma of pomp in the air, banners dating back to 1923 when Kansas claimed what was then a mythical national championship, and an atmosphere made for college basketball. If you can't have fun watching a game in this old place, then you can't have fun.

"If you like this sport then it doesn't get any better than this," Kansas assistant Alvin Gentry said while the crowd lustily booed Missouri as the Tigers came out to warm up. "You walk on the floor for a game like this, you get chills up and down your spine."

Sadly, Gentry's boss, Larry Brown, felt almost none of this. An hour before tip-off he sat in the end zone half-watching the last minutes of the women's game, a morose look on his face.

"I'm so depressed right now I don't know which way to turn," he said. "This was going to be such a great year and now all this has happened. I'm not dealing with it very well and neither is Danny [Manning]. We're both very frustrated."

"All this" had started ten days earlier in New York during the final of the ECAC Holiday Festival in Madison Square Garden. The opponent was St. John's, a team the Jayhawks had beaten just two weeks earlier in Lawrence. Midway through the first half, during a scramble underneath, Archie Marshall's knee had collided with someone. There were so many players involved that even on tape it was tough to tell where the major contact had occurred.

That didn't matter. What did matter was that Marshall had come out of the crowd screaming in pain, then collapsed in a heap on the floor right at Manning's feet. For a split second, Manning thought he was dreaming; he knew that his friend, who had worked so hard to come back from his 1986 knee injury, could not possibly be hurt again.

"I just knew, I mean I *knew* that it wasn't that serious," Manning said. "It couldn't be. But when I looked down he was all curled up in the fetal position screaming."

As Manning stood frozen in his tracks, Brown and trainer Mark Cairnes raced to Marshall's side. While they worked on him, the assistants were telling the players, "Don't worry, it's just a sprain. It's not the bad knee, it's the other one. He'll be all right."

But as Brown leaned over Marshall, he heard him say through clenched teeth, "My God, Coach, I think this one is worse than last time."

When Brown looked at Cairnes he just shook his head. Even just a quick check told him the injury was bad—ligament damage again. "All the kids I've ever coached, I've never coached a better kid than Archie," Brown said. "That's easy to say when he's hurt but it's true. When they said it was ligaments again, I couldn't take it. I just broke up completely."

When Brown came back to the bench, he was weeping uncontrollably. The players knew right then that this was no sprain. "It was a nightmare," Manning said. "Archie had worked so hard to come back. The whole time he had never gotten down or depressed. He was just so upbeat all the time. He had learned to play differently because he didn't have the same explosiveness in his legs.

"And then just like that he was gone again. I felt sick. I didn't want to be out there playing anymore. I don't think any of the other guys did either."

The Jayhawks went through the motions the rest of the night. St. John's won easily. The next day, back in Lawrence, they got the official word on Marshall: ligament damage. More surgery. His college career was certainly over. There was a good chance he would never play again. It was not a Happy New Year.

Five days later, in their first game without Marshall, the Jayhawks struggled past a mediocre Washington team, having to come from 19 points down in the first half to win. Before that game, Manning wrote Marshall's number—23—on his wristbands. He also shaved a tiny 23 on the side of his head. "I just wanted Archie out there with me in some way. In spirit, if not in body."

Marshall was still in the hospital recovering from the surgery when Missouri came to town. Manning went to see him daily, sometimes twice a day. Brown went too, but found each visit difficult. "Every time I see him lying there," he said, "I lose it again."

The day before the Missouri game, Brown got more bad news. Marvin Branch, the junior-college center whose role had become even more important with Marshall gone, was academically ineligible. It would not be official until the following Wednesday, but unless a grade was changed, Missouri would be his final game.

Marshall's injury had saddened Brown. This infuriated him. He was angry with Branch for getting into this trouble. He was angry with his academic support people who had not, in his view, kept a close enough watch on Branch's progress. And, he was angry with Kansas. Branch had gotten a C— on the final in the course he had to pass to stay eligible. And yet, he had flunked the course because his papers during the semester had been F's.

Brown felt a C— on the final should at least get you a passing grade in the course because it showed you knew something about what had gone on during the semester. He was not about to directly involve himself in the situation, though. A couple of years earlier he had gone with a player to talk to a professor about a grade and he had been publicly accused of trying to intimidate the professor into changing the grade.

This time, Branch was in the hands of the academic counselors, which didn't thrill Brown. He felt that if Branch was capable of passing the final, he should have been capable of writing passing papers during the semester. The academic counselors were paid to keep on the kids to do their work. In Brown's mind, they hadn't done their job.

Branch would play against Missouri. But unless something drastic happened, it would be his last game. That would leave Kansas without two starters and leave Manning to face double- and triple-teaming up front. "We're right back to where we were last year," Brown said. "Only this feels worse."

There was one other note of good cheer: Chris Piper, the team's other senior, had been struggling all season with a groin injury. He wouldn't start against Missouri and how much he would be able to play the rest of the season was also questionable.

Missouri had different problems. When the starting lineups were introduced, Derrick Chievous was not among the starters. This was not the first time Stewart had benched him. Apparently, Chievous had been late for the team bus that morning; his car had hit a patch of ice and spun out. He was unhurt, but also not playing when the ball went up.

Amidst all these troubles, the two teams played a sterling basketball game. Manning was Manning, scoring 28 points, getting 7 rebounds, and blocking 4 shots. But the key for Kansas was Milt Newton, a fourth-year junior from Washington, D.C., who had patiently waited for his chance to play and had seen it come when Marshall went down. Newton scored 21 points, hitting 8 of 10 from the field, giving Kansas the boost it had to have.

Missouri was a talented team searching for a rudder. Chievous, who only played twenty minutes, wasn't about to supply it. Sophomore point guard Lee Coward, a talented player who seemed to save his best games for Kansas, wasn't consistent enough. Stewart didn't help. Chievous threw a bad pass, he came out. When it is apparent that the best player and the coach aren't getting along, the whole team is affected.

No one ever had command of this game. The biggest lead came ten minutes in when Kansas went up 19–10. No one led by more than six in the second half and that margin, 70–64, didn't last long because Chievous promptly buried a three-pointer.

Manning made the big plays at the end, scoring 8 of the Jayhawks' last 12 points, most of those coming while Missouri was trying desperately to rally. His two free throws with thirty-three seconds left made it 74–69, but Coward nailed a three-pointer to cut it to 74–72. Then, with Missouri screaming for time-out, Manning threw a long pass to Pritchard for a lay-up. That made it 76–72. Greg Church scored quickly to make it 76–74, and this time Missouri did get time-out. Eight seconds to go.

As soon as the ball came inbounds, the Tigers fouled Jayhawk Scooter Barry. The son of Rick Barry, Scooter isn't as tall (6–2 to 6–7) or nearly as talented as his father. And, unlike his father, he shoots his free throws overhand, not underhand. But, like his father, he can shoot them well. Calmly, he stepped to the line and made both ends of the one-and-one with six seconds to go, icing the game.

"I've been doing that in my backyard since I was a little kid," he said. "We all do it, pretend we're shooting free throws to win a big game. That's the first time I've ever *really* done it though, even in high school."

Manning didn't linger long in the locker room after the game. "Got to go," he said to a TV crew looking for one last comment. "I want to get to the hospital and see Archie."

As always, Brown and the coaches headed for the Mexican restaurant of which Brown is part owner. This is a postgame tradition in Lawrence and it had now produced fifty-four straight victories, dating back to Brown's first season. Manning had never lost a game in Allen Field House. "We come here," said assistant coach R. C. Buford, "after every game, win or lose." Buford had been on the staff four years. "Of course, I've never been here for a loss. I *guess* we come here after a loss."

The victory had cheered Brown up, especially since it was over Stewart. But looking ahead, he was concerned. "Oklahoma may be the best team in the country," he said, not innacurately. "Missouri is very talented, you saw that today. And Kansas State is darn good. So is Iowa State. I've never won up there and we have to play them next. I'm telling you, Coach, it's gonna be real, real hard."

Brown wasn't speaking to a coach. He calls approximately 60 percent of the people in the world "Coach." After a couple of drinks, it goes up to 90 percent. His two favorite words—besides coach—are "um" and "special." He begins almost every sentence with the word "um," and describes almost every person or event in his life as special. His coaches joke about this often. How was practice today, guys? Special. How tough will Iowa State be? Very tough, they're a special team. Johnny Orr is a special coach. Jeff Grayer is a special player.

That is Brown, though. A good friend of his once said, "Larry believes everything he says when he's saying it. It's just that five minutes later, he may believe something completely different."

Because of that, the coaches had absolutely no idea where Brown would be coaching next year. It might be Kansas. It might be UCLA. It might be Texas. It might be in the NBA with Charlotte. Or Houston. Or San Antonio. Brown didn't know either. He liked it in Kansas but worried about whether he could recruit players good enough to legitimately compete for a national title. And, at least on some days, Brown was certain the worst mistake he had ever made had been leaving UCLA in 1981, which he did because he wasn't making enough money.

In an ideal world, Brown would stay at Kansas. Strangely, for someone who has been accused so often of disloyalty, Brown is a man who craves loyalty. He knew the people here were loyal to him and that feeling of belonging was important. But as he looked ahead and saw Ames, Iowa, looming, Brown knew that all the loyalty in the world wasn't going to produce any more points or rebounds. And right now, Kansas needed some of both.

Danny Manning was stretched out on his couch, a just-finished pizza lying on the table in front of him. In the background, the Norm Stewart show was on. "I like to watch Band-Aid's Court," Manning said with a smile, referring to the segment of the show done by Chievous. Chievous's nickname is Band-Aid because he always wears one.

For Manning, this is the last day for a long time he can take it easy. Tomorrow, he will miss the first day of class for his final semester of college because Kansas will be flying to Ames to play Iowa State. He has decidedly mixed emotions about the impending end of his college career.

"I never pictured this year turning out this way," he said. "First, Archie, now Marvin. Pipe is hurting too. People just don't know what kind of competitor Pipe is.

"I knew when I decided to come back that I would still see zones and double-teaming and all. But it wasn't going to be like last year. Now, it *will* be. It isn't like I'm not used to pressure. I am. Coach Brown has put pressure on me since the day I got here. I know I'm the best player, so if we lose I think it's my responsibility. But sometimes, I just like to get away, come back here and be by myself. It seems like everyone is always looking at me to see how I react to things. You know, 'What does Danny think of this? Is he upset about that?' "

This was a time when it might have been easy for Manning to wish he had turned pro. That same day his mother, thinking aloud, would say, "Sometimes I wonder if I did the right thing talking him into coming back."

Her son, however, had no doubts. "I'm not thrilled with everything that has happened. How could I be? But this has been a good year for me. I think I've grown up a lot. Before, when I needed my laundry done, I took it home and let my mother do it. Now, I do it myself. If I ran out of food, I just went home for dinner. I don't do that anymore.

"Is any of that a big deal? No. But this is like a transition year for me in terms of learning to grow up. I'm twenty-one, I can do almost everything there is to do legally but in a lot of ways I'm still a kid. This is a good way for me to start acting like an adult without doing it in a crash course on the road in the NBA.

"If I had turned pro and then Archie had gotten hurt and I had looked at this team now, I would have felt terrible, like I'd left the guys in the lurch. The one thing that Coach Brown yelling all the time does is put us all in the same boat. We've shared a lot of suffering together and we're very close. That's what I think will get us through all of this now, that closeness.

"I know I get tired of the yelling. It gets old, Coach Brown has taught me a lot in the last four years but on some things, philosophically, we're just different. We clash at times."

Often when they clashed, the man caught in the middle was Ed Manning. On one side, he had his boss saying, "Why isn't he tougher?" On the other, he had his son saying, "Why isn't he ever satisfied?"

"I understand both of them," Ed said, diplomatically. "Larry's like me, though. He sees the potential. Danny still doesn't know how good he can be. Sometimes, during a game he stops concentrating or doesn't go as hard as he can. That upsets you."

Most of the time, when Danny wanted to talk about something, he would talk to his mother. That was the way it had always been. But lately, he had been dropping by the house and waiting for his father to open up the conversation. Then, the frustration would come pouring out. "Why," Danny would ask his father, "is Coach Brown always so negative?"

Now, with Marshall and Branch gone, Manning will be asked to do even more, if that's possible. "I've got a good feeling about this team though," he said, as Band-Aid's Court flickered off the air. "I just feel like something good *has* to happen to us. Maybe it will start at Iowa State. I've got a good feeling about that game. Of course, I've had a good feeling going up there the last three years and lost every time."

He smiled. "One thing I know for sure, though, it's going to be great when their band plays 'Here's Johnny,' and Coach Orr comes down the runway. Now that's what I call fun."

January 13 . . . Ames, Iowa

It is exactly zero degrees outside when the Jayhawks land in Des Moines the next day. The airport in Ames is so small that even their thirty-seat plane can't land there. So, they must bus the sixty miles over from Des Moines.

It has been seven years since Johnny Orr shocked the college basketball world by leaving Michigan to come out here to Iowa State. Orr had one of the top programs in the country at Michigan, but big money and long-term security lured him away. He has built a solid program at Iowa State and become a local folk hero.

Brown is a big Johnny Orr fan. Unlike Kansas–Missouri, there is no animosity in this rivalry. In fact, Manning and Jeff Grayer, Iowa State's best player, are good friends. The Kansas players enjoy playing in Hilton Coliseum, a shiny fourteen thousand-seat arena where the fans love their basketball and their Cyclones and trek through the cold and snow faithfully to watch them play.

Iowa State is resurgent this season. In 1986, Orr reached the NCAA round of sixteen by upsetting Michigan in the second round, as sweet a victory as he had ever had. But in 1987, the Cyclones slumped to 13–15. Now, though, they are 13–2, a national surprise, and in addition to Grayer they have the surprise player of the season, 6–8 center Lafester Rhodes.

As a junior, Rhodes scored 34 points—total—for the season. This year, he is averaging almost 20 points a game and, unbelievably, scored 52 points during Iowa State's December upset of arch-rival Iowa. The Kansas coaches have with them a copy of Iowa's scouting report for that game.

In it, Assistant Coach Rudy Washington wrote, "They have three players who like to pop out to the top of the key to take the jump shot: #44 [Grayer], #25 [Elmer Robinson] and #5 [Rhodes]. I would recommend letting #5 do it."

He did it that night for fifty-two points. The Kansas assistants get a laugh out of this because it is the kind of thing that can happen to almost anyone. Who can explain how a 6–8 lefty with a funny-looking shot-put-type jump shot suddenly becomes unstoppable?

The Jayhawks arrive at Hilton Coliseum for an 11 A.M. shootaround, a little sleepy after leaving campus at 7:30 A.M. The coaches prefer these one-day trips: get in, get out, get home. They will spend a few hours at a local motel this afternoon, then fly home right after the game.

Brown is in an upbeat mood. He squeals with delight when he walks into his suite and finds a heart-shaped Jacuzzi in the bathroom. This doesn't quite fit in here in Ames, especially with the Iowa Pastoral Conference headquartered in the motel.

To win, Kansas will have to handle Iowa State's press. Beat it and there will be lay-ups galore. Turn the ball over and the lay-ups will go the other way. Until now, Brown has said little about the loss of Branch, who has been officially declared ineligible. Before the game, in the locker room, without mentioning anybody's name, he addresses the question.

"You know last year we lost guys and we won twenty-five games," he says. "And I guarantee you that team wasn't as good as the one we've got in this room right now. I'm tellin' you that's the truth if you guys will just believe it. You guys know how to play, you know how to win."

Brown shrugs. "I get on you guys a lot. But you know I think basketball should be fun. You play it right and it is. So let's just go out and do that. We've got a long trip back. Let's enjoy it."

Before the game starts, they will definitely enjoy one thing: Orr's entrance. If there is a better act in college basketball, no one has found it yet. It usually comes with no more than a minute left on the clock. Everyone else is on the floor when the band strikes up *The Tonight Show* theme. Orr comes down the runway and everyone comes to their feet. Orr waves, shakes his fists, blows kisses, the whole routine. If Iowa State really wants to blow the roof off some night, it will fly Ed McMahon in to stand at center court and say, "Heeeeere's Johnnnny!"

As it is, everyone loves Johnny. Brown, usually tight as three drums before tip-off, breaks up as Orr comes down to give him a pregame shake of the shoulders. The players all stop to watch, fully appreciating the moment.

Unfortunately for Kansas, Orr's entrance is not the climax of the evening. The Jayhawks, with Keith Harris starting in Branch's place at center, struggle almost from the start. Manning and Newton are soaring, but everyone else is having trouble. The turnovers mount and so does the score. Up 28–21, the Cyclones go on a 10–0 run to build a

38–21 lead with four minutes left in the half. Kansas fights back to 42–31 at half.

"Goddammit, we just should not be behind these guys by 18 [actually 17] at any point in the game!" Brown yells during the intermission. "It just shouldn't happen. You know, we all sit around and talk about how tough we're going to play and then we go out and don't come close to doing it. I hate watching this shit, I really do."

The Jayhawks try to come back. They fall behind by 16, then rally to within 6 with more than 15 minutes left. But they can't get closer. Even with Grayer quiet—15 points—Iowa State gets 20 points from Robinson, 19 from Rhodes, and 13 from guard Gary Thompkins. The Cyclones force 25 Kansas turnovers and coast to an 88–78 win.

"We play like this," Brown says when it's over, "and it's gonna be a long season."

As always, Manning is the last one out of the locker room, having stayed to answer all the questions about all the problems. He is patient, but when he walks to the bus, he has a look on his face that says, "Where is the light and where does this tunnel end?"

The Jayhawks are now 11–4.

10
WEEKEND
WITH A
BALD MAN

January 15. . . Clemson, South Carolina

On October 27, 1986, college basketball lost one of its true characters. On that morning, Charles G. Driesell, the man known to one and all in his sport as Lefty, resigned as coach of the University of Maryland basketball team, walking out of Cole Field House with his wife on one side, his teenage daughter on the other, both pressed tight against him.

It was a sad sight, a sad scene, and a sad day. Driesell had been caught in the middle of one of college basketball's great tragedies. Four months before his resignation, on June 19, Len Bias, who had just become the No. 2 pick in the NBA draft a day earlier, died moments after overdosing on cocaine, in a Maryland dormitory.

Bias's death was one of the most stunning things to happen in college sports in many years. He was an athlete so gifted, so strong, so full of life. He had been the heart and soul of Driesell's program, a two-time All-American and ACC player of the year. When the Boston Celtics drafted him to eventually play alongside Larry Bird, his entire life was ahead of him. He would be rich, he would be famous, he would be a superstar.

Instead, he was dead.

Naturally, Bias's death brought the Maryland program under microscopic scrutiny. It turned out that Bias had stopped going to class once his eligibility had been used up. The other two seniors in his class had also failed to graduate that spring. Several other players were academically ineligible.

Driesell had made mistakes. He had put too much faith in his academic counselors and assistant coaches to keep a rein on the players and had not done enough checking on things himself. He had recruited some players who probably should not have been in college—though that didn't make him unusual.

But Driesell had not messed up as badly as Chancellor John Slaughter claimed he had. Remarkably, Slaughter contended that he had been "concerned" about the direction of the basketball program before Bias's death. If so, then why had Driesell been given a new ten-year contract just seven months before Bias died?

In any event, Driesell and Athletic Director Dick Dull were set up by Slaughter as the fall guys in the tragedy. If they were guilty, Slaughter was at least as guilty. He had been at Maryland for more than three years and showed up at most games to pal around with the jocks and the big-bucks contributors. If things had been so bad, where had Slaughter been before June 19?

A lot of coaches would have wanted to leave Maryland. Why fight a chancellor who is out to get you, a tragedy that won't go away, and a situation that is clearly untenable? Driesell, being Driesell, wanted to stay. His trademark in the '80s had been, "Aaah can coach," the product of a tirade in 1981 against detractors who thought maybe he couldn't. He *could* coach and he wanted to prove it again. Slaughter wasn't going to give him that chance.

Driesell finally went, kicking and screaming, after lengthy negotiations which ended with Maryland agreeing to pay him for the balance of his contract while allowing him to keep his summer camp, his car, and the title of assistant athletic director. All for about $150,000 a year.

A pretty good deal. What's more, Driesell had to do almost nothing to earn his salary because Slaughter didn't want him involved in the athletic program. The chancellor had hand-picked Bob Wade, a highly successful high school coach from Baltimore, to succeed Driesell. Wade had been recommended by Georgetown Coach John Thompson.

To say that this galled Driesell is a giant understatement. He and Thompson had barely spoken since a 1980 Georgetown–Maryland game during which Thompson had called Driesell a motherfucker, screaming the word in front of several thousand people in the D.C.

Armory. Much later, Thompson apologized for the incident. Driesell, asked if he accepted the apology, answered, "Of course I do. To err is human, to forgive is divine and I'm divine."

Thompson didn't think having to apologize was so funny. And, since his team had beaten Driesell's in that game and in the NCAA Tournament the following March, he saw no reason to play Maryland again. He canceled the series between the two schools and he and Driesell sniped at each other from afar. Now, Thompson had chosen Driesell's successor, a man who, in the past, had made no bones about the fact that he didn't want his high school players going to Maryland.

Driesell's new office was no more than one hundred feet from his old one. Yet he and Wade studiously avoided one another. It was not an easy season for either one of them. Maryland finished 9–17, going 0–15 against ACC opponents. That was certainly no fun for Wade. What was no fun for Driesell was picking up newspapers and reading about how Slaughter and Wade were "rebuilding" Maryland's program with a new emphasis on academics.

Driesell knew who Wade was recruiting. He knew there were a couple of players on his list who would have been inadmissible to Maryland when he was the coach. Slaughter was fooling people and Driesell couldn't rebut anything Slaughter was saying because he was still under contract to Maryland.

At the same time, Driesell was putting his life back together. He was hired by Jefferson-Pilot Sports to do TV commentary on their weekly ACC telecasts and he was in great demand as a speaker. That, combined with his camp and a little work at Maryland, kept him busy.

Now, in his second year of exile, Driesell had grown quite comfortable. He still chafed when he read what great work Wade was doing, now winning a respectable number of games with a team made up largely of Driesell-recruited players. But he was learning, slowly, to put that behind him and enjoy his current role. At fifty-six, he was getting to spend time with his wife and family for the first time since he had gotten into coaching. And, everywhere he traveled, he had folk-hero status. Once, he had been the man in the ACC everyone loved to hate. Now, they just loved him.

Why? Driesell is Everyman. He is big and bald and blunt and funny and charming and self-deprecating. He is vulnerable. People feel they can touch him in some way. He makes them comfortable. He is always friendly and never intimidating.

What's more, it has always been hard for Lefty. He built two programs, Davidson and Maryland, from ground zero to a spot just below the top. Somehow, he never quite got to the top. He won 524 games, but never made the Final Four. He made the ACC Tournament final six times before he finally won one. People identify with The Struggle. Clearly, Lefty has struggled. In fact, he's never *stopped* struggling.

Being a television commentator doesn't come naturally to him either. With his cornpone southern accent, Driesell is bound to strangle some words. For example, he cannot say the word "statistics." Always, when he says it, the word comes out "sastistics." Point this out to him and he will say, "Aah say it right. Sastistics. See, aah said it."

But he works at the job. He studies the teams he is going to be covering, calls the coaches to talk to them, and spends hours looking at tape. "I tried to get my wife to look with me," he said. "But she just gets bored and leaves the room."

Lefty's biggest problem as a commentator is a tendency to coach on the air. He says things, like, "Now Sam, don't you put the ball on the floor. You do that, you gonna get stripped." And, "Grayson, son, you gotta take that shot when you're open."

But he can be funny, too: "Jerry, if you keep takin' shots like that, Coach Ellis is gonna pull out all his hair and end up lookin' like me." And he can be insightful. Early in January, working a Clemson–Virginia game, he predicted that Virginia's John Johnson would try to go the length of the floor with the ball for a winning basket with the score tied and five seconds left. Johnson did exactly that. Clemson Coach Cliff Ellis had figured Virginia would go to Mel Kennedy. He was wrong. Driesell was right. He could coach . . . Still.

Now, on a balmy January weekend, Driesell was bound for Clemson. He was doing double-duty on this Saturday, working the Clemson–Wake Forest game Saturday afternoon, then being whisked by private plane to Chapel Hill to do Virginia–North Carolina that night.

"I ain't crazy about those little planes," he said, settling into his seat en route to Clemson. "They say they're safer than jets but when you're bouncin' around in one of 'em, it sure don't feel safe."

Driesell is a nervous flyer anyway. It is an interesting phenomenon that many coaches, who have to fly all the time, are nervous flyers. Driesell can still remember a flight to New York on a recruiting trip years ago when all of a sudden the oxygen masks in the plane came down. The cabin was losing pressure.

"I thought to myself, 'My God, I'm gonna die and it ain't even goin' to see a good player.' If it had been Moses, it would have been different. Moses was worth dyin' for."

Moses Malone was the best player Driesell had ever signed at Maryland. But before he ever enrolled, he was enticed by agent Donald Dell and the Utah Stars of the old ABA into becoming the first high school player ever to turn pro. For years after that, Driesell would say at least several times a week, "You know, if I just had Moses . . ." He was still saying it long after Malone would have used up his eligibility.

This flight, even with a change of planes in Charlotte, is routine, although the stewardess does insist on an autograph for her boyfriend. "You know," she says, "you're a whole lot cuter in person than you are on television."

"Oh really?" Lefty answers. "You might want to get your eyes checked."

Tell Lefty anything and the first two words out of his mouth are always, "Oh really?" They are his trademark. That and answering almost any question he is asked by saying, "Aah dunno, you know."

Once, when someone told Driesell he did this, he denied it categorically. A few minutes later, responding to the first question of a press conference, Lefty said, "Aah dunno, you know."

"Lefty," someone said, "you said it."

"Oh really?" Lefty answered.

When the plane lands in Greenville, Lefty isn't quite sure what to do. He knows he is supposed to rent a car and drive the sixty miles to Clemson. "I don't know how to get there," he says. "Usually, I just get on the team bus and tell the driver to follow the tiger paws."

When one drives into Clemson, there are tiger paws on the road for the last several miles. Lefty finds the tiger paws and Clemson and pulls up to Littlejohn Coliseum just as the Tigers are about to start practice.

"*Lefthander!*" Coach Cliff Ellis screeches, greeting Lefty. It is this way almost everywhere Lefty goes. He sits through practice, then Ellis invites him to the house for dinner. Lefty would like to go but he is committed to eating with his TV brethren. "I'm a member of the media now," he says with a laugh. "I got to eat with my own."

Before dinner, Lefty goes for a walk. This is a daily routine with him, a thirty-minute walk. He turned fifty-six on Christmas Day. He isn't so committed to exercise that he is willing to run, but he does walk every day. Walking through the dark back streets of Clemson, kicking at patches of snow, he talks quietly about his family.

"I got lucky with Joyce," he says of his wife. "We've been married thirty-six years. I don't know how she's put up with me that long. Her patience is amazing. The best thing about all this is that we've had more time together. If I went back into coaching, I would miss that."

His son, Chuck, is a coach now after having played for his father at Maryland. He is coaching the Navy Prep team and, after two good seasons, he is struggling this year. "I called him the other day and said, 'Son, you better start winnin' some games or they'll ship your ass to the Persian Gulf.' "

Talking about the Navy reminds him of his favorite movie: *Patton*. "I used to show it to my team to get 'em fired up sometimes," he says. "My favorite part is when Patton comes on and says, 'We ain't never lost a war and we ain't never *gonna* lose a war.' "

Patton's diction was no doubt a little different, and it is pointed out to Lefty that we have lost a war: Vietnam.

"We didn't lose, we just pulled out."

"No, we lost. The communists took over the country."

"Oh really? Well, maybe we should send Patton over there. Except he's dead so maybe we should send Bobby Knight."

After a huge dinner of catfish and fried chicken, Driesell stops in to see Ellis. They talk about the coaching business and Driesell's ouster at Maryland. Ellis is like most coaches. He thinks Lefty got screwed.

By eleven o'clock, Lefty is back at the hotel. "One beer and I'm going upstairs to study my game notes," he says. In the bar, he runs into Art Eckman, his broadcast partner. As the two of them sit at a corner table, they are approached by several of the Clemson locals.

"It *is* him, I told you it was him," one woman says to another. "Lefty, can we have your autograph?"

Lefty signs and the group insists on buying a round of drinks. Lefty would really rather go study his notes but he is too polite to say no. Midway through the drink, one of the locals says, "Come on, we're going to show you the *real* Clemson. You can't find it in a hotel bar."

"I got to go to bed," Lefty says. But they are insistent. One drink, they say. So Lefty, Eckman, and the group pile into two cars and head out. They pull into a place called Whirl's. The only way to describe Whirl's is to say it is next to the Christian Book Store and behind the Exxon station. It is also packed with humanity from wall to wall.

Lefty's arrival causes no more of a stir than, say, the arrival of the President and Gorbachev might cause. Actually, the President and

Gorbachev would not be recognized as quickly. People start screaming his name as soon as he walks in, unmistakable at 6–5 with that bald head. Everyone wants an autograph. Or a handshake.

Somehow, it is now almost midnight. That means it is time for the nightly Whirl's sing-along. Everyone is given a shot of schnapps and the bartender, using a yardstick to point at the words that are printed on an easel, leads everyone in a song.

This is a special night at Whirl's, though. So special, it calls for a guest pointer. Yes, it is the man who can coach, proving he can also point, The *Lefthander!*

"I ain't doin' it," Lefty says. "Aah got to get back to the *mo-*tel." (Lefty calls all hotels *mo-*tels.) But Lefty is outnumbered. Reluctantly, he walks behind the bar and takes up the yardstick.

The song is "La Bamba." Sure enough, the Lefthander *can* point. He leads the crowd in the song, pointing the yardstick at those he catches sloughing off. He finishes to a thunderous ovation and walks off, saying, "I think I point better in English than Spanish."

The local tour guides aren't quite finished yet. Once the sing-along is over and everyone in Whirl's has an autograph, it is time to go to Crazy Zack's. Lefty has given up fighting it by now. Sure enough, the minute they walk into Crazy Zack's, which is much more a college hangout with a huge dance floor, Lefty is spotted. The DJ starts screaming into his microphone, "Ladies and gentlemen, look who has joined us, yes, it's *Lefty Driesell!*" He will repeat himself at least a dozen times.

Lefty is standing as close to the door as he can manage but he is still being besieged. Teenage boys keep coming up and asking Lefty if he will dance with their girlfriends, who are too shy to ask themselves.

"No, I can't," Lefty says. "I can't dance." Actually, he is a pretty good dancer. "I know that," he whispers, "but Joyce would kill me."

Joyce would probably understand—she has already understood a lot in thirty-six years—but Lefty is taking no chances. He takes several bows, waves to the crowd, drinks a Perrier and, finally, at 2 A.M. escapes.

"I am too damn old for this," he says, walking out of Crazy Zack's. "Now, I got to get up at seven to read those notes."

Sure enough, he is up at seven. The notes, by the way, are in English, not Spanish.

The games go fine. Lefty is funny at times, coaches at others, and mangles a couple of words. But, in all, he ain't bad. The four-seat plane

lands safely in Chapel Hill without incident and Lefty gets home
Sunday in plenty of time for the Redskins–Vikings playoff game. Just
another weekend. But Whirl's and Crazy Zack's will never be quite the
same again.

January 20. . . Knoxville, Tennessee

Don DeVoe saw the flashing light in his rearview mirror just after he
had started across the bridge. "Uh-oh," he said, "I'll bet it's that damn
registration tag the guy hasn't sent me yet."

He pulled the car over and got out. The police officer recognized him
right away. "Coach, you got a dead tag there on your license plate."

DeVoe nodded. "I know, I know. The guy who supplies me with this
car is supposed to be coming to the game tonight to give me a new one.
I know that sounds like a weak excuse . . ."

The cop waved his hand to stop DeVoe. "Look, Coach, I don't want
to give you a hard time. But if the state police stop you, they have to
give you a ticket. I'm surprised you haven't been stopped before this.
I'd make sure that guy gets you the tag tonight because so far, you've
been lucky."

DeVoe thanked him and got back in the car shaking his head. "He
thinks I've been lucky," he said with a laugh. "He hasn't seen my team
lately."

It was a joke . . . sort of. Lately, DeVoe's team had been, in a word,
horrid. "Shows you how times have changed," he said. "A few years
ago I was racing out of my house on the morning we were going to play
Kentucky and I was just so fired up I was flying. A cop pulled me over.
I told him I was sorry, I knew I was speeding but if he let me go, I
promised that we'd beat Kentucky that night. He let me go and we
won.

"I don't know that I'd make that kind of promise now."

It had been a tough seven days for DeVoe. The Volunteers had
played well through most of December, finishing the month with a 7–1
record. The only loss had been a bad one—at home to Ohio University.
But there had been some solid victories too, over decent teams like
Florida State and Pepperdine.

Then they had started Southeast Conference play with victories at
home over Mississippi and Vanderbilt. The Vandy victory was espe-

cially encouraging because the Commodores were a Top Twenty-type team (as they would prove in March by reaching the round of sixteen in the NCAA Tournament).

That win had put Tennessee at 9–1. For a coach fighting to save his job, that was exactly the kind of beginning that was needed. Then, Louisiana State came to town. There is probably no one in coaching DeVoe enjoys beating more than Dale Brown. They are complete opposites: one the consummate salesman, the other a no-nonsense farm boy. One coaches every trick defense he can think of, the other hates playing anything but man-to-man.

And, over the years, they have clashed. Most recently, they had exchanged angry words during the SEC media day in November. DeVoe, angered by Brown's hiring of Stanley Roberts's high school coach as part of the 6–10 center's recruitment, ripped Brown during his time with the writers. "I think what he did was unethical," DeVoe said. "I just think it's wrong."

When Brown's turn came he was asked to respond to DeVoe's comment. "I think divorce is unethical," he responded.

This was a cheap shot. DeVoe had been divorced and was remarried. But that certainly had nothing to do with basketball or recruiting. Before the game on January 13th, DeVoe and Brown talked. "I should have called to apologize," Brown said.

DeVoe shrugged him off. "Dale, I just think you're wrong recruiting this way. You make us all look like prostitutes. It's bad for the whole profession. And you know what else? You don't need to do it. You're a damn good coach."

Brown was certainly a good coach that night. With Tennessee leading 51–44 and a little more than two minutes left, it looked like the Vols had a victory wrapped up. But the Tigers held them scoreless the rest of the game and pulled out a 52–51 victory that left twenty thousand Tennessee fans in shock. DeVoe too. He tossed and turned all night, replaying the last two minutes in his mind over and over again.

"That's exactly the kind of game we've been losing the last few years," he said, pulling his car safely into a restaurant parking lot without any further trouble with the law. "We had a big game won and then, somehow, we find a way to lose it. We go from being on top of the world to somewhere underneath it. You just can't lose games like that."

The timing hurt too. Tennessee had its roughest weekend of the season coming up right after LSU: a trip Saturday to Kentucky followed by a game Sunday at Illinois. It would take a Herculean effort just to stay in those games and now the team was going into them depressed.

It showed. Kentucky, pressuring Tennessee's guards every step of the way blew to a big first-half lead and cruised to an easy victory. The next day at Illinois, things didn't get any better. The Illini overpowered the Volunteers, DeVoe, frustrated, drew two technical fouls in the second half.

"We were never in either game," DeVoe said. "I just didn't do a very good job of getting the team ready to play over the weekend. The LSU thing definitely lingered with all of us. At our very best it would have been hard for us to win either one of those games. But we weren't even close to our best. When we aren't near our best, teams like that are going to make us look bad."

So now, Tennessee stood 9–4 with Auburn, a team that had just beaten Florida and Kentucky, coming to town that evening. DeVoe is a man who does not get down very easily. He is almost always upbeat and gets excited talking about his basketball team. But as he sat eating a club sandwich for a game-day lunch, he sounded like a man searching for a missing piece in a jigsaw puzzle.

"It just boggles my mind to think that I can't get this team playing well enough to get the wolves off my doorstep," he said. "A week ago, we were the big men in this town, sitting at 9–1. Now, we're a bunch of dogs. LSU was a killer. We sent twenty thousand people home angry. Tonight, the boo-birds will be out. I always say that's just fine, let 'em boo just so long as they keep coming out. But it is frustrating when you have a team that does some things well, then does some other things so poorly. There's just no consistency."

The only consistency at Tennessee seemed to be in the luck department—all of it bad. The latest mishap, hardly a minor one, had occurred the night after the victory in the SEC opener over Mississippi. Rickey Clark, a freshman whose play had prompted DeVoe to seriously consider moving him into the starting lineup, had gone out with a group of friends and ended up out late in a Knoxville bar.

Clark and his friends were drinking and they weren't alone. An argument started. Clark ended up in the men's room with a couple of antagonists. Outnumbered, he reached for what he thought was a beer bottle sitting on a wall. It was a broken beer bottle, the jagged edges hanging loose. Clark put his hand practically through the jagged edges, ripping it open.

"He was lucky he didn't hurt himself worse than he did," DeVoe said. "As it was, he tore tendons in the hand, lost a huge amount of blood. And it still could have been worse than it was."

It was bad enough that Clark was through for the season. DeVoe, in need of every break he could get, was only getting bad ones.

There was also the continuing problem of Doug Roth, the one-time prodigy center. DeVoe had come to understand that, because of his vision problem and a lack of quickness, Roth was never going to be a great player. But there were things Roth could be doing, DeVoe thought, that he wasn't. Like taking the ball aggressively to the basket.

"We throw the ball in to Doug, he catches it, but instead of going to the basket, he just throws it back out," DeVoe said. "We've played thirteen games and he's shot ten free throws. That just shouldn't be with a guy his size who also has good hands.

"I still look at our guys and think we can win eighteen or twenty games, get this thing turned back around. But other times, I wonder. It's a battle just getting them to battle."

DeVoe had talked to his wife, Ana, about the possibility of having to leave Tennessee. Since she was from Knoxville, she was not thrilled about the possibility. But Ana DeVoe is a religious woman. When her husband talked about getting fired, she would often tell him that, either way, it was God's will and he should accept it.

DeVoe laughed when his wife said this. "I wish," he said, "God would will us some wins."

It was ironic that Auburn was in town at such a crucial time. Years ago, Auburn Coach Sonny Smith had been DeVoe's top assistant at Virginia Tech. Now, with DeVoe in trouble, one name being mentioned as a possible replacement was Sonny Smith, who had been born and raised in East Tennessee. DeVoe heard the same rumors everyone else heard. But he wasn't about to lose his sense of humor. In fact, he clung to it like a life raft.

Shortly before tip-off that night, Smith walked up behind DeVoe. He put his arm around him and said, "I'd like to wish you luck tonight, but the hell with you."

DeVoe laughed. "You better be nice to me," he said. "You may need a job someday."

"Would you take me back?" Smith asked.

"Hell no," said DeVoe.

If he was tight, it didn't show. His prediction about the boo-birds was half right. Many of the 20,380 who had bought tickets for the game didn't show up. The actual turnstile count was 14,771—almost six thousand people had paid *not* to see the game. Those who came didn't do much booing, but they didn't do much cheering either. Thompson–Boling Arena had the atmosphere of a bright orange mausoleum.

If it bothered the Volunteers, they didn't show it. They raced to an early 13–4 lead with Roth nailed to the bench. DeVoe had decided that it was time to be aggressive with Roth in order to try to get him to be aggressive. The first eighteen minutes could not have gone much better for the home team. With the exception of 6–11 freshman Andy Geiger, Auburn was cold. When Dyron Nix hit a fall-away baseline jumper with 1:58 left to make it 40–29, the once-silent crowd was suddenly alive and noisy.

But careless basketball the last two minutes allowed the Tigers to close the margin to 40–33 at halftime. Given that impetus, they came out of the locker room and promptly scored the first six points of the second half to cut the margin to 40–39. Nix hit two foul shots to stop the 10–0 run, but Geiger made a gorgeous spinning lay-up, was fouled, and tied the game at 42–42 with his free throw.

Tennessee was in trouble. With the score tied at 44, Derrick Dennison hit a jumper after a Nix miss to make it 46–44. A moment later Travis Henry, one of the favorite targets of the boo-birds—his nickname among many fans is Travesty Henry—turned the ball over. When Chris Morris of the Tigers swished a three-pointer, it was 49–44 with 11:37 left.

Silence would have sounded golden to DeVoe at this moment. The boos were coming from all over. The Auburn run was 20–4, going back to the first half. If the Volunteers folded here, the season could become a very long one for everyone.

They didn't fold. Down 54–51, Nix made a steal for a lay-up to cut the lead to 54–53. Ian Lockhart, who had been as far down the bench as Roth during the first half, hit a jumper in the lane and Tennessee had the lead back, 55–54. He hit again thirty seconds later to make it 57–54.

DeVoe had tried some zone defense to sag on Geiger earlier in the half. But now he had his team playing man-to-man, and the players were playing it for dear life. Chris Morris missed with Nix in his face, then Nix came down and drilled one to make it 59–54. When Lockhart scored his third basket in ninety seconds, it was 61–54 and Smith took a time-out. The crowd had changed direction once again and, as Tennessee set up on defense, DeVoe turned and waved his arms to the crowd. They responded.

A few seconds later, Roth actually caught the ball in the low post, turned and shot—and was fouled. DeVoe was jumping up and down with excitement now. Down the stretch, Roth suddenly wanted the ball inside. He went to the line seven times during the last five minutes and helped ice the 75–64 victory.

DeVoe heaved a huge sigh of relief and walked off with a win he knew he had to have. Still, the tension he was feeling showed through in the postgame press conference. When Ron Bliss of the Kingsport *Times–News,* a reporter who had been critical of DeVoe at times, asked about the switch to man-to-man that had turned the game around, DeVoe said to him, "Give me credit for that one, Ron, okay? You get on my ass enough times, give me credit when I do something right."

He stopped. "I'm just joking, Ron, you say what you want. I'm coaching this team right now and that's something you'll never have a chance to do."

This was not typical DeVoe. But these were not typical days. They were tough ones, with or without the Knoxville police.

January 21. . . El Paso, Texas

In the annals of college basketball, among the thousands and thousands of games that have been played, one stands out as more meaningful, more important, more significant than all the rest.

It was played on March 18, 1966, in Cole Field House on the campus of the University of Maryland. On that night, tiny Texas Western College defeated all-powerful Kentucky, 72–65, to win the NCAA basketball tournament. What made the game significant was not that Texas Western beat oh-so-lordly Kentucky. What made it important was that Texas Western did it with five black players in the starting lineup. It would be five more years before Kentucky Coach Adolph Rupp would recruit a black player.

That game marked a turning point in the history of the game. Until then, very few southern schools had recruited black players. Most schools that did recruit had quotas. You could have only so many blacks on your team and you could put only so many on the floor at once.

Texas Western changed all that. It didn't happen overnight. In fact, even now, in 1988, there are southern coaches who will tell you they wouldn't dare start five blacks. But it did happen.

Adolph Rupp, who won four national championships, the last in 1958, never made it back to the Final Four. Kentucky forced him into retirement when he turned seventy in 1973 and he died several years later. The man who beat him that night, the man who profoundly changed college basketball, has never been back to the Final Four either.

But Don Haskins still coaches. He hasn't changed schools in twenty-seven years, although his school has changed names. Texas Western is now the University of Texas at El Paso, and the man they call "The Bear" is still churning out twenty-victory seasons and getting his team into the NCAA Tournament more often than not.

If Haskins coached in the ACC or the Big East, he would probably have a building named after him by now. He would be a media star. But because he has done all his coaching just across the border from Mexico in a corner of West Texas, he remains almost anonymous to most people who follow his sport.

Not here, though. Here he is just "The Bear" to most people, a legendary figure who really has little interest in being a legend. This is a man who wears a clip-on tie to games because he is so uncomfortable wearing a real one. He walks down the ramp to the floor wearing his tie, then simply pulls it off when the game begins.

UTEP's Special Events Center is a modern, handsome twelve thousand-seat arena. Like most arenas that house successful teams, it is full of banners ballyhooing various conference titles and tournament appearances. But one banner stands out. It is older and more worn than the others but it catches your eye as soon as you walk into the building. It reads: "Texas Western College, NCAA Champions, 1966."

This is, make no mistake about it, The Lair of the Bear, and very few teams come in here and win. UTEP plays in one of the most underpublicized conferences in America, the Western Athletic Conference, better known to one and all simply as the WAC.

No conference has ever been as far-flung as the WAC. UTEP sits on one end and Hawaii sits on the other. In between are schools like

New Mexico, Utah, Brigham Young, Wyoming, San Diego State, Colorado State, and Air Force. There is no such thing as an easy road trip in the WAC.

Even if you didn't need the Pony Express to help get you to many of the WAC locations, the road in the WAC would be difficult. No place in America is tougher to play in than New Mexico's Pit. But the Special Events Center at UTEP is right up there, and so is the Marriott Center at Brigham Young. As for Wyoming, few people have lived to tell about how tough it is to play there.

Into the Bear's Lair on a windy, snowy night came Brigham Young. The Cougars are always one of the country's more interesting teams, even when they aren't one of the best. Because most of their players are Mormons, there are inevitably several who have gone on two-year Mormon missions overseas.

Religious missions are the only exception to the NCAA's rule that requires an athlete to use his four years of eligibility within five years. A player who goes on a religious mission is exempt from this rule. Other WAC schools cry quietly about the fact that BYU has an unfair advantage because it constantly has teams filled with older, more experienced players. New Mexico Coach Gary Colson refers to some of the Cougars as "those seven-year guys."

Brigham Young is also one of America's whitest teams. There are very few blacks in the Mormon Church and very few non-Mormons at BYU. There are exceptions of course. Jim McMahon played quarterback there and Jeff Chatman, who is black, is one of the captains on this year's team.

"But they converted me," said Chatman, who became a Mormon on December 6, 1987. "They were such nice guys, they made me one of them."

There is irony, of course, in a matchup between a team famous for being white and a team famous for having won with an all-black starting five. UTEP's starting five this year is all-black too. Now though, it hardly matters.

Very quietly, BYU has put together a 12–0 record. The Cougars have solid guards, an excellent post-up shooter in Chatman, a solid center in Jim Usevitch, and they have Michael Smith.

To say that Smith is unique would be an understatement. He is, to begin with, a superb basketball player. At 6–10 he can shoot to twenty feet, is the best passer on his team, and a good rebounder. He plays a lot like Duke's Danny Ferry. Ask him if he buys the comparison and he will smile and say, "There's one difference. People have heard of Ferry."

People will hear about Smith, a junior, who went on a two-year mission two years ago. Smith is one of four Cougars fluent in Spanish; sometimes when they are all on the court they will call plays in that language to confuse the other team.

Smith loves to play basketball. And, he loves to talk. About basketball. About his team. About the Mormon Church. You name it, Smith will talk about it. When you ask Smith if it bothers him that his undefeated team hasn't gotten much national notoriety yet, he smiles and talks about football.

"You know, in 1984 nobody talked all year about the Brigham Young football team. Well, they just kept winning and winning and people kept ignoring them and when the season was over, they were Number One."

Then, in the same breath, he will add: "I couldn't believe it when everyone was making such a big thing about Wyoming before the season started. I mean, they finished tied for third in our conference last year and people were acting like they were the greatest thing going."

Right now, BYU is the best thing going in the WAC. The Cougars have already won in Wyoming but now they are in the Bear's Lair. No visiting team has won here since BYU did it a year ago. As they leave their locker room to walk to the floor, the Cougars can be heard chanting: "Coogs, get ready to roll! Hey Coogs, get ready to roll!"

The sight of eleven white guys and one black-guy-turned-Mormon walking into a basketball arena repeating a rap chant over and over is unusual to say the least. But BYU is an unusual team. "We picked it up last year from Alabama," Smith says. "After we lost our first game in the NCAA Tournament, we were walking off and Alabama was going on. We heard them chanting, 'Tide, get ready to roll! Hey Tide, get ready to roll.' We liked it."

Smith smiles. "Of course, we don't have a whole lot of soul on this team but Jeff has worked hard with us. We've definitely gotten better."

Smith is the first Cougar introduced. He turns to each of his teammates, shakes their hand and says, "I love you." Then he walks onto the court.

"I say it every game," he says later. "I say it because I mean it. I do love the guys on this team. We all love each other. Really, we do. Now, some people may get the wrong idea about a bunch of twenty-one- or twenty-two-year-old guys going around saying they love each other, but we've been through a lot together. A lot of us [six] have been on missions and come back. That brings us closer. We really do love each other."

The UTEP fans, 12,222 strong, do not love the Cougars. They love their Miners, who use their quickness to take a 30–27 lead late in the first half. But Smith hits a double-pump baseline jumper to put BYU back up 35–34 and the Cougars lead 37–35 at halftime.

Smith goes out with his third foul five minutes into the second half and he sits on the bench fidgeting, begging Coach Ladell Anderson to let him back into the game. "Coach, I don't want to sit here and watch us lose," he keeps saying. Anderson has no interest in losing either. But as long as he has the lead he has the luxury of resting Smith. When third guard Nathan Call, a Radar O'Reilly lookalike, hits a three-pointer with 6:33 left, BYU leads 71–58 and looks safe.

But UTEP charges back to within 73–67 with four minutes left. The Cougars spread their offense, the Miners have to foul, and BYU makes all its free throws for an 81–71 victory.

"No one back east knows how hard it is to win on the road in the WAC," Anderson says when it is over. "Sooner or later, people are going to have to start realizing this is a great league."

Michael Smith agrees. "We've only done half the job, though," he says. "We've still got to go to The Pit."

January 23 . . . Albuquerque, New Mexico

It is the most famous ramp in basketball. If you walk down it too quickly, you will lose your balance because it is so steep. If you walk up it too quickly, you will lose your breath for the same reason.

One night in 1983, Jim Valvano walked down this ramp a basketball coach and walked back up a legend. Most visiting basketball teams walk down hopeful and walk back up beaten. Three weeks ago, Arizona walked down this ramp 12–0 and ranked No. 1 in the nation. Two hours later, the Wildcats walked back up the ramp 12–1.

When you reach the bottom of the ramp and walk into a sea of red-clad fans, you can look up into the balcony and see a sign which proclaims, "Welcome to the Legendary Pit." A few feet away is another sign. It reads: "Elevation, 5,200 feet."

The playing floor is not that high, however, because it is below ground. One enters The Pit at ground level, walks down to the floor, then looks up at more than seventeen thousand very loud New Mexico fans.

Today, Brigham Young walked down the ramp, calmly rapping away—"Coogs, get ready to roll! Hey Coogs, get ready to roll." They almost seemed glad to be here. "Games like this," said Michael Smith, "are fun."

Certainly for a spectator. New Mexico has not been to the NCAA Tournament since 1978 and the Lobos are scrapping to put together enough victories to get a bid. Colson, once viewed as a savior when he took over what was left of the program after numerous NCAA violations put the school on probation for three years, is now being questioned. A year ago, New Mexico won twenty-five games and still only made the NIT.

The natives are getting restless. In a crowd where the cheer of preference is "Eat em up, eat em up, wuf, wuf, wuf!" that can make you nervous.

New Mexico has won thirteen straight here. Quickly, led by their two talented forwards, Hunter Greene and Charlie Thomas, the Lobos build a 17–10 lead. The Pit is rocking. But BYU is not a team that rattles easily. Chatman hits two straight jumpers, then Smith hits to cut the margin to 19–18. New Mexico builds the lead back to 30–22 and is still leading 37–31 with 3:44 left in the half. But Chatman hits a drive and center Jim Usevitch produces a three-point play and a post-up jumper; suddenly the Cougars are up 38–37. At intermission, just like at UTEP, they lead by two, 44–42.

And, just like at UTEP, they slowly take command in the second half, even with Smith again fighting foul trouble. This is a day for Usevitch and Chatman to shine. Usevitch, the blue-collar center, scores 24 points while Chatman, shooting what Smith calls his "automatic All-American jump shot," has 22. Smith, even on an off day, has twenty. New Mexico never gets the game even in the second half and the Cougars win, 89–82. They are now 14–0.

The disappointed fans chant, "Social Security!" at the Cougars, a shot at their older players, and Colson can't resist another shot when talking about Usevitch. "Hell, I got a freshman who can't even *say*

Usevitch, much less *guard* him," he says. "Got to give the guy credit,
though. You'd never know he was twenty-nine years old."

Usevitch is twenty-four. Despite the humor, this is a tough loss for
Colson because it is at home. "It just means I have to do my shopping
at six in the morning," he says with a laugh. Sadly, this will turn out
to be gallows humor. A month after the end of the season, Colson will
resign under pressure, perhaps the first coach in history to build a
program from rubble to twenty-plus victories a season and then get run
out of town.

Someone asks Colson if there is any way to fight the advantage he
thinks Brigham Young has, the older players coming back from missions. Colson thinks for a minute. "The best thing to do," he finally
says, "would be to go out and get some Mormons."

It might not be a bad idea. One thing is for sure: Missions or no
missions, age or no age, they can play. To survive in the WAC on the
road, you have to be able to play.

January 24. . . Tucson, Arizona

In a hectic basketball season, this has been a very hectic week for Steve
Kerr. Once a year his mother comes to visit him during school and this
has been the week.

Ann Kerr arrived in Tucson on Monday and was greeted by a very
tired son. Arizona had played the previous weekend at Oregon State
and at Oregon, the roughest road trip of the season—travel-wise—and
Steve was still recuperating.

Ironically, Ann Kerr came to town on the fourth anniversary of the
assassination of her husband. That weekend, mindful of that anniversary, CNN did a piece on Steve, focusing on the success he and Arizona
were having this season. But in the middle of the piece was a tape of
the first game Kerr had played after his father's death, against Arizona
State.

Sitting in a hotel room in Eugene, Oregon, Kerr suddenly saw himself on his TV screen. Seeing himself on television isn't unusual for
Kerr, but this was different. There he was, breaking down during the
moment of silence for his father and then hitting jump shots during
the game.

"It was weird," he said, "sitting there realizing this was going out on national TV. First of all I noticed that I looked like Shaun Cassidy or something. My hair was really weird. But then when they showed the moment of silence, I caught myself looking away from the TV. It was such a personal thing and there it was on television again."

Kerr and Arizona got home Sunday and Steve went home to bed to prepare for his mother's visit. As usual, Ann Kerr would stay with Steve and even go to class with him. "If I was in high school it might be embarrassing having my mother go to class," he said. "But this is different. I'm taking graduate courses and it's kind of nice taking her along."

Shortly after the death of Malcolm Kerr, the *Los Angeles Times* ran a lengthy profile on the Kerr family. The writer spent a day with the Kerrs in their Pacific Palisades home and wrote that, in the aftermath of the tragedy, the Kerrs "seem to cling to one another."

This was in no way a put-down, but a commentary on the closeness of the family. One senses, however, that this closeness existed long before Malcolm Kerr's death. To all of Tucson and much of America, Steve Kerr is the All-American boy. It is an image that makes Kerr laugh.

"It's nice that people like me the way they do," he said. "But to tell you the truth, sometimes I get tired of it. I mean, if I hear or read one more time that I'm Huck Finn or Tom Sawyer, I'll throw up. I'm like any other guy my age. I like to have fun, I like to drink a few beers, and there are times when I'm an asshole. When my family reads all this stuff about how great I am, they think it's really funny."

Not that they aren't proud of him, but the other Kerrs don't have quite as heroic an image of Steve as the rest of the world does. "He can be brutal," said younger brother Andrew. "Sometimes he can get on people and really take them apart. But most of the time he's funny about it, so he gets away with it."

Ann Kerr says that one of her children was never a very good traveler: Steve. And one of her children really hates getting out of bed in the morning: Steve. And one of her children can be quite lazy: Steve. "Really though, I think of him as special, just like everyone else does," she said. "But I think of all my children as special."

Steve Kerr says he now thinks of his mother more like a trusted older sister than anything else, and there is reason for this. Like him, she is at a crossroads in her life. She has just started teaching at the American University in Cairo. It is all quite new to her. At the same time, Steve is winding up five years at Arizona and preparing to start a new life somewhere. His older sister and her husband have just moved to Oxford. His older brother is with his mother in Cairo. And Andrew is a freshman at Arizona. So, ironically, all the Kerrs are in some form of transition in their lives.

"It does makes us closer," Steve said, "because we all know that the people in our family are the ones who are going to be there for us no matter what happens."

That is why Kerr is delighted to have his mother in town, even if it means having to clean up his apartment. The season is at that point where things begin to drag a bit. It is not close enough to March to start thinking about postseason and yet there is little left for Arizona to do in the regular season. The Wildcats have dominated the Pac–10 from the start and, barring a collapse, are almost locked in as the No. 1 seed in the West Regional. But there are still a lot of games to be played.

Kerr is tired, but he is also having the time of his life. "I'm trying to enjoy every minute of this," he said one morning. "Because I know nothing like this will ever happen again in my life. This is an ultimate, something that will only happen once."

While it has been fun, it has not been that easy for Kerr. After the Wildcats vaulted into the top five in the Great Alaska Shootout, then to No. 2 the third week in December after their victory at Iowa, the spotlight began to shine brighter on Kerr than ever before. He had always been in demand locally—speaking at every school, Boy Scout, and civic function there ever was in Tucson, or so it seemed. And, he had always attracted attention from the western media because he was a good player, a good story, and an excellent interview.

But now the attention went national. Kerr's mail increased so much that, to his embarrassment, he was having trouble answering it. He got so many phone calls from fans, media, and well-wishers that he started having his roommate answer the phone most of the time. He was also still trying to maintain his relationship with his girlfriend, Margot Brennan, who had graduated from Arizona and moved to Los Angeles.

The arrival of the national press, while flattering to Kerr, meant being asked repeatedly to relive his father's assassination, since the story was not that familiar to people outside Arizona. If he had wanted to, Kerr could have told people he didn't really want to talk about it—an understandable position to take—but he was too polite for that. Intellectually, he understood why the question was asked and so he patiently dealt with it. Over and over and over again.

And then he would read the story, find the Huck Finn reference and head for the bathroom to get sick. It may have been boredom with the goody-good image that prompted the practical joke he played on Olson two days before New Year's.

The Wildcats were playing Duke in the final of the Fiesta Bowl, the tournament they host each Christmas. This was a much ballyhooed matchup. Both teams were unbeaten and Duke had just crushed Florida the night before in the opening round.

Arizona played superbly, especially Sean Elliott, who lit Duke defensive specialist Billy King up for 31 points. The Blue Devils, who like to play a very physical man-to-man defense, were unhappy with the constant whistles from the Pacific 10 referees. Early in the second half, inbounding in front of the Arizona bench, Danny Ferry turned to no one in particular and said, "Boy, is this a home job."

Trainer Steve Condon answered Ferry, saying, "Oh, isn't that just too bad." Ferry thought the response had come from Olson and started yelling at him. Olson told Ferry to just play the game. There was another whistle. At that point Duke coach Mike Krzyzewski walked to center court and began shouting at Olson not to talk to his players during the game.

"We're supposed to be the professionals here," Krzyzewski said to Olson, who walked up to talk to him. "You shouldn't be talking to my players. That's not professional."

"Come on, Mike," Olson said. "That's bullshit."

Kerr, standing a few feet away, was shocked. He had never heard Olson use profanity before. "I knew right then," he said, "that this was really a big game. I knew it before, because it was the toughest game I ever played in physically, but after that I knew it was big. He didn't even curse at Iowa."

The Wildcats went on to win, 91–85, extending their record to 12–0. After the game, Kerr spent close to ninety minutes in the locker room answering every question under the sun. Finally, he was pulled over to a phone to do a postgame radio show hosted by a friend of his, former Arizona Manager Todd Walsh. Near the end of the conversation Walsh asked Kerr if he had made any New Year's resolutions yet.

"Yeah, as a matter of fact, the whole team has made one," Kerr said. "We've resolved to work really hard to try to help Coach Olson kick this heroin habit of his because it's really been getting us all down lately."

The notion of Olson, who is cleaner than squeaky clean, having a heroin problem might well have sent any number of Arizona fans who were en route home off the road. It undoubtedly had others fiddling with their radios—there was no way they had just heard Steve Kerr say that Lute Olson had a heroin habit.

But that's what they had heard. Kerr, for once, was a little embarrassed, thinking he had probably gone too far with this joke. "For the next couple of days I didn't even look Coach Olson in the eye at practice," he said. "I knew he must have heard about it, but he didn't say anything. But then his wife told me that people thought it was pretty funny and I was relieved."

There was another side of Kerr that enjoyed the whole thing. "Yeah, I really did," he said. "I just like the thought that maybe some people were saying, 'Steve Kerr said *that?*' It made me feel a little more normal."

And why did Olson let Kerr get away with such outrage? "Because," he said, "Steve is Steve."

Three days after the Duke/heroin game—having moved to No. 1 in the polls—Arizona's unbeaten string ended. Still a little worn out emotionally and physically after Duke, the Wildcats went to The Pit and played a horrendous first half, falling behind New Mexico by 16 points. No shot would drop and, with the crowd going crazy, the Lobos played their best basketball of the year.

Still, Arizona came back in the second half, chipping away at the lead, even though Kerr and Craig McMillan were ice-cold from outside. Finally, with the score 61–59, McMillan had an open three-pointer with fifteen seconds left. It wouldn't drop and New Mexico hung on for the upset . . . barely.

"I don't see how we could have played much worse," Kerr said, looking back. "None of us could make a shot except for Sean. I really don't think they're a very good team. We were just so bad the first ten minutes that we gave them a lot of confidence and then they hung on."

Olson wasn't happy with the loss but figured if his team had to lose this was the right time: Arizona had won enough to get some national attention. Now, having been beaten, they would be removed from the glare of No. 1, at least for a while. Still, practice two days after the loss was the most intense of the season.

"I feel sorry for Cal," Kerr said that night. "They're coming in here with a lousy team and we're pissed off. We may beat them by 40." He was close: the final was 79–41. The Wildcats kept on going from there, easily beating Stanford at home and both Oregons on the road. Then, with Ann Kerr watching, they struggled for a half against Southern California (leading by just 11) before humiliating the Trojans with a 27–2 burst to start the second half. That brought UCLA to town for a Sunday afternoon game.

Even in its weakened condition, UCLA was still UCLA. The Bruins were also the defending Pac–10 champions and they had beaten Arizona twice in 1987. Olson wanted a big victory. That was apparent Saturday when he kept the team at practice for two and a half hours, considerably longer than usual. Kerr, who had just seen his mother off the day before, yawned all through practice.

"The funny thing about UCLA is, except for Sean, they're probably just as talented as us," Kerr said after practice. "If they got as much out of their talent as Coach Olson gets out of ours, they would be very, very good."

Kerr's point was well taken. Arizona was one of those special basketball teams where the whole was far greater than the sum of the parts. The backcourt of Kerr and McMillan wasn't very quick. Anthony Cook, though improving rapidly, was an inconsistent offensive player, and Tom Tolbert was big and strong but not a one-on-one scorer.

But it didn't matter. In a sense, what made the Wildcats so good was their ability to recognize and understand their limitations. Other than Cook, whose game was still developing, all the Wildcats knew exactly what they could do and what they could not do. Kerr was a perfect example of this. One of the reasons he almost never turned the ball over was because he never tried to make the too-hard pass that a better athlete might attempt. McMillan and Tolbert were similar. Each had enough experience and had made enough mistakes to know their limits, to know what was impossible. Younger, more gifted players often think nothing is impossible. They usually find out the truth the hard way.

Other than Elliott, the Wildcats rarely did anything spectacular. But doing something stupid was even more unusual. When Olson went to his bench, he had talent that was more standard: good athletes who could be wonderful on one play, awful on the next. One reason why Kerr never came out with a game still in doubt was that Olson wanted someone on the court who could tell the other players "No!" when they started to get frisky. When Kerr said "no," he always got an immediate response.

UCLA came to Tucson on one of those days the local Chamber of Commerce would like to bottle. While the East and South were digging out from under snowstorms, the temperature was close to 70, the sun climbing high into the sky. Students in shirtsleeves played touch football outside the McKale Center before tip-off.

Because basketball is a newfound obsession in the desert, the crowd at Arizona games is still more innocent than those back east or in the Midwest. It is still more of a family crowd since it's only recently that tickets have become tough to get. Fathers take their sons instead of their bosses, everyone dresses in red, and there is a festiveness surrounding the games that one can't find amidst the tension of the Big Ten, ACC, or Big East. Here, it is still sort of "neat" to be in the top ten.

It is also sort of neat—and spine-tingling—when Kerr is introduced. When the crowd roars "Steeeeeevee Kerrrrrrrr" in answer to hearing his name, it gives you chills. Kerr almost blocks the sound of his own name out by now; he is a little embarrassed that he is singled out this way. "When I get older though, I'm sure I'll love showing tapes of it all to my kids," he said. "They'll say to me, 'Gee, Daddy, you must have been a great player,' and I'll say, 'Yeah I was.' Then I'll put the tape away before the game starts so they won't find out the truth."

Kerr is so popular here that freshman Matt Muelbach occasionally tells women that he is Steve Kerr, yes, *the* Steve Kerr, to try to impress them. "He says it works," Kerr says, laughing. "Funny, it never worked all that well for me."

The game starts very well for Arizona today. A Kerr three-pointer— "Steeeeeve Kerrrrrrrr"—breaks a 6–6 tie and starts a 12–0 run. UCLA looks completely frazzled. Trevor Wilson, the Bruins' best player, consistently gets himself open for good shots and clangs them off the rim so hard he's fortunate that nothing breaks. The Arizona lead is 36–22 when Kerr hits a short bank shot with 5:36 left and it looks like a romp. But UCLA revives long enough to get within 45–34 at halftime.

This is a potentially dangerous situation for Arizona. When you are playing a fragile but talented team, you are well advised to blow it out early before the players get any notions about an upset. When Elliott hits a three-pointer to make it 56–41 four minutes into the second half, all seems to be under control, but UCLA promptly rips off the next nine points. Olson calls time.

Too late. The Bruins, suddenly unbothered by the raucous crowd, have found their stride and their range. Guards Jerome (Pooh) Richardson and Dave Immel are on a roll and Wilson has discovered that there is a net underneath the rim. When freshman Kevin Walker hits a three-pointer that seems to come from about the fourth row, UCLA leads 66–64 with 5:50 left.

The crowd is in shock. This was supposed to be easy. UCLA is 7–9. The good guys are 17–1. This has become an interesting test for Arizona. Suddenly, the Wildcats are under pressure from a team they are supposed to handle, not a top ten team like Syracuse or Duke or a fired-up home team like New Mexico. If they lose, there will be a lot of questions. "What happened?" will definitely be the phrase of the week.

Kerr, smart enough to recognize a crisis, gets the ball to Elliott, who hits a lean-in jumper that ties the score. Wilson throws up another clanger and Kerr, seeing an opening, surprises the Bruins by going straight to the basket. "I surprised them with my speed," he said. "They didn't think I had any. Actually, I just have very little."

Kerr gets fouled and hits both shots for a 68–66 lead with 4:23 left. Immel misses a short baseline jumper and Tolbert hits a spinning jumper from the low post to make it 70–66. Eighteen seconds later, McMillan puts in a jumper to make it 72–66.

Wham! Arizona has run off eight straight points when it had to and four different players have scored. Pressure? *What* pressure? Any more questions, Bruins? The final is 86–74. Kerr has a typical Kerr game: 40 minutes, 13 points, 6 assists, 3 steals, and 2 turnovers—the last number matches his season high and gives him 20 for the season.

Hazzard, after saying all the right things about Arizona, whines about the officiating, saying that Elliott gets star treatment. This is a symptom of Hazzard's problem at UCLA. Someone *else* is always at fault when the Bruins lose.

Kerr is just glad to have the game—and the week—over. After dinner with some friends, he trudges back to his apartment (already a mess only two days after his mother's departure), opens some apple juice and turns on the television. "I'm too tired to even drink one beer," he says.

It is not easy for Kerr to get much rest when he is home. Besides the nonstop phone ringing, the door opens more often than the door in the ship cabin scene in *A Night at the Opera*. Kerr shakes his head. "Never in my wildest dreams did I think my life would ever get this hectic. But then sometimes when I think about it all ending soon, I get kind of sad. Next year, no matter what I do, play ball, coach, go to school, whatever, it won't be like this."

Just then, Kerr's face appears on the television screen. "Who is that," Kerr asks, pointing a finger, "Huck Finn?" The TV Kerr is explaining to the camera that Coach Olson probably won't be very happy that the game was such a struggle.

Seconds later, Olson appears, saying, "It was good for us to have to struggle."

"Wrong again," Kerr murmurs.

Olson continues: "I thought we were a little bit winded in the second half. We need to be more careful about using our bench."

"Or maybe more careful about not practicing for two-and-a-half hours the day before a game," Kerr says to the TV and laughs.

The phone rings for the tenth time in an hour. It is a friend calling to kid him about his erroneous soothsaying on TV. "Yeah, yeah," Kerr says. "Nobody's perfect, you know."

Not even Steeeeeeve Kerrrrrr. But don't try to tell that to anyone in Tucson.

11
COLD,
COLDER,
COLDEST

January 25. . . Pittsburgh

They are expecting snow here any minute but it is water that has Paul
Evans concerned. Evans awakened this morning to find his basement
flooded. "Sewer's backed up," he said. "I hope it isn't an omen."

Like most coaches, Evans is superstitious. The opponent tonight is
Providence, a team that is wobbling. Playing at home, the Panthers
should have little trouble with the Friars, who are a shadow of the team
that stunned college basketball by reaching the Final Four in 1987.
Rick Pitino has left to coach the New York Knicks and, in addition to
seniors Billy Donovan and Pop Lewis, he has taken his magic wand
with him.

In his place is his top assistant, Gordon Chiesa. Already, promising
sophomore center Marty Conlin has quit the team and, even though
the Friars did upset Georgetown, they are struggling. Naturally, Evans
is worried. "The way our team is, they're apt to come in here just
figuring showing up is enough, he said. "I'm a lot more comfortable
when we're playing a ranked team. Then I know they'll come to play."

Since the loss to Georgetown that opened the Big East season, Pitt
has come to play pretty consistently—which doesn't mean that the
road has been a smooth one for Evans.

He was gratified and somewhat surprised by the reaction he got to his comment after the Georgetown game that John Thompson had run roughshod over the school administration. "I've got a bunch of letters from people, a lot of them Georgetown people, saying they agreed with what I said. They seem to think that there's more to a college than winning basketball games."

There was more controversy waiting for Evans ten days after Georgetown. After victories over St. John's, Duquesne, and Connecticut, the Panthers hosted Villanova. This brought Rollie Massimino to town, Evans's off-season antagonist. Neither coach was looking for a confrontation, yet one occurred.

A few days before the game, Evans was quoted in the *Philadelphia Daily News* as saying, among other things, that Massimino had "fallen in love with himself" after winning the national championship in 1985 and had alienated many of his friends in the process.

Massimino was enraged. Evans insisted that he thought he was talking off the record. Either way, the comments were ill timed, to say the least. Pitt won the game easily, but when it was over, the coaches didn't shake hands. Massimino said he looked for Evans but Evans had left. Evans said Massimino never looked for him. Either way, there were headlines . . . again.

A week later, Pitt went to Oklahoma for a national TV game. For twenty minutes, the freshman guards couldn't handle the Oklahoma press. The deficit was 14. But the Panthers rallied in the second half, getting the ball to Lane and Smith inside. They lost, 84–81, but Evans was pleased. On the road, against a top team, his team could easily have folded—but had not. They were 13–2.

"There are a lot of good signs with this team right now," Evans said. "They're finally beginning to show some maturity."

Evans's reference was not to the four freshmen—Sean Miller, Jason Matthews, Darelle Porter, and Bobby Martin—who were playing extensively. It was to the three talented veterans: Charles Smith, Demetrius Gore, and Jerome Lane. All had been recruited by Evans's predecessor, Roy Chipman, and even after a season and a half under Evans, they still lacked discipline and toughness. Sometimes it was there, sometimes it wasn't. When it wasn't, they clashed with their coach, who didn't think his team could come anywhere near its potential until the three older players grew up.

"I still think we're going to play our best basketball in this program when I get all my own players here," Evans said. "That's why no matter what happens this year, the experience the freshmen are getting is bound to help us."

Evans is working on the future throughout the day. That and his basement. At lunch, he and his assistant coaches are joined by Darren Morningstar, a recent Naval Academy dropout. Like Nathan Bailey, who is currently a sophomore on the Pitt team, Morningstar ran afoul of the Academy's honor code. He is 6–9 with potential and Vanderbilt is also interested in him. He will eventually enroll at Pitt.

Back in his office, Evans gets a call from Don McLean, the 6–10 blue chipper from California. It was McLean that Evans and Calipari were visiting when they got caught in the earthquake and were on the plane that lost the engine. They have put in a lot of effort trying to get him already.

Evans is not one of those coaches who gets on the phone with a recruit as if hearing the kid's voice has transformed his life. He isn't capable of that kind of false enthusiasm.

"You doing all right?" he asks, picking up the phone. "I hear you're playing pretty well."

They talk for a while. Calipari, who has been out of the office, comes back and Evans turns McLean over to him. Calipari is the enthusiastic one in the group. While Calipari is talking to McLean, Evans slips out so he can go home and check on his basement.

It is just starting to snow when Evans gets in his car to drive back to campus. Once, basketball was little more than a sideshow at Pitt. And, ironically, football is making the headlines today because running back Craig (Ironhead) Heyward has decided to turn pro with one year of eligibility left. Evans has been through all that once with Charles Smith and will go through it again in the spring with Jerome Lane.

Now, though, his mind is focused only on Providence. "If you guys don't play with the kind of intensity you had during the second half against Oklahoma, you'll be right back where you were at halftime of that game," Evans tells his players. "This team can beat you if you don't realize it can beat you."

Even on an ugly, snowy night, Fitzgerald Field House is packed. Basketball was meant to be played in gyms like this one. The crowd is on top of the court and into the game, the ceiling is low and the noise-level high.

The start is routine. Two Lane free throws give Pitt a 6–5 lead with 15:45 left. Providence comes down and Carlton Screen misses a jumper. The rebound comes long to Miller, who feeds it quickly to Lane, racing down the right side.

Lane has a step on Screen as he goes to the hoop. He goes up, the ball tucked in his right hand and *slams* the ball through. As soon as Lane's arm makes contact with the rim, it collapses and the backboard shatters, shockingly and stunningly, into thousands of pieces. The effect is similar to that of a supernova exploding. The glass goes flying in all directions. It is amazing that no one is hurt.

For a second, Lane stands stunned, looking at what he has done. Then, as his teammates come to greet him, he goes wild—and so do they. Everyone is hugging and high-fiving and generally losing it. The crowd is doing the same thing. No one is quite sure what to do next. Lane has just become the first player in college basketball history to shatter a backboard during a game.

The coaches and the officials consult. It will take at least thirty minutes to bring in a new backboard and get it in place. The teams are sent to the locker room.

"What happens if you do that in the NBA?" Lane asks Gore.

"You get ejected."

"Coach," Lane asks Evans, "you ever see that before?"

"Not live," Evans says. "Anyway, at least now I know where you'll be the next forty-eight hours. You'll be home replaying the damn thing on television a thousand times and getting turned on every time you see it."

The players have already decided on a new nickname for Lane: Conan, as in "the Barbarian." Evans leaves them to relax.

"I hate this," he says. "Once the game starts you get over the nervousness and the butterflies. Now, I've got them all over again. Plus, I don't know how the players will react to this."

Evans reminds his team that the score is only 8–5; he says they should forget about the dunk and think about the game. But, heading back for the court, he says to Smith, "Why don't you let Jerome lead you guys out."

The delay is thirty minutes. As soon as they start playing again, Evans's worst fears are realized. The first two times Lane touches the ball, he throws it into about the fourth row. Evans takes him out. "Wake up," Evans yells. "Forget the damn dunk!"

Slowly, the Panthers get their act together. They build a 37–24 lead—including another Lane dunk—but a careless flurry in the last minute allows Providence to creep within 39–28.

Evans isn't happy at halftime. "Eleven turnovers!" he yells. "Eleven! How many times have I told you not to dribble against the zone press?"

Lane starts to argue. Evans cuts him off. "You see, you guys still don't have the fucking mentality to be great. You make one dunk, Jerome, and then the next two times you touch the ball, you throw it into the stands! That's ridiculous. If you don't learn to put teams away, it will do you in, I promise you it will."

Evans has no idea how prescient his words will turn out to be. On this night, he gets what he wants, though. The Panthers score the first nine points of the second half, building the lead to 48–28. From there, it is a joyride to a 90–56 victory.

Lane is the center of attention afterwards. "This is like a dream," he says. "I keep thinking I'm going to wake up." He smiles. "Oh well, another fantasy gone."

In the meantime, Evans heads for Hemingway's, the hangout at the bottom of the hill where he and his friends go to eat and drink. His team is 14–2 and he is upbeat. But not overwhelmed.

"This is still an immature team," he says. "I'm still not sure how we're going to react when it matters most. It's still only January."

And there is still water on Evans's bathroom floor.

January 27. . . Fairfax, Virginia

Rick Barnes walked into his basketball team's empty locker room, walked to the blackboard and wrote in large red letters: *9–0.* Just below that he wrote: *0–9.* It was forty-five minutes before George Mason would play American and Barnes's players were on the floor loosening up. He wanted these numbers waiting for them when they returned.

"They've never beaten us," Barnes said, talking about American. "We've won nine straight and I know it's got to end sooner or later. I just don't want it to be tonight."

Even as a rookie coach, Barnes had already developed one characteristic of a veteran: He lost sleep over every game. George Mason, after struggling through December with a 5–4 record, had played well in January and was coming into this game with a three-game winning streak.

Nonetheless, it had not been an easy month for Barnes. He had started to wonder if his hard-line regime might not be *too* hard-line.

The team wasn't playing badly, but he wondered if anyone connected with the team was having any fun.

"We went on the road trip at the end of December to St. Bonaventure and West Virginia and when I got back I was just so depressed I thought the season was never going to end," he said. No doubt, part of it was losing both games and the fact that Olean, New York, and Morgantown, West Virginia, are not the most wonderful places to be in December.

"But it was more than that. I didn't let Earl [Moore] play at St. Bonaventure because he was late for practice. We might have won if I'd let him play but I couldn't go changing the rules just because we needed him. I just wasn't enjoying myself, even after wins. If we won, I started worrying about the next game. If we lost, I brooded about it. Either way, I wasn't happy."

Part of Barnes's anxiety related to his wife, Candy, who was expecting their second child at any minute. He hated going on the road knowing he might miss the birth of his child. Finally, on the morning of January 9th, Candy woke him at 4:30 A.M. saying she thought she was going into labor. George Mason was opening conference play that night against East Carolina at home, and Barnes had been lying in bed awake worrying about the game most of the night.

He took Candy to the hospital and stayed with her until the baby was born, shortly after 1 P.M. He was excited and thrilled watching the birth. Within an hour, though, he had left the hospital to drive back to Fairfax for his team's pregame meal. The Patriots won that night, making Barnes two-for-two on the day. But two nights later, they lost at home to North Carolina–Wilmington, then went to Richmond and lost, dropping their record to 7–6.

Barnes knew he needed to back off, for his sake and the team's. He decided to stop going to pregame meal, hoping that would take some pressure off the players. He decided to drop the Pride Sheet. Instead, he and the academic counselors met individually with each player once a week to talk about class work. "This way, if a kid is having trouble it's a private thing, not something everyone on the team knows about," Barnes said.

He began trying to work the younger players into the games more to make them feel more a part of the team; that also let the older ones know that if they didn't produce or work hard he wasn't afraid to take them out. None of these changes happened overnight. Barnes was learning on the job and he told the players that. "I can make mistakes too," he said. "As long as all the mistakes we make are because we're trying like hell to do the best we can, we'll be okay."

The team responded. They beat Liberty—as they were supposed to—William and Mary, and Navy. That made them 10–6, 3–2 in the league, and brought American to the Patriot Center on this cold January night. It seemed as if everyone at the game was secretly wishing to be home, curled up in front of a fire.

American was a team that after a slow start, was just beginning to find itself. The Eagles were also 3–2 in league play and were as healthy as they had been all year, except for Coach Ed Tapscott, who had been sideswiped by a falling tree branch while taking out the garbage. He had scratched the cornea in his right eye and was wearing a Captain Hook eye patch.

Barnes had a lot of respect for Tapscott as a coach and a person. "I can't figure Eddie out though," he said. "How can anyone smart enough to be a lawyer [Tapscott has a law degree] be stupid enough to be a coach?" Tapscott often wondered the same thing.

In spite of all the talks he had given himself about loosening up, Barnes was tight. "This game could make or break us," he said to the assistants, probably marking the seventeenth time in seventeen games he had made that statement. "What kind of crowd we got out there? Nothing, I'll bet. This weather on a Wednesday night, we won't have any kind of crowd."

Frank Novakoski, the trainer, walked in. He had started a pregame ritual in which he handed Barnes a safety pin for good luck just before he went in for his last pregame talk to the team. "This one is number four," Novakoski said.

Barnes looked at the pin like a scientist studying a specimen. "Looks lucky to me," he said, and stuck it in his pocket as he walked across the hall from the coaches' dressing room to the players'.

"Okay, see these numbers," he said, pointing to the 9–0 and 0–9. "You know the 9–0 is us against AU. But I guarantee you that right now Eddie Tapscott has this number [0–9] written on his blackboard and he's circling it. Your job tonight is to get a good start and make them think they'll never be able to beat you. Do that and we'll be all right."

As the players headed for the floor, Barnes shook his head. "I've got

absolutely no feel for this game. I just wish it was ten o'clock right now
and we had won."

It would not be that easy. It was American that got the good start,
jumping to a 17–9 lead during the first seven minutes. Barnes had been
right about the crowd—the attendance was only 2,561—and the building was both cold and quiet. Everyone in the place could hear every
sneaker squeak, and the coaches felt as if they had to lower their voices
in the huddle to keep from being overheard.

The Patriots came back after the poor start and pushed to a 26–22
lead, thanks to two pretty baskets by Steve Smith, the lanky 6–3
sophomore who was the team's most improved player. But AU came
right back and, helped by an awful last ninety seconds during which
GMU committed three straight turnovers, the Eagles led 37–33 at
halftime.

Barnes was almost out of control at halftime. "How the fuck can you
have fourteen turnovers in the first half?" he demanded. "How? Have
you guys got any pride at all? How can you come to a game like this
and not be ready to play? I don't fucking understand it! I really don't!
You go out there and play like a bunch of damn pussies! You do that
in the second half and you'll get beat, I promise you."

He walked out. In the hallway, he turned to his coaches with a
half-smile on his face, feeling sheepish. "I swore I wasn't going to curse
anymore," he said. "For thirty-two years I never used that kind of
language, now I can't make myself stop." Then he went back in and,
calmly, talked about what had to be done in the second half.

The second half was just plain old good basketball on both sides. AU
built the lead to 53–45 and then to 59–49 with eleven minutes to go.
Barnes abandoned his zone for man-to-man, feeling he had to do
something to get his team to play more aggressively. It worked. The
Patriots came back, cutting the lead to 63–60. From there, every
possession mattered, the lead seesawing. AU had the lead, 77–75, and
the ball with ninety seconds left, but Daryl Holmes missed the front
end of a one-and-one and Kenny Sanders tied it at 77–77 with two free
throws. Both teams had chances to win in the last minutes but couldn't
convert.

It was ten o'clock and Barnes still didn't have his win. The overtime
started poorly for the Patriots. AU grabbed an 84–80 lead on two
baskets. But the Patriots tied it at 84–84 before Mike Sumner put AU
back up, 85–84, hitting one of two free throws.

The Patriots ran the clock down, looking for a shot. Finally, with time running out, Davis drove into the middle and went up. Holmes blocked the shot. The whistle blew. Foul on Holmes. "I've only got one eye so I couldn't see it," Tapscott said later. "But from what they tell me . . ."

He had a complaint. The call was close, the kind that many officials will let go at the end of the game. But Davis got two free throws with seven seconds left. He made both. George Mason led, 86–85. American called time.

Both coaches were thinking the same thing. Tapscott wanted his best player, point guard Mike Sampson, to penetrate and look either for a shot or a pass as the defense came to meet him. Barnes wanted to cut Sampson off and force someone else to take the last shot. But in denying penetration, he wanted to be sure his defense didn't get lazy and allow Sampson to surprise them by pulling up for a jumper.

The ball came in to Sampson. Sure enough, he drove the middle. The defense came to him. Sampson coolly kicked the ball to Dale Spears on the left wing. He was open from seventeen feet. The ball went up and, as everyone held their breath, it hit the front of the rim, rolled around and off as the buzzer finally sounded.

Both coaches had gotten what they wanted. Tapscott had put the ball in the hands of his creator and told him to create a good shot. He had done that. Barnes didn't want Sampson to shoot the ball. His defense had done that. The only difference was in execution. Spears had been unable to make a makeable shot. That was basketball, though. If Spears had made the shot, Tapscott would have been no smarter, Barnes no dumber. It was a perfect example of the limits of coaching. In the end, all you can do is hope the players can play.

Barnes knew he had been lucky, but he wasn't complaining. "I called you guys pussies and you proved me wrong," he told the players. "Coaching didn't win that game at all. You guys did. It wasn't pretty, but you guys got the job done. That's what matters."

Back with the coaches, Barnes sighed. "I almost cost us that game," he said. "I got them uptight because I was uptight. I made American into a monster instead of a good team. I've got to back off."

He shook his head and smiled. "Live and learn, I guess. I guess I'm lucky. Tonight, I didn't have to learn the hard way."

January 29. . . Jeffersonville, Indiana

A winter Friday night in the state of Indiana means one thing to most people here: high school basketball. In most of the small towns in the state, the fate of the local high school team ranks in importance just ahead of the fate of Indiana University's basketball team. The Hoosiers' fate ranks in importance only slightly ahead of the fate of the free world.

For two years now, one high school basketball player in Indiana has received more attention than most college players will receive in a lifetime. His name is Damon Bailey, and his notoriety is best summed up by the simple fact that at age sixteen he is already in that rare category of athlete who, at least in this state, needs no last name for identification.

Here, he is just "Damon," the same way Dr. J. is Dr. J. and Magic is Magic. For a high school sophomore this is quite an honor—or burden.

Damon first began to become "Damon" as an eighth grader at Shawswicke High School when Indiana Coach Bob Knight made a couple of trips to see him play. Bob Knight going to see an eighth grader is an event that, in this state, is treated about the way Moses' return with the stone tablets might have been handled if there had been advance publicity.

Anointed by Knight, Damon somehow lived up to his clippings as a freshman, leading Bedford–North Lawrence High School to the state Final Four. Now, as a sophomore, he is averaging 29.3 points, 9.5 rebounds, and 4 assists a game. BNL is 14–1.

The opponent tonight is formidable, though. Jeffersonville is also ranked in the state's top ten. A town of twenty-two thousand, Jeffersonville is located at the state's southern tip. It is actually a suburb of Louisville, just across the bridge into Indiana. Both schools are members of the Hoosier Hills Conference, which consists of schools in the southern part of the state.

There are very few high school gyms in Indiana that are merely gyms. Jeffersonville is no exception. The William S. Johnson Arena seats 5,300 people—about a thousand less than BNL's gym seats—and almost five thousand less than the gym Steve Alford played in when he went to high school in New Castle.

The place is packed, partly because this is a big game, partly because a sizable contingent of fans has made the drive down from Bedford. And partly because Damon is in town.

Damon hardly looks the part of an icon. He is listed at 6–3, but standing next to him it is impossible to believe he is much more than 6–1. *Maybe* 6–2—standing very straight. He wears a brace on his left knee, has freckles and light brown hair, and doesn't look a day older than sixteen years, three months, and eight days—which is exactly what he is. In a pinch, he could easily pass for Beaver Cleaver. He even has a teammate who looks like Lumpy Rutherford.

Damon is not a bombs-away shooter like so many high school phenoms are. Damon's forte is the head fake and pull-up jumper, a move that has become something of a lost art in college basketball, especially since the invention of the wretched three-point rule. Most of his shots come from twelve to seventeen feet, and he rarely takes a bad shot. Knight, in a romantic moment, once said that Damon was ready for college basketball. But if he is to be a great college player, he will have to improve his range during the next two years.

On this level, though, his athletic ability and court sense make him dominant. Damon is one of those special players who is gifted with a feel for the game. It is not something that can be coached. The great players—Magic, Bird, Erving, Jordan—all have it. They have much, much more than just that, of course, so Damon's gift doesn't guarantee greatness. But still, it is a rare gift, and it is a pleasure to watch in a player so young.

He also has a remarkable maturity. For a youngster to have received so much adulation and attention yet kept a level head is almost miraculous. Friends credit his parents, who have refused to be swept up in all this and have continued to treat Damon like a teenager.

"I just like to play basketball and have fun playing basketball," Damon says. "If we lose a game and both teams have played well, I don't mind losing."

This is not an attitude that will serve Damon very well should he end up playing college basketball in Bloomington. But for now, he can still be a sixteen-year-old kid enjoying his gift for the game. And this is the kind of game Damon enjoys. From the start, it is apparent that Jeffersonville is going to make life difficult for BNL. The score is tied at 20–20 after one quarter. At halftime, the Jeffs lead 43–37.

The arena/gym is rocking. Damon has 16 points on 6-of-12 shooting. For a mere mortal, a very good half. But for Damon . . .

Jeffersonville takes command in the third quarter, building the lead to 50–39 on a basket created by a (gasp!) Damon turnover. The lead is still 10 in the final seconds of the third quarter when Jeffersonville starts a three-on-one break. This is where Damon becomes "Damon." He steals the ball with four seconds left, turns and heaves it upcourt to a teammate. As the buzzer sounds, the youngster flings a twenty-seven-foot shot at the basket. *Swish*—for three. Instead of leading 68–56 after three, Jeffersonville leads by only 66–59.

The fourth quarter belongs to Damon. He scores 14 of his 38 points, makes a backdoor cut with forty-five seconds left that puts BNL up 78–77, and sinks two free throws with seventeen seconds to go that makes it 80–77. The final is 81–77. In the second half, Damon is nine-for-eleven from the field. That's pretty good even for an icon.

"That was just a good time," Damon says when it is over, surrounded by reporters. "The Jeffersonville kids are really good guys, I enjoyed playing against them. I like an atmosphere like this even when the crowd is against you. It makes you feel like you're really into the game."

Someone asks if all the attention bothers him. He smiles the smile of someone who has heard all the questions before. And even at his age, he has. "No, it doesn't bother me. When I was in eighth grade, Steve Alford took my parents and me to dinner and told us what to expect. He told me to just play basketball and let the rest take care of itself. He knows what he's talking about."

The dinner with Alford was arranged by one Robert M. Knight. Damon is certainly aware of Knight's interest in him. "A lot of people want me to go to Indiana," he says. "But they're not going to be mad at me or get upset if I go someplace else. They'll still back me."

Damon may be a little naïve on that one. If he chooses a school other than Indiana he may acquire a new first name: Benedict. But that is a ways off. For now, Damon is just Damon, a hero in his hometown. Now that isn't such a bad thing to be, is it? Especially in Indiana.

January 30. . . Bloomington, Indiana

The oldest cliche in sports is the one that says, "When these two teams get together you can throw the record book away."

Most of the time, the record book tells you a lot. But when Purdue and Indiana meet in basketball it is definitely fair to say this: Regardless of record, a victory can salve a lot of wounds, a defeat can make a string of victories seem meaningless.

Purdue is a basketball team with a mission: Win the national championship. Indiana achieved that last year, and when the Boilermakers walked onto the floor of Assembly Hall they could see the national championship banner hanging there—along with four others. Purdue has many, many banners in Mackey Arena, but not one of them says "National Champions" on it.

What makes it worse are the strange air currents in Assembly Hall. On some days, the place actually has a breeze blowing through it. When that happens, the banners billow back and forth. This is one of those days. The banners just keep swaying in the wind, a reminder to the Boilermakers that they are in Bloomington, and that they have never achieved the status of Bob Knight's team.

For the three Purdue seniors, Troy Lewis, Todd Mitchell, and Everette Stephens, playing here has never been anything less than strange. As freshmen, they were innocent bystanders in the infamous chair-throwing game, an easy Purdue victory that was completely overshadowed by Knight's chair toss and subsequent ejection.

As sophomores, they had the Hoosiers beaten, leading by five points in possession of the ball, less than three minutes to go. But they managed to score just one point in the last four minutes of regulation and overtime and somehow lost the game, 71–70. Then, a year ago, they played perhaps their worst game of the regular season—until the finale at Michigan—and Indiana won easily.

The game today then, is a chance for the seniors to finish 2–2 in Bloomington. It is also an opportunity to inflict a loss on the Hoosiers they know will be painful.

The Boilermakers are a team riding very high. Having survived the crises of the early season and the controversies surrounding Dave Stack and Jeff Arnold, they are rolling. They have not lost since the November 24 NIT loss to Iowa State—two months and sixteen games ago. They are 17–1 overall and 6–0 in the Big Ten, giving them firm control of the race.

Indiana's situation could hardly be more different. Throughout the Hoosiers' season, everyone has been holding their breath, wondering what will happen next. Six days ago, a decisive loss at home to Michigan dropped their Big Ten record to 1–4, their overall mark to 9–6.

During that game, Knight had shoved his own player, Steve Eyl, as

Eyl was coming out of the game, and a rare sound had been heard in Assembly Hall—boos for the IU coach. The next day Knight decided to radically change his lineup for his next game, against Ohio State. He decided to elevate two freshmen, Jay Edwards (who had briefly been off the team—academic ineligibility) and Lyndon Jones. Benched were Rick Calloway and Keith Smart.

This was the most radical lineup move Knight had made since the disastrous 1985 season when he had benched four starters, including Alford, for a game at Illinois. Calloway, a junior, had been a starter since his second game as a freshman. Smart, a senior, was merely the hero of the '87 national title game, having hit the winning shot with five seconds left.

Clearly, Knight was desperate. Such a move can go one of two ways. It can cause panic on a team and make a bad situation worse. Or it can be a tonic, the new players giving everyone else a boost. This time, the latter proved true. Jones and Edwards played excellent basketball at Ohio State and the Hoosiers beat the Buckeyes 75–71.

But it easily could have gone the other way. That morning, during the game-day shootaround, Knight had thrown Calloway out for not working hard as part of the second team. Calloway never moved off the bench that night. Smart played two minutes. If Ohio State had managed to win the game, who knows what would have happened next?

But Indiana won and that same lineup was intact for Purdue. With Assembly Hall as loud as it ever gets, the Hoosiers roared out of the blocks like a sprinter who has timed the start. It was 4–4 after two minutes. Indiana scored the next 10 points. Purdue scored to cut the margin to 14–6. Indiana scored 7 more. Finally, Purdue awakened, scoring 6 straight points to trim the margin to 21–12 nine minutes into the game.

Jones hit a jump shot and then Edwards made a play that seemed to stun Purdue. He reached in on Mitchell, stripped him of the ball, raced the length of the court and hit a spectacular spinning lay-up to make it 25–12. A moment later, center Melvin McCants was called for a charge and Coach Gene Keady hurled his sports coat into the stands—the second time in three years his jacket had failed to make it to halftime in Bloomington.

After a Todd Jadlow jumper, the next, Dean Garrett scored six straight points and, by the time Keady had called his second time-out, the score was an amazing 33–12. Indiana, which less than a week ago had looked ready to go completely down the tubes, was humiliating the No. 2 team in the nation.

"We'll make a run," Lewis thought to himself. "We know they can't keep this up and we know we aren't that bad." But, glancing at the scoreboard, Lewis also thought, "We sure have dug ourselves a hole here."

It was Lewis's running mate, Stephens, who finally stopped the bleeding, hitting two straight three-pointers to nudge the margin down to 33–18. But, with seven minutes still to go in the half, Knight was so confident he even let Smart get into the game briefly, and Smart responded by immediately hitting a baseline jumper. It was 40–22 and it was Indiana's day—or so it seemed.

Except Purdue didn't die. A three-point play by Mitchell cut the lead to 43–32. IU built the margin back to 50–34 before Mitchell hit a three-pointer with eighteen seconds to go, 50–37. But Joe Hillman ended a near-perfect first half with a jumper just before the buzzer and it was 52–37 at intermission.

"During that first half," Knight would say later, "I thought we played the best basketball I've seen anywhere this year."

It wasn't a boast, just a fact. But, as Knight expected, Purdue came back. "They've played everywhere, seen everything," he said. "Those seniors weren't going to just roll over because we had a good half."

Lewis, zero-for-four in the first half, finally found the basket three minutes into the second period, hitting a three-pointer, chipping the lead down to 56–48. The lead went back up to 12, then down to 8 and back to 12 at 67–55. But Lewis hit a short pop and Stephens stripped Edwards for a lay-up to make it 67–59. After a Lyndon Jones turnover, Stephens hit a three-pointer. Suddenly, it was 67–62. Garrett missed inside and Lewis bombed from three. Amazingly, it was 67–65. Knight called time, hoping to regroup.

Purdue had now made this a game that would be remembered regardless of outcome. Would this be the day Indiana built a 21-point lead and hung on to upset the No. 2 team in the country? Or would it be the day the Hoosiers blew that big lead and allowed this Purdue team to truly establish greatness?

When Lewis tied it at 69–69 with a baseline drive, greatness seemed very possible. A minute later, after Indiana had missed three shots inside, McCants posted up and put Purdue in front, 71–69. In a span of less than twenty-three minutes, the Boilermakers had come all the way back, outscoring IU 59–26 to take the lead.

But Bob Knight teams don't usually fold their tents and go home. Edwards, who would finish with 22 points, calmly swished a three-pointer. It was 72–71. Purdue went back ahead 74–72 on a McCants free throw and a Mitchell lay-up. So Edwards simply nailed another three to make it 75–74 with 3:45 left. Then, with the score 76–76, Stephens hit what appeared to be a huge shot, a three-pointer. With 1:51 left, Purdue was up 79–76. Garrett came back, cutting it to 79–78, then Purdue, trying to spread the floor, turned the ball over with less than a minute to go.

The Hoosiers didn't call time. They came down the court with everyone standing—the crowd, the benches, the coaches—looking for the lead. The ball went inside to Garrett. He missed. Jones rebounded. *He* missed. The ball was alive on the board and then there was Todd Mitchell, grabbing it in his huge hands and covering up, holding the ball like a mother protecting her child from the rain. Quickly, Indiana fouled. Mitchell, who had been superb during the second-half rally, scoring 15 of his 24 points, was going to the line with fifteen seconds left. If he made both ends of the one-and-one, Indiana would have to hit a three-pointer to tie.

"It's exactly the kind of situation you dream about being in," he said. "You've come all the way back, on the road against your arch-rival, and now you have a chance to just about clinch it. I knew I was going to make the shots. I just knew it."

Indiana called time to let Mitchell think about it. He thought about it, knowing he was going to make the shots, squared himself to the basket, spun the ball off his right hand and then watched in horror as the ball hit the back rim.

Garrett grabbed the rebound and quickly flipped the ball to Hillman. Indiana rushed down. Again, as usual with a Bob Knight team, no time-out. Hillman swung the ball to Jones. The freshman had no intention of shooting. Garrett was planted in the low post to the right of the basket, a spot he had been in so long all afternoon he should have been paying an occupancy tax. Jones threw him the ball. Garrett turned and softly shot the ball over McCants. *Swish*—his 31st point. Four seconds left. Purdue screamed for time-out. There was still time.

"No need to panic," Lewis said. "We had time to get a good shot."

Instead, they got no shot. Tony Jones inbounded to McCants, who quickly threw the ball back to him. Jones was to take the pass and race upcourt and either shoot or, if there was time, find one of the seniors for a shot. Instead, Jones's brain got ahead of his body and he started running before he remembered to dribble. Traveling. It was over. Lyndon Jones's lay-up at the buzzer was just a twist of the knife that made the final score 82–79.

If a January basketball game can have major implications, this was it. Purdue had showed guts coming back but hadn't been able to finish Indiana off. "It's a shame when you have seniors," Keady said, "and they can't get it done at the end."

He was angry and frustrated and it showed. Once again, Indiana had stolen the show. Purdue, with a sixteen-game winning streak, was ranked No. 2 in the nation. The headlines all week had been about Indiana's lineup changes. Now, the headlines would be about how they had worked and how Knight had proven himself a genius once again. Keady wanted to scream.

"All I know is we work our ass off to get recognition in this state and we don't get it," he said. "Obviously, you've got to win in March to get recognized. Winning the Big Ten doesn't mean anything. Nothing means anything."

Someone asked Keady if he was surprised by Knight's new lineup. "Are you shitting me?" he roared. "Nothing surprises me over here!"

It was Mitchell who took the loss hardest. He sat on the bleachers waiting for the bus to leave to go back to West Lafayette, his head down, looking up only when Dean Garrett and Rick Calloway came over to offer condolences. "Hey Todd, you played really well," Calloway said.

Mitchell nodded, and in a voice that was barely a whisper said, "Good players play well. Great players win games."

12
REFS

Joe Forte felt good. In fact, he felt better than good. He was an hour outside Philadelphia, the weather was beautiful, and he was about to spend the evening doing what he loved to do best: referee a basketball game.

"This is my favorite time of year," he said. "Once you hit February, it's all downhill. You can see the finish line so you don't feel tired. And the games are better because everyone is sharp. I walk on the floor every night and look around and say, 'This is exactly where I belong.' There is nothing I would rather do than referee a basketball game. To me, it's like I'm still playing the game. Only now, my shots are my calls and my goal is to hit at least ninety-five percent of them."

On any list of the top officials in college basketball, Joe Forte's name will appear, usually right at or very near the top. At the age of forty-two, he is one of the most respected men in his profession, a fact reflected by five Final Four appearances in the last eight years and two appearances in the national championship game.

To Forte, like most of the men who officiate college basketball games, refereeing is a profession. True, most college officials have another job, but during the winter that job usually takes a backseat to refereeing. A top college basketball official will work about eighty games during a season, usually averaging a minimum of four games a week.

Forte has gone a step further than other officials. He has just quit his job as a salesman for a food products company to devote full time to the marketing of the new whistle he and fellow official Ron Foxcroft invented. The whistle is called, cleverly enough, "The Fox40." Forte's name is pronounced "Fort-A," but Fox40 is close enough.

The whistle is the product of four years of work. It came about after Forte and Foxcroft, working a tournament together in South America, realized that in certain situations, their whistles couldn't be heard over the din of the crowd. "What if we could invent a whistle with a higher pitch that could be heard anywhere?" they said to each other one day, and the concept was born.

It took four years, lots of time, and lots of money, but eventually they developed a pealess whistle with a higher pitch than the old whistle. Now, more and more officials are using it, Forte and Foxcroft are marketing it nationally, and they are starting to make some serious money.

"A lot of people say to us now, 'Gee, I wish you'd have told me, I would have invested in you guys at the beginning,' " Forte said. "But the fact is, when Ron and I first started doing this, a lot of people laughed at us."

No one is laughing now. Except perhaps for Forte.

He has been involved in sports all his life. He was born in the Bronx and one can still hear the twelve years he spent there in his voice. His parents moved to Levittown when Forte was twelve and there he played high school baseball and basketball. One incident, his sophomore year, may have had as much influence on the way Forte works today as anything that ever happened to him.

"We were playing in a big Christmas tournament," he said. "You know, big deal type games if you're a kid. In the second quarter, I was bringing the ball up and this guy was guarding me tight. I went by him and he tripped me. It was an accident, but the ref didn't see it at all. I fell and he called me for traveling.

"I got up, really upset and said, 'Come on, call the damn foul!' He nails me with a technical. My coach was a really strict guy. He yanked me out of the game right there. I sat down, figuring I wouldn't play until the second half. Then, at halftime, the coach tells me I'm off the team for cursing at the ref and getting a technical. I couldn't believe it. I went home that day and it wasn't until five days later that I got reinstated after a lot of negotiations.

"Now, when I work a game and a kid gets upset at a call, you know, reacts instinctively and says something he shouldn't, I try to remember what happened to me. I know it isn't personal, it's just an emotional reaction. It takes a lot for a kid to get a technical from me."

Having survived his outburst, Forte went on to star in both sports first at Brevard Junior College and then at High Point College in North Carolina. In basketball, he played on two teams that reached the NAIA Final Four. In baseball, he was a good enough prospect that the Cincinnati Reds signed him and sent him to the Florida State League.

But after one season of minor league baseball, Forte figured out that the major leagues wasn't in the cards for him. When a friend of his from college landed a job coaching football at Ballou High School in Washington, Forte went there as an assistant coach and a physical education teacher. Two years later, looking to make more money, he got into sales.

It was during this time that Forte began to officiate. He had done a little refereeing in college, working intramural games to make some extra money, and he had enjoyed it. When he got out of coaching, he looked into refereeing some junior high school games to keep his hand in the game. "I just wasn't ready to grow up completely and give up sports altogether," Forte said. "I'm still waiting to grow up I guess."

Forte got hooked on refereeing. He started working any game he could get—at any level. "There were nights when I refereed four ten-and-under games," he remembered, laughing at the memory. He was dating his future wife, Lois, at the time, and she got so tired of his obsession with refereeing that for a while she told him not to bother to call. "She dumped me," Forte said. "I had to beg her to take me back."

But the hours began to pay off. He began getting better assignments at the high school level. In 1971, Forte was offered the chance to referee freshman games in the Southern Conference and in the ECAC. He accepted. Two years later, he was elevated to varsity games and a year later was offered a job in the Eastern League, one of the minor league forerunners of the Continental Basketball Association.

In 1976, the NBA referees went on strike at the start of the season. Forte was one of several Eastern League officials asked to work in their place. There was the promise that those who did good work would have a chance either to stay in the league or be elevated in the near future. Forte turned the chance down. He wouldn't break the strike.

"It broke my heart," Forte said, "because there was nothing in the world I wanted to do more. But I believed in what the referees were striking for. They made their living this way and they wanted some long-term security. As much as I wanted to work I don't think I could have looked at myself in the mirror if I had done it. Saying no was one of the toughest things I've ever had to do in my life."

Forte went back to the Eastern League and then, after the season, he received an application in the mail from the Atlantic Coast Conference. He filled out the application, sent it back to the ACC office, and several weeks later received a notice in the mail informing him that he was now an ACC referee. To this day, Forte has no idea who recommended him or if the ACC ever scouted his work before hiring him.

Forte did have limited experience working college games. In fact, his introduction to college officiating had been unique, to say the least. It had come in 1974 when he was working as a freshman referee in the Southern Conference.

"I was home on a Saturday when my phone rang just after noon. I was fixing lunch. It was the league office. There was a game that day at Fort Myer between American and Drexel. One of the officials assigned had thought it was a night game. The game started at one o'clock and he couldn't get there. They said, 'Get out there as fast as you can.'

"I threw on my [officiating] clothes, raced to Fort Myer [he was living in Maryland at the time], and came running into the gym just as Clark Folsom, the other ref on the game, threw the ball in the air. I was standing at the end of the court where the play was coming and I caught Clark's eye and waved to him. He didn't see me. So, I thought, 'Should I wait for a whistle?' I figured I'd just take a chance, so I stepped onto the court and got into position. Clark saw me then and everything was okay.

"But as soon as I got onto the court I heard a voice in the stands yell, 'Hey, ref, what's the matter? Don't you know when the game starts?' That started a little booing, no big deal. But there I was, working my first college game and I got booed before I'd even blown my whistle once."

Welcome to the business, kid.

Forte was welcomed warmly into the ACC, quickly establishing himself as a top official. He made the NCAA Tournament for the first time in 1978 and just kept rising. He worked his first ACC Tournament in 1981 and was assigned to the final. He has worked every final ever since.

Now, though the ACC is still his primary assignment, Forte works games in seven different leagues: the ACC, the Big East, the Atlantic 10, the Colonial Athletic Association, the Southeast, the Sun Belt and the Metro. Most weeks he works a minimum of four games, often more. This week he'll work six games, assigned out of five different leagues. Before the season is over, like most top officials, Forte will have worked in the neighborhood of eighty games. There are some who contend this is overwork, that officials work too often and as a result are not always as sharp as they should be.

Forte insists that isn't so. "I think by working a lot you stay sharper," he said. "If I'm off for a few days it takes me a few minutes to really get into the game. I like to keep working. Especially now, with the three-man crews, you aren't running that much of the court. It isn't as tiring. As long as you're in shape, you're okay."

The reason officials work so much is simple: money. The top of the pay scale is $350 a night (in the ACC, Big East, SEC, and Big Ten) and with per diem and expenses added, officials may receive $650 on a top pay night. But most nights aren't top pay nights and even so, a referee who works eighty games a year will probably net no more than $35,000. That isn't bad for four months of work but it isn't all that much; it is only made by the very top officials and those guys lose money taking time off from their full-time jobs to make that money.

So, officials tend to cut corners to save money. Often, they stay in cheap hotels, they will drive rather than fly when they can do it, and they will take work wherever they can, whenever they can. If the NCAA was smart, it would hire a group of full-time officials to work big games and the NCAA Tournament and pay them well enough so that they didn't have to cut corners.

Forte admits that being one of the top officials in the country puts pressure on him, regardless of what league he is working in. "It's nice when I hear guys say that I do a good job and they feel comfortable when I'm working," he said. "But knowing I have that kind of reputation means I have to go out there every night and try never to be down or sluggish. Every game you work is a big game to *somebody* and if you act like a game isn't important or is beneath you, they're going to notice and they're going to get mad and they're going to be right. I try to look at every game and say, 'Why is this game important?' There's always a reason why it is."

There will be no problem finding significance in tonight's game: Villanova–Georgetown. This is one of the Big East's great rivalries. Both teams are scuffling to try to wrap up NCAA berths and both have been struggling a bit of late. For Forte, there is another concern: Georgetown has been in two fights in three weeks and he and his partners will have to be conscious of trying to avoid a fight when the game starts.

Forte reaches Philadelphia by 4 o'clock. The game is at 7:30. Since he is driving back to Washington after the game to stay at a friend's house (he lives in Atlanta now), there is no hotel for him to check into. He stops at the Days Inn to meet Nolan Fine, one of the other officials working the game.

Forte calls Fine "Wonder Boy." He likes giving other officials nicknames. Fine's comes from a story in a refereeing magazine (yes, they exist) in which he was called the "Boy Wonder" of college officials. Last March, at thirty-three, Fine had worked the NCAA final along with Forte and Jody Silvester. Forte, who didn't become a college official until he was thirty-one and worked his first final at thirty-seven, immediately dubbed Fine "Wonder Boy."

Wonder Boy, who sells insurance and mutual funds in Virginia Beach when he isn't officiating, is trying to sleep when Forte arrives, but he is quickly roused. Forte wants to talk plays (referee talk for calls that are questionable or tricky) and catch up on the gossip. Officials are very much a fraternity and there is little that goes on that all the brothers don't know about very quickly.

"Officials learn to stick together," Forte said in explaining the fraternity feeling. "I think we feel like we're misunderstood by most people. We're always seen as the bad guys. We don't see ourselves that way. Most officials are good guys, very good guys, but most people don't want to hear that. So if you're going to be understood by anyone, it's going to be another official. We all really like spending time together."

That is not to say that officiating isn't competitive. Just as teams want to make the NCAA Tournament, advance to the Final Four, and get to the national championship game, so do officials.

In 1987, for the first time the NCAA brought nine officials to the Final Four instead of six. Prior to 1986, three of the six officials assigned to the semifinals advanced to the final. Under the new system everyone worked one game. When the officials met on Saturday morning to receive their assignments the first three names called were those doing the first semifinal; the next three called were doing the second. "In other words, the last thing you wanted to hear was your own name," Forte said. "Because hearing it meant you didn't have the final. Everyone wants the chance to work the final."

Forte's first final had been in 1983. That was during a period when games were assigned according to crew, meaning either the crew from the first semifinal or the crew from the second would work the final. Forte was working in a crew with Hank Nichols and Paul Housman. All three were ACC officials.

When N.C. State beat Georgia in the first semifinal, Nichols turned to Forte and Housman as they prepared to go out for the Houston–Louisville game and said, "Well, guys, it looks like this is our last game of the year."

Like everyone else, Nichols never dreamed that three ACC officials would be assigned to a final with an ACC team playing. In fact, as the other crew came off the floor after working the first game, Rich Weiler had turned to Larry Lembo and said, "We're in the final."

Forte laughs telling the story. "I remember telling Hank and Paul, 'Let's go out there and work such a good game that we'll make things really tough on the selection committee.'"

They made it tough enough that the committee indeed selected them to work the Houston–State final. And, when Lorenzo Charles soared over everyone on the last play of the game to dunk Dereck Whittenburg's air ball to win the national championship, what was Forte thinking? "I was thinking, 'Thank God he's nowhere close to goaltending,' because if he had been it would have been my call to make."

Forte says he loses sleep if he thinks a call of his in a crucial moment may have been wrong. He constantly looks at tape of his games, looking for general things like positioning as well as for specific calls to check up on himself. Before each season, he goes back and looks at tapes from the previous five seasons to see if he has made any changes—good or bad—in the way he works a game.

Now, he is telling Wonder Boy about his most recent strange call. "I have a game up at Rhode Island, okay? Kid from Rhode Island is inbounding. He can't get the ball in and the defender is in his way. So, he reaches out with his off hand and pushes the defender out of the way."

Forte stops like the guy in the TV commercial. "What's the call?"

"Player control foul," Fine says.

"Right, Wonder Boy," Forte says, nodding in appreciation. He laughs. "I go over to the scorer's table and this is what I said: 'Guys, you aren't gonna believe this one, but I got a player control foul on number twenty-three.' They were all cracking up."

Fine asks about another call, this one in a game between Providence and Miami that Forte had worked. In the last minute, with Providence down one, Tito Horford had blocked a shot that could have won the game for Providence. Forte had, as the officials say, "no-called it," ruling the block was clean.

"Was that one all right?" Fine asks.

Forte nods. "I was really worried about it. I thought I had it and Larry [Lembo] and Timmy [Higgins] both said after the game it was a good call. But it bothered me. I wanted to see the tape. Well, I went to dinner with Larry and his wife after the game and as we were walking to the elevators all of a sudden we hear [Providence Coach] Gordy Chiesa behind us. He goes, 'Joe, Larry.' I'm thinking, 'Oh boy, here we go now.'

"He walks up to me and he says, 'Joe, I looked at the tape on Tito's block. Tito got it clean. You made a good call.' What a relief that was. Gordy really showed class coming over to tell me that."

Forte likes most coaches and players. Naturally, officials don't socialize with coaches. They stay in different hotels and learn to keep a certain distance. But working with people for years, you are bound to develop some feeling for them.

That is not to say that Forte's career has not been devoid of run-ins. Georgia Coach Hugh Durham called him some ugly names in the newspaper several years ago after a close loss, and has never apologized. Forte won't talk about Durham—at all. And, several years ago, Forte had problems with Virginia guard Othell Wilson, a gifted but troubled player who refused to keep his mouth shut during games. Wilson's ACC career ended in 1984 with him chasing Forte off the floor after Virginia lost a first-round game in the ACC Tournament.

Wilson ran up behind Forte, screaming profanities at him. Forte turned and said, "Othell, you better get into your locker room." Wilson kept screaming. Forte kept his cool and kept walking.

"I felt bad about the whole thing because I never felt like Othell was a bad kid," Forte said. "But he just couldn't control himself at times on the court. What was bad about it from my point of view was that it put me in the spotlight. That's the last thing you want. You just want to work the games, make sure the kids are the ones who decide the winner and the loser, and go home."

Forte has a simple motto when working a game: "neither seek nor avoid."

Forte and Fine leave for the Spectrum at about 5 P.M. Officials are required to be in the arena ninety minutes before tip-off. Forte always leaves extra time in case of traffic or, if he is unfamiliar with a place, bad directions. Pulling up to the VIP lot at the Spectrum, Forte rolls his window down.

"Refs," he says, and the security guard waves him through. "It's funny," Forte says, "no one ever asks you to prove it. I guess they figure no one would claim to be a referee if he wasn't one."

The officials' locker room in the Spectrum has all the ambience of a dungeon. It is tiny and dirty with three small changing benches and one shower. It is remarkable that, in a major arena, no one has bothered to think about decent facilities for the referees.

Larry Lembo is the third official tonight. He will drive in from New York, where he is a teacher and tennis coach at Queensboro Community College. Twenty-five years ago, Lembo was a 6-4 center at Manhattan College, and he is still described by everyone who saw him play with the same word: "bitch." As in, "He was a bitch to play against."

Lembo has also been to several Final Fours and worked the 1980 final between UCLA and Louisville. In short, a top crew is working this game. Lembo, whose primary league is the Big East, is the referee. Forte is U-1 (umpire one) and Fine is the U-2 (umpire two). The U-2 is known as the "U-boat." His job, off the floor, is to make sure the door gets locked on the way out and is unlocked either by security or by carrying the key himself when the officials return at halftime and after the game.

The difference in responsibility among the three officials in a game is minor. The referee runs the pregame meeting, throws the ball up for the center jump at the start of the game, and is responsible for getting the teams back on the floor after a time-out. The U-1 is responsible for the home team: getting them out of their huddle, controlling them if a fight breaks out. The U-2 does the same with the visitors.

Like the teams, the officials always review the game before they go out to work it. Different officials use different methods of running a pregame meeting. Lembo likes to let the two umpires mention situations that should be looked for before he does any talking. He saves the thing he likes to talk about least for last.

"God forbid, I mean God forbid, if we should have a fight, let's break it up as fast as we can and then consult with each other before we adjudicate."

Forte nods. "Let's watch the stuff off the ball very carefully," he says. "A lot of times, especially with the pressure defense, that's what gets things started."

All three officials know that a Georgetown game is very tough to work. Part of it is the Hoyas' pressure defense, always trapping and slapping at the ball. But another part of it is that the shooting in Georgetown games is almost always poor on both sides. The Hoyas can't shoot, but they can defend.

"The more missed shots you have, the more rebounds you have and the more contact there is," Forte says. "The hardest game to work is the kind with a lot of missed shots and no dominant rebounder."

This game has the potential to be hard.

The pregame meeting over, the refs relax. Forte is talking about technicals. When officials talk about technicals they say, "I teed him up," as in, "Coach so-and-so kicked his chair over so I had no choice and I teed him up."

Lembo is talking about the Georgetown–Pitt debacle of early January, Jerome Lane's "intercepted" technical that kept Paul Evans from being ejected. "That was the worst game I ever worked in my life," Lembo is saying. "I mean, right from the beginning. The kids were all over each other, the clocks didn't work right for most of the game, it was really awful. I thought the game was never going to end.

"Then, in that last minute, we had to tee up both coaches. First, Evans goes crazy and Jody [Silvester] and Jimmy [Burr] both tee him up. Then, I'm about to give him another when Lane comes along and says, 'Come on, man, please give us a break. He already got two.' I figured, okay, let it go.

"Then the clock breaks again and John [Thompson] comes screaming out of the box. He was right about the clock so he was okay coming out of the box, but he was screaming and gesturing so much I had to tee him up, too. The whole thing was a nightmare."

Forte tells a story about a completely different kind of technical.

"Last year my partner and I are working North Carolina at Notre Dame." Forte always refers to Gerry Donaghy as his partner since they often work together in the ACC. "In the last minute, Notre Dame is going to win the game and, after a foul call, the fans go wild, throwing things on the floor. Gerry tells the PA to announce that if they don't stop it'll be a technical.

"Next time there's a whistle, they start throwing stuff again and the leprechaun comes onto the court. That's it, Gerry tees him up. He goes over to the scorer and signals the tee. Digger [Phelps] comes over and he says, 'Who is the tee on?'

"Gerry says, 'The leprechaun.'

"Digger never misses a beat. He says, 'The leprechaun is from Carolina.'

"Gerry just looks at him and says, 'Oh yeah? Then what's that ND on his uniform?' "

It is time to go. A security guard comes to escort them to the court. "If by some chance things get hectic," he says, "we'll take you out through the side tunnel." Fine, the U-boat makes sure the guard knows to come back at the end of the half to open the door for them.

On the way out, Forte delivers his nightly line: "Guys, let's call 'em right, so we can sleep tonight."

Lembo laughs. "Let's go paint a Picasso," he says, and they walk onto the floor to the scattered boos that are as much a part of an official's life as his whistle, Fox40 or otherwise.

The game is, relatively speaking, an easy one, even though Georgetown shoots a putrid 32.5 percent for the game and the two teams combine for 41 turnovers. The only real problem is caused by the weather. During the day, the temperature in Philadelphia hit 65 degrees, a record for the date. Because of the warmth, the ice underneath the basketball floor at the Spectrum is melting and the floor is full of wet spots. From the first minute, players are slipping and sliding as if they are trying to run on ice.

Early in the game, the officials call John Thompson and Rollie Massimino together to tell them they're going to have to call all the traveling calls that will be caused by the wet floor. Letting the coaches know this early may keep them from becoming frustrated later.

At halftime, with Villanova leading 34–27, the talk is about the floor. "I'm afraid to do anything but take baby steps," Lembo said. "You slip now, you're done for the season."

Forte is concerned about Villanova's Rodney Taylor, who slipped coming down with a rebound and did a split, pulling something in his leg. "I just hope the kid isn't hurt badly," he says. "It'll be a miracle if we get through this without a serious injury."

Somehow, they do. Villanova wins 64–58 and the three officials leave the floor the way they like to leave at game's end: unnoticed. "Very good job," Lembo says as the three men shake hands in the locker room. "I can't think of anything we could have done differently."

"Nice job, guys," the security guard says, bringing them postgame sodas.

"We always hear that," Forte says, "when the home team wins."

He is back in the car heading for Washington thirty minutes after the final buzzer. He will arrive at his friend's house shortly after 1 A.M. and will stay up an extra ninety minutes, winding down and watching a tape of the game. By noon on Tuesday he will be on the road to Richmond to work Old Dominion–Richmond that night.

"Good game," he says, looking forward to it. "I'm with my buddy [John] Clougherty and my partner, Ron Foxcroft. Should be a good day."

February 2. . . Richmond, Virginia

Not even the power of the word "refs" can get Forte as close to the entrance of the Robins Center as he wants to get tonight.

It is pouring rain when he and Ron Foxcroft pull into the parking lot and Forte wants to park the car on the sidewalk next to the back door of the arena. "Can't let you do that," a security guard says.

"Oh come on, pal," Forte says. "We'll get soaked walking up from the lot. There's no one using this door, anyway."

"Sorry," the guard says, "I got orders."

Forte knows he is going to lose this argument. He can't even tee the guy up. So he goes for a laugh line. "Let us park here and we'll give you a couple of calls."

The guard, who is probably too wet to have a sense of humor, doesn't even crack a smile. Forte retreats to the parking lot and he and Foxcroft sprint from there for the door.

Inside, John Clougherty has already arrived, having driven up from his home in Raleigh. With Hank Nichols now semiretired to run the

NCAA's two-year-old officiating program, Forte and Clougherty are generally considered the top two officials in the country.

They are friends, but there is also an unspoken sense of competition between them. One of them will be chosen to represent the U.S. in the Olympics next fall.

Before focusing on the game, the three men exchange gossip. There are two members of the fraternity fighting cancer, Pete Pavia and Charlie Vacca. Both have had to stop working, at least temporarily, to receive treatment. "I worked with Charlie in Hawaii over Christmas," Forte says. "He seemed fine. Then I heard he had an attack down in Alabama and Lou Grillo saved his life."

Forte has heard right. Driving through an ice storm after a game at Alabama, Vacca had lost consciousness in the backseat of the car Grillo was driving. Grillo pulled the car over, yanked Vacca out of the car and tried to find a heartbeat. Finding none, Grillo administered CPR. Vacca started breathing again. Fortunately, because there was little chance of getting an emergency vehicle to them in the horrible weather, a passing car told them they were little more than a mile from a hospital. Vacca recovered.

Later, telling the story, Grillo would shake his head and say, "Actually, we were lucky in a lot of ways. Suppose a police car had happened by and seen this black guy sitting on top of a white guy pounding on him? That wouldn't have been too good a deal for me."

Forte is the referee tonight. He goes through all the various possibilities, talking in referees' lingo. As in most professions, referees have a language of their own. Some of the slang expressions they use are things like:

- *Freight-training:* When a trail official races downcourt and takes a call away from the lead official who is in better position.
- *Pop the whistle:* Blowing the whistle when you think maybe you shouldn't.
- *Spraying:* Too many calls.
- *Phantoms:* Never make a call if you can't see what happened. If you call something that isn't there, you're making phantom calls. A good official will resist the urge to pop the whistle and in doing so won't be guilty of spraying or calling a bunch of phantoms.
- *Rubber-banding:* A good crew rubber-bands, all three men moving, in effect, together, so that they are always in position.

- *Straight-lining:* Officials need angles to make a call. If you have a straight line between yourself and the play, the odds are you can't see what's going on.
- *A marriage:* Tonight's game is a marriage between the Sun Belt Conference and the Colonial Athletic Association. In other words, a split crew of officials.
- *Laramie:* Strictly a Forteism as in, "You give the head coach more Laramie than the assistants." Laramie is rope.

Tonight, Foxcroft has a play for Forte. "Saw it on television last night," he says. "Guy shoots a three-point shot. Defender deflects it. It goes in. Two points or three?"

"Two," Forte says. "The three-point shot is dead as soon as the ball is deflected."

Foxcroft and Clougherty shake their heads. "Wrong. It's still three. The latest Atlantic 10 directive talks about it."

Forte is already reaching for his rule book. "That's wrong," he says. "I'll prove it." He is still looking through the rule book when it is time to go onto the floor. As they leave, he presents Clougherty with a new Fox40, complete with a ridge that has been added for comfort.

"It's the new improved Fox Forty," Forte says.

"Yeah, just like Kellogg's corn flakes," Foxcroft says. "It means we can raise the price."

Even though this is a nonconference game, it is an important one to both schools. Each is scrambling for postseason position. Richmond is 15–3, Old Dominion 13–5. Early in the game, Richmond Coach Dick Tarrant is on all three officials. "I think they let an old guy [fifty-seven] like me get away with more than a young guy," Tarrant says later. "I take advantage of it. Why not? You need every edge in this game."

During one argument, Forte points down at Tarrant's foot, which is across the line of the coaching box.

"Dick," he says, "you've got a wing tip on the line."

"Joe," Tarrant shoots back, "I'm glad the game's so easy you've got time to look at my feet."

Forte laughs. Officials will often cut a coach extra slack if he says something funny. Hank Nichols, generally considered *the* referee of the last twenty years, tells a story about an argument he had one night with Jim Valvano. "Jimmy was all over me about a call. So, finally, I said, 'Okay Jimmy, that's enough. I don't want to hear another word.'

"Jimmy says to me, 'Hank, can you tee me for what I'm thinking?'

"I said, 'No Jimmy, I can't tee you for what you're thinking.'"

"And he says, 'Okay then, I think you suck.' I had to let him go. It was too good a line to tee him up for."

Richmond controls the game until a flurry of missed free throws in the closing minutes makes it close. The Spiders finally win, 82–75, after a drawn-out last few minutes.

"I didn't think it would ever end," Clougherty says.

"Tom Young never quits," Foxcroft answers.

Forte has his head buried in the rule book, still trying to prove he is right about the deflected three-point shot. He is well on his way to losing his second argument of the night. No matter really. He is happy with the game.

"Last night, when I looked at the tape of Villanova–Georgetown I noticed that when I was in the center position I was much too close to the play. I was so close on a couple of plays the kids could have passed me the ball. Tonight, I backed off. It was better."

He is back in Washington by midnight. On Wednesday, he will fly to Raleigh to work Virginia–N.C. State. "Good game," he says. "The kind that gets you pumped up very easily."

He will be up early in the morning, though. "I want to call around and see what I can find out about that three-point deflection play."

February 3 . . . Raleigh, North Carolina

As soon as Forte's plane lands, he races across the street to the Triangle Inn, the airport motel, knowing that Nolan Fine and Tom Fraim are there. He has confirmed that he was wrong on the three-point deflection play, but he wants to see if they will answer the question correctly or not.

They both come up with the right answer. Fine is in town to work Duke–Georgia Tech in Durham. Fraim will be with Forte and Rusty Herring at Virginia–State. They leave Fine to his afternoon nap and head off in search of food.

Once again, Forte is working with a strong crew. Fraim is retiring at the end of the season after twenty-three years as a ref. He worked the infamous regional final in 1987, during which Bob Knight pounded the courtside telephone after Fraim teed him up for coming out of the coaches' box. Fraim's only regret is that he didn't tee him up again after the outburst.

Rusty Herring, the third official, is a rising young referee. He reached the Final Four for the first time last year and drives a car with a license plate that reads, "Luv2Ref." His wife's license plate reads, "LuvARef."

Fraim is the referee tonight. His pregame talk is very detailed. He even has notes that he refers to. Fraim is into details: "On a foul-out, make sure the guy coming in is coming in for the guy who fouled out . . . If there's a time-out called after a foul-out, make sure they sub before the time-out . . . Be careful administering free throws. Make sure you get the right shooter. Watch for guys going into the lane. We've been getting beat on that . . . Let's have good visible counts . . . Try not to get straight-lined . . . Remember to suck on the whistle sometimes. Let's not pop it too much in this game . . . Make sure you give the player's number on a time-out call."

This last detail is one of those little-known things about officiating. Why does it matter which player on the floor called a time-out? Answer: If there is confusion later in the game about whether a time-out was called by a team or by television, there is a specific reference in the scorer's book as to which player called the time-out.

Fraim also makes reference to the emotions involved in calling a technical foul. "If we tee someone up, let's help each other. There's always that extra shot of adrenaline when you do it, so let's not look dumb by going to the wrong foul line or something. Let's call it, administer it, and get it over with."

Technicals are taken very seriously in the ACC. Any time an official calls a technical in an ACC game he is required to call ACC Supervisor of Officials Fred Barakat that night to tell him what happened and why he called the tee.

Fraim adds one more thing: "If a coach comes out of the box because he's coaching, give him some leeway. If he's bitching, it's automatic, tee him up."

Forte, drinking his nightly ration of pregame honey, has one more thought when Fraim is finished: "Let's not call anything cheap early. Let's talk to the kids, rather than whistle them. This is an important game so the coaches might be hyper, especially early."

Reynolds Coliseum is slightly less than sold out. Although Virginia is 4–2 in league play, they are still thought of as a doormat. For State, this is a big game. The Wolfpack is 3–2 in the ACC and has a four-game losing streak against Virginia. The Cavaliers always give them a hard time.

Tonight is no different. No one leads by more than four points during the first half. Seven minutes in, when Herring calls a foul on Charles Shackleford, Valvano is up screaming. Forte stands directly in front of him, facing the floor, saying out of the side of his mouth, "Easy Jim, easy." He was right. Valvano is hyper.

When Herring calls an illegal screen on the last play of the half that allows Virginia to tie the game at 39–39, Valvano screeches all the way across the court, heading for the locker room.

In the locker room, Fraim asks Herring about the last call. "The screen gave them an open jump shot, Tom," Herring says. "I didn't have any choice."

"Absolutely right," Fraim says.

In preseason clinics, officials were instructed endlessly about advantage/disadvantage. The point being that not all contact is a foul, that if something mildly illegal happens that doesn't affect the play, it should be no-called. The good officials are living by the rule. A lot of bad ones still call every touch foul they see.

"I almost popped the whistle on your toss, Tom," Forte tells Fraim. "It was a little short."

"Good thing you didn't," Fraim says laughing. "At my age I can only get it up good once a night."

"It's a pretty slow tempo," Forte notes. "That means every call is an important one."

The game is close until State goes on a 10–2 run for a 62–52 lead. Virginia comes right back with an 8–0 run. The game goes to the wire. A Mel Kennedy three-pointer cuts State's lead to 71–69 with 1:14 left. But Vinny Del Negro hits a crucial drive with thirty-five seconds to go that ices it and State wins 75–69.

"Great game," Forte says when it is over. "Both teams really played well. Del Negro is a hell of a player."

Nolan Fine, who insists that Forte is by far the best official in the country, believes that Forte's appreciation for the game is one of the things that sets him apart from other officials. "He played the game and loves it so much that he's studied it to the point where he just *feels* the game better than the rest of us," Fine says. "Joe never looks like he's working out there. It all looks easy because he loves it."

This game Forte loved. "A game like that, I stand on the floor before it starts, looking around, hearing the band, and I get needles in my legs," he says. "I feel so lucky to do something I love and get paid for it."

On Thursday, Forte will be in Washington for a game in an almost empty arena between two struggling teams, St. Joseph's and George Washington. "But to them, Forte says, "it's a big game. So to me, it's a big game."

February 4. . . Washington, D.C.

The crew working St. Joseph's–George Washington is a remarkable one, considering that this is a game between two not very good teams in the Atlantic 10. Forte is the referee. Luis Grillo is the U–1. Tim Higgins is the U–2. In April, all three of them will work the Final Four.

Higgins is one of the more popular officials around. His colleagues call him Barney Rubble because he looks and sounds exactly like the Flintstones' cartoon neighbor. Before the game, Barney is talking about arenas he would like to work. "I've never had a game in Rupp Arena," he says. "I'd like to work there."

"I've never been in Pauley Pavilion," Forte says. He turns to Grillo. "Of course, I love working at Mount St. Mary's."

Grillo is assistant athletic director at Mount St. Mary's, a Division 2 school.

Forte's pregame is simple. "Let's remember that both these teams need a win," he says. "They're probably both going to be tight and maybe a little frustrated."

It is GW that is frustrated. The Colonials have been playing horribly since New Year's and are buried near the bottom of the Atlantic 10. Tonight will be another miserable game for them. They stay close for a half, leaving with the score tied at 27–27. But from a 36–all tie, St. Joseph's goes on a 20–4 romp that puts the game away. The Hawks go on to win, 67–55.

It is not an easy night for Forte. He gets poked in the eye on a first-half play and needs Grillo and Higgins to up-periscope and freight-train in to make a call he can't see. Late in the first half, one of the St. Joseph's players sidles over to him and says, "You know that guy ain't got no game."

"Who?" Forte asks, thinking the player is talking about one of the GW players.

"Him," the kid says, pointing at Grillo. "That ref ain't got no game." Forte resists the urge to tee the kid up and instead tells Grillo the story at halftime.

Late in the game, with St. Joseph's on the foul line, Forte makes the GW cheerleaders stop pounding their megaphones against the wall, which in the quiet, empty gym reverberates all over. "Why did you do that?" Higgins says afterward.

"They shouldn't be doing that," Forte says.

"But they were doing it all game," Higgins answers.

"They were?" Forte says. "I didn't notice until then."

He is tired. Friday, he will fly home to Atlanta for a day off. On Saturday, he will be in Columbia, South Carolina, with his partner Donaghy to work Clemson–South Carolina.

"Intrastate rivalry," he says. "Big game."

Every time Joe Forte walks on the floor, he tells himself he is working a big game. That is one of the reasons why he is so good at what he does. He's a ref. And proud of it.

13
BUCKLING
DOWN

The days are passing too fast for Billy King.

"I was sitting with some friends the other day and one of them said, 'Do you realize it's just eighty-eight days to graduation?' I hadn't even thought about anything like that. The time is just slipping away so quickly. College is almost all over for me."

Many college basketball players see their last game as the end of their college experience. Billy King isn't one of them. His last game will, in all likelihood, be an ending for him because he is not likely to play pro basketball. But it will also be the start of many beginnings for him. At twenty-one King knows what many basketball players never know: There is life after hoops.

"I've taken the approach this season that this is it, my finale, and I want to make it memorable," he said, eating Chinese food one afternoon. "If I get a shot to play pro ball, that's great, wonderful. But the odds are I'm going to be working nine-to-five next year. This is my last time around. The last time I'll hear the cheers and be the center of this kind of attention. I want to savor it all."

King is in a perfect place to have that kind of season. He and his roommate, Kevin Strickland, are the only seniors on a young but talented Duke team. Two years ago, when King and Strickland were sophomores, Duke won thirty-seven games, the ACC Tournament, and the East Regional, and came within two baskets of beating Louisville for the national championship.

Five seniors, four of them starters, two of them All-Americans (Johnny Dawkins and Mark Alarie) graduated off that team. In 1987, picked for sixth in the ACC, the Blue Devils won twenty-four games and reached the NCAA round of sixteen. Now, four starters are back from that team. Still, in most preseason polls, Duke went almost unnoticed. They were in almost no top tens; some national polls didn't even rank them in the top twenty-five.

By the end of December, the Blue Devils were 6–1, their only loss at top-ranked Arizona, and they were in everyone's top ten. But it was a month of turmoil and, although none of it directly involved him, King felt partly responsible.

Duke began the season with four very easy victories over Appalachian State, East Carolina, Northwestern, and Davidson. But on December 13th, sophomore center Ala Abdelnaby ran his car off the road into a tree. He was charged with reckless driving (although he later pleaded guilty to "unsafe movement") and was fined twenty-five dollars and court costs.

King was hardly surprised by Abdelnaby's mishap. The first time he had ever driven with him, Abdelnaby had wheeled out of a parking lot so fast that King almost got out of the car. Abdelnaby was bright, funny, and popular with his teammates. But he was also immature. It showed up in his play—and his driving.

By this time, exams had started and two members of the team were struggling. One was Joe Cook, a freshman. The other was Phil Henderson. That was the more serious problem. Henderson had flunked out the previous year as a freshman, so if he flunked out again he was gone. Four days after Abdelnaby's accident, Coach Mike Krzyzewski called a team meeting.

"He was as angry as I've seen him in four years," King said. "He couldn't believe how undisciplined we had all been. Three guys out of twelve in trouble is a lot. Here we were with a chance to have a great team and we might screw the whole thing up before we'd played one big game. He told Kevin and me that part of being a friend is to crack down on guys when they need to be cracked down on. He was really, really pissed."

Things calmed down. Henderson and Cook got their minds on their books and came through finals okay. The players went home for four days at Christmas to regroup for the tournament in Arizona, which would be their first real challenge of the season.

The tournament in Tucson was good . . . and bad. On the first night, Duke blitzed Florida, a team that had won the preseason NIT a month earlier. King, in his role of defensive stopper, guarded All-American Vernon Maxwell and shut him down. For King, this was something of a revenge game. In high school, during an AAU summer tournament, Maxwell had made two free throws to win a game after King had thrown a bad pass. After the game, Maxwell was gracious. "Makes us even," he said to King, who had been thinking the same thing but wouldn't say it.

The next night, though, Sean Elliott got even for Maxwell—and more. He torched King for 31 points and Arizona beat the Blue Devils 91–85 in one of the better games of the year. "The best I've ever guarded," King said. "He's 6–8 and has those long arms. Most guys I can get up and give them trouble when they take their shot. But he just shot over me all night. He was great."

King has had a reputation as a defensive specialist since high school. Krzyzewski can still remember a summer camp game in which King was assigned to Michael Brown, a hotshot shooter from Dunbar High School in Baltimore. "He just shut him down totally," Krzyzewski said. "I turned to my assistants and said, 'I have to have him.' "

King, whose father died when he was four, was raised by his mother, grandmother, and sister. They did good work. King is articulate, funny, and bright. He is the kind of person everyone likes—except for the people he is guarding.

"I've always loved defense," he said. "Even when I was little, I was never a great shooter. I can remember when I was ten years old, I couldn't make free throws. I still can't. But I could always play defense and it was always fun for me. I liked to think I could do things on defense other guys couldn't."

Krzyzewski saw this in King. He had thought when King first came to Duke that he would improve his offense as the years went by. But by his senior year he knew that wasn't going to happen. "Billy is unique," he said, "in that he focuses so much of his concentration on defense. Even when we're on offense, I think his mind is on defense. Most kids are the other way around."

Krzyzewski would have liked for King to produce more on offense.

He had pushed him for three years to work on his shooting. At times he had threatened to bench him if he didn't improve on offense. But he never did, because even when he wasn't scoring, King's defense and his leadership on the floor were imperative for Duke to be successful.

After the Arizona loss, Krzyzewski lectured his team about being soft in tough games. This was something he worried about with this team. There was no one on this Duke team, he felt, like Danny Meagher or David Henderson, two of his past players who would break an arm to win a game. He told his players they had lost to Arizona because they had thought winning would be *nice*—instead of thinking winning was an *absolute necessity.*

The next four games were relatively easy victories: William and Mary, Miami, Virginia in the ACC opener, and St. Louis. But Krzyzewski wasn't happy. Their play was sloppy. After St. Louis, he told his players, "If you improved a lot you'd be deplorable. You're ripe to be picked."

Players almost never believe coaches when they hear things like this, especially when they are 10–1 and ranked fifth in the country. But Krzyzewski knew what he was talking about. Two days later, Maryland came to Duke and stunned the Blue Devils, who immediately got down 12–2 at the beginning of the game and were then outscored 8–0 in the last three minutes to lose, 72–69. Now, King and his teammates understood what Krzyzewski had been talking about.

"What really made us mad was that Maryland didn't even play very well and we still let them win," King said. "We gave them too much respect. We knew they were talented but we forgot that so are we. We played tentative. The next few days in practice were like preseason again. We had a lot of cockiness knocked out of us. We didn't like the way losing felt and the only way to make up for it was to win at Carolina."

Duke wins at North Carolina about as often as the Chicago Cubs contend for the pennant. The Blue Devils won there in 1966. They repeated the feat nineteen years later in 1985. Twice in twenty-two years. But they had to win now. No big deal, right?

To change things a little, Krzyzewski took his team to shoot in the Dean E. Smith Center the day before the game. To everyone in the world, the 21,444-seat palace was the Deandome. At Carolina they always call it "Smith Center." It is a reflex action. Say "Deandome" in front of someone from Carolina and they say, "Smith Center," as if you had pressed a button and gotten a tape. "Smith Center, this is a recording."

The Deandome is a tough place for a visiting team to play for one reason: the opposition. Carolina is always good, more often than not excellent, occasionally great, and once every ten years virtually unbeatable. But Krzyzewski is not intimidated by Dean Smith, a fact that was evident the very first time they met.

Carolina won the game 78–76. This was in the last year of the old Big Four Tournament. Krzyzewski, then thirty-three, was brand new to the ACC. When Smith, thinking he was victorious, ran over to shake his hand, there was one second still on the clock. Krzyzewski shook him off, saying, "The damn game's not over yet, Dean!"

Smith won that one and eight of the first nine in which the two men met. But slowly, as he built his program, Krzyzewski began to catch up. They had split their last six meetings going into this game in the Deandome, uh . . . "Smith Center, this is a recording."

Duke blew to an early eleven-point lead, which was hardly unusual. Over the years, Carolina had made a habit of falling behind early at home, often way behind, then rallying and finding a miraculous way to win.

In the ACC this phenomenon is known as The Carolina Piss Factor. A Piss Factor game is one where you are winning, you are about to win, you have the game won, and then something strange happens, you lose and *you are pissed*.

Duke has been the victim of as many Piss Factor games as anyone. In 1974, the Blue Devils led Carolina by eight points with seventeen seconds left—and lost in overtime. Walter Davis scored the tying basket on a forty-foot shot that banked off the top of the backboard and went in at the buzzer. Piss Factor. In 1984, trying to deny Carolina a perfect ACC regular season, Duke had a two-point lead with nine seconds left and Danny Meagher on the foul line. Meagher missed, Matt Doherty raced downcourt, appeared to travel, shot off-balance, and the ball went in at the buzzer. Carolina won in double overtime. Piss Factor.

In 1986, in the inaugural game in the Deandome—Smith Center, this is a recording—Krzyzewski was hit with two first-half technical fouls that were so bad that Fred Barakat, the league's supervisor of

officials, criticized the calls on television at halftime. Carolina won by
three. Piss Factor.

This one had all the makings of another Piss Factor game. Slowly
but surely, Carolina whittled the lead away in the second half. But
there was another factor at work in this game—the King Factor. King
was guarding Jeff Lebo, Carolina's point guard and best outside threat.

In high school, King and Lebo had roomed together at summer
camp and they had remained good friends. Lebo was an anointed
player, a coach's son who seemed born to play basketball. He had been
recruited by everybody, yet there had been little doubt that he would
play at Carolina. He had been an All-ACC player as a sophomore and
was this year's Designated Talker in the Carolina locker room. If you
wanted to hear some pablum, you headed for Lebo.

In a Piss Factor game, Lebo would be the guy who hit the off-balance
three-pointer at the buzzer. But King wasn't going to let Lebo do much
of anything in this game. Everywhere Lebo went, King went. When
the game was over, Lebo had taken fourteen shots—and hit two.

In the final two minutes, neither team could make a big play. Caro-
lina got the last shot—twice—and couldn't hit either time. When
Lebo's last shot of the game hit the rim and bounced to Danny Ferry,
Duke had a 70–69 victory. It wasn't pretty but it didn't matter—it was
only the second game Carolina had lost during three seasons in the
Deandome—Smith Center, etc. . . .

King felt this was a breakthrough victory for his team, not just
because they had *competed* with a top team—they had *beaten* that
team. Two years earlier when the '86 team had won this kind of game,
the key players on the '88 team—King, Strickland, Ferry, and Quin
Snyder—had been complementary players. And the fifth starter, Robert Brickey, had been a high school senior.

"I think until that Carolina game, we were still trying to find an
identity as a team, King said. "Kevin and I still hadn't really made this
our team as captains. We knew we were good, but *how* good? Coach
K kept telling us we had to learn how to fight our way through tough
situations. In Chapel Hill, we did that."

The King–Krzyzewski relationship was an interesting one. Although
Krzyzewski remembered King's impressive performance against Michael Brown, King remembered a summer camp game in which he
guarded Reggie Williams, the future Georgetown star, as the one
where he established his reputation as The Defender. Other than that,
they disagreed on almost nothing.

Krzyzewski was a defensive coach and King the ultimate defensive player. "Of all the kids I've had at Duke, Billy probably knows what I'm thinking during a game and takes pride in it more than any of them," Krzyzewski said. "Kids believe in what you're saying in varying degrees. Billy, I think, more than anyone, has always believed in me. If I say something is so, he believes it and, as he's gotten older, he's become the guy who gets the other kids to believe it."

Even though the Carolina victory was gratifying, Krzyzewski still wasn't convinced this team had the kind of get-down-in-the-mud guts that the '86 team had. When he watched the tape of the Carolina game, he saw a lot of things he liked, but he also saw some plays at the end when his team had looked scared. The difference in this game and others against the Tar Heels was that Carolina had looked just as scared.

The next two games were virtual walkovers for Duke: a victory over an outmanned Wake Forest team and a not-too-pretty win at Stetson. That set up the biggest week of the season: four home games in seven days, against Clemson, Georgia Tech, N.C. State, and Notre Dame, the last one a national TV game (clearly the type of game a coach plays only because the athletic director tells him to).

Well rested, the Blue Devils started the week by hammering Clemson, 101–63. "That's the best team I've seen in the four years I've been in the ACC," Clemson Coach Cliff Ellis said. "They don't allow you to do anything."

Two nights later, the Blue Devils were almost as good. They built a big lead early against Georgia Tech, let the Yellow Jackets get back to within four, then put the game away early in the second half, winning 78–65.

The defense was there every night for Duke. The question, as had been the case in 1987, was the offense. Against some teams, like Clemson, the defense created so many easy baskets that the opposition was never in the game. But against the really good teams, if they had to run a halfcourt offense to score, the Blue Devils were vulnerable.

That was Krzyzewski's concern with N.C. State coming to town. If Valvano got the kind of pace he wanted and was able to run *his* halfcourt offense, State would have the advantage. With Shackleford and Brown inside, the Wolfpack had a combination Duke simply couldn't stop.

Valvano had mixed emotions approaching the game. He still wasn't sure what kind of team he had. Since Hawaii, the Wolfpack had been up and down. They had opened conference play with a great victory, beating Georgia Tech in Atlanta on a tip-in at the buzzer by Brian Howard. But then they had turned around and lost at Wake Forest, a game so disheartening that Valvano couldn't even look at the tape afterward.

"We had the game won," he said. "We've got a five-point lead in the last two minutes. It's over. My teams don't lose those games. But we lose it. I want to be sick just thinking about it."

That loss was followed by a 77–73 loss at home to North Carolina; it wasn't a shock to lose but it hurt. If you are going to have a big year, it is the kind of game you win. Then came a crossroads game at Maryland. Valvano told his team this was a game it *had* to win and, after blowing a big lead, the Wolfpack won it, 83–81. Vinny Del Negro hit the winner just before the buzzer. "We lose that one, we maybe go in the toilet," Valvano said. "Instead, we feel good about ourselves, go home and beat DePaul and Virginia."

The Virginia victory put State at 13–4, 4–2 in the league. Duke was 15–2, 5–1 in the league. Valvano was convinced the Blue Devils were the best team in the conference. "They are a great college basketball team," he said. "They do a great job taking you out of your offense, they have a great player in Ferry, they're deep and they are well coached."

Valvano believed all this. He also believed he could go to Duke and win. He had always had success at Duke and against Krzyzewski—ten wins in sixteen games. Some of the time this had been because State just had more talent. But there were psychological factors involved too. When Valvano took a team to Carolina, he almost never believed he could win there. As a result, his players followed his lead. Valvano was 0–8 in Chapel Hill. But Duke, even when it has an excellent team, never has overwhelming athletic talent. Valvano always thought he had a chance against Duke and that belief filtered down to his players.

There was also this: Valvano believes he will win most close games because he has Valvano on his side. His former coach, Bill Foster, once said about him: "Jimmy thinks he's the best coach there is, period."

Valvano denies this . . . sort of. "I've never put my mind into coaching 100 percent of the time the way some guys do," he said. "Those guys are the best coaches. If I put my mind to it all the time, then, yeah, I think I could be the best coach."

But for one game, give Valvano his choice of coach and he would, without question, take James T. Valvano. So, as the Wolfpack made the twenty-mile trip from Raleigh to Durham, Valvano was both confident and curious.

As *they* waited for the Wolfpack to arrive, the Blue Devils were antsy. They wanted to prove that the so-called State jinx was a myth. They also knew that a victory would put them in command in the ACC race.

The afternoon was a recruiters' dream: sunny and warm, the Duke chapel bathed in sunlight, making it impossible to believe it was still winter. Inside Cameron Indoor Stadium, hours before tip-off, the students were jammed in tight.

Cameron is college basketball's best-known fun house. It is ancient, small (8,564 seats), and because Duke is one of the few places left that believes the students deserve the best seats, they sit surrounding the court on all four sides. What's more, they honestly believe that part of their job at a game is to come up with some clever way to throw the opponent off.

Over the years, when State has been the visitor, this has meant doing things like throwing aspirin at Moe Rivers after he had been arrested for stealing a bottle of aspirin, throwing red-and-white underwear at two players who had stolen some underwear, delivering pizza to Lorenzo Charles after he was involved in the mugging of a pizza delivery man, and waving car keys at Clyde Austin after it came out that he had two cars, a Cadillac and an MG.

Sometimes, the Duke students go too far. In 1984, they had spelled out R-A-P-E at Maryland's Herman Veal and thrown condoms and women's underwear at him after he had been accused of sexual assault on another Maryland student. Scolded for that, the students made a superb comeback the next week against North Carolina: They presented Dean Smith with two dozen roses before the game, eschewed the "bullshit" cheer that has pervaded gyms everywhere in favor of "We beg to differ," and, instead of waving their arms at foul shooters, held up signs which said, "Please miss."

In short, when you came to Cameron, you never knew what was waiting for you. Today, the students were mild. When they saw referee Lenny Wirtz come on the floor, they serenaded him with their traditional "Oh no, not Lenny" chant. When Valvano came out they chanted, "Sit down" at him. Ever clever, Valvano sat—on the floor.

The students liked that, but they had a comeback: "Roll over, roll over." Valvano wasn't going that far.

The game was as tense as the pregame had been fun-filled. King was guarding Del Negro and holding him in check, but Chris Corchiani, now entrenched as State's point guard, was taking advantage of Duke's overplaying defense, consistently penetrating to either score or set other people up. And, Rodney Monroe was coming off the bench to give State a boost when it most needed one.

Duke's defense took command in the last four minutes of the first half. Trailing 29–28, the Blue Devils finished the half with a 14–3 binge, helped by a stupid behind-the-back pass by Shackleford that King stole and fed to Strickland for a three-point play. For ten minutes in the second half, Duke stayed in control. Two Ferry free throws with 10:44 left made it 59–44. What jinx?

This jinx: Monroe hit a three-pointer. Corchiani made a pair of free throws. Monroe hit another three, Corchiani two more foul shots. That made a 10–2 run, courtesy of the freshman guards, and it was 61–55. The Duke students were less jovial now. Quin Snyder, clearly nervous, threw a silly pass and Del Negro got loose for his first field goal of the game. Howard made a three-point play and Shackleford powered inside. *Wham-Bam* the run was 17–2, and State led 62–61 with 6:01 left.

From there, it was anyone's game—except that one team was *hoping* to win, the other believed it *would* win. Krzyzewski put King on Corchiani down the stretch and King cooled the little guard off. But Del Negro now had room and he took advantage of it, hitting a ten-footer that put State up 73–72 with 1:50 left, and a gorgeous, jump-catch-and-shoot backdoor lay-up that made it 75–72. Duke had one last chance, trailing 75–74 with seven seconds left when Del Negro missed a free throw.

Ferry rebounded and thought he saw Phil Henderson open for a lay-up. But as he reached back to try to throw the long pass, Ferry, who almost never makes fundamental mistakes, lost control of the ball. His pass went right to Chucky Brown. Seconds later it was over, 77–74 State.

For Valvano, this was the biggest win of the season. His team had gone into a hostile gym, hung in for thirty minutes against a good team playing well, and made the big plays in the clutch. Everyone had helped: Monroe had 17 points, Shackleford had 16, Corchiani 15. Del

Negro, held in check most of the day, only had 12 but he got them when they counted most.

"We could be a pretty good club before this is over," Valvano decided. "But now, we've got to play like this consistently." Every coach can find a "but" line in a victory. This time, though, Valvano was hard pressed.

The feeling on the other side could not have been more different. The Blue Devils weren't just unhappy, they were angry. King, normally the last one out of the locker room because he will answer every single question, was out in a flash. "I'm just so pissed off I don't know what I could say to anybody," he said. "There's no way you can be a good team and blow a 14-point lead at home."

That was exactly the way Krzyzewski felt. Again, he had the sense that, when it counted most, his team had played scared. He was most upset with Snyder, who had been outplayed by a freshman—Corchiani —and hadn't seemed to know what to do in the final minutes. "Quin is playing to protect his spot, instead of being aggressive," Krzyzewski said. "To one degree or another they're all protecting. That's just no good."

He glanced at a picture of the 1986 team that hung on his office wall. "I'll tell you one thing. This team isn't anywhere near where that team was," he said. "It isn't so much talent, although that team did have more talent. What this team doesn't have is a motherfucker."

In the coaching vernacular a motherfucker was a guy the other team just didn't want to mess with. Del Negro was that kind of player; so, to some extent, was Corchiani. Meagher and David Henderson had played that role in the past for Duke. Now, there was a void, and Notre Dame was coming to town looking to knock off a top team. The Irish were rested, the Blue Devils tired and frustrated.

It was a game Duke easily could lose because in the long run, it didn't matter. The team was going to be in the NCAA Tournament regardless. It would have been easy to rationalize a loss and go on from there. But King wouldn't let it happen.

In pregame the next day, he was on his teammates in a very un-Kinglike manner. Snyder, who was being benched by Krzyzewski, caught the brunt of King's anger. "You can't play scared, Quin," he told him. "Go out and be angry. Prove to Coach K that he's wrong."

King had a major assignment for the day himself: He was to guard David Rivers, the All-American point guard. Rivers's importance to Notre Dame was best summed up by the Duke students who, as the Irish were introduced, chanted, "One-man team, one-man team."

That wasn't true in this game. Sophomore guard Joe Frederick, averaging 6 points a game, was 9-for-13 and had 23 points. At halftime, the Irish led 35–32. King had held Rivers in check for twenty minutes, but could he do it for forty? And would fatigue set in after two games in twenty-four hours and four games in seven days?

With 12:20 left, Notre Dame still led 48–44. King was giving Rivers absolutely no room to breathe. When Forte called him for a foul early in the second half, King, who calls all the officials by their first names, yelled, "Come on, Joe, don't protect him because he's a star."

"I'm not, Billy, you fouled him."

King smiled. "I know."

Rivers saw no humor in the situation. "After he told the ref not to protect me, they never called anything on him the rest of the day," he complained later. Rivers had no right to complain; the fact that he did was a mark of how frustrated he was by King. Rivers is not a whiner. After this game against Billy King, he whined.

It was Snyder, playing aggressively, who made the basket that got Duke going. He hit a three-pointer that cut the lead to 48–47. A moment later, King drove the baseline and put the Blue Devils up for good, 49–48. Then, to put an exclamation point on the day, he hit a ten-foot jump shot, something he had done in most leap years during his career.

It was over after that. Duke cruised home, 70–61. This was King's day. Rivers finished with 9 points on 3-of-27 shooting and turned the ball over 4 times. "When he started slapping at my hand on inbounds plays, I knew I had him," King said.

King, the nonscorer, also hit 5 of 7 shots and had 11 points. It was the first and only time in his senior season that King would score in double figures. For Rivers it was the first and only time in his senior season that he would *not* score in double figures.

With thirty seconds left, Krzyzewski took King out to what was undoubtedly the loudest standing ovation ever given in Cameron for a player who had scored 11 points. King, being King, understood how special this day was for him.

"A year from now David Rivers is going to be playing in the NBA as a first-round draft pick," he said. "He'll be making six figures and then some. I'll be working at a desk somewhere, fighting rush hour traffic every day."

King smiled. "But I'll always have the tape of this game. And when I'm old, I'll pull it out and show it to my kids and say, 'You see, the old man could play a little defense in his day.' "

February 9–10. . . Philadelphia

If you care about college basketball as a sport, about its history and its traditions, then you must make a pilgrimage at least once a season to the Palestra.

The Palestra is to college basketball what Fenway Park and Wrigley Field are to baseball. It is a place where you *feel* the game from the moment you step inside. The popcorn smells like college basketball, the noises are those of the game: the crowd, the bands, the players, the coaches. All of it. Even though the old (born in 1927) place was given a $1 million sprucing up in 1986, complete with new paint and new seats, it still feels old. Most of the seats are still bleacher-style. The locker rooms are tiny and the seats are close enough to the floor that the crowd is always part of the game.

Things have changed, as they inevitably must, over the years at the Palestra. Once, all the schools in Philadelphia's Big Five—Villanova, Temple, LaSalle, St. Joseph's, and Pennsylvania—called the Palestra home. All of the traditional city games were played there, usually as the second half of a doubleheader. The first game would bring a major national power to town, then would come the Big Five game. The gym was smack in the middle of the Penn campus but it belonged, really, to the city and to The Game.

The Palestra still considers itself at least a part-time home for all five schools. It is the only arena in America that has national championship banners hanging for two schools: LaSalle (1954) and Villanova (1985).

But when big dollars came into college basketball, the Big Five schools were lined up like everyone else to grab some. Villanova joined the fledgling Big East while Temple and St. Joseph's joined the Atlantic 10. LaSalle became part of the Metro Atlantic. The conferences were where the TV money was—especially in Villanova's case—and were the schools' route into the NCAA Tournament. The City Series games became less and less important until, in 1986, it looked as if they might end completely.

Temple and Villanova no longer wanted to play home games in the Palestra. Villanova had built a new arena and Temple wanted to build one. What's more, when you played in the Palestra, you split the money, taking away the financial home court advantage.

More and more in recent years, local rivalries in college basketball have gone the way of the dinosaur. The teams in power don't want to play the weaker teams because they somehow fear that a loss might knock them off their pedestal. And, they know that a big local win could revive a rival that is down, making them a threat again. The attitude is: Forget the fans, who love local rivalries, and forget the fact that there is plenty to go around for everyone these days.

Georgetown Coach John Thompson is a perfect example of this kind of thinking. Every year Thompson sprinkles his schedule with teams like St. Leo's and Morgan State, teams so bad that no one should be asked to pay money to watch them play. In the meantime Thompson has dropped Maryland, George Washington, and American from his schedule. He also refuses to play Howard University.

He is not alone. For years, Kentucky would not play Louisville. Dean Smith won't play any in-state teams other than the ones in the ACC. Alabama will not play Alabama–Birmingham. Heck, Hawaii won't even play Chaminade.

Dan Baker, the executive secretary of the Big Five, did not want to see this happen in Philadelphia. He knew he had no chance to keep the City Series in the Palestra as it had been in the past. So, he struck a compromise. Beginning with the 1986–87 season, the designated home team in a City Series game could choose the site. This meant that Temple and Villanova would get their home games on campus and it meant that Penn, LaSalle, and St. Joseph's could continue to have theirs in the Palestra. The new contract was for ten years.

"It took hours and hours and hours of talks to get this," said Baker, an unfailingly polite, soft-spoken man. "I think it's a shame that some of the people involved don't have more feel for the tradition of Philadelphia basketball. But this was better than losing the whole thing altogether."

That much is true. There are not nearly as many games in the Palestra as there used to be. But they do still play here and, when they open the doors on a cold winter night, there are few better places to be.

Tonight is a doubleheader night. Game one is LaSalle–St. Peter's, two teams unbeaten in the Metro Atlantic Conference. Game two is one of the great traditional rivalries in the sport: Princeton–Penn.

Jam-packed, the arena can seat almost ten thousand people. The crowd tonight is 6,297. They come streaming in off 33d Street, working their way to the front door. Only when you are within ten feet of the building can you read the sign that says, "The Palestra." Since the building opened sixty-one years ago, it has hosted more college basketball games than any gym in America. It is a place where even the bathrooms could tell stories if they could talk.

LaSalle–St. Peter's will not go down with any of the Palestra's more memorable games. LaSalle has the best player on the floor in Lionel Simmons and, even on a night that is not his best, Simmons is good enough, with fifteen points and eight rebounds, to produce a 56–47 victory.

Princeton and Penn is the main event. For the last twenty years, these two teams have *been* the Ivy League. Since 1968, when Columbia beat Princeton in a playoff to win the league championship, only Brown, in 1986, has interrupted the Penn–Princeton stranglehold on the league. Penn has won ten titles, Princeton eight during that time.

The difference between the two schools, besides the fifty miles that separates the two campuses, is in coaching. Tom Schneider is in his third year at Penn and is one of five different coaches to win the Ivy League at the school during the last twenty years. He is forty and ambitious. Like his predecessors, he probably won't be at Penn for life.

One man has coached Princeton since 1967. He is Pete Carril. He has won eight Ivy League championships, several of them with mirrors. Carril is fifty-six and, in all likelihood, will end his career at Princeton. When he retires, he will do so as one of the most revered figures in his profession. The consensus on Carril among his peers is that he could probably take five charter members of the Daughters of the American Revolution and find a way to contend in the Ivy League.

Certainly, the Ivy League isn't what it was in the 1960s or even in the 1970s, when Princeton had Bill Bradley and the Hummer brothers and Chris Thomforde, and Penn had Craig Littlepage, Dave Wohl,

Steve Bilsky, Bob Morse, Phil Hankinson, and Tony Price. In 1965, Princeton reached the Final Four. In 1979, Penn equaled the feat. No Ivy League team is likely to get that far any time soon. But that doesn't mean the intensity in the league is any less or the games less fun.

In another life one suspects that Carril was Yoda, the diminutive *Star Wars* Jedi who taught Luke Skywalker about The Force and how to use it. In his blue sweater, Carril waddles around, scrunching up his face in anger when his Jedi screw up.

No game in the Palestra can really get underway until the traditional throwing of streamers after the first basket by the Philadelphia team is complete. Hassan Duncombe (pronounced *Dunk-em*), a huge Penn freshman from Brooklyn, scores the first basket, and the blue-and-red streamers come from everywhere.

But this is, after all, the Ivy League, and no self-respecting Ivy League school is going to come to a game as big as this one without an answer for a bunch of streamers. So, when Princeton freshman Kit Mueller ties the game, the Princeton fans pelt the court with blue-and-orange marshmallows. Take that, Big Five.

That out of the way, Yoda puts his team into the weave he loves to use to confound the opposition. Stop running for one second against a Princeton team and you will be back-doored into oblivion. Even if you know the Tigers are looking for just that, you're still going to get burned.

Yoda loves these games. He is into every play. When he spots an illegal screen that the referees miss, he turns to press row and screams, "That's an illegal screen—write that down!" Everyone writes it down for fear of ending up on the dark side of The Force. Princeton leads 34–26 at halftime. Penn, with superior athletes, rallies in the second half to within 36–34.

But the Quakers never get even. They get to within 58–55 with twenty-one seconds to go but John Thompson, Jr., the son of the Georgetown coach, calmly makes two free throws to ice the game. Princeton wins 60–57.

It is career victory No. 364 for Yoda. No big deal. He puffs on a dead cigar, squints through his glasses to look at the statistics, and sounds very much like the wise old Jedi that he is. Someone notes that Penn did a good job defending against the weave in the second half.

"Defending us well is no surprise," Yoda says. "We have a lead, we blow the lead. This senior class has been doing that since they walked into school. The school paper says I should play more guys. Maybe they're right. I have about half a brain so I'm a little slow."

He goes on. "Coaching isn't very hard, you know. My players tell me how to coach. The way they play tells me what I tell them to do. If a guy can drive, I tell him to drive. If a guy can shoot, I tell him to shoot. If a guy can pass, I tell him to pass."

Of course. Yoda shrugs. "You do what you can and then at the end of the game, everybody's grandmother makes three-pointers against you and none of it matters."

Someone wants to know what Dave Orlandini, a senior and a leader of the team, has given Carril this season.

"Headaches," Yoda answers.

"It's not a hard game to figure, you know," he says, still lecturing. "Take Tim Neff. He was fifth in a class of five hundred. He always does his schoolwork. You can't separate the player from the man. If a guy is a clown on the court, he'll be a clown in life."

Yoda waddles out. His team is 12–5 now and 4–1 in the Ivy League but he isn't impressed. The clock and the three-point shot have taken some of his control of the game away. He knows this team is vulnerable. When the season is over, Cornell will be the Ivy League champion. But on the last night of the season, Yoda will give young Mike Dement, the Cornell coach, a lesson he will remember; Princeton will beat the Big Red by 29. That will be career victory No. 369 for Yoda. He will shrug, light another dead cigar, and be back next year.

In the meantime, on a cold night in February, he and his team have added one more memory to a building already full of them.

The next morning, Rollie Massimino was up before six o'clock. He was on one of his exercise kicks and before he went to the office, he would stop at Pat Croce's gym to work out. "I'm gonna lose at least 15 pounds and get down to 210," Massimino vowed. His friends found this amusing. They figured the workout regimen might last a month. They were closer: It would be three weeks and the six pounds lost would be eaten back on in March.

But it didn't matter. Massimino was happy again. He was back to being Rollie the Magician, the Little Coach Who Could. Villanova was also back—16–6 and on its way to the NCAA Tournament. As for the dire predictions of a finish near the bottom of the Big East, the Wildcats were 7–3 in conference play; Rollie didn't have to carry out his threat to jump in the Schuylkill River if his team finished in the league's second division.

All fall, Massimino had suspected that he had a pretty good team. But it wasn't until the first weekend of the season, playing in the Maui Classic in Hawaii, that he knew for certain 1987 would soon become just an unhappy memory. "Before then I thought we were okay, but I didn't know," he said. "I was still a little afraid. We needed to get a win over a good team early to get our confidence back."

That crucial win came in the second game of the season. After beating Nebraska easily in the opener—Massimino's thirty-second straight victory in an opener on the high school and college level—the Wildcats played Illinois. Every season, Lou Henson has one of the more talented teams in America. And every season, one way or the other, the Illini don't live up to their potential. One night they are devastating, the next night they are devastated. In 1987, two weeks after beating the Indiana team that would win the national title, Illinois was knocked out of the NCAA Tournament in the first round by Austin Peay. Name the city where Austin Peay is located and you win two tickets to Illinois' next game against the Governors.

In Kenny Battle and Nick Anderson, Illinois had one of the best forward combinations in the country. But Villanova upset the Illini 78–76. The next night, in the Maui final, the Wildcats led Iowa at halftime before getting blown out in the last five minutes. That was okay, though, at least as far as Massimino was concerned. They had found out they could play with good teams again. "The whole week over there was critical for us," Massimino said. "We practiced outdoors, had pool parties and spent time together. We started getting the old Villanova feeling back again."

There are many who look cynically at Massimino and his claims that his team is a family. Big-time hoops is big-time hoops, right? Wrong. This is a program where the kids eat milk and cookies together after early morning preseason workouts and call the coach "Shorty" for the very simple reason that he's short. Winning is important but so is having fun. And yet, there is no doubt about who is in charge, first, last, and always.

The Hawaii tournament set up a solid December, marred only by a pair of one-point losses, one to St. Joseph's and one to Auburn. There was an early league game thrown in, a victory at home over Connecticut, but that didn't prove much.

Then came January and a trip to St. John's. Alumni Hall is as tough a place to win as there is in the Big East. Yet Villanova went into the game completely confident of victory. "Sometimes, you look at the kids before a game and you know they're going to win the game," said Assistant Coach John Olive. "That was the way we felt before St. John's."

The feeling was right. Villanova led the whole night and won, 69–62. Eyebrows went up around the East Coast. A victory over Boston College followed, and then came the stunner, an 80–78 upset of Syracuse. The Orangemen had not played up to their No. 1 preseason ranking, but they were still as talented as anyone in the country. When Villanova beat them to go 4–0 in the Big East, a lot of the 'neers started to come back.

Massimino didn't want to make a big deal of anything yet, although he was starting to get excited himself. Publicly, all he would say is, "We're more mature this year. A little more aggressive. Tom Greis has grown up into a player, Plansky is more confident, Doug West has become a star, and Kenny Wilson is confident running the team."

All of this was true. But it didn't take Massimino to tell people this. Anyone watching the Wildcats play could see that Greis had truly become a force inside and that West, when he was on, could play with anybody. What people couldn't see, and what Massimino didn't talk about, was what was going on inside the team. Villanova was having fun again.

Winning games was certainly part of this. Putting the Gary McLain ordeal behind them was part of it, too. But there were also factors people couldn't really fathom unless they were there. Like Pat Enright.

If there has ever been a Walter Mitty story in college basketball it is Pat Enright. As a freshman at a Division 2 school, Merrimack College in Massachusetts, he was cut from the team. A year later he transferred to Villanova. He dreamed of following in the footsteps of his brother Mike, who had played for Massimino as a walk-on, graduating in 1984. "I worked out all summer before my sophomore year," Enright said. "I really got better. When tryouts came, I was ready."

And he got cut again.

He went back to work. All summer, once again, he worked. When a friend asked him why he was working so hard at a sport where he clearly didn't have the ability to be a star, Enright shrugged and said, "I just like to play."

He went out for the Villanova team one more time in the fall. One more time he was cut. But during semester break that winter, reserve guard Veltra Dawson decided to transfer. Massimino had an extra spot on the roster. He called Enright, who was home on Christmas vacation, and asked if he was still interested in walking on. Enright was back in Philadelphia the next day.

He got to play fifteen minutes in mop-up roles that season and forty-five more minutes in 1987. He worked hard and was popular with his teammates. When the Wildcats played their last home game against Syracuse, Massimino started him—as a farewell gift. The season ended, Enright got his degree in communications and began thinking how he wanted to go about pursuing a career in radio and television.

But, at the same time, Massimino came out of his recruiting season empty-handed. He was player-shy, especially at guard. Enright had only played two seasons in four years of college, so he had another year to play if he wanted. Once again, Enright didn't hesitate. He came back, took out a second major in English, and began to get some playing time.

More than just a backup guard, Enright was important because he made the team laugh. He is a gifted mimic who did, among others, a brilliant Massimino. His rendition of Assistant Coach John Olive doing a scouting report usually brought the house down, and his back-of-the-bus Frank Broyles—"Keith, aah have never seen an ath-a-lete laak Bo Jackson in maa laaaf"—was always in demand.

"That little strap," Massimino liked to say. "I don't think I'm ever gonna get rid of him."

Massimino didn't want to get rid of Enright or anyone on this team, not with all the pleasure they were giving him. The undefeated Big East joy ride had ended in Pittsburgh on January 16 in a game that left Massimino more than unhappy and not just because the Panthers won easily. Once again, he and Paul Evans were jousting, each claiming the other had ditched the postgame handshake. The publicity surrounding the nonhandshake was unpleasant for Massimino, who admitted that he had planned before the game not to shake hands with Evans but changed his mind because the Wildcats lost and he didn't want to look like a sore loser.

This time, Massimino was angry with Evans for comments that had appeared in the *Philadelphia Daily News* just before the game. Evans had been quoted as saying that Massimino had "fallen in love with himself" after winning the national championship and had "alienated a lot of friends." Evans said later he thought he had been off the record when he made the comments. On or off the record, Massimino was incensed. Knowing this, Evans might have assumed Massimino wouldn't shake his hand and walked off the floor too soon. Either way, it made for more childish sniping back and forth. "He wouldn't shake my hand . . ." "Wrong, he wouldn't shake mine." And so on.

Safely out of Pittsburgh and with Evans behind him—at least for four weeks—Massimino and the Wildcats came up with victories at Connecticut and at home against Seton Hall before hitting their first real slump of the season, a home loss to St. John's and a shocking loss at Providence in which an 18 point second-half lead evaporated.

Now the team faced its first true crisis of the season. Georgetown was coming to town and that was never an easy game. A loss would drop the Big East record to 6–4, and with the heart of the schedule still coming could be disastrous. But in the very strange "humidity" game that Joe Forte refereed to in The Spectrum, Villanova built a big lead thanks to horrid shooting by the Hoyas and hung on to win 64–58. "We lose that one and the kids start to wonder all over again," Massimino said later. Providence was exactly the kind of game we had never lost before last year. It brought back bad memories. We wanted to get rid of that in a hurry."

The key to the game was Greis who refused to back down to Georgetown's swarming big men and came up with 21 points and an amazing nine blocked shots. That was more blocks than he had produced his entire freshman year and continued his extraordinary one-year improvement program. "He's still such a strap," Massimino said. "I have to kill him more than anybody to keep him going. He's still got sixty floors to go before he gets anywhere near his potential."

Massimino wasn't complaining. Without Greis, work ethic or no, it would be very difficult for this team to Find a Way against the good teams. After Georgetown, Villanova played well enough to win and got past Boston College in the Boston Garden. That gave the team a 16–6 record—one more victory than it had produced in all of 1986–87.

That victory put the Wildcats back in the Top Twenty—at No. 20—and set up a showdown with Temple, which had just ascended to No. 1 in the polls. Remarkably, in all the illustrious years of the Big Five, this was the first time one of their teams had been ranked

No. 1 in the regular season. The game would be at Temple, at McGoni-gle Hall. Its 4,500 seats would be packed to the rafters. The Philadelphia papers placed the game—in importance—only slightly ahead of developments in the Middle East.

"I love it," Massimino said, staring at a huge front-page headline ballyhooing the game. "This is the way it oughta be."

He had finished his workout and was back in the office with his assistants, looking at tape. Massimino looks at tape the way archaeologists study hieroglyphics. You can never look too often and there is always something you will miss if you don't look that one extra time.

Massimino had no doubts about how good Temple was. He respected John Chaney as much as any coach in the business and he knew the Owls wouldn't turn the ball over, partly because point guard Howard Evans was one of the most underrated players in the country, but partly because Chaney's teams *never* turn the ball over. They fear his wrath too much to do so.

Which was all fine with Massimino. He now believed that this team could compete with anyone. Beyond that, he knew that most people hadn't figured that out yet. It was exactly the position he loves to be in: a good team that isn't taken seriously. The underdog.

"This team isn't as good as the '85 team was," he said as a Temple–LaSalle tape droned on in the background. "But I have the same kind of feeling with these guys that I had in '85. They're a bunch of nuts but they know how to win. They find a way."

That the Wildcats are nuts is apparent during their pregame meal. Before the meal, Father Bernard Lazor, the team's chaplain for the last fifteen years, performs a mass. Then, everyone eats. And then the talent show starts.

Remember, this is about four hours before tip-off. Some coaches do not allow their players to *talk* during pregame meal because they are supposed to be focusing all their thoughts on the upcoming game. Massimino thinks that's silly. So do his players. There is only one rule at pregame meal: All rules are null and void. Anyone can be a target.

Today's show begins with a sing-along. Senior Manager Neil McShea (doing the high notes) and freshman redshirt Paul Vrind—a 7-2 center from the Netherlands—(doing the low notes) lead the team in a raucous and fairly decent version of "Under the Boardwalk."

Then it is Enright's turn. First, he does Olive, hunching his shoulders, dropping his voice, and hollowing his cheeks. It's very good. Then, urged on by his teammates, Enright does Massimino. "Remember, you *must* rebound the basketball." He is just starting to go into the part about having fun when a familiar voice in the back interrupts.

"You little jag, you better sit down."

Enright sits. Even Massimino can't keep a straight face.

"I think," Olive says as Massimino heads home for his pregame nap, "we're ready to play."

As it turns out, *both* teams are ready to play. The only shame in this game is that it isn't played in the Palestra, because in the storied history of Philadelphia basketball this game will rank right near the top. In his pregame talk, Massimino speaks about what this kind of game means.

"In all the years you kids will play basketball, this is an opportunity you will get very few times," he says. "You are playing the number one team in the nation and that means the whole nation is watching. But there's more. You are getting to play in Philadelphia as an underdog. That doesn't happen very often at Villanova.

"The game Saturday against Boston College was a lunch-pail game. We just had to get the job done and we did. Now we can put the lunch-pail under our arms and step out into the limelight."

He paused. That was Olive's signal to take the players through the matchups. More fuel, no doubt, for Enright's imitation. When Olive was finished, Massimino went through highlights of the scouting report on the board. Each time he finished a diagram, one of the managers jumped forward to erase the board. When he was finished, he had one last thing to tell them.

"In terms of attention, this is the biggest game many of you guys have played in. A lot of people would love to be in your shoes tonight. Go out and enjoy it."

With that, he sent them out on the floor to warm up. He sat down and shook his head. "I'm getting too old for this," he said. His eyes were shining with anticipation. Clearly, he would *never* be too old for this.

The game was a classic. Villanova was up 8–0 before Temple had a chance to breathe, West nailing two three-pointers in the first minute. Calmly, Temple came back, tying the score at 12–12 on a jumper by Mark Macon, the baby-faced freshman whose scoring had given Temple the added dimension that made it a special team this year.

From there, they raced to halftime like two sprinters not willing to back off from a torrid pace. It was 41–40, Temple, at intermission, Macon's soft baseline jumper giving the Owls the lead.

Massimino floated through the intermission on a cloud. On the outside, he was his usual unraveled self: hair disheveled, shirt hanging out of his suit, tie undone. But inside, he was Gene Kelly, singin' in the locker room.

"If you guys think after that half that you need to take a backseat to any team in the country, you're nuts," he said. "Temple has shot the hell out of the ball, we're playing in their house and we're down one. This is a great game. You have to be a great team to play in this game."

He wanted some changes. To Wilson: "Kenny, you are not going to make Howie Evans eat the basketball. Don't jump out at him. Jump straight up." To Gary Massey: "Don't chase Macon so much. Drop back a step every once in a while." To Rodney Taylor: "Don't foul back. The officials always see the second foul. You foul back and I have to take you out of the game."

Overall, though, the plan was the same. Rebounding was still the key. "Box out and play and you'll win the game," Massimino said. "You know you can play at this level. You've done it for twenty minutes. Now let's just go out and find a way."

They went out as if they fully intended to do that. A Plansky three-pointer put them up 45–43 and a Wilson jumper made it 47–43. A couple of minutes later, Wilson grabbed a rebound, raced through the Temple defense and hit a gorgeous, driving scoop shot as he was fouled. The free throw made it 53–47 with 15:51 left. McGonigle was stunningly quiet.

But Temple had not gotten where it was just on talent. It was not about to wilt. Mike Vreeswyk, the Rambo-look-alike junior, hit a three-pointer. Tim Perry hit a hook. Wilson answered and Vreeswyk hit another three to make it 57–55.

It was the kind of basketball that you see once a season—if you are lucky. Every shot was contested, yet they kept falling. Every possession was vital, both teams trying to dig in and take control. There was no dirty play, no yapping between the players, no whining at the referees by the coaches. Just chest-to-chest basketball.

With 9:40 left, Macon, who seems to float into the air for his jump shot, tossed in a three-pointer. Temple led 66–65. West promptly answered from seventeen feet. But Vreeswyk came right back with yet another three and Temple was up 69–67 with 8:43 left.

As it turned out, Villanova never got even again. Temple just wouldn't make mistakes and Macon was in a zone that only great players are able to reach. He stripped Greis and went all the way for a lay-up. Then, with the shot clock running down, he cut across the lane and hit a *lefty* hook shot. If any shot did in the Wildcats that was the one. It was unanswerable.

Forced to foul down the stretch, Villanova watched Temple hit all its free throws—twelve of twelve in the last two minutes. The final score was 98–86, but it had been closer than that and everyone knew it. Temple had shot 56 percent from the field including 9 of 13 three-pointers. Macon was 14 of 20 and had 31 points. Vreeswyk had 19 and Evans had 17 and 20 assists—2 shy of the all-time NCAA record. For Villanova West had 27 and Wilson had 25.

"Temple just played a national championship game, they were that good," Massimino told his players. "You did everything we asked of you. Don't hang your heads for even a minute. We're going to do a lot of good things before this season is over."

They had already done a lot of good things. But Massimino was right. There was more to come.

February 13. . . Fairfax, Virginia

In the seventeen days since George Mason's overtime victory over American, the Patriots had been riding high. American had been their fourth straight victory, a streak they had since extended to nine. They had won at James Madison, at East Carolina, and at North Carolina–Wilmington, all important conference road victories. They had also beaten Virginia Commonwealth in a nonleague game—an impressive victory.

On the surface it seemed that all the screaming and yelling and disciplining that Rick Barnes had done early was finally paying off. To some degree, that was true. But just as important, Barnes felt, was his decision to back off, to give the players a little more breathing room.

"It's a little bit like with your first kid," he said, finishing breakfast on a rainy winter morning. "You make all your mistakes with them. That's the way I guess it is with your first team as a head coach.

"I was making the kids too uptight. I think they probably felt like they were in the army or something. So, I stopped going to breakfast with them every morning so they wouldn't feel like I was watching them. I stopped making them wear jackets and ties on the bus. Instead, I told them to all wear their George Mason sweats—they would be comfortable but would clearly be part of the same team. I stopped bringing them back to walk-through the night before games. Instead, we just give 'em pizza and send them home. I started coming to pregame meal at the end instead of being there the whole time.

"I think it's helped. They feel more relaxed but they know the discipline is still there. We still talk to them once a week about their schoolwork, or more often if they get in any trouble. This team has been through a lot, most of it because of me. Now, some of it's paying off. I'd be disappointed if they didn't finish strong."

Barnes had loosened up a little but he hadn't become Mr. Chips by any means. One night after practice he had asked his three seniors—Amp Davis, Brian Miller, and Darren Satterthwite—why they thought the team was playing better. Miller had answered for all three: "Coach, we just don't want to deal with you when we lose."

That answer didn't thrill Barnes. He didn't want basketball to become something his players dreaded. He wondered if that's what had happened. He had ridden his best player, Kenny Sanders, unmercifully at times. He had made them practice day and night at others. But they *were* producing. "Next year I'll be a better coach," Barnes said. "But for now, I think the kids understand why I've done what I've done. At least I hope they do."

Barnes was much too high-strung to be happy with a 16–6 record (or even with the fact that his team was first in the Colonial Athletic Association with a 7–2 record). Richmond was coming into the Patriot Center for what was shaping up as one of the biggest games in school history. The American game had drawn less than three thousand fans. This one would draw closer to seven thousand. Richmond and George Mason were clearly the class of the CAA. Just as clearly, only one of them—the postseason tournament winner—was going to get an NCAA bid.

For just that reason, Barnes didn't want his team making this Richmond game into too big a thing. He wanted to win, to establish in his players' minds that they could beat the Spiders. But he also wanted them to understand that win or lose, their biggest and most important games would be the ones in the Hampton Coliseum during the first week in March—the tournament that would determine the NCAA invitation.

Barnes had been telling his players that all season: Their goal was the NCAA Tournament and they should work toward being at the top of their game by the CAA Tournament. He thought that they finally understood that. He thought that until he walked into the locker room before the Richmond game.

It was quiet, much quieter than normal. None of the normal banter and whisperings. The players had been reading and hearing what a big game this was. They had believed it. "You know, no matter what we do tonight, win or lose, you're going to walk off the floor with a piece of first place," Barnes said. "This is like any other game. Play defense and rebound and you'll win. But *don't* think this game will make or break your season. It won't. If you win, you're still going to have to beat them again in March. If you lose, they're still going to have to beat you again in March. So go out, play like hell, and come back in here spent. That's all I ask."

As soon as the team had left to warm up, Barnes shook his head. "They're too tight. That's what I was afraid of."

He walked down the hall to where the Patriot Club, the GMU booster group, was having its pregame party. Barnes may be the only Division 1 coach in America who goes to talk to his team's fans while his team is on the floor warming up before a game. At a place like George Mason, he does those little things to build the program.

Barnes will usually talk for two minutes or so about the game, then pray there aren't any questions. Usually, someone will ask why someone isn't playing more or about changing defenses. Tonight, though, there are no questions. "I think," Barnes says going back down the hall, "they sort of knew I didn't want to hang around."

Barnes has one other concern: the officials. Twelve days ago, during the game against Virginia Commonwealth, Barnes had angrily charged a couple of feet out of the coaches' box to yell at one of his players. Hank Armstrong, generally considered the CAA's top referee, had been refereeing the game.

If Hank Armstrong has a problem as an official it is ego. Older and wiser people in his profession have counseled him to be less of a "tough guy" on the floor, always trying to prove that he is in charge. Armstrong was standing between Barnes and his player during this incident. When Armstrong saw Barnes screaming in his direction, he thought Barnes was getting on him. Angrily, he pointed Barnes back to the coaching box. As soon as Barnes realized that Armstrong thought he was yelling at him, he jumped back, avoiding a technical foul.

The next day when Barnes saw the tape of the game he realized that from Armstrong's angle it easily could have looked like Barnes was going after him. Knowing Armstrong would be working his games again before season's end, he called him to apologize.

"But he really didn't accept my apology," Barnes said. "He was angry. He said I had shown him up and I better not ever do it again. I tried to explain to him that he had misunderstood. But I don't think he heard me. He was upset."

It is exactly this kind of reaction by officials that makes coaches crazy: *"You showed me up."* Jim Valvano tells a story about an official walking over to him in the middle of a game while Valvano was getting on him and saying, "If you show me up, I'll tee you up."

Valvano was furious. "Did the guy think that fourteen thousand people came to the damn game to see him work? Did he think all eyes were on him? What crap that is, 'Don't show me up.' That's the problem with so many of these goddamn guys. They think they're the fucking stars. They're not. But they don't know it half the time. That's why I'd rather not shake hands with them before the game. They're not my friends. They have a job to do and so do I. Leave it at that. But don't give me this 'Don't show me up' crap. I don't want to hear it."

Barnes, hearing it on the phone, felt the same way. Now Armstrong was working Barnes's biggest game so far. So was Donnie Vaden, a talented young official Barnes liked. But he also remembered the notebook Joe Harrington had left him, listing the strengths and weaknesses of the league's officials. Next to Vaden's name Harrington had written, "gutless."

The officials had little to do with the first half. Richmond was as tight as George Mason. The Spiders did lead 11–4, but GMU came right back to lead 12–11. They proceeded that way until the last 3:30 of the half when both teams virtually shut down with the score tied 34–34. After Rodney Rice put Richmond up 37–34 with 3:15 left, neither team scored the rest of the half.

Barnes wasn't happy, but he was calm. "These guys don't think we can play with them," he told the team. "You have to get the ball inside where we can score. You're giving up on the offense too quickly."

Walking back to the floor, Barnes said to his assistants, "I could rip them but they might overreact if I did. Let's just stay calm for a while."

The second half was much like the first. Richmond led for the first twelve minutes, but never by more than four points. Finally, Amp Davis, who had been struggling all night, hit a three-pointer that put the Patriots up 52–51. The lead got to 56–51 before Rice hit a three-pointer to make it 56–54. With 4:18 left, Ken Atkinson, the Richmond player Mason most wanted to see shoot, hit another three-pointer. Richmond led 57–56.

Now, both teams struggled on offense. The Spiders hit a free throw, the Patriots missed several shots. But Kenny Sanders was fouled while going for a rebound. He hit both foul shots to tie the game at 58–58 with fifty-five seconds left.

Then came confusion. When Sanders went to the line, Barnes told Amp Davis that if Sanders hit both shots, Davis should call for a zone defense. But if he missed, Davis should call man-to-man. Davis heard wrong—and with the score tied called for man-to-man. With Barnes screaming for his players' attention, the ball went inside to bulky Peter Woulfolk who scored easily with thirty-nine seconds to go.

Now it got wild. Davis missed from three-point range with fourteen seconds left. Sanders got the rebound but it slipped out of his hands and out of bounds. There were eleven seconds left on the clock. Richmond inbounded and Mason immediately fouled Mike Winiecki—put in the game by Coach Dick Tarrant because he could shoot free throws. Winiecki made two with ten ticks left to make the score 62–58. Davis came down and hit a drive to cut it to 62–60. Now there were only four seconds remaining. Again, Mason fouled right away, this time getting Scott Stapleton. He missed, Sanders rebounded and urgently called time. There were two seconds still to go.

Barnes had two things he wanted to try on the last play. He wanted to throw a pass to midcourt to Sanders, knowing he was the player Richmond would focus on. There was a chance the Spiders might get overzealous and foul. If Sanders caught the ball and there was no foul, he was to throw it immediately to Miller, who'd be cutting for the corner. Miller would then catch the ball and shoot in one motion.

Before the ball was inbounded, Barnes walked over to Armstrong and

Vaden and said, "Watch carefully on this play. They're going to foul Sanders. Be watching."

Sure enough, as Sanders cut crosscourt to catch the pass, Steve Kratzer bumped him. Vaden was right on the play. Was it a foul? Maybe. But in this kind of situation, very few officials are going to call anything. And, it can be argued, they *shouldn't* call anything—unless the action is so flagrant and strong it legitimately changes the result of the play. In this case, no foul was called.

Sanders caught the pass, turned and flipped it toward Miller. But the pass was deflected. By the time Miller caught up to it, the buzzer was sounding. He grabbed the ball and threw it up from the corner anyway—and it went in.

Clearly, the shot had come after the buzzer. But Barnes tried to steal the call, racing out with his arms up, giving a three-point signal. The officials weren't buying it. They knew the shot had been late.

So did Barnes. Walking off the floor, he turned around and said, "No way the shot counted, right?" Right. That didn't bother Barnes. Vaden's noncall did, especially when he remembered what Harrington had written about him.

"Joe called that one," he said. "It would have taken a lot of guts to make that call and he didn't make it."

In fairness to Vaden, it took guts not to make the call. Sanders had caught the pass, meaning that the bump had not caused him a disadvantage. But Barnes isn't paid to be objective. He asked his managers to get him a tape right away. Barnes looked at the replay and saw the bump. That was enough for him.

Barnes strode down the hall to where the officials dressed and asked if they were still inside. Told they were, he was about to knock on the door when it opened. Armstrong, Vaden, and the third official, Allen Felts, emerged. "Donnie, I just looked at the tape and you missed a foul on the last play," Barnes said to Vaden.

The officials didn't stop. "I'll look at it," Vaden said.

"*Look* at it? What good does *that* do? I told you there was going to be a *foul* and you looked right at it and didn't call it. You know it and I know it."

Vaden kept walking. Armstrong didn't. He stopped, turned as if to say something, then just shook his head and turned to leave.

Barnes looked at his athletic director, Jack Kvancz, who had witnessed the scene. "Now I've really got 'em pissed off, don't I?"

Kvancz nodded. But neither one of them knew yet just *how* pissed off.

February 17. . . Knoxville, Tennessee

Don DeVoe still had his sense of humor. "Maybe I'll just walk onto the floor tonight and wave a white handkerchief," he said. "Or maybe I'll just tell the team in the locker room to go out there without me and bring back a win. They walk out there without me they'll probably get cheered."

This was a day for gallows humor. "It's almost time for my dealer to give me a new car," DeVoe went on. "Maybe, I'll ask him for a van."

Times could hardly have been tougher for DeVoe. Kentucky was coming to town that evening for what was always the biggest game of the season. The Tennessee team it would meet was reeling. In the four weeks since the Volunteers had beaten Auburn, raising their record to 10–4, they had lost five of seven games, dropping to 12–9. Even more damaging, they were only 5–7 in the Southeast Conference.

But even that didn't begin to tell Tennessee's tale of woe.

After the victory over Auburn, the Vols had played Florida. The game had been close for thirty-five minutes. But in the last five minutes, with Tennessee fouling, Florida pulled away. The final was 76–56. It was Tennessee's worst home loss in twenty-six years.

A victory over Mississippi State soothed things briefly, but then came a loss at Alabama—and Alabama was clearly beatable.

Things quickly went from bad to worse. Two days after the Alabama game, starting guard Elvin Brown was arrested in a Knoxville record store for shoplifting. When DeVoe asked Brown what happened he admitted his guilt. DeVoe felt he had no choice. Brown was the team's third-leading scorer and best defensive guard but he had admitted to shoplifting.

"I'm just not going to have guys on my team who do that sort of thing," DeVoe said. "I told Elvin that. I told him that if he needed help, we would get him help and that I would try to keep him in school but that he couldn't play on my basketball team. If it means losing games or losing my job, so be it. I just can't coach any other way."

In their first game without Brown, the Volunteers, led by Dyron Nix's 28 points, pulled together and beat Georgia, 92–81. But then they lost at Mississippi and next, in their first national (cable) TV game of the year, they were pummeled, 90–62 at Vanderbilt. Three days later at LSU, also on ESPN, they were embarrassed again, this time 92–73.

DeVoe felt helpless and he could hear the wolves baying at his door. He was angry with himself, with his team, and with the situation. "No matter what I do, I can't seem to get this group to care enough about winning," he said. "When we lose, they don't *hurt* the way you should after a loss. The other night, Anthony Richardson had six turnovers. He's a *senior.* But he wasn't really hurt by it. Mark Griffin shot zero-for-five and didn't get a rebound in seventeen minutes—and he wasn't that hurt.

"Do I yell at them, scream, go crazy? Sometimes I really think they get tired of my bitching, but it hurts the way they play. To go into Vanderbilt and LSU and get beaten up that way, especially on television, was just awful."

DeVoe was exhausted when he got home Sunday after the LSU game. And discouraged. These were not easy times for him. The person he talked to most about his troubles was his wife, Ana. "After the LSU loss I said to Ana that, if truth be told, it would be a lot easier for Doug Dickey if he just made a change. That would give him a two-year honeymoon with a new coach. It might work out perfectly because there are five top juniors in this state next year and, for the first time since I've been here, none of them are from Memphis.

"A new coach can walk in here and if next year's senior class doesn't get it done, he can go out and recruit those kids with the new building as a lure and maybe be in Shangri-la in a couple of years. But I also told her that because Doug used to coach [football], I thought he understood coaching and that whatever happened he would be fair."

That evening, DeVoe and his wife went to bed early. Not wanting to be awakened, DeVoe turned off the telephone. Shortly after 8 P.M., he heard a loud knocking on his door. He got out of bed, went downstairs, opened the door and found Dickey standing there. He let Dickey in and then went upstairs to tell Ana who it was before going to talk to his boss.

Ana DeVoe was terrified. "She was sure Doug had come over to say he was releasing me," DeVoe said.

That thought had never really crossed DeVoe's mind. Dickey had come over because he had tried to call and, getting a constant busy signal, figured DeVoe had taken the phone off the hook. He had missed the Vanderbilt–LSU trip and was leaving town the next morning so he wanted to stop by just to give DeVoe a pep talk. DeVoe appreciated it. But his wife's frightened reaction triggered something in him.

"If *she* felt that way," he said, "I wondered what in the world the players were thinking at this point."

DeVoe had never directly addressed the issue of his job security with his team. He knew they were aware of the situation because it was impossible to be anywhere near Knoxville and not be aware of it. But he had never said anything to them because he thought doing so might make it a larger issue than it was. Now, however, he felt he had no choice.

"They had been asked about it all through preseason, then when we won nine of our first ten it faded for a while. But now it was back stronger than ever. It had become *the* thing to talk about in Knoxville."

The following day DeVoe walked into his locker room and, instead of talking about the Kentucky game two days hence, he talked about himself. "It doesn't matter what you've heard or what you've been told," he told his team. "If you think I'm quitting or if you're going to let up because you think you're going to have a new coach next season, you're mistaken.

"We still have one third of our conference season left. We've proven we can play good basketball. Kentucky may be a better team than we are. But on Wednesday, all we have to do is be better than them for forty minutes. That's all. No matter how good they are, they can only put five guys on the court at once, just like us."

Now it was six hours before the Kentucky game and DeVoe had no idea how his team would react to his talk. He only knew what a victory over Kentucky could mean. "In this town if you ask people in April what our record was during the season they won't be able to tell you," he said. "But if you ask them about the Kentucky game in Knoxville, they'll know all about it. That's the way it is. This is the biggest game of the year to people here.

"But I have no idea how we'll react tonight. I knew before the season started that this was a swing team. Right now, it's swung down."

DeVoe shook his head. He was a baffled, confused man. Always, he had known success in coaching, but now he was fighting for his job.

For the first time in his career, he found himself wondering exactly what the best thing was for him.

"You get to a point in a job where, if the people are really down on you, it might be best to leave, even if you think you're doing the job," he said. "I've thought about what I would do next year if I wasn't here. Maybe I would take a step back, take a year off and try to get some perspective on things. I have a young family, I could spend some time with them, then start back in another year, refreshed.

"But when I think about that I wonder what would happen in a year. In this business you take a year off and maybe getting a job isn't so easy. I don't mean just any job. With my background, I can't see myself coaching in a place where, realistically, you have no chance to win a national championship. I just couldn't do it. Basketball has been the most important thing in my life for forty-one years now. I just can't see myself coaching someplace where it isn't as important to everyone else as it is to me."

There were other frustrations. "I've always felt that Tennessee wanted a clean program and that's the way I've run the program here. In the last ten years, Vanderbilt and Tennessee are the only two schools in the SEC that haven't been under some kind of NCAA investigation at one point or another and I'm proud of that. I've never felt I could coach kids you made deals with, anyway.

"But is there a reward for that somewhere along the line? Maybe there is. Maybe running that kind of program will help me get another job if I lose this one. I don't know. I had seven straight good seasons at Tennessee and then two bad ones. Does that make me a bad coach? Or is Tennessee just going through the down cycle that almost every program goes through sooner or later? The whole thing has really been an ordeal. I lie awake at night wondering how in the world I can be coaching a team that accepts losing the way this one does. We work hard in practice but we just don't have a relentless drive to win. Whose fault is that? Mine? Maybe it is, I really don't know.

"I told them Monday that they were too concerned about themselves individually. Dyron Nix has been a great player for us this year but he needs to be more verbal and get on the other kids so I don't have to do it all the time. I really got on them, even though I didn't want to have to. I just didn't want them thinking that I had thrown in the towel. We're taking on water fast here—but we haven't sunk yet."

He smiled the gallows humor smile. "Of course, by ten o'clock tonight we could be doing some serious bailing."

By game time that evening, things had only gotten worse. A local TV station had reported that a deal had already been cut between DeVoe and the university. The newscaster said that DeVoe would resign at the end of the season and still be paid for the final year of his contract.

The report was wrong. DeVoe knew it and Doug Dickey knew it. But everyone else in Thompson–Boling Arena wondered—including the Tennessee players.

But one thing was correct: DeVoe's instinct that Kentucky would bring out the best in his team—and in the fans. The place was close to full, and when the ever-reticent Doug Roth started the game with a driving lay-up, the fans went wild. Tennessee roared to a 13–4 lead, the last three points coming when Griffin, who comes from a tiny town six miles from the Kentucky border, nailed a three-pointer.

Suddenly, the nightmares of the last few weeks were forgotten. Everything was falling for the Vols. When Greg Bell hit two free throws with 4:14 left in the half, the lead was 39–26. Three baskets by UK's superb point guard, Ed Davender, cut the halftime margin to 44–36.

Still, Tennessee had to feel good. It had kept Rex Chapman, The Boy King, in check and, for the first time in a while, was getting some solid outside shooting, most notably from Griffin, who had knocked in three three-pointers. And yet, DeVoe knew Kentucky would come back. At halftime he told his team that but also reminded them, "You've been better than them for twenty minutes, now just go and do it for another twenty."

It would not be easy. Down 50–42, Kentucky ran off nine straight points. Freshman Eric Manuel hit a jumper. Senior Winston Bennett got inside for a three-point play. Manuel hit again and Rob Lock posted up with 12:30 left to put the Wildcats up 51–50. Tennessee was in trouble. Once again, the cheers were turning to boos.

But the Vols didn't die this time. They stayed right with Kentucky, trading the lead back and forth until Nix scored three straight baskets, the last on a shattering dunk to make it 64–59 with 6:20 left. Kentucky came right back with an 8–0 run of its own. Tennessee went scoreless for more than three minutes. When Chapman, who would finish the night just five-of-fifteen, hit a turnaround jumper off the baseline, it was 67–64, Kentucky.

Now, Tennessee was surely finished. But no. Griffin hit one more three-pointer to tie it, then rebounded a Manuel miss and fed Nix. He was fouled and made both free throws for a 69–67 lead. Then came a flurry of turnovers. On the last of them, Roth was called for an intentional foul on Davender.

DeVoe was ready to tear his hair out after that call. By now, the crowd, which had been swaying back and forth with each basket, was almost limp from the intensity of the game. Tennessee had been just as good as Kentucky for thirty-nine minutes. But forty?

Davender made one free throw. Kentucky kept possession because of the intentional foul call and Lock scored to put UK up 70–69 with 1:15 to go. This time, Griffin's three-pointer hit the back rim. But Nix rebounded and was fouled. He could only make one, but it tied the score at 70–70. There were forty-seven seconds left. Kentucky brought the ball upcourt and called time. Thirty-seven seconds to go.

At this juncture, DeVoe did what very few coaches have the guts to do. Rather than lay back on defense and let Kentucky take the last shot, he decided to attack. "If they back-door you, fine," he said later. "But you don't want to watch the last basket go in on you as the buzzer sounds."

It makes sense, but few coaches are willing to chance it. DeVoe was. As Kentucky tried to set up on offense, Tennessee was trapping every pass. Finally, Manuel was trapped on the sideline. Clarence Swearengen slapped the ball loose. Manuel reached for it but it rolled off his hand and out of bounds. Tennessee ball. Ten seconds left. Time-out.

Now DeVoe wanted to spread the floor and let Swearengen use his quickness on Chapman. He had been effective all night, getting inside for 10 points and 8 assists. Swearengen caught the inbounds pass and went right, Chapman with him. He started a drive and as he did, Chapman slipped and fell down. Swearengen kept going. Now the defense had to come to him. When it did, Swearengen looked and saw Bell just behind him to his right. He fed the ball back to his teammate and as Manuel tried desperately to get to him, Bell, off balance, tossed up a ten-footer from the lane.

Swish. The buzzer went off before the ball was all the way through the net. It was over. Tennessee–72, Kentucky–70. Bell, lying on the ground, was being mauled by his teammates. Griffin, tears pouring

down his cheeks, was pounding on him and so was everyone else. The
arena was complete bedlam. DeVoe didn't need to wave any white
handkerchiefs on this night.

Games like this *make* college basketball. An undermanned team,
fighting for *something*—pride, a coach, an injured teammate—whatever it may be, finds a way to beat a superior team and the victory
produces memories that everyone in the arena will share for years to
come.

DeVoe was thrilled, but realistic. "We still have to go on the road
and find a way to win there," he said when the celebration was finally
over later that evening. He looked around at the huge arena, now dark
and empty. "Either way, though, I'll remember this one for a long
time."

He wasn't alone.

February 20. . . Chapel Hill/Raleigh, North Carolina

They weren't really sure how to feel in the Deandome today. North
Carolina had won a basketball game. That was hardly unusual. But the
way the Tar Heels won was both unusual and unsettling.

They had been facing a team that was struggling. Maryland had
talent, loads of it. But it was a team still searching for itself. Coach Bob
Wade had yet to figure out which parts went where and because of that
the Terrapins were not playing up to their vast potential. When they
came into the Deandome and promptly fell behind 28–11, there was
every reason to believe Carolina would go on and cruise to an easy
victory.

But it didn't happen. The Tar Heels couldn't take care of the
basketball and they couldn't hold on to the lead. Maryland cut the lead
to 30–25, thanks largely to the kind of mistakes Dean Smith-coached
teams almost never make. J. R. Reid, Carolina's superstar, turned the
ball over seven times.

Before the game was over, Jeff Lebo, Carolina's resident brain, had
committed as stupid a foul as can be committed—he jumped into
Maryland's Steve Hood while Maryland was trailing by four points and
out of time-outs. If Lebo had stayed away from Hood, even if his shot
had gone in, the game would have ended without Carolina even having

lack of improvement. As good as J.R. was, he still committed foolish turnovers (witness Maryland) and took bad shots. That had been okay a year ago, but not now.

There was more. Lebo wasn't comfortable at point guard. The only senior, Ranzino Smith, was so limited that Smith had to take him out of the starting lineup, something he hated doing. His replacement was Kevin Madden, a redshirt sophomore who had been forced to sit out a year because of poor grades. The top recruit for next fall was Kenny Williams, an excellent player but a suspect student who had yet to meet Proposition 48 requirements. Why was Dean Smith—whose greatest strength was his clean, untarnished reputation—suddenly recruiting bad students?

Smith doesn't talk about recruiting, one of his many rules. Everything is relative, of course. The chinks in Smith's armor might be considered strengths in many programs. And yet, sitting in the Dean-dome listening to 21,444 people make no noise at all while the Tar Heels were winning an important ACC game, one had the sense that all was not well in Paradise. . . .

Twenty miles and a lifetime away in Raleigh, things were pretty good. Georgia Tech was in town to play N.C. State and Jim Valvano was feeling good about his team. The Wolfpack, buoyed by its victory at Duke, had almost won at North Carolina for the first time in Valvano's eight years at State. They had lost in overtime but the sense was there that State could play with anybody. A win at Clemson on a night when Shackleford had to sit out with a bad ankle had reinforced that notion.

Georgia Tech was a hot team, too. After struggling through January, the Yellow Jackets had won four in a row, a streak started when freshman Dennis Scott hit a twenty-five-foot three-point shot at the buzzer to beat DePaul 71–70 on national television.

Tech's program was an interesting one. Bobby Cremins had become the coach there in 1981, taking over a program that was in shambles. Tech had been in the ACC two years and had a conference record of 1–29. Within three years, Cremins turned everything around. Recruiting with boundless enthusiasm and aggressiveness, he brought players like Mark Price, John Salley (now a star with the Detroit Pistons), and Bruce Dalrymple into the program.

to inbound. As it was, Hood made the two free throws and, because Lebo had stopped the clock by fouling, the Tar Heels had to inbound the ball again and make two more free throws before their 74–73 victory was secure.

"I didn't think Jeff fouled him," Dean Smith said, avoiding the question of what in the world Lebo was doing anywhere near Hood. "Give Maryland credit for a great comeback."

Wrong, Dean. If Wade had known what he was doing on the bench, Maryland would have won the game. Something was wrong at Carolina and no one, least of all Smith, really wanted to talk about it.

To make such a statement about a team that was 20–3 sounds ludicrous. But it was true. It had started in October with the murder/ suicide of Scott Williams's parents. Shortly after that, Smith started having trouble with nose bleeds. His doctor ordered him to cut back from two packs of cigarettes a day to eight cigarettes a day, which he did, often lighting a cigarette, taking three or four drags and then putting it out delicately so he could relight it a few minutes later.

Then came the J. R. Reid, Steve Bucknall assault/spitting incident in the Raleigh nightclub. Smith's initial comment on the incident was that Bucknall and Reid shouldn't have been in Raleigh. "I told them that going over there once a year to play was plenty," he said.

Two weeks after that incident, Smith, his wife, and his parents went to church at the Duke Chapel. When the service was over, Smith went to get his car, a brand-new Cadillac. As he was pulling out of his parking space, he was sideswiped by a Duke transit bus. Damage to the bus: about $20. Damage to Smith's car: about $2,000. No one said anything to Smith about not going to Durham except to play.

Once the season began, the Tar Heels, as usual, won a lot of games. Playing without Reid, they upset Syracuse in the opener and moved to No. 1 in the polls. They were upset by Vanderbilt, so they dropped. But for the most part, they won. They did lose to Duke at home but they beat N.C. State on the road, then Maryland and Virginia.

They were in first place in the ACC after the Maryland victory but something wasn't quite right with this team. Reid was such a big star, with his distinctive haircut, wide butt, and ability to take over a game, that it made Smith uncomfortable. This was a coach who had kept Michael Jordan from becoming bigger than his program, so he certainly didn't want Reid doing it. What's more, Smith was annoyed by Reid's

In 1985, Tech beat North Carolina three times—a remarkable achievement in itself—won the ACC Tournament, and reached the Final Eight of the NCAA Tournament. Cremins was *the* hot young coach in America. He was easy to like with his Bronx accent and his malapropisms. Cremins had been a very good player at South Carolina in the late 1960s, but had left college unsure of what to do with his life.

"Let's be honest," he said. "All coaches will tell you they want to help people and teach. That's nice, but it's a crock. If we all wanted to help people and teach, we'd go join the Peace Corps. Even that may not be the answer. When I played basketball in South America after I got out of college, I knew some Peace Corps guys and all we ever did when I was with them was hang out and smoke dope."

It is just like Cremins to casually admit that once upon a time he smoked dope. Most coaches would be too frightened about what it might do to their image, but Cremins is secure enough to know that in 1988, very few people are going to judge him on something he did in 1970 unless he decides to become a Supreme Court judge. Or unless he starts losing.

Deciding the Peace Corps wasn't the answer, Cremins got into coaching. He landed the job at Appalachian State, stayed there for five years, then moved on to Tech. By the fall of 1985, with the guts of the ACC championship team back for '86, Georgia Tech was everyone's preseason No. 1 pick.

But things didn't work out for the Yellow Jackets that year. The one starter they had lost, center Yvon Joseph, proved to be more critical than anyone had anticipated. And, in the big games, the shots that had fallen so easily on the way to the top weren't falling anymore. Tech lost the ACC final by a point to Duke and was upset in the NCAA round of sixteen by LSU.

Price and Salley graduated off that team, and even with a superb pair of young forwards in Duane Ferrell and Tom Hammonds, Tech dropped to 16–12 in 1987. Now, with super-freshman Scott to go with Ferrell and Hammonds and senior point guard Craig Neal finally playing up to his vast potential, Tech was one player short—a big center—of being a great team. Even without that center, it was still a dangerous team.

Valvano liked Cremins as much as he liked anyone in the league. And he respected him. Like everyone else, he loved to tell Cremins stories. "A few years ago I asked Bobby how old he was. He said, 'Thirty-six or thirty-seven.' I said, 'Well, what year were you born in?' And he said, 'Oh, I think it was '46 or '47.' "

Valvano still isn't sure how old Cremins is. But by halftime in Reynolds Coliseum he knows that, regardless of his age, Cremins has a hot basketball team. Tech is leading 47–28. Valvano has gotten so out of sorts in the first half that he has drawn a technical foul, something he almost never does. "I think that's my second one in eight years."

The technical came from Dick Paparo, who is known to one and all as "Froggy" because he sounds just like a frog. Froggy is a very good official. He is also a no-nonsense official. In the last two seasons Dean Smith has drawn four technical fouls—all of them from Froggy. A few weeks ago when Froggy teed Smith up, someone asked the coach what the technical was for.

"I just said, 'Mr. Paparo, I think J.R. was fouled on that play,' " Smith answered. The last time Smith called a referee "Mr." he was playing Peewee ball in Emporia, Kansas.

Valvano's tee comes after Froggy calls a goaltending against Shackleford. The call is a correct one but, in making it, Froggy had freight-trained, racing from beyond halfcourt to make the call. Over the years, this has been a Froggy staple—the freight-train call—and he has cut back on it in recent years because supervisors have talked to him about it.

Valvano, incensed at the sight of Froggy running in to make the call, screamed at him, "You can't see that play. How can you make that call?"

Once upon a time, an official in this situation might have walked to the bench and said, "Jimmy, I know I was a long way off, but I saw it clearly. It was goaltending."

But this year, officials are not supposed to talk to coaches except to interpret a rule or to say—once—"Coach, that's enough," before teeing them up. So, as Valvano rants, Froggy ignores him. Valvano knows the rule and he knows it's nothing personal. But his team is getting blown out at home and he's frustrated. So, he keeps yelling, finally saying, *"Damn it, talk to me!"*

Froggy doesn't talk, but he does tee. "That no-talk rule is so stupid," Valvano says later. "It makes me crazy."

Surprisingly, down by 19 at halftime, he doesn't go crazy on his team. "We have been thoroughly embarrassed so far," he tells them. "But you know what? We can still come back."

Valvano had no idea how right he was. Amazingly, the game turns around completely during the first five minutes of the second half. Tech, which could do no wrong, pushing the ball up the floor on every possession, suddenly can do no right. Passes that were going right to Yellow Jackets are now going right to the Wolfpack. In a span of 5:07, State goes on a 23–3 spree that ends with a Corchiani three-pointer, putting the Wolfpack up 51–50.

This is a stunning turnaround. Cremins's team stands an excellent chance of folding up, rolling over, and being in serious trouble with two weeks left in the regular season. But Ferrell and Hammonds get things calmed down. Tech slows the pace, shows some patience, and gets the ball inside. State is exhausted after its wild run and Tech builds the lead back to eight. State comes back again but each time it gets close, Ferrell, the silky-smooth senior forward, has an answer. He finishes with 29 points and Tech hangs on to win, 87–84 when three-point shots on State's last two possessions are off the mark.

"So, it's an L [loss] in the books," Valvano says. "Our comeback doesn't matter. Nothing matters, when we come back in here on Monday it will still be an L. We were a little bit tired from the Clemson trip, Shack's ankle still hurts some and he's missed some practice. But it doesn't matter, it's an L."

Valvano can't get too upset with this team. It has played close to its potential most nights. Even this loss was just a matter of catching a hot team on a hot night. He sits and talks about the game and the season and almost any subject that comes into his head until way past midnight, much too wound up to think about going home.

"The other day I got a speeding ticket," he says, telling a story as he is wont to do during these sessions. "I was going fifty-four in a forty at eleven o'clock in the morning on an empty street and the guy nails me. Okay, I was daydreaming and I did it. But then it becomes a story in the newspaper. Why is that newsworthy? I wasn't drinking. I wasn't doing drugs. I wasn't endangering anyone. I wasn't out late at night."

Before he can continue his tirade, Valvano's late-night reference reminds him of another story. "A couple of years ago I was still doing this morning radio show I do out of the studio, going by and taping it. One night after a game, I forgot to go tape it. Just went home and went to bed. Four o'clock in the morning the phone rings. It's the radio station. I say, 'Oh God,' and I get in the car and start driving down there. At that hour, I was going very fast.

"A cop pulls me. Before I can even explain to him what's going on, he wants me to get out of the car and walk a straight line for him. I said, 'Officer, take a look at me. I'm in my pajamas. Call the radio station and ask them if they just woke me at home. I have not been drinking. Look at these pajamas. Would you go around town drinking dressed in these pajamas?"

The pajama-clad coach made it safely to the radio station. As Valvano finishes the story and is about to launch into another one, Don Shea, who hosts Valvano's TV show, pokes his head in the door. "Oh God, Don, I forgot!" Valvano says.

With that, he is off, at one in the morning—not dressed in pajamas—to tape his TV show.

February 21 . . . West Lafayette, Indiana

As Troy Lewis, Todd Mitchell, and Everette Stephens walked into the restaurant, there were stares. But only for a moment. Then, everyone in the place started applauding. Some of them stood up. Earlier that day, when 14,123 people had been standing and cheering them, Lewis, Mitchell, and Stephens didn't bat an eye. Now, in this more intimate surrounding, dressed in street clothes rather than white-black-and-gold, they were embarrassed.

"It's a good thing," Lewis said, "that we won."

"Yeah," Stephens added. "If we had lost, they might not have served us in McDonald's."

They were a far cry from McDonald's but that was as it should be. That afternoon, Purdue had beaten Indiana 95–85 in a game so scintillating that Bob Knight, in defeat, expressed admiration for both teams. "I don't think there was a kid on that floor on either team who shouldn't be proud of the way he played today," Knight said.

Extraordinary words, particularly considering who had spoken them. But these were rather extraordinary times at Purdue, especially for the three seniors. After all the rockiness of preseason and December, it had all come together in January and February; the Boilermakers now found themselves sitting on top of the Big Ten with an 11–1 record.

They also found themselves sitting on Temple's shoulder, ranked No. 2 in the country with a 22–2 record.

"Of course, if Temple had lost today, they probably would have jumped somebody over us into number one," Mitchell joked.

Temple had not lost today. In fact, the Owls had gone into the Deandome and trashed North Carolina, proving that the Tar Heels were indeed as vulnerable as some suspected. The Owls hadn't just beaten Carolina, they had wiped them out, 83–66, starting the second half with a 19–0 run that left everyone in the place, including Dean Smith, agape.

That didn't much matter out here, though. On a day when Indiana and Purdue were playing in Mackey Arena, Neil Armstrong could be stepping on the moon and the reaction here would be, "Yeah, fine, but what's the score over at Mackey?"

Purdue people have a complex about Indiana. They can't understand why Knight and the Hoosiers get so much attention while they go virtually ignored outside the state. "When I think about how different things might have been if we had made the Final Four last year instead of them I get sick," Mitchell said. "We've got to change that this year."

Naturally, there is nothing Purdue likes doing more than beating Indiana. Mitchell–Lewis–Stephens are undefeated in Mackey against the Hoosiers and they certainly didn't plan for their last game against IU to be a loss. But winning would not be easy. Indiana was a very different team from the one that had parlayed that remarkable 33–12 start into an 82–79 upset of Purdue in Bloomington three weeks earlier.

Indiana was now on a 6–1 roll. It was getting good play out of freshman guards Jay Edwards and Lyndon Jones—especially Edwards—and was also getting production out of Keith Smart and Rick Calloway, the two players who had been benched during Knight's January purge. Having beaten Purdue once, Knight's Hoosiers saw absolutely no reason why they couldn't do it again.

It didn't look good early for Indiana, though. Center Dean Garrett picked up three fouls in less than five minutes and had to come out. Purdue soon had a 22–12 lead and it looked—and sounded—like this might be the day when the Mackey roof finally did blow off. But, as they had been doing in recent weeks, the Hoosiers kept their cool. Led by Smart, they rallied, taking a 27–26 lead.

Purdue regrouped, holding a 49–47 lead at the half. The game stayed torrid in the second half. Purdue scored 9 straight points to lead 62–53, but Indiana came right back with 9 straight points of its own to tie. Smart, who would finish the day with 23 points, made the play of the day, soaring over everyone and dunking a Joe Hillman miss with one hand, not a move one sees a 6–1 player make every day.

Down the stretch, though, the Purdue seniors took over. Trailing 73–72, Mitchell posted, took a pass from Lewis and hit a soft jumper. Lewis fed Melvin McCants for a layup. A moment later, he fed Mitchell again, then, after IU had closed to within one again at 78–77, Stephens nailed a three-pointer with 4:25 left. Mitchell hit a ten-footer. Lewis hit a three. Stephens hit two free throws. Lewis hit two more. It was 90–81. Indiana rallied one more time, but Mitchell iced it with a jarring dunk with thirty seconds to go, and everyone celebrated.

"That was just a great basketball game," Keady said. "I think everyone here felt that way."

Knight, who had barely spoken to Keady for three years, was impressed enough with what he saw that, as he shook hands after the game, he said, "You've got a hell of a team. I hope you go all the way."

The contrast between the feeling in the Purdue locker room after this game as opposed to three weeks ago in Bloomington was 180 degrees. Mitchell had scored 24 points and had 9 rebounds. Lewis scored 22 and had a career-high 14 assists, a total that left everyone blinking in disbelief. Stephens had scored 16 points and had 7 assists of his own.

The mood was so light that Mitchell and Lewis did a brief comedy act during the postgame interviews. Glancing at the stat sheet, Lewis said, "I had 14 assists?"

"Where does it say that?" Mitchell said, grabbing the sheet from him.

"I better frame this," Lewis said.

"You better blow it up real big," Mitchell answered.

For Mitchell, perhaps more than anyone, this victory was a sweet one. He had felt like the goat after the loss in Bloomington. Even though he had scored 24 points in that game, he had missed the front end of a one-and-one with his team up by one and fifteen seconds left, a miss that probably cost them the victory.

The following day, still stewing about the loss and about the team's horrendous first half, Keady had destroyed Mitchell in front of his teammates. "I told him he was worthless, playing the way he was," Keady remembered. "I told him he might as well go ahead and quit and do everyone a favor if he didn't care more than he did. I buried him. He cried, but he's turned around since then and gone to war, every night out."

Mitchell had been stung—and stunned—by Keady's tirade. It was not the first time that the hard-nosed coach and the laid-back player had clashed. His tears had been brought on by embarrassment and by anger. "He hurt me that day," Mitchell said. "I know he's a good man and I know he cares about us and would do anything for us. But sometimes he thinks because he cares he can say anything he wants and it's okay. Well, it's *not* okay. Sometimes he goes too far. That day he went too far."

Keady believed that, as good as his two senior guards were, Mitchell was the key to this team. He had called Mitchell in the previous spring and had told him that. He had been on Mitchell more than any other player because he believed he had to pull Mitchell's potential out of him. Mitchell was not the natural that Stephens was or the competitor that Lewis was. But he was a superb athlete, a player who was capable, at 6–8, of scoring inside and outside and of taking over a game—when he chose to.

But Keady thought that Mitchell had a languid attitude and the only way to cure that was to infuriate him. He had questioned his manhood, told him not to listen to his father (who was telling him to shoot more), and told him to quit. Whatever the reason, Mitchell was now playing the way Keady hoped he would and the team had come out of Indiana to reel off victories over Wisconsin, Michigan, Michigan State, Iowa, and now Indiana. Winning at Michigan had put them in control of the Big Ten race and now, inevitably, all eyes were beginning to turn to March. As Mitchell said, "That's where our fate will be decided."

This had been the theme all season, of course. That very afternoon, moments after the Indiana win, Keady had said of the seniors: "The jury is still out on how they're going to react when the pressure's really on."

Keady wasn't being critical. Just as the three seniors loved him in spite of his faults, he loved them. But he wanted desperately for them to play their best basketball when it mattered most. He wanted them to erase all doubts about the greatness they had brought to Purdue. The seniors understood. They had understood that all season.

"Six more games," Mitchell said softly over prime rib and strawberry daiquiris. "And then, once and for all, we find out."

February 22. . . East Rutherford, New Jersey

This was Bobby Martin's chance to be a star. He was just a freshman on a team of big-name veterans, but now all eyes in the Meadowlands Arena were on him. He lined up, eyed the basket and, from forty-seven feet, he fired. For a moment, everyone held their breath. When the ball swished through, the place exploded.

Twenty people were clapping and cheering and Martin, with a huge grin on his face, was picking ten dollars off the floor and stuffing it into his warmups. "I called it," he said. "All the way."

It was noon on a freezing Monday morning and Pittsburgh was wrapping up its game-day shootaround the way it always did. Assistant Sports Information Director Kimball Smith put up ten dollars and each Panther took a shot from halfcourt for the money. The seniors went first, then the juniors and so on down the line. As soon as someone made a shot, the contest was over. Martin was the last shooter of the day.

"That's an omen," Coach Paul Evans said, heading for the team bus. "The only problem is, I don't know what kind."

Most of the omens had been good ones for the Panthers of late. They had just survived round two with Georgetown two days earlier and were here to play Seton Hall, a game that worried the hell out of Evans. "We haven't had time to relax and come down from the Georgetown game," he said. "We could use a rest tonight, not a game against a team that has to win to get into the NCAAs."

This had been a season without much rest for Evans. Even with a 19–3 record, it had been full of controversy and turbulence. After the victory over Providence in the Jerome Lane backboard-shattering game, Pitt had gone on the road to beat Boston College and rout St. John's. The latter victory, by an 88–71 margin, was especially pleasing to Evans because his two starting seniors, Charles Smith and Demetrius Gore, had never beaten St. John's before this season. Now they had done it twice. Putting bugaboos behind the older players was crucial, Evans thought.

The high of St. John's was followed by a low, a loss at home to Syracuse. When the Orangemen were on, they were as good as anyone in the country. They were on against Pitt, outrebounding them 44–23, a figure that astounded and mystified Evans.

Still, his team bounced back and played very well to beat Villanova at Villanova three days later, 87–75. But that victory was obscured by yet another outbreak of the Evans–Rollie Massimino feud. Once again, the postgame handshake caused problems. Massimino had vowed not to shake Evans's hand after the no-handshake incident in Pittsburgh the month before. But late in the game, with Pitt in command, he turned to his assistants on the bench and said, "I can't not shake his hand after we get beat. That wouldn't look right, especially at *our* place. I'll shake his hand."

When the game was over, Massimino went to shake hands. Evans wasn't sure exactly what was going to happen when the two of them crossed paths, so when Massimino put his hand out, Evans, at the last moment, pulled his back. That was it for Massimino. "How dare you!" he screamed. "How dare you embarrass me that way in my house!"

Evans responded with several profanities and for a moment it looked as if the two men might square off. Fortunately, their assistants guided them away from each other and the incident ended there. But the aftermath did not. Lane's 24 points and 13 rebounds were forgotten and everyone focused on the Evans–Massimino war. Even Big East Commissioner Dave Gavitt, who would have denied that the *Titanic* was in trouble, took a few minutes out from his TV career to try to convince the two men to cool it. Gavitt does not like seeing his league's dirty laundry washed in public, and this had become a very public no-rinse cycle.

Still distracted by the publicity, Pitt went to Providence and played horribly. Only two three-point shots by Jason Matthews in the last seventy-six seconds saved the Panthers from a defeat. They finally escaped, 87–86.

That brought them to Georgetown II. Georgetown I six weeks earlier had produced a major brawl, two Evans technicals, and a loss. Now, Evans's whole family was in town for the sequel: his parents, his brother, and his sister with their families. For Evans, it got the weekend off to a hectic start.

It was a hectic game, too, and an excellent one, with 16,721 jammed into the Pittsburgh Civic Arena. Down the stretch, Charles Smith, who finished with 25 points, made every big free throw and Pitt hung on for a 70–65 victory (Evans's first in four tries against Georgetown). But just when it seemed the game would end as a hard-fought, clean game, all hell broke loose.

With four seconds left, Sam Jefferson went to the foul line for

Georgetown. He missed. In the ensuing scramble, Perry McDonald turned around and put an elbow into the back of Jerome Lane's head. Lane went after McDonald and, before it was over, police had to help break up the fight and the officials declared the game over with those four seconds still left.

John Thompson closed his locker room to the press and acted as if this fight was terribly upsetting. Why this fight was any more upsetting than any of the others Georgetown had been in over the years was anybody's guess. On CBS-TV, former Seton Hall Coach Bill Raftery, now an analyst, watched the replay carefully. After seeing clearly that McDonald had started the fight, Raftery commented that this happened all too often in Georgetown games. He said it was Thompson's responsibility to put a stop to it.

These comments were not only correct, they were extremely reasonable. Others might have been much harsher. Coach Thompson, however, does not take criticism well. The next night on his local TV show in Washington—a show he is paid handsomely to do—Thompson ripped Raftery, saying that Raftery had no right to make such comments since he had been a failure as a coach himself.

This was classic Thompson: Deflect the issue. To begin with, Raftery was a good coach, one who had a winning record at a school where winning was very difficult. But even if he had been a terrible coach the point was moot. One did not have to be a good coach—or a coach at all—to be appalled by Georgetown's oncourt behavior over the years.

Only one person could stop the fighting: Thompson. He was the only person who had enough sway with his players to say, "Don't fight or else," and know they wouldn't fight. The shame of the whole thing was that all the fighting obscured what a superb coaching job Thompson was again doing.

Evans wasn't happy about the brawl. But he was delighted that, for once, the onus was on the other team and the other coach. The tape was all the defense Pitt needed. But the emotion that had been poured into the game—and the battle—worried Evans as he relaxed in his hotel suite waiting for the Seton Hall game.

"I'm still not sure about the maturity of the older guys on this team," he said. "I'm still not sure if they're as serious about winning as they should be. I know they were all out partying on Saturday night. I told them to take it easy because we had this game coming up so fast, but I know they didn't. I don't think they ever will.

"But the other side of it is they've played really well and consistently almost all year. It's taken Charlie Smith until the last two weeks to really get over all the negatives of his first three years. Saturday he makes all his free throws. That's progress.

"This has really been a strange team to coach. I look at the four freshmen and they don't need any fire-and-brimstone speeches. I don't need to go bullshit with them. They know what has to be done to win and they just assume that we'll go out and do it.

"But the older guys I've always got to be on. There's something about this program left over. I call it the Pittsburgh mentality. The other night I was on a radio show and a guy called in and said we never won any big games. We've beaten Florida, St. John's twice, Villanova twice, Georgetown. I call those big games. But he says Syracuse was a big game.

"To him it was—because we lost. Those are the only big games in Pittsburgh. Last year we beat Syracuse twice, so those weren't big games. The older kids have heard that for a long time and it affects them. They wonder about it too. That's why it's important that we win the regular season title because then I can say to them, 'You won big games. You won a title. Now, let's keep going.'

"This is a good team. And yet, in the back of my mind, I still think we're going to be better when these freshmen are juniors and seniors and it's their program and their team. Tonight will be interesting because the older guys think we can just show up and win. If I can't convince them otherwise, we'll get beat."

Evans's pregame talk focuses on exactly that theme. "There's a label on this basketball program," he tells the whole team, his eyes moving from Gore to Lane to Smith. "The label is 'fat cat'. The bookies out there, the experts, everyone will tell you that when Pitt wins a big game they become fat cats and play lousy their next game. That's what everyone is expecting tonight. That's why you're only one-point favorites—because you're fat cats.

"Seton Hall [which is 16–10] has to have this game. They figure they win tonight, they'll make the tournament and that's what their whole season is built around. Play like fat cats and you'll get beat. Play the way you can and you'll shut a lot of people up."

Evans also reminds the players about fighting. On the floor, before the game, he had talked to Seton Hall Coach P. J. Carlesimo about the Georgetown fight. Finally, the Big East had been roused into action and would issue an edict declaring that any player involved in a fight would receive an automatic suspension. Why it had taken so long for the Big East to act no one but Gavitt knew. But Carlesimo was afraid the referees would overreact.

"If they start calling every contact and not letting it be a basketball game, I'll tell them they're full of it," he told Evans. "My team doesn't get in fights. I hope they understand that."

Evans wanted his team to understand that he wouldn't tolerate fighting. "Just to remind you," he said. "I don't care about anybody else's rules. If you get into a fight, you're suspended, regardless of what the league does. Don't do it."

Lane, who is never one to let anything get by, said, "What if the other guy starts it, are you suspended then?"

"Jerome," Evans answered, "you're playing tonight, aren't you?"

Before Lane could answer, Gore, sitting next to Lane, just looked at him and said, "Damn, Jerome."

The whole room cracked up. "I just wanted to be sure," Lane said, "because . . ."

"Jerome," Evans interjected, "shut up." That broke everyone up again.

The game, however, was no laughing matter. Evans had not been talking hyperbole when he said this game was a season-maker for Seton Hall. It was more than that. Carlesimo's job was on the line. After the encouraging start in the NIT, the Pirates had gone through preseason 11–3. But when Big East play began, their problems began again. A loss on January 30 to St. John's dropped them to 13–9. They were now 16–10 but the boos that Carlesimo was hearing from the 7,471 on hand for this game had become as much a part of a Seton Hall game as the national anthem.

"I'm so used to it," Carlesimo said, "that I don't even hear it anymore."

Pitt started well, bolting to a 32–24 lead. But careless play, most notably by Gore, got Seton Hall going. By halftime the margin was down to 44–42. All of Evans's concerns were coming into play. Smith was being outplayed inside by Seton Hall's Mark Bryant. Gore was way off his game. The offense was stagnant.

"You get up six points and you get fat-headed and lazy," Evans told them at halftime. "This time when you build the lead, don't look back. Keep on going. Finish them off."

They never got the chance. Seton Hall had been close against good teams before: a two-point loss to Florida, a two-point loss to Syracuse; one- and three-point losses to St. John's. With another top team in their sights, they weren't going to lose another one. Down 56–50 with fourteen minutes to go, Bryant took over the game. He dunked once, then twice. Smith fouled him. He hit a jump shot and a drive. With the score tied at 66–66, Seton Hall went on a 16–2 run and the score was never even close again.

For Carlesimo, this was a breakthrough victory. His team had been *close* before but this was a *win*, an overwhelming one, over a team ranked sixth in the nation. Did he think he had saved his job?

"Who knows?" he said. "But if I don't get a new contract I can walk away feeling we did everything we could, feeling like the kids went out and dealt with it all and played up to their potential. I wanted this team to make the tournament. We should make it now. After that, what happens, happens."

What happened is that Seton Hall would make the tournament and Carlesimo would get a new contract. That it took the school as long as it did to renew him was more a reflection of the administration not understanding how much had gone into turning the program around than anything else.

Even Evans, upset as he was with his team's play, would concede later, "If we had to lose a game like that, I'm glad it was to P.J. If anybody deserves good things to happen to him, it's him."

Evans had watched those last few minutes, listening to the cheers of the suddenly enthused Seton Hall fans, feeling helpless. His hope had been that his team would assert its superiority early before Seton Hall began to feel it could win. That hadn't happened and as Bryant pounded away—32 points and 16 rebounds—Evans knew that all his worries had been justified.

In the locker room, his voice was menacingly low as he prowled around the room. He walked over to Smith, who had shaved a small star into the side of his head. "Why don't you shave a star into the other side of your head, Charlie? Do you realize you shot an air ball from the foul line? An air ball? And you let Bryant just kick your ass all night long."

He reached down as if to touch Smith's head. "Another star right there, huh, Charlie?" Smith was so frustrated that when Evans reached his hand out, he slapped it away.

Evans turned to Lane, "How many rebounds did you get, Jerome? Five? How many, fat cat?

"I told you guys Saturday: Take it easy. We have another game in forty-eight hours. But you had to have beer blasts and strippers and just party all night. And the worst thing of all is that except for [Sean] Miller, every one of you quit at the end. That's just terrible.

"Okay fat cats. Curfew tonight is ten-thirty. We'll be up to leave the hotel at six-forty-five. I would advise you to get all the sleep you can tonight because you're going to need it."

The next afternoon, Evans gave his team the day off. He didn't need to kill them in practice. He had already made his point.

February 24. . . Norman, Oklahoma

For once, Larry Brown was relaxed, comfortable—even happy. If there was an afternoon when he should have been nervous, this was it. Kansas was about to play at Oklahoma, taking on what Brown thought was probably the most talented team in the country.

Brown wasn't worried. "We'll probably get beat," he said. "But I can't be upset about it. The way these kids have played the last couple of weeks, there's no way I can be mad with them. To tell you the truth, I've enjoyed these last three weeks as much as any time I've ever had in coaching. It's been an amazing experience."

The experience had started with a four-game losing streak, a string that had capped a month of sheer frustration for everyone connected with the team. After the loss of Archie Marshall and Marvin Branch and after the loss at Iowa State, the Jayhawks had won a walkover nonconference game against Hampton University to raise their record to 12–4. Then came the losses.

First at Notre Dame, 80–76, the kind of game Brown hates to lose. Then a real killer, 70–68 at Nebraska. The Jayhawks blew a 16-point lead in the last twelve minutes and, holding for the last shot with the score tied, Danny Manning dribbled the ball off his leg. Beau Reid then hit at the buzzer for Nebraska.

"That was the low point for me," Manning would say later, looking back at that night. "Losing was awful, but feeling as if *I* had lost the game was worse. It wasn't like there was any doubt about it, either. I lost the game for us. I shot terribly [five-for-thirteen] and dribbled the ball off my leg. It was a nightmare."

On the trip home that night, the coaches huddled at the front of the plane, looking through the schedule, trying to see if they still had a realistic chance to get into the NCAA Tournament. "We kept saying, 'If we can get to eighteen wins, the committee will take us because of Danny,' " assistant coach R. C. Buford remembered. "But looking at the schedule, eighteen wins weren't a lock by any means."

It got worse before it got better. Kansas State came into Allen Field House and, playing a textbook second half, ended KU's fifty-five-game, four-year home winning streak, 72–61. It was the first time Manning had ever lost a home game. And yet, it was in that game that Brown first saw a glimmer of hope. "K-State just played great that night," Brown said. "Mitch Richmond [35 points] was unbelievable. I told our kids after the game that if they played as hard every night as they had that night that we'd be okay. I'm not sure they believed me right then, but I really believed that."

Brown had become a salesman during this time. With the team depleted physically and struggling emotionally, he felt it was his job to convince his players that they could compete. He wanted help from Manning, but he wasn't really getting it. Manning was playing well, very well in fact, but he had to do even more. That fact was never more apparent than during the fourth loss in the streak. Manning scored 28 points and had 16 rebounds, but Kansas still lost to Oklahoma, 73–65. The rest of the team was 15-for-40 that night and that just wasn't good enough.

Now, the Jayhawks were 12–8 and the school began making phone calls to NIT officials to find out what their chances would be of hosting a first-round game. A victory over Colorado—even that game was a struggle—finally broke the losing streak but did little to pick up anyone's spirits.

Then, during a ten-day period, everything turned around. Two things happened that turned a season spinning hopelessly out of control into what would become a memorable one.

First, Brown decided to move Kevin Pritchard to point guard. This was not a move he was comfortable with because Pritchard, a 6-3 sophomore, was not a point guard in any sense of the word. He was not a great ballhandler, he was not a natural leader, and all of his instincts were those of a scorer, not a creator.

But Brown felt he had no choice. All season, he had hoped that one of the two junior-college point guards he had brought in—Otis Livingston and Lincoln Minor—would step forward. He even talked about putting Clint Normore, the ex-football player, on the point. Nothing worked. Often the Kansas offense looked like a sailboat with no rudder, just floating around in the ocean with no direction.

"I made a mistake at the beginning of the season," Brown said. "I forgot that it takes kids a while to really understand me, especially point guards. Kevin, at least, was used to me."

When Brown put Pritchard on the point, he did two other things: He moved Jeff Gueldner, a little-used but hard-nosed sophomore, into the starting lineup at Pritchard's old spot. He also told Manning to help bring the ball upcourt at times and to help Pritchard call plays. If this team was going to sink, it was going to do so with Manning as the chief sailor.

The new lineup made its debut at Oklahoma State on February 10. It worked—at least this time. Pritchard, who had been having shooting troubles, was 6-for-8 with 20 points. Manning had 23 points and nine rebounds. Gueldner only had 5 points but his presence on defense seemed to help at that end. KU won the game 78–68, its first Big Eight road victory of the season.

Back home, the Jayhawks got even with Iowa State and with Nebraska, beating both teams convincingly. Against Iowa State, Manning was unconscious, scoring a career-high 39 points. Against Nebraska, he only had 21 but the defense, improving every game, held Nebraska to 48 points.

It was shortly after that game that Brown and Manning had a run-in—not their first or their last, but possibly their most serious. During practice one afternoon, Normore and freshman center Mike Masucci exchanged some angry words and elbows. After practice, back in the locker room, the two of them were still angry. More words were exchanged and, finally, punches. The other players watched, letting their two teammates settle their differences. When Brown heard what had happened, he was furious—at Manning.

Like everyone else, Manning had watched Masucci and Normore go at it. Brown felt he should have broken the fight up, that his sitting by and just being one of the guys was exactly the reason why he had never become the leader Brown insisted he had to be.

"You are not one of the guys!" Brown screamed at Manning in his

office two days before the Jayhawks were to play at Kansas State. *"How many goddamn times do I have to tell you that?!"*

Manning had heard this speech a hundred times if he had heard it once. His tendency was to tune it out. He had grown weary of Brown's yelling and felt that the whole team had grown weary of it. But now, Brown brought up David Thompson, and when he did, his voice turned from harsh to soft.

Brown had coached David Thompson in the NBA, in Denver. Many who saw David Thompson play at North Carolina State still insist that, Michael Jordan or no Michael Jordan, Magic Johnson or no Magic Johnson, David Thompson was the most gifted basketball player ever. As in *ever.* Thompson was 6–4 but he could block anyone's shot, as he proved in the Final Four in 1974 when he cleanly stuffed Bill Walton during N.C. State's double-overtime victory over UCLA. Thompson could shoot, he could jump, he could ball-handle. He could do *anything.* He was a star among stars. But, more than anything else, David Thompson wanted to be one of the guys.

"He never wanted the responsibility of being the best player," Brown said. "David wanted to be one of the guys and people protected him. They made things easy for him. Whatever David wanted, he got. Everyone wanted to keep David happy."

Brown didn't have to tell Manning the rest of the story. Thompson eventually became a cocaine addict, hurt a knee, and was out of basketball before he turned thirty. Today, he is clean and trying to get back into basketball. When people talk about talent wasted, the first name often brought up is David Thompson. Brown wasn't really trying to tell Manning that he was going to end up like David Thompson. The analogy went only so far as the refusal to take responsibility for being the best player. "The best player has to be the leader, Danny," Brown said. "It isn't a matter of choice. By the time you've been in the NBA for two years, you're going to have to be the leader on your team. You won't have any choice."

Manning and Brown talked for a while that day. Brown told him not to worry about his statistics, that if he was only the second player chosen in the NBA draft instead of the first he would still be a very wealthy young man. Manning told Brown he thought a little less yelling would be positive for the team. Each listened to the other. When it was over both felt better.

"I'll tell you what, Danny," Brown finally said. "I don't want to yell

so much. You get on the guys sometimes when they mess up in practice
and I won't have to do it. Do it your own way, but *do* it."

Manning nodded. Later, he told his teammates, "In the end, we can
only be as good as you guys are. Not one of us in this room can win
by ourselves."

Two nights later, Kansas went to Kansas State and shocked the
Wildcats, 64–63. Manning, double- and triple-teamed all night, only
had 18 points. But Milt Newton had 14, Gueldner had 10, and Pritchard had 12 (and 6 assists), including the three-pointer with twenty-nine
seconds left that won the game. The Jayhawks had won five straight,
they were 17–8, and they had stopped making phone calls to the NIT.

Two days later, with a display of superb defense, they jumped to a
23–8 lead on Duke. But the Blue Devils came back, forced overtime
and won the game 74–70, even though Manning scored 31 points and
had 12 rebounds. The loss was a bitterly disappointing one. Duke had
beaten Kansas twice during Manning's sophomore year, once in the
preseason NIT final and then in the Final Four. That was the game
in which Manning only scored 4 points and Marshall tore up his knee
for the first time. Now, Duke had come into Allen Field House and
come from way behind to steal a victory.

Yet, amidst the disappointment, there was hope. Kansas's defense
had made life miserable for the Blue Devils. Only Duke's defense, as
good as any in the country, had kept it in the game. And in the
overtime, Quin Snyder, the long-struggling point guard, had stepped
forward, hitting two big shots, including a three-pointer, to finish with
21 points.

That was why Brown felt very little fear as his team prepared to play
Oklahoma. Duke didn't have as much sheer talent as Oklahoma but
it played just as hard, and the Jayhawks had proved they could match
that intensity. The feeling that his team would go out and play just as
hard as Oklahoma made Brown feel good.

"This team is playing as hard right now as any I've ever coached,"
he said. "Since Danny and I had our talk, he's been great. He's done
everything I could possibly ask. It's funny, all season long Ed [Man-
ning] has been on me to get on Danny more. He's been worried
whether Danny was going to be mature enough to handle the pros next
year. Now, I think he feels like he's taken that step forward. Right now,
we all feel good about the way this season is turning out. A month ago,
we were all miserable."

Manning had a chance to make a little history in this game. He needed 28 points to break the Big Eight scoring record set by Wayman Tisdale during his three years at Oklahoma. Tisdale had left after his junior year and had a much higher points-per-game average than Manning, but a record was a record—and Manning had a chance to break it on Tisdale's home floor.

Naturally, when the Jayhawks walked into the Lloyd Noble Arena that night the first sign they saw read, "Hey Danny, Wayman did it in three."

"Nothing but class in this place," Buford murmured, looking at the sign.

Actually, Oklahoma had offered to stop the game and present Manning with the ball if he broke the record. Brown had turned down the invitation because "their fans will probably be booing the whole time anyway."

Oklahoma's fans were a strange group. This was a team ranked No. 4 in the country. It had a record coming into this game of 24–2 and it had been *destroying* teams all season long. The opponent tonight was a bitter rival that came in led by the best player in the country. Yet the Lloyd Noble Center was nowhere near being sold out. There were 9,785 people in the arena—one thousand shy of a sellout. This is, after all, football country. That the Sooners were as good as they were, yet largely ignored, was evidence of that. That the fans who *did* come spent most of the game sitting on their hands was further evidence of that. Undoubtedly they were all waiting for spring football to start.

Brown honestly thought the setup for his team was pretty close to perfect. "Nobody in the world expects us to win this game," he told the players. "Whenever you play these guys you're always in the game, no matter what the score is. They're going to take bad shots. You'll make mistakes, but don't get frustrated. So will they.

"These guys aren't any better than Duke. Remember, when we get to the NCAA Tournament we aren't going to play anybody any better than Duke or these guys and you'll see tonight that we can play with both these teams."

The one problem going in is Gueldner. He twisted an ankle in practice and, after testing it in pregame, tells Brown he can't play on it. Normore will start in his place.

"The only thing I ask of you," Brown says in conclusion, "is that you walk out there thinking you're going to win."

Kansas didn't win. But it came close. Manning was, as was now the norm, brilliant. Pritchard and Newton played well and so did Scooter Barry coming off the bench. But Oklahoma's inside combination of Harvey Grant and Stacey King was a little too good on this night. King scored 22 points, Grant scored 17, and Mookie Blaylock, the lightning-quick guard, had 19 points and caused at least half of the Jayhawks' 24 turnovers.

With 4:42 left in the game, Manning hit a turnaround twelve-foot jumper that closed the lead to 75–72. The PA announcer told the crowd that with that basket, Manning had become the Big Eight's all-time leading scorer. The fans booed lustily, easily their most animated reaction of the evening. Brown's prediction had been right.

The Jayhawks hung in until the final minute. A Newton three-pointer made it 83–80 with 1:59 left, but eleven seconds later Manning fouled out—finishing with 30 points and 11 rebounds—and that was all for KU. The final was 95–87.

Brown was not unhappy with his team. But he felt they could have won the game. "If you guys play a little smarter, take care of the ball after you get a rebound, we win," he said.

In the press conference, Brown couldn't resist a swipe at the officials. "Danny plays inside all the time, goes to the basket constantly, and he takes four free throws," he complained. "I don't understand it. I don't like to bitch but every other coach in this league does it so tonight I will too."

Manning, overrun by writers who want to talk about the record, shrugs it off. "Tonight, it doesn't mean anything because we lost," he said. "But in a few years when I look back I think it probably will."

As he walks out of the locker room, Manning isn't as down as he often is after a loss. "We're not that far away," he says softly. "We may still be a good team before this is all over."

February 25. . . Beaumont, Texas

If you are looking to get off the beaten path of college basketball, this is the place to come. They love football and oil down here but lately there hasn't been very much of either. Surprisingly, though, they have always played pretty good basketball.

Lamar University is located eighty miles east of Houston and forty-five miles from the Gulf of Mexico. It has slightly more than fourteen thousand students—average age twenty-four—and a basketball tradition that is largely unknown yet fairly illustrious.

Billy Tubbs played and coached here; Pat Foster, now the Houston coach, followed him and continued to have success. In Tubbs's last three seasons and in all six of Foster's seasons, Lamar made either the NCAA or the NIT. In 1980, Tubbs's last season, the Cardinals reached the round of sixteen. When Foster left in 1986 and Lamar needed a new coach, no one in college basketball could have known who the school was going to hire. When the word went out who the new coach was, basketball people shook their heads in amazement.

The new coach at Lamar was Tom Abatemarco. To the casual follower of the sport, the name Tom Abatemarco means nothing. To those inside the sport, Abatemarco is a legend in his own time.

He has been an assistant coach at six different schools. At Iona, working for Jim Valvano, he was largely responsible for the recruitment of Jeff Ruland, a player every big-time program in the country wanted. Abatemarco drove to Ruland's house each morning that winter and, knowing that contact with him was against the rules, would leave a note on his car windshield each morning, telling Ruland how much he could do for Iona and how much Iona could do for him.

From Iona, Abatemarco went to Davidson, Maryland, and Virginia Tech before finally landing at N.C. State back with Valvano. It was there that he wrote to Chris Washburn over two hundred times while the Wolfpack was recruiting the 6–11 center. Once again, Abatemarco got his man—even though Washburn ended up making more impact at State as a stereo thief than as a player.

Abatemarco is the ultimate recruiter. Unlike most of his peers, he loves it. He loves to talk to teenagers on the phone at night—"Why not, he thinks just like them," Valvano often says—and he will do just about anything to get a player. One of his favorite tricks while at State was to howl like a wolf into the telephone to let a player know just how much the Wolfpack wanted him.

Abatemarco was the perfect foil for Valvano. Whenever State, at Abatemarco's urging, signed a player who turned out to be more suspect than prospect, Valvano would just roll his eyes and say, "You know T-man." Next to Abatemarco, Valvano came off as low-key. They were a perfect combination.

Lost occasionally in all the stories and jokes about Abatemarco was the fact that the guy was, in fact, one hell of a recruiter. In 1983 when State was guard-desperate after winning the national championship, he convinced Valvano to bring in a junior college guard from Texas for a visit. The guard's name was Spud Webb.

When Spud arrived at the airport in Raleigh, he went right to the baggage carousel, somehow missing Valvano and Abatemarco, who were waiting for him at the gate. When the two coaches finally went downstairs they found him waiting for his bags. Looking at the baby-faced, five-foot-seven-inch, 145-pound Webb, Valvano turned to Abatemarco and said, "If that's Spud, you're fired."

It *was* Spud, Abatemarco *wasn't* fired, and Webb went on to be a star for them (and the Atlanta Hawks). By the spring of 1986, Abatemarco had been with Valvano at State for four years and there was no reason to believe he would go anywhere else. He was making good money, he had the V-man (V-man and T-man—get it?) at his side and all was right with the world. And then he took the Lamar job.

"I know everyone in the world thought I would stay with V the rest of my life, but I didn't want to do that," Abatemarco is saying in the rat-a-tat, rapid-fire way he talks, the words gushing out. "See, I always thought I could coach. I know no one else thought I could but I could. At least I wanted to find out. So, they have a pretty good program here, they've got some tradition, the money is, you know, not that bad, so I come."

Abatemarco stops for a second to catch his breath. He is sitting in the living room of his house a few hours before his team is going to play New Orleans. This is a vital game for Lamar. The Cardinals are 18–8, a major improvement from the 14–15 record of Abatemarco's first year. Abatemarco just wants to get into postseason play. The new league Lamar is in, the American South, does not have an automatic NCAA bid. That may mean that all four teams in the league with winning records will be NIT candidates. "We need to win twenty to get into the NIT," he says. "And we need to get into the NIT because last year when we didn't make postseason it was the first time in nine years and holy shit, were people pissed.

"See, the problem here is that they don't really understand the real world in college basketball. They think, like, Lamar is a big deal. Hey, we've got a real nice new building. Montagne Center seats ten thousand, it's only four years old, it's nice. But we almost never sell it out.

There's interest here but it's not the ACC. Or the Big East or any of those leagues. But the people here don't understand that. They think this is, like, the best job in the country or something."

He stops for a moment as his three-year-old daughter, Tracy, toddles in. Tracy loves going to games because the Cardinal mascot always comes over to talk to her. "I'm glad I took this job, I really am, because I think I've proven to people I can coach. That was important to me.

"But you know what?" He lowers his voice and leans forward. "I gotta get out of here."

Strange thing about southeast Texas. It's a whole lot different from Long Island, where Abatemarco grew up, or, for that matter, Raleigh. Recently, a Raleigh newspaperman had put together a story on ex-Valvano assistants who had gone on to head-coaching jobs. When he asked Abatemarco about Lamar, Abatemarco had told him that he liked the job but he missed Raleigh. "All the Italian food down here is canned," he joked. He also said that basketball fans in Texas didn't know the sport quite the way the ones in North Carolina did.

Well, he might as well have said the mayor of Beaumont's wife had fleas. The folks here were ticked—especially the proprietors of the local Italian restaurants. Abatemarco responded with a letter to all the local newspapers explaining his comments. That soothed matters a little but didn't change the basic problem: Boys from New York don't fit in down here unless their record is about 25–2. Abatemarco was 18–8. Not good enough, Yankee.

Driving to the game, Abatemarco stops at a 7–Eleven for his good luck cup of coffee. He is as superstitious as any coach, maybe even more so. He is also excited about the team he will have a year from now. "If I can take it down here one more year, I can have a great team," he says. "Wait till you see this guy Adrian Carwell. He's a transfer from SMU. The guy is huge. Boy, could we be good in a year."

He sips the coffee and stares glumly ahead. It is almost seventy degrees as the sun sets, delightful for February but a reminder of the summer months ahead. "Whatever happens," he says, "at least I found out I can coach."

To basketball people, Abatemarco has been a revelation as a head coach. Brad Greenberg, chief scout for the Portland Trail Blazers, is in town to scout New Orleans's Ladell Eackles and Lamar's James Gulley. He has seen Lamar earlier in the season.

"I like Tom and I was really concerned the first time I saw them play that they would look really uncoached, as if they didn't know what they were doing," he says. "I was so impressed by what he was doing I wrote him a note and told him so. He's done well."

Abatemarco's teams mirror many of the things Valvano does, but it is common for an assistant to do the same things his old boss did. What is most amazing is to stand in the locker room before the game and listen to Abatemarco talk to his team. Close your eyes and you will swear you are hearing Valvano.

"You see that number on the board?" Abatemarco says, pointing to where he has written a '1,' and circled it just like Valvano would. "That is how many games you need to win to get into the NIT. One. Get this one tonight and you'll be in the NIT.

"Okay, do we understand? Are we ready to go get this club? Okay, let's go!"

As the team heads for the floor, forward Anthony Bledsoe pauses long enough to take his earrings out. Abatemarco won't tell him not to wear them but won't let him wear them on the court. College basketball is a different game in 1988 than in the old days.

The crowd is one of the largest of the season, 7,504, and the game is a good one. Lamar trails 39–32 at halftime and Abatemarco is so wound up his assistants have to calm him down. "The only good thing," he tells his players, "is that you're playing terrible and only down seven."

Carwell, the SMU transfer, is screaming at his future teammates. "Enough of this shit! Enough! Let's go back out there and kill those suckers!"

They try. They lead briefly but can't hang on against New Orleans's consistency. The final is 75–69.

Abatemarco is disconsolate. He tries to be calm—"Keep your heads up, okay?" he tells the team initially. "I saw some good things out there. Now we have to beat Southwest Louisiana to get into the NIT." Finally, though, he explodes.

"Goddamn it, how could you let them come into your own house and beat you! You just played yourselves right out of the NIT!" He takes the six markers sitting on the board and hurls them across the room. "You could have had ten thousand people here Saturday. Now you'll have five thousand. I wouldn't come to see you play either."

He starts scribbling numbers all over the board à la Valvano and finally says, "Practice is at three-thirty. Anyone who is one minute late doesn't play Saturday. It's time we get some fucking discipline on this team."

He walks into his office and opens a beer. "I wonder," he says, "if V would take me back."

He is joking . . . sort of.

February 27. . . Columbus, Ohio

For a man who is doing perhaps the best coaching job of his life, Gary Williams looks exhausted. Somehow, with a team that really isn't ready for prime time, he has entered the last two weeks of the season fighting for an NCAA bid. Ohio State has beaten Michigan, Iowa, and Illinois and, with five games left in the season, has a 14–9 record, including 7–6 in the Big Ten. Before the season began, Williams thought he had no chance to finish at .500 in the league.

But today is a Big Day. A game the Buckeyes must win to stay in contention for the NCAAs. Michigan State is in town, and though they are one of the league's doormats this season, they have the kind of athletic talent that gives Ohio State trouble. In East Lansing four weeks earlier, they had beaten the Buckeyes rather easily.

After today there are home games left with Minnesota and Purdue and road games at Indiana and Michigan. Realistically, the best Williams can hope for is a split of these four games—and that is being optimistic. So if Ohio State is to get the seventeen victories Williams figures will lock up an NCAA bid, it has to beat Michigan State.

It has already been a hectic week for Williams. His wife, Diane, has been away visiting her parents for a few days; he and his seventeen-year-old daughter Kristen have been keeping house. In truth, it means Kristen has been keeping house.

"Hey, Kristen," he yells, pulling frozen orange juice from the freezer on game morning, "do you know how to make this stuff?" Kristen, who is blond like her mother and fortunate enough to have inherited her looks, knows how to make the juice. And coffee. Williams sits in the living room, glances at skier Alberto Tomba on his television set, and worries.

Williams has been going in three different directions all season. He has tried hard to focus on *this* team, not wanting to shortchange his seniors, trying to get the most he can from *this* group. That's why he was so excited that they still had a chance to get into the NCAAs; at the start of the season he honestly thought a losing record was all too possible.

At the same time, Williams has been looking ahead. For the second straight season he has put together what he thinks is an excellent recruiting class. Four players, three of them from Ohio, are signed while a fifth will sign in the spring. Two of this year's freshmen are sitting out as Proposition 48 victims. When he assembles his team in October of 1988, Williams will have seven new players to work with. That is a lot of turnover—and a lot of inexperience.

"But also a lot of talent," Williams says. "I've been a head coach ten years now [four at American, four at Boston College, two at Ohio State] and people have always said my teams have overachieved. Well, that's nice, it's a compliment to me. But I've always wanted to see how I could do with a lot of talent.

"Sure, we'll make mistakes next year, but we'll do a lot of good things too. And, if I am any good, we'll get better. We'll be pretty good by the end of next year. The year after that we should be very good. And, if we add Jackson to the group, then, well, we can be what I really want to be—a national contender."

Jackson is the third direction that Williams's mind has been going in this season. James Jackson is a 6–6 high school junior who lives only a little more than an hour from the Ohio State campus. He has also become a big name in the basketball cult world, considered a "franchise" player. Rudy Washington, an Iowa assistant coach who is vigorously recruiting him, describes James Jackson this way: "A-*Men*. James Jackson is A-*Men*."

That's amen—as in the last word.

Gary Williams knows the recruitment of James Jackson will be more intense than any he has ever been involved in. Already, the games are starting. Jackson's coach was invited by the Iowa state high school coaches association to speak at their annual banquet; he was flown out there in a private plane. "Just a coincidence," Washington says, grinning.

Everyone will be involved. North Carolina, Michigan, Illinois, Kentucky—and others. But Williams thinks he has a chance. Jackson is from Ohio and so far, early as it is, the vibes he has gotten have been positive.

"Put him with what we've got and I could really have a good time,"

Williams says, almost daydreaming. He soon snaps back to reality, though—which is a gray February afternoon and a game that promises to be difficult.

He meets before the game with his staff to go over Michigan State. He also checks with assistant Fran Fraschilla on Fraschilla's trip to Dayton that morning to see Mark Baker play. Baker will be Ohio State's point guard next year—if he qualifies academically. Chris Hall, another recruit, is going to be in the stands today with the rest of his high school team. Always, it seems, the present and the future are crossing paths here.

The present is Michigan State. On the blackboard before tip-off Williams writes three keys to the game—ball movement, rebounding, and transition defense—and below them he writes, "better team."

After going through the basics he points to the last two words and says, "Who is the better team, us or them? They got us last time. What you need to do today is go out with a lot of confidence and show them right away that you're better than they are. Why are we 14–9 and they're 9–14? We've beaten Iowa, Illinois, and Michigan. Who have they beaten? Right now, they got *us* the one time. But they aren't in contention for an NCAA bid, we are. Why is that? I think it's because we've worked harder than they have and we've done a better job than they have.

"We need to go out and show them that. Show them why we're better. Show them some pride and walk off the court feeling proud of what you did today.

"If I were playing on this team, I would want to play in this game more than any other since we last played them. I'd want to get back— and that thought would have been in the back of my mind ever since then. Now, it's four o'clock on Saturday and we have a chance to go get these suckers again."

The team headed for the floor. Williams turned to his assistants. "You see the way they go out there," he says, a little despondently. "No one wants to break the damn door down and charge out there. They just trot out. We haven't got that kill-those-bastards kind of leader we need yet."

Williams's hope that Ohio State will assert its superiority quickly goes by the boards quickly. Michigan State jumps to a 6–0 lead in the first ninety seconds, then leads 25–15 after twelve minutes. Williams is not happy and, as always, it shows. He is as animated on the bench as any coach in the country, working from a crouch in front of the seat he never uses. Williams is up and down, arms flailing, face turning red, right in the heat of the battle for forty minutes. Friends often wonder how he can stay so intense for forty minutes every night of the season. His answer is simple: "You don't get that many chances to compete every year."

This game is as competitive as it gets. The Buckeyes rally in the last few minutes of the half, getting even at 35–35 before Steve Smith gives Michigan State a 37–35 lead at halftime.

No one takes control in the second half. The Buckeyes always seem to be going uphill. They fall behind by five and get back to within two. The lead goes back to five and they tie it. They finally take their first lead of the entire game when freshman Perry Carter powers inside for a layup that makes it 67–66 with 3:13 left.

Nothing is easy for this team. Jay Burson is the only real outside threat and he is so small at six feet and 145 pounds that he often has trouble getting a shot. None of the inside players is quick enough, big enough, or strong enough to dominate. Carter may get there, but he is still only a freshman.

Ed Wright puts Michigan State back up at 68–67 with a jumper and they scrap back and forth for the last three minutes, Curtis Wilson's free throw the only point either one scores. That ties it at 68–68.

Ohio State has the last chance to win. With time running out, Wilson misses a jumper. The rebound is back-tapped. Burson grabs it and, as time runs out, goes up to shoot. He has no chance to get the shot off though because Smith jumps into him. The three officials, Gary Muncy, Mike Stockner, and Ted Valentine, look at the play, see the contact, watch Burson go flying and do not blow their whistles. Time runs out. Overtime.

Williams is almost hysterical. He understands that officials are reluctant to call a foul with the game on the line. But this one was extremely obvious. Burson had been creamed and there was no call.

They go to overtime. Ohio State leads by four early but Michigan State comes back to tie. The Buckeyes are patient though and, with eighteen seconds left, they hold a 78–77 lead.

Michigan State calls time. The game will be decided by one possession. In the huddle, Williams reminds his players to jump straight up in defending so there can be no foul called. The Spartans get the ball to Smith. He starts left of the key and dribbles to the right, Wilson right with him. Finally, with time running out, he goes up. Wilson goes up with him. There is contact, but not nearly as much as there had been on the last play of regulation. Wilson has played excellent defense.

The shot is way off. However, as the ball is in the air, Muncy's whistle blows. Having ignored an obvious foul on Burson at the end of regulation, he now calls a highly questionable one on Wilson with one second left in overtime. St. John Arena is stunned into silence. Williams stands in front of his bench simply pointing to the spot where the Burson nonfoul occurred. He doesn't say a word but his message is clear: If you didn't call that one, how can you call this one? It is a good question.

Smith makes both free throws. Michigan State wins, 78–77. Williams can't deal with losing this way without getting a last word in at the officials. As they run off the floor, he runs after them. He is intercepted by a security guard who pushes him. Williams pushes back, then calms down and walks off the floor, hurt and disgusted.

He is angry with the officials but unhappy with his team. "I can't believe we came out like that against this team. I'm as disappointed as I've been all year."

In his press conference Williams is calm, but blunt. "This is arguably the best league in the country," he says. "I don't think the officiating measures up to the play. I didn't think the players decided this game. One of the officials told me there was *no* contact on the play with Burson. He might say to me he didn't want to call a foul but how can he possibly say there was no contact?"

Williams stays to answer everyone's questions. He spends some time in the locker room with Chris Hall and his high school teammates. Finally, still stewing, he retreats to his office. He looks at the tape of the two key plays and becomes angry all over again. He picks up the phone and calls Big Ten Supervisor of Officials Bob Wortman. He isn't home. Williams leaves a message.

He pulls out the book that lists all the Big Ten officials, their background and experience. "Gary Muncy," he reads. "He's been refereeing in the Big Ten since 1970. During that time he's been chosen to work the NCAA Tournament one time. Hmmm. If a guy only gets to the NCAAs once in eighteen years, he can't be very good, can he?"

Unfortunately, the night isn't over for Williams. He can't go home and brood. He has to attend a party being thrown by a friend (who is a big booster) and then he must do his weekly TV show. The show is

televised live every Saturday night at 11:30 with a live studio audience—a first for a coach's show.

At the party, Williams's mood has mellowed. When a taped replay
of the game shows his run-in with the security guard, Williams says to
the assembled group, "I asked the guy who the hell had hired him."

The only sour note at the party is struck by Ohio State Athletic
Director Jim Jones. Jones became athletic director in November in the
wake of the Earle Bruce firing fiasco. Athletic Director Rick Bay, the
man who had hired Williams, had resigned in protest of Bruce's being
fired by OSU President Edward Jennings.

Into the breach stepped Jones, who had first come to Ohio State as
an academic counselor. Jones is one of those men who walks into a
room and sends people scurrying for the door. He is humorless and, to
him, being clever is saying something like, "We'll get 'em next time,
guys."

As Jones gets up to leave, in a room full of Buckeye boosters, he says
in a loud voice to Williams, "Now you behave yourself tonight."

The reference is to Williams's TV show. The tone is one that would
be used on a child. Williams, showing great self-control, says calmly:
"I'm fine. But you know something should be done about the officiating in the league."

Jones turns around, points his finger and says, "You just worry about
coaching and let me do my job."

That's it for Williams. He gets up, finds his wife, politely says good
night to his hosts and walks into the cold night. "Unbelievable" is all
he says about Jones's behavior. "I guess he doesn't think bad officiating
affects my coaching."

The television show is relatively painless. The crowd is supportive,
Williams "behaves," and the tape of the last two plays is the same:
Burson gets creamed, Smith gets brushed, and the officials make the
same call. Ohio State loses again.

When it is over, Williams, Diane, his business manager, Jack
Schrom, and his wife Kathy go out for a beer. Williams stares at the
beer for a moment, looks back on the long day, and holds the glass up.
"To next year," he says softly. A moment later, the glass is drained.

14
SEVEN DAYS
IN MARCH

March 1 . . . Fairfax, Virginia

At last it was March. Perhaps no team in the country had looked forward to this month more than George Mason. Anytime a season begins with four-a-day practices in October, you are going to look forward to the climax—under *any* circumstances. But now they were also playing for an NCAA bid.

All the work and emotion and heartache had come down to seven days. The Patriots were 17–9 and they were coming off a loss at American, which was the hottest team in the Colonial Athletic Association. In front of them was the regular season finale against Navy—a team almost as hot as American—and then the CAA tournament in Hampton, Virginia. One team would come out of that tournament with an NCAA bid. The final would be Monday night, March 7. Rick Barnes's goal for this team was to play in that game—and win it.

"I've probably only said this twenty-seven times, but this one is *real* big," Barnes said, relaxing in his office shortly before the Navy game. "We're not that far from being right where we want to be going into the tournament. Losing to American didn't even bother me that much. They're playing really well and they were bound to get us sooner or later. I'd rather it be now than in the tournament. But we need to win

tonight to be confident. I don't want them having any doubts playing
that first-round game."

The first-round game would be against James Madison. That was
locked in, regardless of tonight's outcome. Richmond, after beating
George Mason two weeks earlier, had locked up the top seed. American, with its late rush, was second, and George Mason was third. That
was why the loss to American hadn't shaken Barnes that much. He
expected to have to play the Eagles in the tournament semifinals; in
some ways, having lost to a team earlier often made it easier to play
them a second time. The losing team often had an advantage in the
rematch.

Barnes had come to the end of his first season as a head coach feeling
sadder but wiser. He had started out confident and now felt even more
confident. He had thought he could coach, now knew he could. The
won-lost record and the improvement of the team from October to
March was evidence of that.

But it hadn't been easy. Being a hard-ass with players he liked wasn't
fun. He had screamed, threatened, cajoled, and used so much profanity
it made him shudder to think about it. He had benched and suspended
and worried and wondered. Tonight was typical. Long ago, he had
promised Amp Davis, his point guard, that he could sing the national
anthem before his last home game. Davis was an accomplished gospel
singer.

But Davis had just been convicted by a student judicial board of the
cheating offense he had been accused of in November. Since the
semester was half over, and since he was not going to graduate on time
in May, the board had suspended him from school for summer school
and the fall semester. This meant that Davis's basketball eligibility was
unaffected but his chances of graduating were damaged severely.

Barnes and Athletic Director Jack Kvancz were stumped. Should
they go ahead and play someone who had been convicted of cheating?
If they benched him, were they guilty of double jeopardy? The judicial
board could have ruled Davis ineligible to play but hadn't. Was it their
place to add to the penalty? Davis still insisted he was innocent. If he
was suspended, he wouldn't suffer alone: The Patriots were not likely
to do much damage without their starting point guard.

All of this, along with the pragmatism that afflicts most people in
making such decisions, led to Davis staying in the lineup. But what
about the national anthem? "If we're letting him play," Kvancz said,

"we should let him sing the national anthem. How can we say he should be penalized that way if we aren't penalizing him by taking him off the floor during the game? If he plays, he sings. If he doesn't play, he doesn't sing."

And so Amp Davis sang—quite well. He and fellow seniors Brian Miller and Darrin Satterthwaite received their farewell flowers and plaques. Then it was time to play. Only Barnes's Patriots forgot about that one little detail. They spent the first twelve minutes admiring the Midshipmen, who ripped to a 29–12 lead, thanks largely to the three-point shooting of freshman Joe Gottschalk, who had been out for almost a month with a leg injury. The layoff didn't seem to bother Gottschalk, who came off the bench and hit three straight three-pointers in ninety seconds to help build the Navy lead. At halftime, the lead was nine points, 39–30.

Barnes didn't scream and yell during the break. Instead, he issued a challenge. "Okay now, we're in March and we're in trouble. So now we'll find out after all these months what you guys are made of. You went out and played scared for a half. Why, I don't know. *You* know these guys can't guard you if you play the way you're supposed to. But you've fucked around for a half like a bunch of fags and now we've got to come back. Well, let's see if you can do it. I know you can. But do *you?*"

If they didn't, they figured it out. Navy briefly built the lead to 42–30, then George Mason just took over the game. Sanders scored inside. Miller hit a three-pointer. Satterthwaite hit a drive. Robert Dykes and Sanders scored inside and Davis hit a three-pointer. That made it 50–46.

It was 50–48 when Hank Armstrong, Barnes's old friend, called a cheap foul on Navy. Coach Pete Herrmann, watching the game go down the drain, screamed at Armstrong and drew a technical. Armstrong then did what referees worry about doing when they are pumped up after a technical—he walked to the wrong foul line.

At that moment, Armstrong's error meant very little. Davis made the two free throws to tie the game and Mason gradually pulled away for a satisfying 85–72 victory. Barnes was able to take the seniors out one at a time and let them hear the cheers of a home crowd one last time. But Armstrong's little faux pas would turn out to be a harbinger of trouble still to come.

For this night, though, it didn't matter. March had come in with a victory and Barnes was happy with the way his team had reacted to his halftime words. "We played, guys, we really played the way we can that second half," he told them. "Now we're going to Hampton. It's all right there for you. Three more games and we're there."

March 2. . . Knoxville, Tennessee

The sunshine that had blanketed the University of Tennessee campus seemed just about right to Don DeVoe. The sounds of spring were in the air and if spring is about new beginnings and rebirth then that was just fine with DeVoe.

In two short weeks his outlook had changed 180 degrees. He had gone from a coach struggling not to completely lose his team—and, in the process, his job—to a coach whose team seemed to be coming together at exactly the right time.

"I knew all along that this team wouldn't be as good offensively as last year's," he said, luxuriating in a banana pudding dessert at his favorite lunch spot.

"But I also knew we had the potential to be better defensively. Before the Kentucky game, when we got blown out those three straight games, we had lost it defensively. If we didn't get it back, we were finished. But we got it back in the Kentucky game and that seemed to convince the guys they could do it every night. So, we've gone out and done it."

One day, DeVoe might look back at Tennessee's dramatic 72–70 victory over Kentucky and say, "That saved my job." But in the aftermath of the win, happy as he had been, DeVoe had said firmly, "For this to mean anything we've got to go on the road and do something."

The road in the Southeast Conference had been a nightmare for Tennessee for three seasons. The Volunteers had a three-year SEC road record of 2–22 as they started on a trip to Auburn and Florida. Their big chance, they felt, was at Auburn. They had beaten the Tigers easily at home in January. Three days later, Florida had come into Knoxville and beaten them by 20. The odds of going to Gainesville and winning were not too good. So Auburn was it.

To add to the road woes, DeVoe learned shortly before tip-off at Auburn that John Ward, Tennessee's longtime radio play-by-play man—The Voice of the Vols—had been taken to the hospital. He'd

been bleeding internally. It turned out Ward was having a bout
of diverticulitis. That night there was fear that tests might show
cancer.

With Tennessee fans listening to the Auburn radio feed, the Volunteers almost won the game. They led by as many as seven points in the
second half. But down the stretch, the jump shots that had been
dropping against the Auburn zone didn't drop and the Tigers ended
up with a 73–68 victory. DeVoe was surprised by his players' postgame
reaction.

"They were actually up," he said. "They knew just how we had lost
but also that we could have won. It was the first time in a while that
we had played a good team on the road and walked away saying, 'What
if?' We hadn't been close enough to do that before."

The team bussed back to Knoxville right after the game. DeVoe
couldn't sleep throughout the five-and-a-half-hour ride. He was too
keyed up, worrying about Ward, a friend, and wondering if his team
could ever find a way to win on the road. Tennessee was now 13–10
on the season, 6–8 in the SEC. Athletic Director Doug Dickey had said
to DeVoe, "Show me improvement, Don." There were four regular
season games left—two at home. If Tennessee split those games, it
would be 15–12 going into the SEC Tournament. That was better than
the 14–15 of a year ago. That was improvement. But would it be
enough? DeVoe didn't know the answer.

He sat awake on the bouncing bus, his mind churning, racing from
thoughts of Ward, to the late turnovers at Auburn, to how to beat
Florida. He got home at 5:30 A.M. and slept two hours before his
children woke him.

The following day DeVoe and his coaches began to prepare for
Florida. Avoiding turnovers, they knew, would be the key. Florida
could embarrass you if you didn't take care of the basketball and
Tennessee had been weak in this area often—especially on the road—
during the season. "We came up with two different plans," DeVoe
said. "Plan A didn't work."

Plan A called for the guards to get the ball up the floor themselves,
clearing the big men out of the way and perhaps looking for Doug Roth
as an outlet cutting down the sideline. It didn't even come close to
working. Florida's quick guards, Ronnie Montgomery and Vernon
Maxwell, wreaked havoc on the Tennessee backcourt, forcing quick
turnovers while the Gators built a 15-point lead. Tennessee looked

dead. But a late flurry in the last minute of the half cut the margin
to 9.

"That was critical," DeVoe said. "We came into the locker rooms
and the guys were saying, 'Hey, we can win this game.' We decided
to go to Plan B in the second half against their pressure. It worked. We
didn't have one turnover in the second half."

Plan B brought all five Tennessee players into the backcourt—if
necessary—to help against the press, while the quicker, more dangerous
Dyron Nix replaced Roth as the sideline outlet. Greg Bell got hot,
scoring 13 straight points during one stretch. Instead of being a Florida
walkover, the game was tight and, as always, the pressure was on the
home team. They were *supposed* to win.

The Auburn experience also came into play here. Before Auburn,
Tennessee hadn't been involved in a close game on the road. Now it
had been, and it was better able to cope with the pressure down the
stretch. With time running out and the score tied at 63, Tennessee ran
a clear-out play for Bell, the hero of the Kentucky game. He drove the
lane and hit a short jumper with two seconds left. Florida called time.
It got the ball downcourt to freshman Livingston Chatman but his
desperation shot from the corner hit nothing. Tennessee had the victory, 65–63.

"When Chatman's shot was in the air I think my heart actually
stopped," DeVoe said. "After everything that had happened, after
getting a bunch of bad calls the second half and then the ball ends up
in his hands, you wonder. But the ball doesn't go in and we've got the
win."

If DeVoe had ever had a bigger win he couldn't remember it. It was
the 300th victory of his coaching career and at least as important, the
fourteenth of the season. The team flew home by charter. When
DeVoe finally walked into his house—it was after two o'clock in the
morning—he found his wife waiting for him. Normally, she would have
gone to bed, but this was too important.

It was their third wedding anniversary.

Don DeVoe met Ana Garcia on a setup. In 1983, shortly after he
and his first wife had separated and decided to go ahead with divorce
proceedings, his next-door neighbors, Bill and Myra Brown, invited
him over to the house for a barbecue. They also invited Ana Garcia to
the house that day, hoping the two of them would hit it off. They did.
Less than two years later, they were married. There are some who say

that DeVoe's second marriage has mellowed him. DeVoe doesn't buy that old cliché but he doesn't downplay the importance of his new family.

"After my separation, I think I went into a shell for a while," he said. "I really don't think it affected my coaching but I do know I didn't want to see people that much and I didn't travel the way I had before. I just wanted to sort of be by myself and feel sorry for myself.

"If I had gone through this past season feeling the way I did that year, I'm not sure I could have handled it. I don't really know what I would have done, if I would have stuck it out. I'd like to think I would have because I'm a competitor, but who knows? Having my family and knowing that no matter what happened they were going to be there for me helped me an awful lot."

Now, he had the chance to share some *good* times with his family. The following night he took Ana to a high school game—after they had celebrated the night before with cookies and milk. For the first time in three years, he felt the kind of warmth from the fans that he had enjoyed in the past.

"It was like the old days," he said. "People coming up, congratulating us on the Florida game, talking about the rest of the season and the future. It was a nice feeling."

This was exactly eight days after DeVoe had been half-joking about trading his car in for a van. Two days later, Tennessee beat Mississippi State in a tough game, 64–62. The letdown was to be expected and the Bulldogs were a much-improved team. They would prove that the following week by beating LSU a second time in a row. DeVoe was delighted to escape with the victory.

That win brought March, the sunshine, and Alabama to Knoxville. This would be Tennessee's last home game. DeVoe thought it crucial that Tennessee win and win resoundingly. Seven straight losses to Alabama stung. This was Wimp Sanderson's worst team in years. It came to town with a 14–14 record, 0–7 on the SEC road. There was no way Tennessee could afford to lose this game.

A victory would make the Volunteers 16–10 going to Georgia for the final game of the regular season. It would put them on the NCAA Tournament bubble, giving them at least an outside shot at a bid. And it might very well earn DeVoe a new contract.

"If we can just get past this [the new contract] we really can get it turned back around here," he said. "I'm convinced of it. With those

five good juniors in the state next year. If we swept them—*wow!*" His
face lit up at the thought. "But we can't do anything without a new
contract."

DeVoe was as upbeat now as he had been down two weeks earlier.
Friends had sustained him all winter. Bob Knight had called and given
him a pep talk. Texas Coach Bob Weltlich had written him a note right
after his 300th victory. C. M. Newton had talked at length about how
people who run programs the way DeVoe did should be given the
benefit of the doubt even when the program was a little bit down. And
Fred Taylor, DeVoe's old coach at Ohio State, had sent him a note
when things were at their low ebb just before the Kentucky game. In
the note, Taylor had written:

"Just remember this. Even though you walk in the valley of the
shadow of death, you have the comfort of knowing you're the meanest
SOB in the valley."

It all made DeVoe feel better. "Nothing's guaranteed in coaching,"
he said. "I lost my job once after going 22–6. You're always on the
bubble if you're a coach. There are always going to be people who think
someone else can do a better job."

He laughed. "Right now, though, it's still my job."

After Alabama, DeVoe was even more confident it would continue
to be his job. Tennessee rolled from the start, leading 36–22 at halftime
and then embarrassing the Tide in the second half, eventually building
a 77–49 lead. DeVoe cleared his bench with five minutes left, getting
everyone, walk-ons included, into the game. The only bright spot for
Alabama came when Bryant Lancaster, who had come into the game
3-of-19 from the free throw line, made two in a row.

Wimp Sanderson spent most of the second half with his head buried
in his hands. "No point looking," he said. "I knew it wasn't gonna get
any better."

It all looked wonderful to DeVoe. The final was 81–58 and it was
even easier than it sounded. Win number sixteen might be the one
DeVoe needed.

"I haven't slept well at all these last couple of weeks," he said. "The
other night I dreamt that I brought back [suspended] Elvin Brown for
the SEC Tournament and we beat LSU in overtime. I woke up at five
in the morning with a smile on my face. The problem was it was five
in the morning and I couldn't go back to sleep."

He was smiling as he told the story. Elvin Brown wasn't coming

back. But DeVoe sensed that he was. That night, when the Tennessee
fans sang, "Nah, nah, nah, nah, Hey, hey, goodbye," it was directed
at Alabama, not DeVoe.

From where DeVoe had been two weeks earlier, that was major
progress.

March 5. . . Tucson, Arizona

Steve Kerr munched on the chocolate chip cookie, kicked his feet up
and let his body relax. At least for a minute. He had a couple of hours
to rest before he had to venture from his apartment once again, duck
into a nearby phone booth and emerge as that great superhero,
Steeeeeeve Kerrrrrrrr, defender of truth, justice, and the basketball
whenever Arizona had it.

The apartment, especially at its messiest, was Kerr's refuge. Although he would have been well advised to put in a revolving door to
save people trouble, everyone who wandered in and out came in search
of nothing more than a beer or sunglasses or suntan lotion. No autographs. No words of wisdom. And, at least for now, if the phone rang,
his girlfriend, Margot Brennan, was there to answer it. Kerr was safe
. . . for a moment.

"Margot, you want a cookie?" he yelled.

"No, I don't like that kind."

"Why, don't you like nuts or something?"

"I like you."

Ba-boom. Kerr wasn't the only wit in this group.

It had been a long month for Kerr. Tonight, Arizona would play its
final regular season game against Washington. Although the Pacific 10
tournament would be played in the McKale Center, meaning that Kerr
and fellow seniors Craig McMillan, Tom Tolbert, and Joe Turner
would play here again, this was, technically speaking, their last home
game. A major pregame ceremony was planned.

Kerr was looking forward to it but was also glad that a little of the
emotion involved would be deflected by his knowledge that this wasn't
really his last game. "If this really was the last one, I might get choked
up about it all," he said. "This way, it will be nice, but not that big
a deal."

Kerr didn't need any more big deals or any more attention right now.

He wanted to get some rest, focus his mind on the NCAA Tournament, and put the month of February behind him. It had not been an easy one.

There had been the now-standard crush of demands on his time. Interviews, speeches at local schools and to charity groups, appearances. The team ended January with a 20–1 record, then had gone a little flat. The spark that had carried them through their tough December schedule had gone out; faced with the desultory competition of the Pac–10, they weren't the same team.

"In a way it was inevitable," Kerr said. "Let's face it, playing Oregon and Washington wasn't the same as playing Syracuse and Duke. We knew it, the coaches knew it, everyone knew it. We kept having team meetings saying we had to get emotional again but the fact was we were dragging a little."

They dragged into Stanford and found themselves up against an inspired team, perhaps the only one in the Pac–10—other than underachieving UCLA—that had a reasonable chance to beat them. The Cardinals came up with their best game of the season, the Wildcats didn't score in the last three minutes, and Stanford pulled the upset, 82–74. "That woke us up," Kerr said. "But only a little. It wasn't like we went into Cal two days later saying, 'Hey, these guys can beat us.' We knew they couldn't."

Nonetheless, Kerr had managed to get himself into hot water in Berkeley. The week before the game he had gotten a phone call from Michael Silver, the sports editor of the *Daily Californian.* Silver and Kerr had gone to Palisades High School together and had co-written a column called "The Riptide" in the student paper. Silver wanted Kerr to write a column about Cal and it's often-funny fans for the *Daily Californian* prior to the game.

Kerr, naturally, loved the idea. And this is what he wrote: "Well Cal fans, the roles are reversed. The shoe is on the other foot. After four years of taking more abuse from you than Larry Holmes's face took from Mike Tyson's fist, I finally get my chance to get back. At last I can throw insults your way, fully aware that you will see them, read them, and know them. Yes, Cal fans, the Tuna is on the other sandwich."

The last was a reference to Cal students' picking a "Tuna of the game." Kerr was always the tuna when Arizona was in town.

Kerr went on: "I'd like to take this time to respond to some of the more prominent insults I've heard during my career. First, to the guy in the referee shirt in the front row who mockingly shouted, 'How's the knee?!' for two hours straight last year, I say, 'It's doing quite well, thank you. How's your brain?'

"To the earthy-looking, Birkenstock-wearing girl who, during one game two years ago, repeatedly yelled, 'Kerr, what kind of hairspray do you use?' I say, 'Before you and all the rest of Berkeley ask for advice on hairspray, try thinking about the simple basics of personal hygiene—like showering.'

"Also, to the Shakey's employees who double as Cal [Straw Hat] band members, and who each year obnoxiously parade across the floor as we attempt to warm up, I ask, 'Why don't you stay off of Pete Newell Court? You're an embarrassment to Harmon Gym—not to mention Harmon Arena. Or is it Newell Pavilion? Or the Harmon Alameda Coliseum? The Kapp Center? The Granola Dome? Or simply, Lou's Bread box?'"

Kerr had one last shot: "Finally, to all of you sophisticated intellectuals who each year cleverly ask, 'Hey Kerr, why don't you go to a *real* school,' I say, 'I wanted to, but Stanford didn't accept my application.'"

Naturally, they were waiting for Kerr when he and the Wildcats arrived at Harmon Gym/Arena/Stop'N Shop/Drive Thru Bank.

The Straw Hat Band not only marched through Arizona's warm-ups but followed Kerr everywhere he went during warmups. They also presented him with a number of Shakey's pizzas, several tunas, and lots and lots of words of advice. It was all in good fun. The only one who didn't seem to understand that was Cal Coach Lou Campanelli, who expressed annoyance with Kerr's irreverence. Come on, Lou, loosen up.

Arizona didn't play very well, but won fairly easily, 74–62.

They slogged on through February, beating up on the Oregons at home. In the Oregon game, a one-sided 89–57 rout, Ducks Coach Don Monson drew a technical foul in the second half. Kerr went to the line to shoot the two shots. When he missed the first, the ball bounced right to Monson. Not wanting to throw the ball to the official he was still angry at, Monson threw the ball back to Kerr.

"He threw it kind of hard," Kerr said. "And I wasn't sure if he was trying to show me up or what. Later, I realized he was doing it to the ref, not me."

In the heat of the moment, angry at missing the free throw, Kerr reacted instinctively: He threw the ball right back at Monson. Fortunately, Monson had turned his back and walked away. He stared hard at Kerr for a moment and Kerr stared right back. Nothing more happened.

After the game, Monson, not in a great mood after a 32-point loss, wouldn't comment on what had happened. Kerr, of course, found humor in it. "He didn't do a very good job of coming to meet my pass," he said.

That night, watching the various replays on the news, Kerr heard over and over again, "Of course, this was very uncharacteristic of Steve . . ."

Kerr laughed. "Uncharacteristic, huh? If it happened a hundred more times I'd do the same thing a hundred times. Throw the ball right back at him."

The next day when Kerr went to speak at a local elementary school there was a new question added to the usual, "Can I have your autograph?" and "Will you win the national championship?" repertoire. It was, "Why did you throw the ball at the coach?"

The Wildcats were on the road the next week, routing USC before winning a tough 78–76 overtime game at UCLA. Kerr found it amazing that UCLA could play so well against Arizona and so poorly against other teams. "You watch them on tape and they don't even get in a defensive stance half the time against other teams," he said. "Then against us, they're like a top ten team."

That left one road game—at Arizona State. Inevitably, every year, this was Arizona's least pleasant road game. The ASU fans had none of the good spirit or sense of humor that existed at Cal and at Stanford. "The only game their fans even come to is ours," Kerr said. "They draw terribly except when they play us and then the fans come in with a chip on their shoulder. It's never any fun playing there like it is at other places."

No fun is one thing. What happened on the night of February 27 went way beyond no fun. It was, without doubt, the most appalling behavior ever displayed by any group (calling them fans would be an insult to fans everywhere) at a college basketball game in all the years the game has been played. Given the ugly incidents that have taken place over the years, this is no small statement.

A little less than an hour before tip-off, Kerr and his teammates went out on the floor to shoot around and warmup. As they began shooting in the still near-empty gym, a small group of Arizona State students, perhaps a dozen of them, began taunting Kerr.

"PLO, PLO, Hey Kerr, where's your dad!" they chanted.

And then, "PLO, PLO, go back to Beirut!"

At first, Kerr couldn't believe what he was hearing. That anyone could possibly be so cruel as to taunt him about his father's assassination in such a manner was impossible. But in the near-empty gym, the impossible words kept echoing: "PLO, PLO . . ."

"At first, I tried to ignore it," Kerr said. "I took a couple more shots but I was shaking and my body actually felt kind of numb. I had to go and sit down. I just couldn't believe anyone would do that."

The other Wildcats didn't know what to do. The thought crossed everyone's mind to just go over and shut the idiots up one way or another. "But that wouldn't have been good," Kerr said. "If we had done that, then we would have ended up coming off as the bad guys."

As Kerr sat on the bench trying to collect his emotions, he felt a tap on his shoulder. He turned around and saw Wally Joyner, the California Angels' star first baseman, standing there. Joyner, unaware of what was going on, had come over to introduce himself to Kerr.

"I just wanted to tell you I'm a fan of yours," Joyner said. "If you can get a chance, come out to a ballgame sometime."

Kerr, in the middle of this trauma, was thrilled that Joyner would come over to introduce himself. Being a big baseball fan, he thought it quite something that a major leaguer would want to say hello to him. But when Joyner walked away, the insane chants were still there. Finally, it was time to go back into the locker room.

"Everyone was really pissed," Kerr said, "including me. For the first time in my life I actually found myself thinking about what I was going to say to the press about something that had happened. I just wanted to *get* those people somehow."

Once again, Kerr was in a situation where if he had backed away or gone into a shell of some kind no one would have blamed him. But he has proven time and again that he is one of those rare people who always seems to rise above being a victim. When the game started, Kerr was a man possessed. "Usually, I wait for an open shot, I don't look to shoot," he said. "This time, I wanted to shoot."

He took a three-pointer and hit, shaking his fist to the crowd. He took another one and hit again. Then another. By halftime he had hit six three-pointers and had 20 points. Arizona only led 47–41 but ASU had had to shoot 61 percent to stay within shouting distance. In the second half, the Sun Devils came out in a box-and-one, focusing their entire defense on Kerr. "They acted as if they hadn't played it much before," he said. Kerr now became the decoy and the rest of the Wildcats ran amok. The final was 101–73. If there was ever a night when Olson and Arizona would have been delighted to run up the score, this was it.

"Actually it was a little unfair to be angry with their players and coaches," Kerr said. "They had nothing to do with it. But I was just so angry I wanted to beat them by 50."

After the game Kerr called the "people" who had been taunting him "the scum of the earth." The reaction to the incident around the country was immediate and universal. Many people called on Arizona State to find out who the culprits were and expel them from school. Arizona State's only response was to apologize to Kerr for the "unfortunate" incident.

Once again Kerr found himself in the role of a martyr when all he really wanted to be was a basketball player. But he understood that, just as he could not escape his father's death four years ago, he could not escape this. As the mail poured in from everywhere, he tried his best to answer it all. "I just can't keep up," he said. "There's like twenty-five letters a day, sometimes more. I'm saving them for after the season when I'll have a chance to answer them."

One of the letters he received truly stunned Kerr. It came from one of the taunters. "I'm sorry if you were upset by what we did," he wrote. "But there's no way you can understand the intensity of the ASU–UA rivalry and some of the things we have had to put up with when we've gone to Arizona over the years." Naturally the letter was unsigned.

Kerr couldn't believe his eyes. "The guy actually tried to justify what they did," he said. "I didn't know whether to hate the guy or feel sorry for him for being so sick."

Now, with the Pac–10 tournament in Tucson the following week, Kerr had another concern: retribution by Arizona's fans against Arizona State. "They wouldn't do anything sick, but still they shouldn't do *anything,*" Kerr said. "The players and coaches didn't do it. They're all pretty good guys."

Kerr, with help from Arizona administrators, was planning an open letter in the local newspapers asking Arizona fans not to retaliate.

Always sensible, Kerr understood that an entire school should not be branded because of the sins of a small group of sick people.

Tonight, though, was not a night for unpleasantness. It was a night for nostalgia and fun—and the Arizona fans came prepared for both. Every corner of McKale Center seemed to have a sign thanking the seniors. One by one, PA announcer Roger Sedlmayr introduced them, along with their families. Each senior came through a giant papier maché cutout with his number on it. Each one heard thunderous cheers. Finally, there was only one senior left.

Sedlmayr paused for a moment, showing a sense of the dramatic. Everyone was standing now, clapping in rhythm, waiting. Finally, Sedlmayr began: "The last of the seniors. He came to Arizona five years ago and . . ."

The rest was drowned out. Everyone knew the story. When Sedlmayr was finished, thirteen thousand people became one. And through the paper cutout came . . . "Steeeeeeeve Kerrrrrrrr." Corny, sure. Overdone, probably. But what the heck. So many people in sports are heroes for all the wrong reasons. Here was someone who was a hero for the right ones. If you didn't feel chills as Kerr stood there drinking in the cheers, you needed CPR to get your heart pumping.

Kerr had been selected as the spokesman for the senior class. "When they first told me that I'd been chosen as the spokesman I was really honored," Kerr said. "But then I saw the alternatives." Typical Kerr. Start out with a wisecrack. A good one at that. But then he added, "I can't begin to tell you what an unbelievable experience this has been for me. You guys are the best. Thank you."

They cheered some more after that and there were some tears, too. Even when you know it's the right thing, it's tough when your son leaves home and that's what was happening now. Tucson's favorite son was going off into the real world, and this was the first of several going-away parties.

The only drawback to the whole affair was the scheduling of the basketball game. When Washington Coach Andy Russo arrived at the arena and was told that both teams were supposed to clear the floor fifteen minutes prior to tip-off, he was furious. "Is this a basketball game," he said, "or an awards banquet?"

Russo wasn't being unreasonable. It was bad enough, coming in as fodder for the Wildcats on a night like this, without being told you couldn't even warm up properly. As it turned out, though, it was

Arizona that wasn't ready to play when the game started. The Wildcats still had their minds on the ceremony. Sean Elliott began the game by missing two free throws, Arizona missed six of its first eight shots, and at halftime the lead was only 34–33, this against a team it had beaten 110–71 on the road.

Halftime solved the problem. Olson reminded the players how embarrassing it would be if they should manage to lose this game after all the accolades and cheers and the Wildcats responded by scoring the first 11 points of the second half. It was a romp from there. Olson took Kerr out with 3:35 left and the score 80–62.

Each senior got one more huge cheer. The final was 89–71.

The only negative part of the evening for Kerr was the onset of a migraine headache. Occasionally he gets migraines and, just as a TV cameraman switched on his light, Kerr started to feel dizzy. His vision blurred. He managed to make it through the interviews, then had to sit down to collect himself.

"This is about the third one this season," he said. "The only time I mind is when I get them during a game. Then they affect my shooting." He smiled. "Against some of the teams we play, it wouldn't matter. But now we're getting to the point where *everything* matters."

True enough. In one sense, this night had been an ending for Kerr. But in another, it was a beginning. Arizona was 28–2. Now, the season the players had been waiting for since December was about to begin.

March 6. . . Durham, North Carolina

Normally, Billy King has no trouble sleeping on the morning of a basketball game. He stays up late, either talking with friends or watching a movie, so that when he goes to sleep he will be tired and sleep soundly.

But this morning, he was up early, lying awake in bed, his mind too full to allow him to go back to sleep. For King, it was hard to believe that in a few hours he would hear himself introduced in Cameron Indoor Stadium for the last time. "I could still remember the first time so vividly," he said. "I kept thinking, 'Can it really be four years already?'"

Not only was it four years, but the senior season that King had wanted to be so special had turned sour. After bouncing back from the

N.C. State loss at home with five straight victories, the last one an impressive come-from-behind overtime win at Kansas, the Blue Devils had lost three straight.

Their record was 20–6 and today they were faced with the task of beating North Carolina in the regular season finale just to ensure themselves of third place in the ACC. This last game was supposed to have decided the regular season title. But Carolina had already wrapped that up and State had clinched second.

Once more, King reviewed the events of the last two weeks in his mind. What baffled him was the way the streak had started. After the Kansas game the Blue Devils had been on a high. They were 20–3 and even though they knew they had three road games coming up, they didn't think anything could be tougher than winning at Allen Field House against Danny Manning.

More important, the Kansas game had been a turning point for Quin Snyder. He had stepped forward and asserted himself as *the* point guard on this team, scoring 21 points and handing out 5 assists. "If we win at N.C. State," King remembered, "then it's a two-team race for the conference championship—us and Carolina."

But the Blue Devils didn't win at State. Once again, they were done in by the spell of the Wolfpack. They led by 11 points in the first half and still led with five minutes left. But State took the lead at 75–74 and the minute that happened, everyone panicked. Hurried three-point shots began going up from everywhere. The offense broke down completely. State outscored them 16–4 in the closing minutes and the final was an embarrassing 89–78—Duke's worst loss of the year.

Coach Mike Krzyzewski was genuinely angry, not so much with the loss but with the lack of poise. Duke teams are not supposed to fall apart in the face of a rally or a tough crowd. But this was a delicate team, one whose offense could disappear at any time. It had done just that *twice* against State. For the next two days in practice, Krzyzewski challenged his team to prove that it was tough; he dared them to bounce back and win at Georgia Tech. The Yellow Jackets were still on the same roll that had victimized N.C. State. And this game, on national TV, was the last home game for Tech's seniors.

Tech blew to a 21–8 lead on the Blue Devils, but this time Krzyzewski's team didn't panic. They came back to trail at halftime 44–42, and the game went right to the wire. But in the last two minutes, Tech got an unlikely basket from Edmund Sherrod while Danny Ferry missed a three-pointer. Tech won 91–87.

This time, Krzyzewski felt better. Tech had played a superb game and the Blue Devils had been about two plays away from winning anyway. But King was concerned. The opposition had scored 180 points in two games and that was too many. "I think we were worrying so much about our offense that we had gotten out of sync with our defense," he said. "Plus, we had gotten to feeling kind of sorry for ourselves, like we somehow deserved better because we'd worked so hard all season. I don't think a lot of the guys, especially the younger ones, really understood what working hard meant."

All of this preyed on King's mind as Duke bussed down to Clemson. He was concerned about this game. Clemson was always the toughest trip of the season because it involved a tedious five-hour bus ride. What's more, Duke had beaten the Tigers so easily in February—101–63—that taking them lightly would be a natural thing to do. King was right on all counts. Duke played its worst game of the season and let a mediocre team think it had a chance to pull a stunning upset. The crowd got behind the Tigers, the Blue Devils got flustered, and Clemson won the game 79–77.

This was rock bottom. Krzyzewski had not lost a game to Clemson since 1984 and had never lost in four years to Coach Cliff Ellis. In fact, no one on the team had ever lost to Clemson before. Now, with the important part of the season just beginning, Duke was floundering.

On the quiet bus trip home, Krzyzewski came back to talk to the players. As they gathered around him, he asked them, quietly, "What do you guys think is wrong?"

One by one, they answered. Some of it was standard stuff: We aren't executing; we aren't being patient; we aren't working hard enough on defense. King was only half listening. He and Strickland, as the captains, would be the last two people to talk. In his mind, King was reconstructing a speech David Henderson, a senior on the 1986 Final Four team, had given to the team just before the start of the ACC Tournament that year. When it came his turn to talk, King, playing the role of Joe Biden, plagiarized a lot of the Henderson speech.

"It's March," he said. "We've worked since October for all the games that are ahead of us. We know how good we can be. We know what our potential is. But do we know about making sacrifices? I'm not talking about coming to practice every day and things like that. I'm talking about little things. Not going to the party you want to go to because you need the rest. Not having a beer or two when you would like one.

"It's easy to rationalize, to say it's not a big deal and why shouldn't I do it. Next month there'll be plenty of time to party, to have a good time, to think about things besides basketball. But right now everything we do should be basketball because if it's not, we may look back at this month and say, 'If only . . .' That's the one thing we don't want to do. We want to know that we've done everything we possibly could to win."

It wasn't a fire-and-brimstone speech and it wasn't exactly like the one Henderson had made. But King sensed that his teammates listened. He knew they wanted to get things right just as much as he did. "The only difference," he said later, "is that they all had another chance. They could say, 'Well, *next* year,' if things didn't work out this year. Kevin and I couldn't say that."

The next day in practice Krzyzewski went back to basics. He wanted each player to understand his role, no matter how simple that might be. Danny Ferry and Kevin Strickland were shooters. Billy King and Robert Brickey were screeners. Quin Snyder was the point guard. On offense he was in charge. On defense, King was in charge. The players knew all of this—they had been practicing for almost five months. But Krzyzewski felt they had lacked focus during the three-game losing streak and needed to reinforce things that should have been automatic. Perhaps things had become so automatic that the players had become sloppy about it.

The Carolina game did not have the meaning it would have had it been for the regular season title, but it was still vital on three levels: First, Duke needed a victory to finish third. That would mean a first-round game in the ACC Tournament against a struggling Virginia team as opposed to an opener against an inconsistent but very talented Maryland team. Second, the bleeding had to be stopped after three straight losses. To finish the season on a four-game losing streak, the last one at home, would be devastating for the team's confidence.

And last, but certainly not least, it was King and Strickland's last home game. As he pulled himself out of bed on that Sunday morning, King thought to himself, "I'm going to remember this day one way or the other. I can't let it be a bad one." He repeated this thought to Strickland as they got ready to leave for the game.

Tip-off was at 1 p.m. because of the NBC telecast. More than one hundred of the students had been waiting in line to get choice seating since Tuesday. This kind of loyalty touched a chord in Krzyzewski. He spent the last three days before the game letting the students inside whenever he could, ordering pizza for them and bringing them blankets. "It's kids like this that make Duke special," he said later.

By noon, the place was jammed. Some of the players had been concerned that, with spring break beginning Friday and the team playing poorly, the students might not stay until Sunday. They had stayed.

The pregame ceremony for the seniors was brief, very different from Arizona's. The ovation was as deafening but the nature of the game that was to come made it different. "I wanted to enjoy it, to stand there and think about the last four years," King said. "But I couldn't. My mind was on the game. I wanted to get back in the locker room and get ready."

Krzyzewski's pregame talk was nothing out of the ordinary. Until the end when he called King and Strickland up front with him. "Our seniors," he said, "don't lose their last home game. Now let's go."

Outside, the students were ready, as they always are when Carolina is in town. They serenaded Dean Smith with a "Dean can't drive" chant, a reminder of his run-in with the Duke bus in the fall. Even Smith, who has been disdainful of the Duke students' antics over the years, laughed at that one.

Technically, this game meant nothing to Carolina. The Tar Heels had clinched first place by beating Georgia Tech on Wednesday. But no game with Duke—especially at Duke—is meaningless to Smith. In 1982, moments before the national championship game, someone asked Smith how many cigarettes he had smoked in the last hour. He pulled out the pack he was working on, looked at it and said, "Less than before the Duke game."

Duke was 10–17 that year.

Duke is not only Carolina's arch-rival, it is the one school in the ACC that when it does beat Carolina, is always doing so with a roster made up entirely of players who are academically superior—usually by a wide margin—at Carolina.

What's more, the irreverence of the Duke students is completely the opposite of the orderly, polite, do-everything-by-the-numbers crowd at Carolina. Smith is not a man who is comfortable with irreverence and he is not comfortable at Duke. The only way to deal with something you are uncomfortable with is to beat it, which, more often than not, Smith has done. In Cameron, he was 13–13 going into this game—but eleven of those victories had come during the last fifteen years.

Today, the Tar Heels begin as if they fully intend to win here again. They lead 12–6 by the first TV time-out. Duke is clearly tight. Sensing this, Krzyzewski tries something new. Instead of substituting a player or two at a time, he sends in five reserves at once. This is an old Smith tactic. Send in five fresh bodies who will go full-bore for a minute or two and then send your starters back in feeling rested.

The tactic works. The second team plays two minutes to a 2–2 tie. When the starters come back, they promptly go on a 7–0 run that puts Duke up 23–20. From there, they seesaw until halftime when it is 36–36.

This is exactly the kind of game everyone expected. King is concerned. Although the Blue Devils escaped with a victory in Chapel Hill in a Piss Factor situation in January, he doesn't want this game to come down to that. At the end of halftime, just before it is time to go back out, he says to his teammates, "If you can't *play* for twenty minutes, don't come back out."

They come back out and they *play.* During the first six minutes, the Blue Devils put on a basketball clinic, the kind that Carolina is used to putting on for other people. After being zero-for-seven on three-point shots in the first half, they catch fire: Snyder hits one. Then Strickland. Then Snyder again. Snyder makes a steal and feeds Strickland for a dunk. Another steal, another Snyder feed and Brickey dunks. Smith's superstar, J. R. Reid, swings an elbow in frustration and is called for an offensive foul. Snyder drives inside.

The place is going bananas by now. Snyder leads another fast break, finds King on the wing, and he dunks. Then, King steals the inbounds pass and feeds Ferry for a jumper. Incredibly Duke has scored 26 points in six minutes and the lead is 62–45. All of a sudden, the struggling team has become a dominant one.

Naturally, there is a letdown. The Tar Heels, rattled briefly, regroup after Smith calls a very rare time-out. Usually Smith hoards time-outs for the last couple of minutes (he hoards to the extent that some people believe Smith thinks that he gets some kind of extra credit in heaven for saving time-outs). Today, he has to call one. Carolina rallies back to within five at 76–71 but Snyder, growing up it seems with each possession, nails another three-pointer and then, after King steals the ball from Reid, Strickland hits another. It is 82–71 and Carolina is done.

The final is 96–81 and with fourteen seconds left, King gets the farewell he has dreamed about. Krzyzewski takes him out to a roaring ovation and hugs him as he comes to the bench. King goes down the bench, hugging everyone, wanting to hold on to the feeling he has for as long as he can. Seconds later, Strickland comes out too, and the two old friends savor their last ticks in Cameron with a warm embrace. It is the right ending, the kind that King and Strickland deserve.

When it is over, the students stampede the court and cut the nets down in celebration. Watching them, North Carolina Assistant SID Dave Lohse shakes his head. "Don't these people realize," he says, "that they just finished third?"

Lohse doesn't understand. Days like this have nothing to do with *where* you finish. They are about the *way* you finish.

March 7 . . . Hampton, Virginia

Rick Barnes stared at the television set blankly. He was trying to go through one last tape before it was time to leave the hotel but he was too wired to concentrate. Barnes's first season as a basketball coach was now down to one game—just as he had hoped it would be—and all he could think about was tip-off, which was now four hours away.

"I hate the waiting," he said. "I liked it the last two days when we played at two o'clock and got it over with. This eight o'clock stuff is for the birds."

The last two days had produced the victories George Mason had to have to get its shot at Richmond in the CAA final. The Patriots had been shaky in the opening round against James Madison, playing not to lose rather than to win. But they had survived, and that was no small thing. American, the other favorite in their bracket, had not. The Eagles had blown a 16-point lead and had lost to seventh-seeded William and Mary. That was a break for George Mason. Barnes had all the respect in the world for Chuck Swenson, like him a rookie coach, but Swenson's team just wasn't as dangerous as American.

The semifinal turned out to be a breeze. William and Mary had used up all its energy upsetting American and the Patriots led by 20 throughout the second half. It was Richmond that had to struggle, the Spiders coming from behind to beat North Carolina—Wilmington by just 3 points. So the final Barnes had hoped for was set: George Mason–Richmond.

In many ways, Barnes should have been relaxed for this game. His team now had twenty victories, no small accomplishment for a first-year coach. If it lost to Richmond that was no disgrace. There might still be an NIT bid in the offing.

But Barnes didn't see it that way. He had primed his team for this since November and he wanted them to play their best game of the season. If they did, he felt they would win. They would make history if they did that. George Mason had never won a conference title and had never been in the NCAA Tournament. Barnes took a long walk along the waterfront that afternoon to try to calm his jangled nerves.

He returned to his room to find a good luck telegram sent by Joe Harrington, the man who had hired him as an assistant at George Mason in 1980. Harrington's departure to Long Beach State had opened the job for Barnes.

"I remember when we first started and the program had nothing," Barnes said. "We'd get down and we'd feel like we were never going to get it going. And Joe would just say, 'Rick, we're going to get it done. Just keep on working.' Sure enough, we did. Actually, he did. We're here tonight because of Joe."

Barnes was in a reflective, almost nostalgic mood, if that is possible for someone who is thirty-two years old with twenty-nine games' experience as a head coach. "I've been thinking all day about what these kids went through back in October and November," he said. "They really went through hell every single day. But they stuck with it, they really did. All I want tonight is for them to go out there and really get after it."

Jack Kvancz, the athletic director and Barnes's confidant, came in to give Barnes his daily calm-down talk. "There's no pressure on you, Rick," he said. "If we win, it's worth $232,000 to the school. Don't think that's pressure. It's only money."

First-round losers in the NCAA Tournament receive $232,000. Kvancz could find about a hundred things to do with such a windfall. But he was only kidding Barnes to try and loosen him up. It wasn't going to work. Not today.

The team arrived at the grimy Hampton Coliseum about two hours before tip-off. This is a building badly in need of major renovations. In the tiny visitor's locker room, the Patriots could look up and see a hole in the wall, the one area of the room where the paint wasn't peeling.

The CAA insists on playing its tournament here because it is a neutral site. If it played at the Patriot Center at George Mason or the Robins Center at Richmond, attendance would be much better and the atmosphere 1,000 percent improved. But the league schools don't want to give anyone a homecourt advantage. So, each year everyone treks down here to play in a building that has all the charm of the Lincoln Tunnel at rush hour.

While Richmond Coach Dick Tarrant sat calmly out in the arena, doing a TV interview here, a radio interview there, Barnes stayed in the bowels of the arena and paced. "I wonder how many miles I've walked today pacing," he said. He turned to Assistant Coach Wayne Breeden. "I need an Advil. I've got my pregame headache."

Breeden pulled one out of his pocket. "I've got an extra. I already took one myself."

Barnes kept talking aloud. He was worried about the officials. His old friends Hank Armstrong and Donnie Vaden were working the game, along with Rusty (Luv2Ref) Herring. "I've got to remember not to get on Hank tonight," he said. "He may be tight, too."

Finally, it was time to talk to the players. "Think back to where we started," Barnes says. "Think back on all the work we've done because that's what's gotten you here tonight. Everything we've done has been because you guys have worked so hard.

"Tonight, though, we've got to go beyond hard work. Tonight, you have to be willing to die for this team. Every loose ball has to be ours. Every one! You may have heard Dick Tarrant say that we have nothing to lose in this game because we're not supposed to win. Well, you know and I know that's bull. We didn't go through all of this not to win. You thirteen guys deserve this.

"When you walk back out there now I want you to look up at that CAA banner. When we come back in here tonight, that banner's ours. Now go get it."

Barnes was certainly right when he told his team that it should ignore Tarrant's comment. But in a sense, the point was well taken. Richmond was 23–6, it was the regular season champion, and it had a string of impressive victories. Mason *wanted* to win. Richmond felt it *had* to win. That kind of pressure could work either way.

Tonight, for a half, it worked in Richmond's favor. The Spiders came out hot, breaking to an early 9–2 lead. Mason got even at 16–16 on a Brian Miller three-pointer but then Richmond went on another binge, opening a 34–24 lead. The Patriots' advantage was their quickness, Richmond's was its strength. The Spiders were forcing a halfcourt tempo and dominating the inside. When Mason collapsed on their big men, they kicked the ball out to Rodney Rice, who made three three-pointers and had 16 points by halftime.

A Robert Dykes basket inside cut the Richmond lead to 34–26 with 5:40 left. Then, after a missed free throw by Richmond's Steve Kratzer, Kenny Sanders had a chance to cut the lead to six. He missed inside, Richmond rebounded and started downcourt. As Sanders missed the shot, Mason part-time Assistant Coach Mike Yohe, easily the most mild-mannered person on the GMU bench, jumped up, thinking he had seen a foul. Yohe never said anything but when he came to his feet, Armstrong, running past, stopped and nailed him with a technical foul.

This was an extraordinary call to make. Technically, an official can call a technical on anyone on the bench other than the head coach any time they stand up. But no one ever does. As long as the bench doesn't become abusive or start making gestures, referees ignore them. If the behavior of the bench does start to get out of hand, most officials will warn the head coach as in, "Coach, I don't want your assistants jumping up off the bench or yelling at us."

Once a coach has been warned, then a technical is his fault if it is called. Barnes had been given no warning and, especially in a game with so much at stake, one would have thought Armstrong would have been giving both teams the benefit of the doubt. If there was ever a game where the old Joe Forte adage—just manage the game, don't dominate it—should have been in play, this was that game.

But Armstrong didn't do that. He nailed Yohe with a technical. Barnes didn't even know who had been called or for what. Armstrong then took a bad situation and made it worse. As Rodney Rice went to the foul line to shoot the two free throws, Armstrong noticed student trainer Dean Ravizzo, who was sitting on the far end of the bench, putting his hand on his neck. Armstrong not only had rabbit ears, he had rabbit eyes. Just as Rice released the ball, Armstrong blew the whistle and teed up Ravizzo.

Armstrong had completely lost control. For one thing, he had messed up the simple act of administering a technical. He had blown

the whistle just as Rice released the ball and the shot had hurtled off
the back rim. "He should get that shot over," Tarrant argued, correctly.
To be consistent, Armstrong turned that down. He did everything
entirely wrong during the sequence.

A good referee does not call a technical foul on a student trainer who
is sitting at the far end of the bench nowhere near the coaches. If he
is so sensitive that he objects to the choke sign—Ravisso denied that
he had done anything later—he should go to the head coach and say,
"I object to the choke sign from that kid on the end of the bench and
if anything like that happens again, I'll tee you." One can be certain
that Barnes, or any coach in a like situation, would clamp down quickly.

Armstrong did none of this. He simply ran amok. Did his past run-ins
with Barnes affect his judgment? Who knows. Armstrong is a good
official most of the time. But he had been counseled by others in the
profession for two years to stop letting his ego interfere with his work.
"Stop being such a tough guy all the time," one supervisor had told him
on several occasions.

Tonight, Armstrong had been a tough guy. And he had cast a pall
over a championship game. Rice made the next three free throws and
on the ensuing possession, Scott Stapleton hit a jumper. Richmond led
39–26. In an amazing twist of irony, Armstrong then pulled up lame
on the next trip downcourt with a torn calf muscle. He had to leave
the game. The Patriots, just as hobbled emotionally, limped into the
locker room down 48–35.

Barnes's assistants had the most work to do at halftime. They had
to convince Barnes not to try to find Armstrong right then to demand an explanation. Outside, Kvancz, normally the cool one in the
group, was raging at ACC Commissioner Tom Yeager and Refereeing Supervisor Dan Woolridge. "I'd like to see that son of a bitch
pull that kind of crap on the North Carolina bench during a championship game," Kvancz raged. "What does he think this is, the goddamn Little League, where he's Mr. Big Shot and can do whatever
the fuck he wants to?

"You send the SOB to my place next year," Kvancz concluded, "and
I promise you I won't pay him!"

In the meantime, the game wasn't over. Barnes's job was to convince
his players of this. "Get your heads up!" he said. "We've been down
before and we've come back. Right now they're sitting in there thinking they've got it fucking won. They're in for a shock. Play our way and

you'll come back. If they get the ball inside, foul them. We can afford to foul. Put them on the line. They aren't good foul shooters.

"There's one key here. You've got to believe you can come back. Twenty minutes is a long time." He paused. "Keep your heads up and go back out there and play like champions."

They did. Sanders, held to five points in the first half, scored right away. Then he stole the inbounds pass and scored again. After that, it was Davis's turn. He nailed three straight three-pointers and suddenly, in less than five minutes, it was 51–48.

Davis, overexcited, committed his fourth foul, reaching in, and had to come out. Richmond built the lead back to 59–52 but the Patriots came back again. Miller hit a jumper, then a drive. Earl Moore, the forgotten man of the last month, hit a three-pointer. Then he hit another one. Amazingly, Mason led 61–60 with more than eight minutes to play.

From that moment on, it was high-wire basketball, two good teams playing with an entire season at stake. No one could get the lead and the ball. Back and forth they went, the old building now full of life as each team's fans cheered and prayed and hung on for dear life.

A Davis three-pointer put the Patriots up 69–67, but Benjy Taylor, a little-used Richmond senior averaging 1.7 points per game, answered with a three of his own to make it 70–69. Davis hit two free throws to make it 71–70, Taylor answered again and it was 72–71 with 1:50 to go.

Moore flashed open. His jumper went in and out. Richmond rebounded. There was 1:20 left. The Spiders would have to shoot. They ran the clock down, then tried to go inside to Peter Woolfolk. The pass was long. Moore picked the ball up in the corner, took a step and slipped on a wet spot. He fell, but on tape, it looked as if he kept his dribble. The officials saw only the fall and called traveling. Either way, a tough call.

That gave the ball back to Richmond. The clock was now down to forty-five seconds. Richmond didn't have to shoot. The Patriots, not wanting to foul, let the clock run to eight seconds before they fouled Taylor, who was 20-of-21 from the line on the season. Coolly, after two Barnes time-outs, he made both. It was 73–70. George Mason needed a three-pointer to tie. Davis, who had been heroic all night, cut to the left wing and with all sorts of hands in his face, fired. The ball clanged off the rim. It was over. Richmond was in the NCAA Tournament.

For a moment, Davis just sat on the floor, staring in disbelief. Barnes went to congratulate Tarrant, still slightly in shock himself. It had been so close. As he walked off, staring at the scoreboard, Barnes couldn't help himself. "Three points," he thought, "and Armstrong gave them three points on the technicals."

Sadly, the technicals had intervened on an evening of otherwise wonderful basketball. The talk in the aftermath should have been about the Patriots' courageous comeback and Taylor's clutch play at the finish. Instead it was about Hank Armstrong. Even Yeager shook his head and said, "I would really like to know the rationale behind those calls."

Unfortunately, the tightness of the officials' fraternity got in the way of what was best for the game. Woolridge, the supervisor, a recently retired official himself, refused to admit that Armstrong had made any mistake at all. Even the next day, after looking at tape, Woolridge still wouldn't admit that Armstrong had messed up.

This is a problem with officiating: When mistakes are made, no one wants to admit it. The fraternity closes ranks. Too many leagues have ex-officials like Woolridge as supervisors. It is very difficult to discipline a former peer, a friend, a pal. Woolridge is a good supervisor but someone else should have been involved in the area of discipline.

Barnes didn't know it but he had just coached his last game at George Mason. On that night, though, he was thinking of the future— one he thought would be at George Mason.

"You proved tonight you're winners," he told his team. "You three seniors have set a standard here and the rest of us are going to live up to it in the future. You should be disappointed, but you should be proud too. I'm proud to have coached you this year. You've put up with a lot.

"We'll be back again," he said finally. "The standard has been set."

Barnes turned around and walked out. His players' tears were more than he could bear.

March 9 . . . New York

From thirty-eight floors up, Paul Evans stared down at the streets of Manhattan, a look of complete relaxation on his face. If ever a coach had reason to feel satisfied, it was Evans. His Pittsburgh team had gone through a season as turbulent as can be imagined and in the game that mattered most, had played its best basketball.

"I would hope winning the regular season will put a lot of the Pitt problems of the past *in* the past," he said. "The whole thing was set up for us to fail and we didn't. That's what makes me feel good."

The Panthers had gone to Syracuse for the last weekend of the regular season with the Big East title on the line. Both teams were 11–4 in league play. After losing on the road to Seton Hall, Pitt had struggled past Connecticut and Boston College. In the Connecticut game, the Huskies had come back from 18 points down in the second half to almost steal the game. Against BC, Evans had intentionally taken a technical foul early in the first half to try and get his team going but then had drawn another one—unintentionally—at the end of the half.

"We weren't playing well, but we were winning," Evans said. "I kept wondering if we were going to just jerk along like this the rest of the season or get it going again. It worried me, though, because it reminded me a little bit of last year. Once we won our twentieth game last year we didn't have a good practice the rest of the season."

Evans was even more worried when his team lost its last home game to Seton Hall. By now, there was no doubt that the Pirates were for real. They had destroyed Villanova after their initial win over Pitt and they were playing superb basketball. Pitt didn't play poorly against Seton Hall. But a loss was a loss and now the Panthers had to go to Syracuse to play in the Carrier Dome in front of more than thirty thousand people for the Big East title.

Strangely, Evans felt confident as he and the team flew to Syracuse on Friday, even though he had left backup forward Steve Maslek home. After Evans had told the team to take it easy and get some rest on Thursday, Maslek had been spotted heading for his girlfriend's dorm at 2:30 A.M. Enough was enough.

Still, Evans was—for him—sanguine. "Playing in the Dome never bothered me," he said. "We'd gone in there when I was at Navy and beaten them by 20 in the NCAAs and we had won up there last year. The question was whether the kids wanted it or not."

On Friday afternoon, Evans called Charles Smith in to talk about his feelings. Evans genuinely liked Smith. He often got frustrated with Smith because Smith was low-key and easygoing, not the kind of blood-and-guts competitor that Evans craved. Even though he wished he could get Smith to hurt more after losses, Evans respected him and looked to him as the buffer between himself and the team.

Evans told Smith he was worried about the team. He didn't think the freshmen were as concerned about winning as they should be. He had no idea where Lane and Gore were coming from. He thought that once again they had become satisfied because they had won twenty games and wrapped up an NCAA bid. Smith agreed. He said he would talk to his teammates.

Evans felt better. But that evening he got a phone call from his trainer. Lane had been scheduled for treatment that night and hadn't shown. He had, instead, gone out with some of the Syracuse players. Evans wasn't pleased. He was less pleased a couple of hours later when he went to make a midnight bed check. Curfew had been at ten. Jason Matthews was on the phone when Evans walked in and Bobby Martin was still dressed. Evans said nothing to the two freshmen. He also said nothing to Lane.

Saturday went by quietly. Evans, who had been having trouble sleeping for most of the season, was up very early Sunday morning. He was angry with his team and he planned to let the players know about it. Before they went to the arena that day, Evans told his players what he thought of them.

"You have the talent to win this game but I don't think you will," he said. "I don't think you guys care enough. Jerome, if you really cared you wouldn't be running around with the Syracuse guys on Friday. You're so good you don't need treatment, I suppose. Jason, Bobby, you're both so cool I don't know if you care at all.

"You guys just piss me off. You don't want to win. You're satisfied to just be good. You don't want to be great."

Evans's words were carefully chosen. "I figured with the environment we were going into, we needed to be pissed off," he said. "If they were pissed at me and went out and played because of it, that was just fine."

Whomever the Panthers were mad at, they played the way Evans wanted—especially Lane. He scored 29 points and had 15 rebounds. "He was on another level," Evans said. "He was possessed."

Smith scored 18 points, Gore scored 15. The Panthers hung on in the face of the screaming crowd and won, 85–84. For the first time in school history, they had won the regular season title in the Big East. "If we had lost we would have gone into the [Big East] Tournament needing to win at least two games just to save face," Evans said. "Now, we've won something that means something and we know we've probably got a number two seed in the [NCAA] Tournament wrapped up. That feels good."

Looking back at the turbulent year—the two players lost to academics, the run-ins with John Thompson and Rollie Massimino—Evans had few regrets. Except about Massimino. "I think we've both hurt ourselves with this thing," he said softly. "I would guess now, it will never really be resolved. Last night, we were both at a high school game and I saw him in the hospitality room at halftime. I started to go over and say hello, maybe break the ice a little, but he had turned around. I don't know if he saw me or not but I really don't think it's going to change any time soon. . . ."

Massimino had seen Evans. That same afternoon, he sat on a bench in Central Park (the Big East Tournament would begin in two days in Madison Square Garden) dressed in a red sweater, smoking a cigar and talking alternately about the joys and frustrations of the season.

Many of the frustrations centered on Evans. Their second meeting of the season had been even more embarrassing than the first. It had come three days after Villanova's loss at Temple. Once again, Pitt had played superbly, killing Villanova on the boards while winning the game going away, 87–75.

Once again, Massimino changed his mind about shaking hands, again feeling that you don't walk away after a loss, especially at home. But the handshake had turned into a shouting match with graduate Assistant Coach Steve Pinone having to step in between the two men to keep it from getting worse.

Massimino was genuinely shaken by the incident. Instead of hanging around his office as he normally does after a game, he left right away. "If I had stuck to my original plan to not shake hands, nothing would have happened," Massimino said. "I'm not a hypocrite, that's why I didn't think I should shake hands. They don't shake hands in the pros and it's no big deal. But then with twenty seconds to go I told [Assistant Coach] Steve [Lappas] that I had to go over and congratulate him, that it would be wrong not to.

"But that incident was it. The whole thing was an embarrassment— to both of us. There just isn't going to be any communication between us. I don't see any reason for it. People in this business know me. I'll let them make the judgments on who is right and who is wrong. The whole thing never should have come to this but it did. Now, it's over and done with. If we play Saturday in the semifinals, I won't shake his hand after the game, win or lose."

Massimino's voice was filled with anger as he spoke. Like any coach who had known success, Massimino has detractors. But he had never had an experience like this with another coach, and it had shaken him.

In truth, though, the Evans affair was the only blotch on a regular season that had been as rewarding as any Massimino could remember. The Wildcats were going into the Big East Tournament with a 19–11 record. They had finished tied (with Georgetown) for third in league play with a 9–7 record, a far cry from the seventh place finish that many had predicted for them.

Since their record included victories over Illinois, Syracuse, St. John's, Georgetown, Seton Hall, and Virginia, they had an NCAA bid wrapped up, even if they were to lose their opening tournament game to St. John's.

"I don't think we'll lose, though," Massimino said. "It will be a very tough game but the way our kids have practiced and prepared the last few days I really think we'll beat them. This will be the eighth time in nine years we've been in the NCAAs. Last year was just a fluke. I knew that but we had to prove it to people. Now, we have. But there's still more to do."

Massimino paused to relight his cigar and leaned back on the bench, watching a female jogger running by. "Great city, New York," he said, giggling for a second like a teenage boy. His mind turned back to his team.

"You know, I could be completely wrong, we might not win another game this season. But I just have a feeling that this team is gonna do something special. We're not as good as we were in '85 and I'm not sure we've got quite the toughness that team had. But these kids have really been something all year.

"When we went to Seton Hall and got absolutely hammered [84–58] we could have been in trouble. That was the one game of the year where we just didn't have it. They were hot. We couldn't stop Bryant and we got killed. I was worried. I thought maybe we were running out of gas, not so much physically as emotionally.

"So the next day I gave 'em one of my talks. I told 'em about the house that we had built at Villanova. That if you play for Villanova, you don't get blown out the way we did at Seton Hall. Every family goes through ups and downs and when you hit a down you pull together and use each other to replenish your strength.

"I screamed and I yelled and I made it clear they hadn't done a goddamn thing yet this season. Villanova teams don't *settle*. They always look for more. When I was finished, I just turned around and walked out. I was drained."

But he wasn't finished with his yelling for the day. "After the kids went home I gave my assistants the same speech. I killed them. I told them that it didn't matter what I said to the kids, this was our fault, not theirs, that we had let up and been satisfied because we had played well early. I said, 'If you catch me doing that, jump on me. I don't want a bunch of yes-men working for me. If I screw up tell me.'"

Two days later Villanova went to Syracuse. Coming off the Seton Hall debacle, there was every reason to believe the Wildcats might be primed for another blowout on the road. It never happened. "When we went up there, they had every reason to kill us. We had beaten them at our place, they were still fighting to win the conference. But our guys went out and played. When we do that, we can play with anybody."

Villanova had a chance to win on its final possession, but Plansky missed a jumper and Syracuse survived. The Wildcats were devastated by the loss. Plansky, normally the most quotable member of the team, sat in a corner of the locker room, his head down, giving monosyllabic answers. Kenny Wilson cried and wouldn't talk to anyone.

"The fact that it hurt that much was good, because it meant they thought they should win," Massimino said. "I was glad because they came out of there believing in themselves again."

Villanova finished the season with a game at Vermont. This was a Massimino special. Vermont was his alma mater and Tom Brennan, the Vermont coach, was a former assistant. The team spent three days in New England, most of it relaxing and getting some much-needed rest.

"It worked out perfectly," Massimino said. "We went and ate every night at the Italian restaurant we always went to when I was in school. It was like a vacation. Mary Jane and I had gone there on our honeymoon, so she loved it. It was a little bit like Hawaii because we got to spend time together as a team and got to feel close again."

He sat back on the bench. "A year ago at this time I was miserable. I felt hurt, betrayed by the whole thing with Gary [McLain]. I wondered how much longer I wanted to keep coaching. Now, I feel young again. I'm fifty-three and I know I want to coach until I'm sixty. Maybe longer. As long as I feel like this about it, I know I want to keep doing it."

He pointed his cigar. "Just remember what I said before the season started. The true guy comes out in adversity. We got some more games to win this season. If I'm wrong, I don't know my kids."

15
TRIPLE CROWN

Almost everyone on the planet has a conference tournament these days. When the Big Ten eventually gives in and starts playing one, only the Ivy League and the fabled American Mid-Continent Conference will not have a postseason tournament.

The reason these tournaments exist is money. People buy the tickets, television shows the games, and the cities that host them rake in all sorts of revenue from the fans who pour in for the weekend.

But there is one conference tournament that is different from all the others. The basics are the same. Money created the tournament and sustains it. But because the Atlantic Coast Conference has had a tournament since it first came into existence in 1954, it is special. The other league tournaments have only been around for a couple of years. The ACC Tournament has always been there.

The nature of the ACC Tournament has changed over the years. Now, the regular season champion comes into the weekend knowing it is in the NCAAs. In fact, most years, the top *four* teams come in knowing they have bids locked up. Some coaches now talk about sitting players out to rest minor injuries. "It just ain't life and death anymore," Lefty Driesell said. "If you win, great. But if you don't, it's no big deal."

Wrong. The coaches could talk all they wanted about the tourna-

ment not meaning as much as it once did. Tradition is tradition. Many
of the players in the league had grown up watching the ACC Tournament on television. They remembered Maryland–N.C. State. They
remembered the infamous 12–10 game between Duke and State in
1968.

They knew that if you won the ACC Tournament you could walk
around all summer wearing a T-shirt that said "ACC Champions" on
it and they knew it was for, as players like to say, "a banner." If you
won, you could hang a banner in your gym that said "ACC Champions" on it.

And then there were the fans. Some had been to all thirty-five
tournaments. Most planned the first weekend in March around the
tournament every year. Year in and year out, there was no tougher
ticket in sports than the ACC Tournament. There was never a public
sale. To buy a ticket you either had to be a student and be selected in
your school's lottery or you had to be a member of one of the school's
booster clubs.

The ACC Tournament, more than anything else, provides the
booster clubs with their revenue. It is a simple case of blackmail. Would
you like ACC Tournament tickets? Yes. Well, they're easy to get. Just
contribute x thousand dollars annually and you will have the privilege
of buying them. Did people object? Heck no. At some schools, there
were waiting lists of people hoping to get a chance to fork over their
money.

The ACC Tournament is more than just a tournament. It is a
social occasion, a part of the lives of the people who participate each
year. "It's like being the king of your neighborhood," Duke Coach
Mike Krzyzewski said. "It's great to have recognition in other places.
But it isn't the same as being considered the best in your own backyard."

For the eight ACC teams, this was their backyard. The rest of the
country didn't much care who won the ACC Tournament, but from
College Park, Maryland, to Atlanta, Georgia, just about everyone who
followed basketball *did* care. A lot.

Winning the tournament could save an entire season. In 1987, N.C.
State had dragged into the tournament with a 17–14 record. The
Wolfpack needed overtime to beat Duke in the first round. It needed
double overtime to beat Wake Forest in the semifinals. And then, in
a game it never should have won, it upset North Carolina 68–67 in the

final. Carolina had also gone two overtimes the day before to get by Virginia.

When the final was over, the State players celebrated as if they had won the national championship. The Carolina players were crushed. So were the coaches. Assistant Roy Williams, normally as outgoing and friendly as anyone in the profession, sat on a stairway, inconsolable.

To an outsider, this kind of emotion can't be explained. In 1988, it would be no different. When the eight teams gathered in Greensboro, four of them had already locked up NCAA bids: Carolina, N.C. State, Duke, and Georgia Tech. All four had twenty victories. Maryland, the fifth-place team, was 16–11. Most people thought that an opening-round victory over Georgia Tech would lock a bid for the Terrapins and that even with a loss, they might still get in.

The bottom three teams—Virginia, Clemson, and Wake Forest—were going nowhere unless they found some miraculous way to win the tournament. This was not terribly likely. Between them, the three schools had won the tournament three times: Wake twice, in 1961 and 1962, and Virginia once, in 1976. Clemson was the only school in the league that had never won the tournament. In fact, the Tigers hadn't reached the final since 1962 and hadn't won a *game* since 1980.

But, as State had proven in 1987, strange things could happen in the ACC Tournament.

Each of the top four teams had a motive for wanting to win. Carolina had not won since 1982, a slump that mystified most ACC people since, prior to that, Dean Smith had won the tournament nine times in sixteen years. Starting in 1983, the Tar Heels had been the top seed three times, but hadn't won. The State loss had been the most crushing, and this year, for the first time since the NCAA expansion, Smith actually admitted that he and his team badly wanted to win.

"We're coming in here pretending it's the old days and we have to win to get to the NCAAs," Smith said. "I think this is important to this team."

Bobby Cremins and Georgia Tech had beaten Smith and Carolina to win the tournament in 1985. The next year, Tech had lost the final, 68–67, to Duke when Craig Neal missed a jump shot with nine seconds left. Since then, Tech's star had faded; to get back on the map the Yellow Jackets needed to do well here or in the NCAA Tournament. They had the toughest first-round game, though, since Maryland felt it *had* to win to get into the sixty-four-team NCAA field.

As for State, Valvano had made a big thing after the '87 tournament victory that winning in March and hanging banners was what his program was all about. Smith, who had had some trouble winning in March since '82, really chafed at that one. Now, after a 23–6 regular season, Valvano had to convince his team that March was as important this year as it was last year.

"Last year, we had a mission because we felt we had to win the whole thing to get into the NCAAs," he said. "The mission should be the same this year. Win, hang a banner, get to play the first two games in our backyard instead of being shipped out west somewhere."

On Thursday, the night before the tournament, Valvano showed his team three tapes: the ACC championship game against Virginia in 1983, the NCAA championship game that year against Houston, and the '87 ACC championship game. When the tapes were over, Valvano reminded his team that this was what the entire season was about. "This is what we've worked for all year," he said. "The chance to do that [celebrate] again. That's what this is about."

But Valvano was concerned. He didn't feel that sense of mission he wanted to feel. They were just a little too comfortable with the twenty-three wins.

The same could not be said for Duke. Like Valvano, Krzyzewski wanted his team to rise to the occasion of a championship. He still remembered the feeling of winning in 1986 and wanted that feeling again. He had been bitterly disappointed the year before when his team had come in as the defending champion, played horribly in the first round and lost to State. On Tuesday, sensing that his team was still basking a bit in the Carolina victory, he threw the whole team out of practice.

"You guys have the chance to do something special and you're throwing it away," he told his team. "Do you want to go into the tournament like you did last year and embarrass yourselves? Or do you want to play like you're capable and win it? You decide."

D A Y   O N E

The opening round of the tournament is always the most unpredictable. Sometimes, the underdogs rise to the occasion to produce remarkable games. Sometimes, they are beaten down by the long season and aren't capable of competing.

Wake Forest certainly tried. Perhaps no team in America had been crippled by injuries more than the Deacons. Even semihealthy, Wake had managed to pull January upsets over Carolina and State. But by February, with only three of his first seven still able to play, Coach Bob Staak was lucky to be able to field a team.

Still, the Deacons came out flying at the start of their game with Carolina. The Tar Heels acted as if noon was just too early to play and were quickly down 13–4. There were some rumblings in the Greensboro Coliseum but for the most part, everyone just waited. Wake would have to stay in the game for a lot longer than seven minutes to win over any fans.

This is one of the phenomena of the tournament. The crowd is divided equally into eight groups. But if an underdog has a legitimate chance to win, the fans from the other six schools will join their fans in trying to pull them through. No one is more conscious of this sort of thing than Dean Smith.

"I noticed the Duke students waving their arms when we were shooting free throws," he would say after the Wake game. "They did a good job. They made it feel like a road game."

Sure, Dean. Two hundred students waving their arms in an arena of sixteen thousand made it feel like a road game. But that was Dean. Before the game, given the choice of benches as the higher seeded team, he had taken what is normally the visitor's bench—because the Wake fans were at the home bench end of the building. The man misses nothing.

The 13–4 start didn't last. Carolina went on a 21–1 spree late in the first half to build a 39–28 halftime lead and eventually cruised home with an 83–62 victory. "We just hit the wall," Staak said. "The kids had hung together and played tough through it all but today we hit the wall. We had nothing left."

Game two of the afternoon doubleheader was, on paper, the best of the day. That is normal since the No. 4 and No. 5 seeds figure to be the most evenly matched. Georgia Tech had beaten Maryland ten straight times. But Maryland needed this game more and played like it. All season, the Terrapins had shown flashes of great talent. But they had never been consistent.

In truth, they were a team in flux. Many of the players were unhappy with Coach Bob Wade. Perhaps no coach in the history of college basketball had been given the free ride granted to Wade when Maryland hired him in the wake of the Len Bias tragedy. Chancellor John Slaughter, after forcing Lefty Driesell out, hired Wade on a recommendation from Wade's good friend John Thompson.

Maryland had gone 0–15 in ACC play and 9–17 overall in Wade's first year. Certainly, under the circumstances, judging Wade on that record would have been unfair. But it was just as stupid to run around shouting that Wade had done a great job—which many people did. CBS voted him the "rookie coach of the year," one of the more absurd acts of that or any season.

This season, with many players who had been forced to sit 1987 out and with two excellent recruits added, junior-college point guard Rudy Archer and freshman center Brian Williams, the Terrapins were vastly improved. They were 16–11 and a respectable 6–8 in ACC play.

Within the team there were problems, however. Even though Slaughter and Wade kept trumpeting a new commitment to academics, the team was full of academic question marks. Reporters' questions about whether several players were in academic trouble were being met with answers like "No comment" and "That's a team matter." What's more, two players, Hood and Williams, were thinking of transferring (and would do so at the end of the semester). Wade could claim that Hood's departure was over playing time. But Williams's departure was a devastating blow. He was the cornerstone of Wade's program and his leaving said, in essence, that he didn't like the way he was being coached and that the so-called new academic emphasis was a crock.

In the short term, though, Maryland had one job: beat Georgia Tech. The Terrapins did that, dominating the game from the start. Ironically, the hero was fifth-year senior Keith Gatlin, a good friend of Len Bias and a man Wade had been ready to write off after he signed Archer. Gatlin had almost left college in the wake of the Bias tragedy. He had lost his eligibility, dropped out of school, wondered if he would ever play again and then come back for one last semester.

A gifted player, he had forced Wade to play him with his brilliance, and today he scored 25 points, knocking in one three-pointer after another when the Terrapins needed them. Tech never could get going and the final was 84–67.

"I never thought I would have this feeling again," Gatlin said. "The funny thing is, after what I've been through, I doubt if losing a basketball game will ever really bother me again."

There were many twists in this story. The last time Gatlin had played

in an ACC Tournament game had been in the 1986 semifinals—
against Georgia Tech. In that game, with five seconds left and the score
tied, Gatlin had tried to throw a crosscourt inbounds pass to Bias.
Duane Ferrell had intercepted it and dunked at the buzzer. He was the
hero, Gatlin the goat. Two years later, Ferrell had played poorly and
Gatlin superbly. Their roles were reversed. Gatlin just smiled when
someone mentioned that.

"You know, I barely remember that game," he said. "It was at least
a couple of lifetimes ago."

Indeed.

That evening, the favorites each had brief scares. State, after a 22–6
start against Clemson, looked to have a virtual off night. For some
reason, Cliff Ellis, whose team was on something of a roll, coming off
wins over Duke and Georgia Tech, started the game in a spread offense.
His players had no clue what they were doing and were soon in a deep
hole. Ellis abandoned that bit of foolishness and the Tigers came all
the way back to tie the game at 63–63 with 4:30 left.

Now the crowd was aroused. During the first half it had been so quiet
you could hear the sneakers squeaking as players made their cuts. But
Clemson is Clemson. With a chance to take the lead, senior Grayson
Marshall missed a jump shot. Vinny Del Negro hit at the other end,
then stole the ball and fed Charles Shackleford for a dunk. That was
that. The final was 79–72. Time for spring football at Clemson—as
usual.

The finale to the long day was Duke–Virginia. Traditionally, the last
game of the first day is a debacle. Although the schedule says 9 P.M.
it never starts before 9:30, and it seems as if the players are tired from
watching the other three games.

"It feels like you're playing in the middle of the night," Virginia
Assistant Coach Tom Perrin said.

For the Cavaliers this would be a sad ending to a sad season. They
came in with a 13–17 record, many of the losses near-misses. In February, they had lost their leader, point guard John Johnson, when he had
tested positive for drugs. *With* Johnson, Virginia wasn't that good.
Without him . . .

"It's a funny feeling," Perrin said as he waited for the game to start.
"In one way, we'll all be glad when this is over. In another, I feel really
sad knowing we'll be watching the NCAAs on television. It's such an
exciting time. It will be a real left-out feeling."

For a half, the Cavaliers acted as if they wanted to give Duke a left-out feeling. Slowing the Blue Devils to their pace—a crawl—they scored the last 10 points of the half and led 26–24. Krzyzewski's concern that his team was still in a self-congratulatory mood had been well founded. Duke was flat.

Snyder had five turnovers during the first twenty minutes, including two passes that had endangered spectators. "His dad's here," Krzyzewski said. "I think he was trying to throw him a pass. I finally said, "Forget your old man and throw the goddamn ball to Ferry."

In the second half, Snyder did exactly as he was told. With Duke leading, 38–35, Snyder took over the game. He hit a three-pointer and then a free throw. Then he stole the ball from UVA's John Crotty and fed King, who would have gone in for a dunk if Crotty hadn't fouled him intentionally. King made one free throw, then Strickland made two more on the ensuing possession. Finally, Snyder stole the ball again and his lay-up made it 47–35 with ten minutes left. Duke was home free.

When it was over, an eager radio man asked Krzyzewski how it felt to get the first one out of the way. "It feels," Krzyzewski said, "like you feel when you get over a sickness."

The semifinals were set just before midnight: Carolina–Maryland and State–Duke.

D A Y   T W O

Strangely, each of the four teams still alive was exactly where it wanted to be today. Maryland didn't care who it played, just so it was still playing. Carolina was delighted not to have to face Tech. State was convinced it would continue its domination over Duke. And the Blue Devils wanted another shot at the Wolfpack.

The opener was your basic yawner. Maryland had shot its wad the day before. What's more, the Terrapins didn't really think they could beat the Tar Heels. After an early 15–12 Maryland lead, Carolina went on a 16–4 binge to take a 28–19 lead. Maryland got back to within six by halftime but Carolina started the second half with a 9–2 run and Maryland never again got closer than eight—and that with a minute to go. The final was 74–64.

The only entertainment was provided by the Duke students who, each time the Carolina band played its fight song, stood and held up their fingers to indicate the number of times the song had been played. There are those who believe the Carolina pep band knows only two songs: the fight song and the national anthem. But, in its defense, the band plays the national anthem faster than anyone in the country, clocked at an average of fifty-four seconds when in midseason form. In an era when some singers stretch the anthem to over two minutes, a fifty-four-second rendition cannot be underappreciated.

The other amusing moment came after the game when Carolina's Jeff Lebo, talking about why it was important for the Tar Heels to win the tournament, commented, "We're probably the only ones who thought we had a chance at the start of the season."

Carolina had been a consensus pick to win the league in preseason. When this was pointed out to Lebo, he said, "Well, I saw some preseason magazines that picked us second, third, even fourth." If a magazine existed that had picked the Tar Heels fourth, no one had *ever* seen it. If it did exist, one might guess that it would cease to exist making those sorts of predictions very quickly. Anyway, Lebo was convinced he and his teammates were the underdogs. His coach wouldn't have it any other way.

Game two was as tense as game one had been dull. Krzyzewski had made a point of not talking about revenge to his team beforehand. Instead, he had just said again and again, "Play *our* game, not theirs."

State's game, as had been proven earlier, was hard for Duke to handle. With the two talented big men, Shackleford and Chucky Brown, and the slashing point guard, Corchiani, State was always going to give Duke trouble. What's more, the Blue Devils were tired; they had played until midnight on Friday and then had to come back and play at 4 P.M. Saturday afternoon. This was the same route State had taken to the championship a year ago. It could be done.

At halftime Duke led 38–36. Just as they had done in Durham, the Blue Devils came out flying at the start of the second half, building a 51–41 lead. But State had seen this before. Valvano inserted Rodney Monroe, his designated Duke-killer, and Monroe began his devastation act again. With some surprising help from backup guard Kelsey Weems, he shot the Wolfpack right back into the game, scoring nine points in four minutes. A Weems free throw tied it at 60–60 and the script looked familiar.

But the Blue Devils were getting some unexpected help of their own. Ala Abdelnaby, the talented but often immature sophomore, came off the bench to score 12 points in nine minutes, giving Duke an offensive spark it needed. Still, when Monroe bombed a three-pointer that Ferry deflected to no avail, State led 67–64 with 5:50 left. Ferry missed a jumper. Shackleford posted and was fouled. Two free throws would make the lead 5.

"This is right where we want to be," Valvano thought on the bench. "We've got them thinking, 'Oh no, not again.' We're on a roll. We're in control."

But standing on the foul line, King was not thinking desperate thoughts. "I looked at Shack and said to myself, 'He's going to miss.' I just thought sooner or later our luck had to change against these guys."

Sure enough, Shackleford missed. Ferry hit to cut the margin to one and then Weems went to the line for another one-and-one. He missed too. Ferry hit a short jumper with 4:15 left and Duke was back up, 68–67.

"Now it's just a battle," Valvano said. "They had a chance to ice us, we had a chance to ice them. No one did it. Now it comes down to one play. Those kind, anything can happen."

Valvano was right. Both teams were reeling with exhaustion. Del Negro, clutch as always, put State back up, 69–68. But then came the shot that should have told people this was Duke's day.

The shot came from Phil Henderson, the enigmatic sophomore guard. With Duke's offense looking totally disorganized and State all over Ferry, he nailed a three-pointer. That made it 71–69. Chucky Brown tied it at 71–71, but missed still another free throw. Duke called time with 2:06 left to make sure to get a good shot.

The person Krzyzewski wanted to see shooting in this situation was Ferry. Even on a day when Ferry's shot wasn't dropping, he was the key to the Duke offense. He was such a talented passer, such an instinctive player, that any time he handled the ball Duke's offense improved. "Good things tend to happen," King said, "when we get the ball to Danny."

This time, they got the ball to Danny and he drove the lane for a short, pull-up jumper. That made it 73–71. There was still 1:45 left. State wanted the ball in Del Negro's hands almost as much as Duke wanted it in Ferry's. He drove the baseline, but with King all over him his shot rolled off the rim. Snyder skied over everyone for the rebound. There was 1:10 left. Duke could not run the clock out. Again, the ball went to Ferry. This time, though, he missed and State had one more chance.

"That kind of situation, last thirty seconds, game on the line, everything is so frenzied it's usually good for the offense," Valvano said later. "Almost always, someone on defense will get confused somewhere along the line and you'll get a good shot. But Duke isn't your average defensive team. I didn't want to call time-out, but I had to."

Valvano called time with twelve seconds left. He wanted to get the ball to Del Negro or Monroe, his two best one-on-one players offensively. Let them do what they could and send Shackleford and Brown to the boards.

On the other bench, Krzyzewski was thinking with Valvano. He also had a picture in his mind that he couldn't get to go away. "It was a Rodney Monroe highlight film," he said later. "In it he makes about a million shots against Duke and the last one is a three-pointer at the buzzer in the ACC Tournament."

For a split second, Krzyzewski was tempted to switch King onto Monroe. But he resisted. Keep the senior on the senior. Del Negro was still State's most dangerous player. Krzyzewski told King to face-guard Del Negro and Henderson to face-guard Monroe. In other words, their sole responsibility was to deny them the ball. They weren't to worry about helping out or double-teaming.

Leaving the huddle, thinking with his coach as he always seemed to do, King had the same disturbing vision of Monroe. He walked over to Henderson, pointed at Monroe and said, *"Don't* let him get the ball."

Henderson listened. The ball came in to Corchiani. King and Henderson were all over Del Negro and Monroe. With time running down, Corchiani tried to throw a lob in to Shackleford, who had gotten behind Ferry. But Corchiani had thrown the ball in to Shackleford on a straight line instead of on an angle. "A straight-line lob, there's time for the help to get there," Valvano said. "On an angle, the help can't get there."

Robert Brickey was the help. He came up behind Shackleford. There was contact. Valvano screamed for a foul. There was no call. The ball rolled off Shackleford's leg and out of bounds with five seconds left. Duke was able to run the clock out. It had won—survived—73–71.

Valvano was crushed. He had thought his team was going to win the game and then find a way to beat Carolina. Now it was Duke that would have the chance. Even so, as he and Krzyzewski shook hands, they hugged. They were an odd couple, these two. For thirteen years— first at Iona and Army for five, then at State and Duke for eight—they had coached against each other. They were as different as two men could be except that each, using entirely different methods, was very successful. Twice, Valvano had beaten Krzyzewski. But in the game both wanted most, Krzyzewski had won.

King felt totally drained by the game. "We worked so hard to win it felt so good," he said. "I was ready to celebrate right then."

It was Snyder who brought everyone back to earth. As his teammates were congratulating themselves in the locker room, he walked around saying quietly, "Carolina. One more. Let's go."

D A Y   T H R E E

There were very few people in the Greensboro Coliseum for the Duke–North Carolina final who gave the Blue Devils much chance. To begin with, history said that Dean Smith did not often lose to the same team or coach three times in a season. In twenty-seven years, three coaches had done it to him: Vic Bubas, the great Duke coach of the '60s; Norman Sloan, when he had David Thompson at State in the '70s; and Bobby Cremins, during his dream season at Georgia Tech in 1985.

There was more. Carolina was rested. The Tar Heels had played early Friday and won easily. They had played first Saturday and won easily. Duke had played very late Friday and won, but not easily. It had played second Saturday and had fallen across the finish line, exhausted.

And, there was the old Smith theory that it's very hard to beat a good team three times in a season. That had worked for Duke on Saturday. Now, it would work against it.

But in an ACC Tournament final, logic is wasted. Like the tournament itself, the final is unique. The atmosphere is different from an NCAA game, or any other game for that matter. The two teams know each other. They are always playing for a third time. The players are often friends. The coaches know each others' foibles. And, there is the Krzyzewski theory of being King of the Block. This is the street fight where everyone stands around in a circle while the two big guys go at it to see who is boss.

On Saturday night, after the team had met to go through matchups, King, Strickland, Snyder, and Ferry sat in the hotel watching the movie

Stakeout. They had become an almost inseparable foursome, the two seniors and the two juniors. All four had been part of an ACC championship in 1986. But that had been different. They had been complementary players then. Now, they were the nucleus. "We wanted one we could absolutely call our own," King said.

It would not be easy and they knew it. King had shut down his friend Lebo twice. Doing it a third straight time would be tough. Reid had played poorly in Durham. He wasn't likely to be so bad again. They talked about the game, the matchups, and how much they wanted to win until exhaustion overtook them and they went to bed.

The referees for the final would be Joe Forte, Dick Paparo, and Tom Fraim. For Fraim, this was special: his first ACC final after twenty-three years of officiating. It would also be his last. He had decided to retire at the end of the season to spend more time with his family. On Saturday night, all the officials got together and took him out for a farewell dinner.

Sunday morning was cool and gorgeous, a reminder that spring was not far away. The arena would be split between Duke and Carolina fans. Many of the other schools' fans had gone home, selling their tickets to Duke and Carolina people on their way out.

Both teams came out blazing. The first four baskets of the game were three-pointers. Brickey picked up his second foul early. Krzyzewski gambled and left him in. King had been right about Lebo. He opened the game with a three-pointer, then hit another. By halftime, he had 13 points.

It was 37–37 at intermission, Carolina outscoring Duke 10–1 during the last four minutes. Walking off the floor, King heard the Carolina players saying, "Yeah, yeah, we got 'em going now." His mind went back seven days to Durham. "It was 36–36 then. I thought, 'Twenty minutes. Just suck it up for twenty minutes.' "

That was Krzyzewski's theme at halftime. He knew his team was tired and sore. But this was no time for nursing wounds. They had to regroup and come back out with as much fire as they had displayed at the start of the game. King wondered if his team could hang on. Reid hadn't scored a single point in the first half. In fact, the Carolina starting front line had two points combined. That wasn't going to last.

In the other locker room, Smith thought his team was right where it wanted to be. He knew that his front line wasn't going to be shut out for forty minutes. He knew Duke had to be tired. "I was very confident," he said. "We weren't shooting well, but my gosh, the effort was certainly there."

The Tar Heels came out blazing in the second half. Ferry missed twice for Duke and Williams and Reid scored for Carolina. Krzyzewski took a quick time-out. He could feel the game slipping away. During the time-out he made a decision. "If they don't show me something quickly, I'm coming in with the kids."

The kids, the second team, had been coming in as a unit in the first half for the last three games. But never in the second half, especially not with an ACC title at stake and Carolina on a roll. But Krzyzewski felt he needed to do something drastic.

Snyder did break the second half shutout—the 4–0 start meant the run had reached 14–1—with a three-pointer that cut the lead to 41–40. But Reid immediately went inside and King was forced to foul him to prevent a dunk. It was his fourth foul. Reid only made one of two but Krzyzewski had made his decision: In came the kids. The starters were surprised.

"Carolina was all wound up," King said. "They were saying to each other, 'Come on, let's make this a big run.' We were definitely down. We were feeling sorry for ourselves. If a couple more possessions had gone by like that, it might have gotten to the point where we just said, 'well, we gave it our best effort.' Sitting on the bench, we watched the young guys. We figured if they cared enough to play that hard, we could suck it up one more time."

The kiddie corps didn't score. But during the two minutes they played, the Tar Heels only stretched the lead to 46–40. Snyder was the first starter to go back in and he promptly hit another three-pointer to breathe some life back into his team. Then, John Smith, still in the game for Ferry, made a spectacular spinning lay-up, got fouled, and made the free throw. The score was tied at 46–46. The rest of the starters came back. The run was done. Duke had its second wind.

From there, the game was anybody's. Fatigue became a factor for both teams. Carolina couldn't score, but neither could Duke. Smith put the Blue Devils up with a neat inside move, 58–57, with 5:07 left. Ferry then hit a huge shot, a three-pointer with 4:14 left. That pushed the lead to 61–57. Both teams kept missing. Scott Williams's two free throws cut it to 61–59 with 2:26 left. Ferry missed. Bucknall charged at the other end.

Carolina fouled King with 1:28 left to keep Duke from using up too much clock. King has always been a poor foul shooter. "When I was eight, I can remember not being able to make free throws," he said. "It just never changed. This time, though, I thought I was going to make it. I just told myself the shot was going in. I was shocked when it didn't."

So, apparently, were the Tar Heels. While Reid and Kevin Madden watched helplessly, Ferry grabbed the ball off the rim and quickly put it back in. Again, something that never happened to Carolina had happened to Carolina. Careless boxing out in a critical situation had been costly. Now, it was 63–59 with 1:16 left. Carolina worked the ball inside again and Madden was fouled. He made both free throws with fifty-seven ticks to go. It was 63–61. Duke had to score again.

The Blue Devils let the game clock run to twenty seconds, the shot clock to ten. Naturally, the ball went to Ferry. But Lebo made a brilliant play, dropping off his man and reaching in on Ferry as he tried to go the basket. He stripped the ball cleanly and took off, heading for a tying lay-up. Freshman King Rice was with Lebo. The only Blue Devil back was Snyder. Lebo fed Rice and they went in on Snyder two-on-one.

"At first I thought sure Rice would go back to Jeff," Snyder said later. "I thought about going towards him but then out of the corner of my eye I saw Kevin [Strickland] coming back and getting close to Jeff. I gambled and stayed with Rice."

Rice also saw Strickland. It would have taken a miraculous play by Strickland to stop Lebo if he had gotten the ball back. But Rice didn't want to take the chance. He went to the basket, looking for a lay-up or a foul. Snyder, 6–3 and perhaps the second-best athlete on the Duke team (behind Brickey), jumped with him. Rice had to try to shoot over Snyder. The ball rolled off the rim. Strickland grabbed it, turned and saw everyone else still sprinting toward him and the Carolina basket.

Except for Brickey, who was a step behind—but now a step ahead—of everyone. Instinctively, he released the ball to Brickey who went in so pumped to dunk that he rammed the ball off the rim. It went high in the air and, remarkably, it was Snyder who grabbed it. He had turned and raced back downcourt, taking nothing for granted. With time running out, Lebo had to foul. Four seconds were now left.

Carolina called time to let Snyder think about the situation. If he missed, Carolina could tie with a two-point shot, win with a three. If he made one, a three could still tie the game. If he made both, it was over.

Snyder was the first one out of the huddle. He went right to the foul line while King gathered the rest of the team to double-check on matchups. Standing on the line, waiting to hand him the ball was Forte, who had made the call on Lebo.

"That was a good call, Mr. Forte," Snyder said, glad to have someone to talk to.

"Thank you, Quin," Forte answered. "You're right."

They both laughed. Both teams were now in position. As Snyder stepped up to the line, King walked up behind him. "End this shit," he hissed. Snyder nodded and took the ball. He stared at the rim and shot. *Swish.* It was 64–61. Snyder took the ball again, his eyes never leaving the rim. He aimed and shot again. *Swish.* 65–61.

Now, it was over. Brickey intercepted the inbounds pass and time ran out. Krzyzewski was so thrilled that he forgot to shake Smith's hand before joining the celebration. He was in midleap when he looked down and saw Smith standing there, forlornly, waiting to congratulate him. "I felt like an idiot," Coach K said later. "That was bad after a game like that. If anyone thinks this tournament is meaningless, they should have watched this game."

No doubt. Snyder and King were locked in an endless hug. In eight short days they had turned their season completely around. The Tar Heels were devastated. "It really hurts to lose this," Smith admitted, "because we put so much into it."

Both teams had put heart and soul into it. Not because it would influence where they went in the NCAA Tournament—even though it would—but because of the championship that was at stake. The ACC Championship.

Two hours after Duke and Carolina decided the ACC title, they learned, along with everyone else, where they would be going to start NCAA Tournament play.

The four No. 1 seeds had been locked in for a couple of weeks: Temple, the top-ranked team in the country, was No. 1 in the East. Oklahoma was No. 1 in the Southeast. Purdue was No. 1 in the Midwest. And Arizona was No. 1 in the West. By their seeding, they were installed as the favorites to reach the Final Four in Kansas City.

By upsetting Carolina, Duke had won the right to stay near home. Instead of being shipped west as the No. 2 seed in the West Regional, the Blue Devils were installed as the No. 2 seed in the East, meaning they would open play that Thursday in the Deandome. Instead of getting to play at home, Carolina had to trek to Salt Lake City as the No. 2 seed in the West. Kentucky was the No. 2 seed in the Southeast and Pittsburgh, in spite of losing to Villanova in the Big East semifinals, was No. 2 in the Midwest.

Villanova, after losing the Big East final to Syracuse, was No. 6 in the Southeast—the highest one of Rollie Massimino's teams had ever been seeded. Kansas was also a No. 6 seed after being bombed in the Big Eight semifinals by Kansas State. The Jayhawks would open in the Midwest against a Xavier team many people thought might upset them. N.C. State was also in the Midwest, with a tough first-round game against Murray State. "I hate playing teams where every guy is 6–6 and can jump," Valvano said. "If we win, we'll win by two."

Ohio State, in spite of upsetting Purdue in the last week of the season to finish 16–12, did not get a bid. Gary Williams and his team gathered in the locker room on Sunday afternoon to watch the pairings. When the last two teams had gone up on the board, Williams clicked the TV off.

"We just didn't play well enough, guys," he said. "We'll get an NIT bid. Seniors, look at it as a chance to go out on an up note. You younger guys, use the experience to learn and get better so we won't go through this again next year." Williams went home that evening depressed. "I expect to have a long career in coaching," he said. "I'll get to the NCAAs again. But the players only get four shots. I feel bad for them."

Don DeVoe's Tennessee team didn't get a bid either. But DeVoe hadn't expected one after losing in the first round of the SEC Tournament to Florida to finish 16–12. Tennessee also received an NIT bid.

One coach whose phone didn't ring at all on that Sunday night was Rick Barnes. He had hoped that George Mason's 20–10 record would earn it an NIT bid even though the Patriots were not the name type of team the NIT looks for to sell tickets. The call never came. Most of the teams in the NIT field had weaker records than George Mason— but records don't really matter to the NIT.

"First thing tomorrow morning," Barnes said, "I get on the road recruiting. We're going to get players so we don't have to wait for a phone call anymore."

Of the 291 teams that started on October 15, 96 were going to postseason play—32 to the NIT and 64 to the NCAAs. The 32 would play for a consolation prize. The 64 would play 63 games. Only one of them would end the season with a victory.

16
WAIT TILL
NEXT YEAR . . .
OR AT LEAST
UNTIL MAY

Camp Lejeune, North Carolina. . . March 14

For David Robinson and Kevin Houston, the NCAA Tournament was just a spectator sport. Houston filled out a pool sheet on Monday morning, picking Temple, Brigham Young, Kansas State, and Arizona to reach the Final Four. Robinson, who had played in the NCAA Tournament the past three years, didn't bother with a pool. "All I know," he said, "is I'm not playing."

Robinson and Houston were playing basketball, though. Both had traveled to this Marine base on the Atlantic coast for the annual Armed Forces Tournament. Each of the four branches had a team and the tournament would be a three-day double-elimination.

Houston had been with the Army team since January. He and his wife Elizabeth had gone west to San Francisco so Houston could try out for the team in mid-January. The trip had not gotten off to an auspicious start. When the Houstons arrived in the apartment building provided for officers stationed at the Presidio, they found themselves back in college. The apartment had a small bedroom and a sitting room with a couch and a TV. The bathroom was down the hall.

"It wasn't a great way to start," Houston said. "We opened the door, looked around and said, 'Oh no.' But after a while we got used to it."

Houston also got used to his new team. The Army All-Stars were, for the most part, experienced Army veterans. Houston was the youngest member of the team. He was also the most publicized and the only white member. This combination guaranteed that Houston would catch a lot of flak from his new teammates.

"It worked out really well," he said, laughing. "I mean, right from the start it was the same old story, guys not believing I was me because I looked so young and all. They all made me feel like part of the group right from the beginning by giving me a hard time."

This was a period of adjustment for Houston. He had not played on a daily basis since his senior season at Army ended the previous March. He had to get used to playing international rules because most of the tournaments the Army team played in were played under those rules. That meant adjusting to the international three-point line, which was nine inches farther out than the college three-point line. A subtle difference but, without question, a difference.

And, being on a veteran, talented team, Houston was not the star anymore. He was a starter and a scorer but not every play was being run for him. He had to share the ball. "In a way, it's fun going out knowing I don't have to score 30 for us to win," he said. "But it's been an adjustment not having the ball as much as I used to. It doesn't bother me. It's just different."

Always, though, Houston's mind focused on one thing, on or off the court: the Olympic Trials. He knew the invitations were going out in mid-April and he had heard that Bill Stein, one of John Thompson's assistant coaches, had inquired about the team's schedule so he could scout Houston at some point. Even just watching games on television, Houston's mind was on his chances.

"I would watch a guy make a move and I'd say to myself, 'Can I do that?' I'd see a guard and wonder if I could guard him. Or, if he could guard me. Some nights I would sit there and think they couldn't choose seventy-five guys without me being one of them. Then, on other nights I would think there was no way I could make that top seventy-five.

"Liz and I would talk about it and she would ask me what I thought and every day it seemed like I thought something different."

Houston was happy with the way he was playing. His scoring average was about half of the 32.9 points per game he had averaged at Army, but he wasn't shooting nearly as often. Once a week, he called the Army basketball office to update them on his progress. Coach Les

Wohtke was surprised when Houston would say softly, "I'm playing pretty well."

"Kevin never says he's playing well," Wohtke said, "unless he's playing great."

In truth, Houston was having the time of his life. For the first time since he had enrolled at West Point he had some free time. He and Elizabeth played tourist all around the Bay Area and they decided to start a family. "I'd like to have about four kids," Houston said, grinning. "All of them white shooters."

The senior white shooter in the family and his team were touring the West Coast and ripping teams up. Their record was 19–2, including four victories over the Navy team that would be playing at Camp Lejeune. "But that's without Robinson," Houston said. "The guys keep asking me what Robinson's like to play against. I tell them I don't know that much. All I know is I'm 0–5 against him."

The difference in the lives of the two former military academy stars was perhaps best illustrated by the way they arrived at Lejeune for the tournament. Houston came with his teammates after a barnstorming stop at Fort Hood on the way east. They arrived two days before the tournament was to begin and found themselves quartered along with the Air Force and Navy teams in an old style barrack—one huge room filled with bunk beds—the kind you see in the movies. All it lacked was the gruff drill sergeant waking them up at reveille.

Robinson spent the day before the tournament began in Kansas City, working for ABC–TV as the color analyst on the Big Eight championship game between Oklahoma and Kansas State. He flew into Lejeune on Monday afternoon and joined the Navy team without having practiced and without having picked up a basketball for most of the past two months. He had spent those months in Oxnard, California, at a civil engineering school.

"All I want to do tonight," he said before the opening game, "is be able to run up and down the court without dying."

Actually, Robinson was in very good physical shape. He just wasn't in basketball shape. "I haven't had the chance to work out with anyone, all I've done is a little work on my own," he said. "The two months in California were just so hectic there was no time to play or even work out, except for some time working with weights."

Robinson's hectic schedule was at least partly self-inflicted. Whenever he had free time, he ran off to do something basketball-related, continuing to live the double life of Navy ensign and millionaire ball-player. One weekend he judged a slam dunk contest. On another, he went to the NCAA convention in Nashville. There, he bumped into John Thompson. "Keep yourself in shape," Thompson said, tapping Robinson on the stomach.

The Navy was certainly doing its best to keep Robinson in shape. One week, Robinson and his classmates were shipped to Camp Pendleton for a week of field maneuvers. "Toughest week of my life," Robinson said. "I came back and said, 'I hope I'm never in a war.'"

Every morning, Robinson would wake up at 4:40 A.M. from a half-sleep caused by the too-small sleeping bag he'd been given. Bathing was no picnic either since Robinson hadn't brought a towel. "I spent the week drying off with a T-shirt," he said.

That was the easy part. The hard part was going into the field for sixteen hours a day under simulated war conditions. "We were supposed to be an advance force," Robinson said. "We were doing these laser drills where they have simulated snipers. If they hit you in a certain spot, you were killed. The only good thing was that you got to stop running for a while if you got killed. I got killed three times."

He wasn't alone. In a group of seventy-three people on the final day, forty-six were killed by the five snipers. "I came back from that more tired than I had ever been in my life," Robinson said. "But I couldn't relax. I had commitments all the time."

Robinson was enjoying himself, though. He played on a softball team in Oxnard, ran into a fence making a catch in center field—"It was an awesome catch"—and was immediately ordered by the officer in charge to get out of center field before he hurt himself.

But in the back of his mind, Robinson was concerned about his basketball. By the time he got to Lejeune, it had been a year since his last game at Navy and seven months since his last game with the Pan American team. He knew he wasn't sharp and he wondered when he was going to get the chance to play. He knew the Navy brass wanted him on the Olympic team but now the trials, scheduled to begin May 18, were only a little more than two months away.

"There's such an irony in all this," he said. "All these years I worked to get better at basketball. The last couple, it really became important to me and, sure enough, I'm the number one draft pick and I'm going to be paid all this money to play basketball. Only I'm not playing.

Here I am, with all this other stuff: The contract, a shoe deal, all the attention, but I'm not *playing.*"

Most of the time, Robinson was able to deal with his situation. He was resigned to the fact that he would be in the Navy until May 20, 1989, and that was fine with him. He wanted to play in the Olympics, a feeling distinctly different from a year ago.

"Losing the Pan Ams certainly affected me," he said. "I can still remember sitting on the bench [in foul trouble] watching that lead disappear during the final. I've talked to guys who played in the Olympics and they all say it was one of the great experiences of their lives, one they wouldn't trade for anything. So I'm really looking forward to having the chance to play."

Occasionally Robinson felt pangs though. Watching his future team, the San Antonio Spurs, struggle was difficult, because he knew he could be helping them if he were in uniform. And some nights it hurt just being detached from the game he had grown to love.

"When I was still stationed back at King's Bay [Georgia] I was in a bowling league one night a week," he said. "One night after we had finished we were all sitting around watching a game on television. I looked at the game and then I looked around me and saw myself sitting in this bowling alley and I said, 'This sucks.' "

But before he concerned himself with his future in the pros, Robinson wanted to concern himself with his more immediate future: the Olympic trials. Unlike Houston, he had no concern about receiving an invitation; in fact he didn't have that much concern about making the team. "But I don't want to just show up and make the team because I'm 7–1 and can run and jump," he said. "I want to go to the trials in shape and really dominate."

That road would start in this tournament. Goettge Memorial Field House was a long way from Seoul. It was an old, dimly lit, 5,194-seat arena. Anyone who wanted to see the tournament simply had to walk in and take a seat. There was no charge for admission. About 1,500 people, many of them in Marine fatigues, showed up on the first night.

In the opening game, Houston shot poorly (5-for-14) but finished with 18 points as his team beat Air Force, 107–106. "We never thought they would be as good as they were," Houston said. "They caught us by surprise."

It was the Navy team that Houston and his teammates were interested in. The Navy had brought two of Robinson's former Academy teammates, Kylor Whitaker and Vernon Butler, in to join the team along with Robinson. Navy routed the Marines; Robinson, looking very rusty, scored 13 points and had 7 rebounds. It wasn't anything wondrous, but it was a start.

"Just playing basketball in a real game feels great," he said afterward. "Hearing myself introduced, the lights, seeing people in the stands—it feels like I'm alive again. I feel like I've been away from the game forever."

While Robinson played, Houston sat in the stands with his wife and watched. "Anything David gets, I'm happy for him," Houston said. "He's going to be a key to our Olympic team. Me, I just want a shot to try out. I know whatever happens, this is my last hurrah.

"But as long as I get the chance to have that last hurrah, one way or the other I can walk away and smile. I just want to show them that I can play."

In a sense, that was the bond between Robinson and Houston. All the ensign and the lieutenant wanted was a chance to play.

Walker Lambiotte could relate to the way Robinson and Houston felt. He had not played in a real college basketball game for a year. Now the 1987–88 season was over and he knew his next college game was more than eight months away.

But when he had made his decision to transfer from N.C. State to Northwestern, Lambiotte had known what he was getting into. He'd hoped the year he had to sit out as a transfer would be a learning one and would give him a chance to get his confidence back after two tough years at State.

For the most part, all had gone according to plan. "I feel much better about myself as a player now than I did last year," Lambiotte said, two days after Northwestern's season had ended with a second straight 7–21 record. "I really feel like I'm going to help this team next year because my game is starting to get where I think it should be."

Clearly, Northwestern needed plenty of help. In Bill Foster's second season, there had been some moments of hope: a win over DePaul and a miraculous victory over Indiana that had set off a net-cutting celebration worthy of a conference championship. Lambiotte had reveled in that victory even though he had only been a spectator.

"We played an almost perfect game to win, which is what we have

to do against Big Ten teams," he said. "When it was over, everyone
went crazy. We all knew that, great as it was, we had to have more wins
like that. You can't build a program on just one win, no matter how
big it is.

"What worried me coming here was the losing. I knew I'd get a good
education and a chance to play against good players in the Big Ten.
That's all there for me. But I want to be part of a team that can
compete. I think we've had a pretty good recruiting year this year and
I hope we're going to be better for it. We had some bad luck with
injuries this year, but with guys coming back and the recruits and me,
I think we have a chance next season. I just wish it would get here quick
because I'm ready to go."

Unfortunately, Northwestern was losing its best player, center Shon
Morris. Often, when he and Morris would work two-man plays in
practice, Lambiotte would find himself fantasizing about playing in real
games with Morris as a teammate and an inside threat. Early in the
season, he would half-joke with Morris, telling him to get hurt so he
could redshirt and come back for another year. If anyone deserved the
chance to play for a good team, it was Morris.

All season, the Wildcats had chances to add to the Indiana upset.
They came close against Ohio State, close against Michigan State, close
against Wisconsin. They played Illinois down to the wire in the last
game of the season. But the big plays just weren't there at the end. "It
would seem like whenever we got in position to win we just didn't know
how," Lambiotte said. "That's when the sitting was hardest to take.
I would sit there on the bench envisioning what I could do if I was in
the game. Sometimes I could actually *see* the move I would make on
a guy if he was guarding me in an endgame situation. But that was all
I could do, fantasize."

One thing that encouraged Lambiotte was the way his coach, Bill
Foster, was dealing with the losses. When he was younger, Foster had
trouble handling defeat, any defeat. When he coached at Duke, Foster
would often get in his car after a loss and drive around all night listening
to country music, trying to escape from the questions gnawing at his
brain. Starting over at Northwestern, Foster understood he couldn't
drive himself so. He didn't take the losing all that well, that just wasn't
in his nature. But Lambiotte was impressed by the way Foster kept
coming back, loss after loss, insisting that there was no reason why the
Wildcats couldn't win the next one if they would just play as well as

they were capable. Like Lambiotte, Foster honestly believed that better things were ahead if he could just make himself stay patient and wait for better players to arrive while the younger ones currently on the team matured. And, there was Lambiotte.

"He definitely will make a big difference in the nature of our team next year," Foster said. "I can't tell you how many times this season, if we had just had that shooter who could knock down the big shot from outside, we might have won ball games. That alone would have made a big difference. Also, he's the kind of player who makes the guys around him better players. We need some of that, too."

Lambiotte had never been part of a losing team in his life, and that was tough to take. But he kept his mind focused on the future in basketball and enjoyed the present away from the floor. Once he got used to the weather, he found himself enjoying Northwestern. "At first, when The Hawk [the wind that blows in off of Lake Michigan] blew through here I said, 'No way can I take this,'" he said, laughing. "I mean it was so cold it was unbelievable. I walked around campus with one of those ski masks that covers your whole face.

"Everyone told me I was the only person on the entire campus wearing one. So for a while I stopped. But I was freezing. So, I said, 'The hell with it, I don't care what anyone thinks,' and I started wearing it again. After a while, though, I started to get used to the cold. The only time I wore the mask was when the temperature went below zero."

A true midwesterner. Lambiotte's grades were solid although he did struggle with a computer science course. One night he locked himself into the computer room at 10 P.M. to figure out a program and didn't come out until 6 the next morning.

"If there's an advantage to not playing basketball, that kind of thing is it," he said. "If I was in the middle of the season, I would never think of staying up all night that way. But because I'm not playing, if I lost a night of sleep it was no big deal. If I'd been playing I might have flunked that course. It was hard as hell."

There were other advantages. Lambiotte got to go home for a real Christmas vacation for the first time in years. "My mom really spoiled me while I was home," he said with a laugh. And, when he suffered through a spate of minor injuries, he didn't have to worry about missed playing time, although he wasn't thrilled to miss practice. "Coach Foster told me he hopes I'm getting all the injuries out of my system this year," he said. "I hope so too because even now they aren't any fun."

More than anything, though, Lambiotte just tried to be patient. In a sense, even though he was sitting and sitting, he was at a point where he could finally see the proverbial light at the end of a long tunnel. For two years at N.C. State he had wondered when his time would come, had wondered *if* it would come. Finally, he had made a very tough decision, one that many ballplayers make without giving enough thought to the consequences. He had decided he would sit for twenty months—from March of 1987 until November of 1988—so that he could start all over again.

Transferring is not an easy thing to do for anyone. All too often, players make snap decisions and they make them when they are frustrated, not knowing the consequences. Lambiotte's decision had been viewed that way by some. But he had never doubted his decision, never questioned it—except perhaps the first time The Hawk cut through him—and now he could begin the countdown to playing again.

"It's been a long twelve months," Lambiotte said. "I feel like I've grown a lot and learned a lot, though. I never realized how much I liked to play basketball until I couldn't play it. I think I'll enjoy the next two years even more because of what I've gone through this year."

David Robinson could certainly relate to that feeling.

17
SIXTY-FOUR
AND COUNTING

March 17. . . Chapel Hill, North Carolina

The best nineteen days of the year began today.

Of all the championships that take place in this country, only the NCAA Basketball Tournament creates such extraordinary electricity in so many different places. Before it is over, thirteen different cities have hosted it, millions of fans have watched it and, unlike any other major team sports event, sudden death is in effect every time the ball goes up. Someone advances, someone goes home.

Pro football fans may argue that the same is true in their sport. But when was the last time a Super Bowl had any suspense in the second half? For that matter, when was the last time a football playoff game started and ended in the same afternoon?

Only one sport produces the upsets, the unlikely heroes that this one does. Only one team wins, but everyone takes home memories. This is an event so good that even the NCAA itself has trouble screwing it up.

The tournament really begins on the last Sunday of the regular season when the field is announced. Three days before the field is officially chosen, the nine members of the NCAA basketball committee gather at a hotel in Kansas City to begin putting the draw together. By the time they arrive there, they probably know who fifty-five to sixty of the teams in the field will be. The tough part of their job is choosing the last few teams, then deciding how to seed them and where to send them. No matter what the committee does, somebody is screaming bloody murder on Sunday night.

What's more, until 1975, the only ACC team that could go to the NCAA Tournament was the ACC Tournament champion. That meant a team could have a superb regular season, dominate everyone for three months, and then go home empty-handed because of one bad night. In 1970, South Carolina went 14–0 in ACC play. But N.C. State beat the Gamecocks in the tournament and went to the NCAAs instead of them.

In 1974, when N.C. State and Maryland had perhaps the two best teams in the country, they met in the ACC final. Only the winner would advance to the NCAAs. For forty minutes, the two teams put on a display of basketball that no one in the building has ever forgotten. It was 86–86 at the end of regulation and neither team had committed a turnover. Not one. State and David Thompson finally won the game, 103–100 in overtime.

After he had finished talking to the media, Lefty Driesell walked out to the State bus, boarded it and told the State players, "Y'all just played an unbelievable game. I'm as proud of you as I am of my own team. Now you make sure you go on and win the national championship."

They did. Maryland went home and watched on television as State went on to upset UCLA in the semifinals and win the national title. The next year the NCAA expanded its field from twenty-five to thirty-two teams, meaning a conference could send two teams to the tournament. In 1980, when the field was expanded to forty-eight teams, all limits were dropped. A conference could send all its teams if all were good enough to be invited.

Five years ago—in a rare moment of TV ingenuity—CBS decided to put together a show to announce the pairings. At 5:30 P.M. eastern time on Selection Sunday, anyone who cares about college basketball finds a TV set, sits down with a draw sheet, and listens as the field is announced. Most coaches nowadays have their teams together to hear where they are going—or in some cases *if* they are going.

"To me, it's the nicest day of the year in college basketball," Rollie Massimino said. "This is what you work all year for and if you're going, it's nice for your whole team to be able to share it."

Massimino did it up right on Selection Sunday this year. His team had played the Big East final that afternoon in Madison Square Garden, losing to Syracuse. No matter. Massimino rented a suite in the Penta Hotel, across the street from the Garden, for his team, ordered a case of champagne and some food, and he and his players gathered around the television to learn that they were going to the Southeast Regional. They'd be playing Arkansas in Cincinnati in the opening round.

"Can you believe it?" Massimino wanted to know. "If we get out of Cincinnati, we're going back to Birmingham." It was in Birmingham in 1985 that Villanova won the regional en route to the national title. Coaches believe in omens.

There were groans and cheers all over the country as the names went up on the board. Arizona got exactly what it expected—a No. 1 seed in the West, a trip to Los Angeles, and a first-round game against Cornell. The second-round opponent would, in all likelihood, be Seton Hall. "That's a tough second-round game," Steve Kerr said. "We're probably in for a tight week."

What about Cornell? Kerr laughed. "We'll be playing five Steve [read slow] Kerrs. We ought to be able to handle them."

Of course for Cornell, even as a lamb to the slaughter, just being part of the tournament is a thrill. The same could be said for all the No. 16 seeds. They weren't going to be there long, but they would be there.

The only real surprise on Selection Sunday this year was the committee's decision not to let teams play at home. For years, the committee had done just the opposite and for years it had heard cries that letting teams play on their home court was unfair. Of course those doing the crying were right. This year, the committee decided to ship teams away, unless they earned the right to stay at home by being a first or second seed.

If North Carolina had beaten Duke in the ACC final, it would have stayed home in the Deandome. Instead, Duke got to play in the Dome as the No. 2 seed in the East. To say that Carolina was less than thrilled with this setup was putting it mildly. Their fans, who had bought up the twenty-one thousand tickets early, assuming they would see the Tar Heels, began taking out ads in the local papers and on local radio stations to try to unload their tickets. The common refrain was this:

"But it's still great basketball."

"Only the Tar Heels play great basketball."

The Tar Heels themselves were in Salt Lake City. In their absence, no one would be using their locker room. Or, for that matter, the hallway on which the locker room was located. It was locked and shut long before any of the eight teams assigned to Chapel Hill arrived.

The opening game of the four played on Thursday was as intriguing as any first-round matchup in the country. It matched Missouri and Rhode Island. In the minds of many, one team—Missouri—had started the season as a dark horse Final Four contender. The other, Rhode Island, had never won an NCAA Tournament game and, even with a 26–6 record, no one took the Rams very seriously. After all, this was a team that had lost to Duquesne twice.

The doubters included Missouri. If ever a team should have been wary of a no-name first-round opponent, it was the Tigers. A year earlier, playing Xavier in the first round, Missouri had neglected to show up and had been upset. Now, playing at high noon in the half-empty Deandome, Missouri was in trouble again. The key man for the Tigers was the ever-enigmatic Derrick Chievous. The day before, as practice was ending, Chievous stood under the basket knocking in lay-ups and baby jumpers. "I just want to spend one more minute on the court where Jordan played," he said to a teammate.

It was a lovely sentiment—but Michael Jordan had played his home games in Carmichael Auditorium, half a mile up the road from the Deandome.

Chievous had already had a strange season, one filled with benchings and bad games and some good ones in between. As with his team, no one ever knew which Chievous would show up.

Today, it was Super Derrick. From the start, he was involved, driving the lane, stopping for pull-up jumpers. If the rest of the Tigers had been as ready as he was, they would have won the game. But everyone else looked like they were waiting for Jordan to arrive.

Rhode Island was a team built around its two senior guards, Carlton Owens and Tom Garrick. In the East, Owens and Garrick were highly respected and highly thought of. But west of Kingston, Rhode Island, few people had heard of them. Quickly, they set out to change that.

Garrick's story was the kind that makes the NCAA Tournament special. He had been unrecruited coming out of high school; given a scholarship by then Rhode Island Coach Brendan Malone because he was a local kid and Malone had an extra scholarship to give. What set Garrick apart, though, from the average late bloomer was his father.

Tom Garrick, Sr., had never seen his son play basketball. In 1944, as part of the U.S. force pushing into Germany, he had stepped on a mine and come home blinded for life. He had met his future wife in an Army hospital and they had produced a family of eight children. When Tom Jr.—the youngest—played, one of his siblings sat with their father and did play-by-play so the father could get a feel for what the son was doing.

"My father is my hero," Tom Garrick said simply. "He's my inspiration. Everything I do, I do for him."

On this day, there was plenty for Garrick's brother John to describe for their father. After a cold (1 for 8) first half, Tom Garrick came to life in the second, hitting 9-for-15 from the field. His 29 points and Owens's 25 were the keys for Rhode Island as they pulled off the first upset of the tournament—which was all of two hours old—beating Missouri, 87–80.

Chievous finished with 35 points. One certainly couldn't criticize his performance. But when the Tigers still had a chance to win, with Rhode Island clinging to a 74–73 lead and more than two minutes left, no one had been able to come up with a rebound. Twice the Rams missed shots, and twice they got the rebound. On their third chance, Owens was fouled. He made both free throws and Missouri never got that close again.

When the buzzer went off, Chievous walked away from his last college game without pausing to shake any hands, without even looking up at the scoreboard. He just walked off, head down, leaving his teammates, his opponents, and four years behind him. In the locker room, he refused to talk to reporters.

"I don't have to do interviews anymore," he said, putting on a Detroit Tigers cap. "I'm just a student now."

It was a sad ending to a strange, often brilliant, career.

Game two that afternoon almost produced an upset that would have made Rhode Island–Missouri a footnote. Syracuse, the 1987 runner-up and the No. 3 seed in the East, played thirty-four minutes against North Carolina A&T, the No. 14 seed, to a 50–50 tie.

North Carolina A&T is a black school that plays in—and dominates—a black league, the Mid-East Athletic Conference (MEAC). No MEAC team has ever won an NCAA Tournament game and so, in spite of a 26–2 record, A&T was rated somewhere between 53rd and 56th in the field, producing its 14th seed. This was Catch-22. If you are always a low seed, you are always going to play a very, very difficult first-round game. If you always play a difficult first-round game you are going to keep losing and keep drawing such games in perpetuity.

"That's not the NCAA's problem, it's ours," said Don Corbett, the A&T coach. "It's up to us to find a way to win one of these games and change things. It isn't up to the NCAA to do it for us."

Another first-day upset: a coach with grace under pressure. But Corbett's team lost again because Syracuse finally figured enough was enough and put together a 15–0 run. Even so, Jim Boeheim wasn't very happy. "Whoever those guys refereeing were, they don't belong here," he said. "They had no idea what they were doing out there."

If this sounds like whining, well, Boeheim is famous for whining. But as it turned out, all three officials in this game were sent home the next day, none of them advancing to the second round. Boeheim, in the opinion of the officiating supervisors, had a point.

That evening, David Rivers made his exit from college basketball. He was far more gracious in defeat than Chievous, but his last game was memorable only because Rivers was outplayed completely by a guard named Kato Armstrong.

Armstrong, Southern Methodist's point guard, lit Notre Dame up for 29 points—Rivers finished with 12 on 5-of-15 shooting—and had his way with Rivers at every key point during SMU's 85–73 victory. "It's not a very happy way to go out," Rivers said softly when it was over.

Rivers had been hoping to get through this game to get another shot at Duke and Billy King in the second round. "David really wants Duke again," Digger Phelps had said the day before. "He doesn't think that game was the real David Rivers."

The real David Rivers was a gifted player who, for four years, was asked to do far too much by Phelps because his supporting cast was never quite up to Rivers's level. This was especially true the last two seasons (after Rivers miraculously came back from an automobile accident that had nearly killed him). Phelps had talked so often about Rivers's courage, his ability, his toughness, his desire, that he had almost become a parody of himself.

But when Rivers's last game was over, Phelps was eloquent. "You know if you coach long enough," he said, "you find out that guys like

[Adrian] Dantley, [Kelly] Tripucka, and [John] Paxson are one in a million. David Rivers is once in a lifetime."

Watching Rivers go down, Billy King felt a twinge of sadness too. He admired Rivers, but at the same time liked the challenge of stopping him. Now, if Duke were to beat Boston University in the first round, King would have to stop Kato Armstrong in the second round.

The Blue Devils were top-heavy favorites to win their opener. It was another middle-of-the-night game, but this time they were in control by halftime. The final was 85–69, the finish marked by sluggish play from the subs.

"If this team is going anywhere in this tournament, it can't play one careless minute," Krzyzewski told King and Strickland during those last few seconds. "You better jump all over these guys before Saturday."

It was going to be tough for King to jump on anyone that night. He was one of six Duke players designated for drug testing. The year before, he had been so dehydrated it had taken him two hours to produce a specimen after Duke's opening game. This time he was a little better: ninety minutes.

For the NCAA drug testers it had been a long day. They had started with Rhode Island at 2 P.M. and their work wasn't done until Billy King produced a specimen at 2 A.M.

March 18 . . . Cincinnati, Ohio

It was snowing when Rollie Massimino woke up this morning at 7 A.M. No matter. Massimino's mood wasn't going to be changed by a little snow, even in mid-March. His team was back in the NCAA Tournament and Massimino couldn't wait to get started.

A lot of coaches around the country have reputations as tournament coaches. Perhaps no one deserves such a reputation more than Massimino. Going into 1988, he had taken Villanova to regional finals four times—without ever being seeded higher than eighth in a regional. In 1985, when the Wildcats won the national championship, they were the eighth seed in the Southeast Regional, meaning they were given a fifty-fifty chance of getting by the first round. Their first-round game that year had been against Dayton—at Dayton.

No one really knows exactly why Massimino's teams did so well in postseason. It may have had something to do with the fact that he looks at postseason as a reward for a good season. "He almost never yells during the tournament," assistant John Olive said. "He thinks that's for the regular season. You get to the tournament by having a good season. Why should the kids get yelled at because they've had a good season?"

Villanova had a noon opener this year against a good Arkansas team. Massimino respected Arkansas but the Razorbacks didn't concern him as much as the starting time. The last time Villanova had played an early game it had been at Seton Hall. The result had been an 84–58 debacle. Mass was at 7:30 that morning, followed by the pregame meal.

"I hope we're all awake by noon," he said. "This game won't be easy. But this time of year, no game is easy."

Riverfront Coliseum is not used for basketball very often. Occasionally the University of Cincinnati plays here. Once in a while, Xavier plays a game here. But it has the feel of a hockey arena, especially on a cold day like this one. With the crowd trickling in at game time, the place was cold.

Massimino believes that tempo is vital in NCAA play, that you can run the game from the bench—even with the introduction of the 45-second shot clock—if your players know what they're doing and if your point guard is in sync with the coaching staff.

For twenty minutes, Kenny Wilson, the tiny Villanova point guard, was in sync with nothing. He played scared, throwing the ball away, missing all five shots he took, and generally looked disoriented. Fortunately, Mark Plansky and Tom Greis were shooting well and Villanova managed a 40–33 lead at halftime.

During the break, Massimino focused much of his talk on Wilson. "Just play your game, Kenny, that's all," he told him. "No more, no less. Don't try to do things you don't normally do. You'll be just fine."

Doug West helped make things fine in the second half. He quickly hit two three-point shots and, at the other end, stuck close to Arkansas' best player, Ron Huery. "He played old man defense," Huery said later. "He was pushing and grabbing all over the place."

Whatever works. Arkansas and Huery found the range eventually, closing the margin to 58–57 with more than ten minutes left. But just when things began to look grim, West rode to the rescue. He hit a jumper, posted up to score again, and then hit a double-pump seven-footer in the lane as he was being fouled.

On the bench, Massimino, his hair going in five different directions by now, took a deep breath. "Doug West is my boy," he often said, "and the other kids know it."

His boy was playing when it mattered most. Arkansas never threatened again. The final was 82–74 and Massimino had won his opening-round game in NCAA play for the ninth straight time. He was so ecstatic that during the postgame interview he referred to Arkansas coach Nolan Richardson as Nolan Ryan. "Nolan Ryan does a hell of a job with that team," he said.

All that and he can pitch, too.

Nothing was going to take away from this victory. After last year's nightmare, to be back in the NCAA Tournament and to advance was pure joy for Massimino. His whole entourage, family and friends, had flown out from Philadelphia on the team charter and now they had a whole weekend to enjoy themselves.

As Massimino went back to the hotel to rest, his assistants stayed behind to scout Illinois against Texas–San Antonio. There was little doubt that Illinois would be the next opponent (they ended up winning, 81–72) and the question was could the Wildcats repeat their November victory over what was now a much more experienced and still very talented team.

"Why not?" Olive said. "If you think you can do something, you can do it. Right now, our kids think they can do anything."

If looking at tape would win a game, Villanova had a great chance. The Wildcats had twelve Illinois tapes with them in Cincinnati. They would all be looked at before Sunday. The work would start that night. First, though, the Arkansas victory would be savored for a few hours. That evening, Massimino took his entourage, thirty strong, to an Italian restaurant near the hotel. Everyone ate, everyone drank, and everyone was merry.

By the time dinner came, Massimino was antsy. He lit his cigar, got up and went into the kitchen to kibitz with the chef and his assistants. Thirty minutes later he was still in the kitchen, signing autographs and talking. It was only one win, but everyone in the Villanova party couldn't help but talk about 1985.

"All I know is, we're in Ohio," said Mary Jane Massimino, who had put up with being a coach's wife for thirty-three years. "In '85 we started in Ohio [Dayton] and went to Birmingham. If we win Sunday, we're going to Birmingham. Something tells me we're going to win."

Her husband, finally back from the kitchen, laughed. "Illinois is a hell of a team, you know," he said to his wife.

"So are we," Mary Jane Massimino answered.

The snow had stopped. Villanova had not.

March 19. . . South Bend, Indiana

By Saturday morning, thirty-two of the sixty-four teams had gone home. There had been two stunning upsets on the second day. The first had taken place in Hartford. There, Richmond, the Colonial Athletic Association champion, the same team that had gone right to the wire to beat George Mason just to get into the tournament, shocked Indiana, the defending national champion, 62–59.

The loss ended a turbulent season for the Hoosiers. They had started well, been in trouble in January, bounced back in February, and then failed in March. In all, their record was 19–10. During the loss to Richmond, Rick Calloway never moved off the bench. One year ago, it had been Calloway's basket with six seconds left that put Indiana in the Final Four. Now, Knight had no use for him. Three days after the Richmond game, Calloway announced that he would transfer for his senior season. It was a sad story.

Knight was gracious in defeat, giving full credit to Dick Tarrant and to the Spiders. He did sound silly, though, when he claimed the outcome wasn't an upset. At one point, he challenged the assembled media: "Who here thinks this was an upset? Does anyone think this was an upset?"

No one dared move. When Purdue Coach Gene Keady heard the story, he giggled like a little kid. "I just wish someone would have had the nerve to stand up and say, 'Bob, that's the biggest goddamn upset since Chaminade beat Virginia,'" Keady said. "I'd have paid to see that."

The other upset, not quite on the Chaminade–Virginia level but stunning nonetheless, took place in Lincoln, Nebraska. Just as Jim Valvano had predicted, N.C. State couldn't handle Murray State's quickness. The appropriately named Racers kept getting big buckets down the stretch, and when Vinny Del Negro's three-pointer bounced off the rim at the buzzer, State's season had suddenly ended with a 78–75 loss.

The team that benefited most from the upset was Kansas. Virtually unnoticed, the Jayhawks routed Xavier, 85–72 in their opener. In a strange twist, Kansas had become the crowd's favorite on what was usually a hostile court. Several of the Xavier players had been quoted, when they heard they were going to Lincoln, as saying that as far as they knew, "Lincoln is Siberia with a bunch of Seven-Eleven's."

The good folk of Lincoln didn't take kindly to that line, and they cheered Kansas—which had suffered its most depressing loss of the season in this same building—as if the Jayhawks had turned into Cornhuskers. After a season of bad luck, Larry Brown couldn't help but notice that the NCAA Tournament had started for his team with two breaks: the crowd turning against Xavier and Murray State upsetting N.C. State.

For Valvano, this was a devastating way to end what had been a terrific season. He had not really thought his team would lose to Murray State, but he had sensed that something had gone out of his team after the Duke loss. The following day, sitting in the stands during the Duke–Carolina final, Valvano had felt a wave of depression sweep over him, almost a precursor of what was to come.

"I cannot for one second put my finger on it, but losing that game was very bad for us," he said, two days after the Duke loss and three days before the loss to Murray State. "It's a funny thing because this has been one of the easiest years I've ever had in coaching. Everything just fell into place. We needed Shack to get better and he got better. The freshman guards gave us an added dimension and great depth. The guy who got benched [senior Quentin Jackson] happens to be one of the great kids of all time, so he deals with it.

"I hear people saying I did one of my best jobs this year and I can't understand it. It was an easy year. But now, I'm worried. I really wanted to win the ACC Tournament and I really thought we were going to do it. We missed some foul shots and didn't win. That should be the end of it.

"But when I was sitting there watching the final, listening to the fans with all the silly things they yell, I suddenly thought just how hard it is to get where those two teams were—in the final. It takes so much effort any year that you get that far. No one understands the work that goes into it. My team didn't get there this year. Just missed—but missed nonetheless. All of a sudden, something in my mind said, 'This isn't our year.' I hope to God I'm wrong because I look at our regional and I think we have the talent to get to the Final Four. But we can also lose Friday."

They lost Friday. Valvano's premoniton was right. In the short run, he was stunned and hurt. But in the long run, he had everyone coming back who mattered for the '88 team except for Del Negro. He would sign three junior college players—exactly one year after juco point guard Kenny Drummond had dropped out of school, causing Valvano to vow never to sign another juco—and would have another very good team in '89.

That was small consolation for Valvano. His team's season ended in Lincoln. *His* season, however, was far from over.

Round two began with play at four sites: Chapel Hill, Atlanta, South Bend, and Salt Lake City. The upset of the day came in Chapel Hill, where Rhode Island continued its unlikely story by stunning Syracuse. Jim Boeheim's pretournament assessment of his team had been correct. "When we play well, we're as good as anyone in the country," he had told a friend on Wednesday. "But we haven't played well all year."

Garrick and Owens were again brilliant. Sore-kneed Kenny Green played the game of his life and Rhode Island pulled the upset. Now, Tom Garrick and his father, unknown outside of Kingston on Thursday, had become a major national story on Saturday.

In the second game in Chapel Hill, Duke easily beat SMU as Billy King shut down Kato Armstrong. The Blue Devils were much sharper than they had been against Boston University, and they ran their record for the year in the Deandome to 3–0. "Sort of like a home away from home," Krzyzewski quipped.

The same could be said for Purdue. After years of frustration with the NCAA draw, the Boilermakers couldn't complain this time around. Not only were they the top seed in the Midwest region, but they were assigned to South Bend for the subregional; many of their fans could make the one hundred-mile trip from West Lafayette. With Notre Dame shipped to Chapel Hill, there were plenty of tickets for Purdue people to buy and they made the Athletic and Convocation Center look like a smaller version of Mackey Arena.

The second round opponent was Memphis State, a team that had been on NCAA probation a year ago and had lost two key players at midseason to suspension (because they had agents). Through all this, the Tigers still had talent; Keady and his three seniors were genuinely concerned going into the game.

"This is something we have to get through," Troy Lewis said. "We've never been past the second round. It's like a barrier we've got to get over. Once we do, we should be okay."

The first half was nerve-wracking. Memphis State led much of the way before a Lewis three-pointer put the Boilermakers on top with only 3:15 left. They led 38–33 at intermission, not home free yet by any means. Then a funny thing happened to start the second half and, strangely enough, it gave Purdue the impetus to turn the game into a rout.

On the opening play of the half, with Memphis State inbounding, no one bothered to cover the Tigers' Elliot Perry. He went one way, Purdue's defense went the other and Perry ended up with an open lay-up to start the half, cutting the lead to 38–35. This was, without question, a screwup. The Boilermakers were so stunned by their own stupidity that they started laughing at themselves. Everette Stephens, suddenly looser than he had been all game, hit twice. Todd Mitchell, so tight the first twenty minutes he didn't come close to hitting a field goal (zero-for-four), dunked. It was 44–35 and MSU Coach Larry Finch called time.

In the huddle, while everyone was still trying to figure out what had happened on the first play, Lewis nudged Stephens. "Donkey show," he said.

Stephens cracked up. He had been thinking the same thing. The reference was to a trip to El Paso when the three seniors had been freshmen. On an off night, seven of the Boilermakers had gone across the border into Mexico in search of "The Donkey Show." They had been told this was must-see stuff, a girl and her donkey at work.

"We got into these cabs and told the drivers we wanted to see 'The Donkey Show,' " Lewis said. "They said they knew all about it, knew just where to go. We drove around and around and around. Stopped a dozen places. We never found the thing."

From that day forth, any time someone from that group got taken, the Donkey Show reference came up. The three seniors were now the only players left from that historic trip. Stephens and Lewis were still giggling when they walked out of the huddle. Mitchell came up behind them. "We're lined up over here, you jackasses," he hissed. He remembered too.

Any sense of dread was long gone now. Lewis hit a three-pointer, Mitchell scored, and the lead was 49–35. Memphis State was through.

The lead just kept growing. Finch, frustrated by the growing margin, drew a technical from referee Woody Mayfield with 10:48 left. During the next time-out, Finch yelled at Mayfield, "I got two more left, Woody, and I'm gonna use 'em up."

The officials were merciful and let Finch vent his wrath without further penalty. Purdue wasn't so kind. Even with Keady clearing his bench, the final was 100–73. The barrier had been cleared.

"It will feel good to be practicing instead of watching next week," Keady said. "This is a new feeling, an awfully good one."

Ironically, Purdue's next opponent would be Kansas State, Keady's alma mater. Mitchell, Lewis, and Stephens were delighted to finally be in the round of sixteen. And slightly amazed at how easy it had been. "For a half they were a tough team," Mitchell said. "Then they just fell apart completely. We played well, but they just died." He shrugged. "I'm not complaining, though."

The donkeys were marching on.

March 20. . . Lincoln, Nebraska

It had snowed in Cincinnati on Friday. It snowed in South Bend on Saturday. But in normally snowy Nebraska, Sunday dawned clear and sunny, the temperature pushing toward 60 degrees.

This was a funny place for the NCAA basketball tournament to come. After all, how many places were there in the country where the basketball arena was named after a football coach? But the Bob Devaney Arena was packed, even if the sports editor from Omaha was on vacation—preparing for the start of Nebraska spring football.

The Pittsburgh Panthers were delighted to be in Lincoln. They had opened the tournament Friday with an easy victory over Eastern Michigan; now they faced Vanderbilt. Paul Evans was mildly concerned about his four freshmen, who had not been shooting well lately. Sean Miller had stayed after practice Saturday to work on that very thing.

"If Sean hits his first shot or two it will give us a big boost," Evans said. "I think the freshmen are a little tight."

Evans was tight too. But that was normal. He is, most of the time, a game-day wreck. His assistants often wonder how he can sit comfortably the next day because on game day he makes so many trips to the bathroom. The gum he chews takes a beating from start to finish. He paces. He sweats. In other words, he's a worrier.

Today, Evans was worried most about Vanderbilt's seven-foot center Will Perdue. It wasn't so much Perdue's scoring that worried Evans—he expected him to score—as his ability to get Charles Smith into foul trouble. Smith had a tendency to pick up quick fouls in big games and Evans didn't think the Panthers could afford to play very long without him.

"If we concentrate, we're fine," he said, pounding away on the gum. "But with this group, I just never know."

His concern was not relieved when, during his pregame talk, Jerome Lane asked Evans if he was to take the ball out of bounds against the press.

"Jerome," Evans said as calmly as he could, "this team doesn't press."

He turned to Smith. "Charlie, it doesn't matter if Perdue scores his 25. What matters is that he doesn't score them from the foul line. You know we need you in the game."

Smith nodded. Pitt had been assigned to the Nebraska women's locker room, which was not only too small but had all sorts of inspirational sayings on the walls. There was even one from Bob Knight: "The will to win has always been overrated as a means of doing so. The will to prepare and the ability to execute are of far greater importance."

Evans had nothing quite so deep to tell his players. "Let's get [win] number twenty-five and let's get to Detroit so Demetrius [Gore] can play at home. We win a couple more and Charlie and Demetrius can go out of here as part of the best Pitt team in history."

They started superbly, leading 25–14 after twelve minutes. Everyone's shots fell. No one was tight. A blowout seemed possible.

But it didn't happen. Pitt went cold. Vanderbilt put together a 12–2 run and cut the lead to 27–26. At halftime, it was 34–all. Evans took his time before saying anything to his team. When he started, he was firm but quiet.

"It's always the same shit with you guys. You don't know how to put people away. Charlie, you pull up and shoot when everyone else is expecting you to pass. There's no one to rebound and we blow a possession. You can't do that at this level! This time when you build the lead up, keep going inside and don't start rushing."

There would be one change. Freshman Bobby Martin had done well against Perdue. He would start on him in the second half in place of Jason Matthews as Evans went to a bigger lineup.

There would be no big leads in the second half. Pitt led briefly, 48–43, but Vandy immediately ran off eight straight points to lead 51–48. It became a game where every possession seemed like life-and-death.

Vanderbilt led 61–57 with 6:20 to go but didn't score for almost six minutes. By that time, Pitt led by three, thanks largely to Darelle Porter, who coolly hit a three-pointer to put Pitt up 62–61 and then hit a jumper to make it 64–61. Eric Reid broke the Vandy drought with a short jumper that made it 64–63 with 1:40 left. Pitt ran the clock down, then ran a clear-out for Gore. Wide open from fifteen feet, Gore missed. But Lane came down with the rebound. Pitt ran the clock all the way to seventeen seconds before Smith was fouled going to the basket.

He hit the first shot to make it 65–63, but missed the second. This time, Lane pulled the ball out of Perdue's hands. It squirted free and went right to Smith. He was fouled immediately but Vanderbilt wasn't over the limit, so Pitt inbounded rather than going to the line. Matthews was fouled right away. Once again, one of the freshmen came through. Matthews hit both shots and with twelve seconds to go it was 67–63.

Vandy had scored two points in 6:28. Now though, desperate, Barry Goheen threw in a three-pointer from the corner to make it 67–66. Vandy called time with five seconds left. Pitt ran a lob play on the inbounds, getting the ball to Smith. He grabbed the pass and was instantly fouled by Perdue. There were four ticks left.

That was Perdue's fifth foul. Dejectedly, he walked to the bench, certain his career was over. "Don't five up yet," Coach C. M. Newton whispered. "You may have more basketball left to play."

That hardly seemed likely when Smith hit both free throws to make it 69–66. Perhaps, here, Evans should have called time to make certain his team knew what he wanted on defense. The clock was stopped anyway, so why not be sure? Evans thought that Porter understood what to do: Foul Goheen right away if he got the ball. That would keep him from having any chance to shoot a tying three-pointer.

Goheen took the inbounds pass and streaked upcourt. Porter never fouled. Goheen bobbled the ball for a moment, got it back and, as the buzzer was about to sound, went up from twenty-three feet. Porter was in his face, but it was too late, he should have been there earlier. As the buzzer was sounding, Goheen's shot swished cleanly. It was 69–69. Overtime.

That shot, for all intents and purposes, ended Pitt's season. The Panthers were a stricken team in overtime. Smith missed a wide-open Lane underneath and took a bad shot on the first possession. Frank Kornet, who had one field goal in regulation, promptly hit to make it 71–69. Smith then missed a dunk and grabbed the rim for a technical in the process. Goheen hit the technical and Eric Booker hit a three-pointer to make it 75–69. Pitt never got even again. The final was 80–74.

Evans didn't have much to say in the aftermath. He started to get on Smith, then realized it was pointless. "Jerome was wide open, Charlie," he said.

"Wide open, man," Lane added.

Smith was fighting tears. "My fault," he said.

"No, it wasn't," Evans said. "It was all of us. I don't want anyone getting on Darelle for not fouling [Goheen] because his shooting got us back in the game. All you freshmen did a great job. You had a hell of a year. Charlie, Demetrius, I wish you were coming back next year."

Evans left the building soon after that. He would fly to California the next day. What he didn't know, when he left, was that Smith and Gore, stunned and hurt by the sudden end of their careers, had made him the scapegoat, claiming he had not told anyone to foul on the last play of regulation. "Anyone who knows basketball knows whose fault this was," Gore said.

He was wrong. No one person was at fault. As Evans had said, it was everyone. Pitt just hadn't been able to rise to the level needed at this stage of the tournament. Evans's concern about this team in January had been correct. "You don't have the mentality to be great," he told his players.

Prophetic words.

Larry Brown watched the end of the Pitt–Vanderbilt game in amazement. First, N.C. State had been upset a round before Kansas would have played them. Now, Pitt had been beaten one round before it would have played the Jayhawks. "You know," he told Ed Manning, "we couldn't have matched up with Pitt. No way."

Maybe all the bad luck of the winter was becoming good luck in the spring. There was still the not-so-small matter of beating Murray State that day. Brown, of course, was nervous. Danny Manning wasn't. He sensed that his team was about to go on a roll. The loss in the Big Eight Tournament had been deceiving because Kevin Pritchard, their point guard, had sat out the game with a bad ankle. Pritchard was healthy now.

Still, there was nothing easy about Murray State. The Racers had a tough-to-guard point guard in Don Mann and a pure scorer in Jeff Martin. The Jayhawks came out flying, taking a 25–13 early lead. But Murray came back to trail just 28–23 at half. The second half was a struggle for twenty minutes. Paul King put Murray up for the first time, 50–48 with 6:50 left. Pritchard answered with a three-pointer. The lead seesawed. A drive by Mann and a follow by Martin put Murray up 56–53 with 3:55 left. Brown called time.

Every team that wins a national championship must survive this type of game. Somewhere along the line an underdog shows up, plays loose from start to finish and pushes the favorite to the limit. If you survive, good things often follow. If not . . .

Manning cut the lead to 56–55, rebounding his own miss. Mann missed a jumper, then Newton hit a twisting jumper to put KU up by one with 2:10 left. They traded misses until Martin hit two free throws to give Murray State a 58–57 lead with fifty-one seconds to go.

Now came the most important possession of Manning's career. A miss here and it might all be over. The thought never occurred to him. "I just never thought we were going to lose," he said later. "We'd all been through so much together this just seemed like something else we had to take care of. I really thought we would get it done."

It was not easy. Pritchard got the ball to Manning to the right of the basket and he calmly tossed a baby hook in with forty seconds left. Kansas was up 59–58. But now Murray would get the last shot. The Racers called time with twenty-four seconds left. Their plan was simple: clear out and let Mann penetrate.

He did just that. With Scooter Barry—playing because Pritchard's ankle was still tender—guarding him, Mann drove right, popped into the clear and was about to toss a scoop shot up with no one near him when, suddenly, Manning slipped around a screen and jumped. He didn't get to the ball. To make sure there was no contact, he only jumped *toward* Mann, not *at* him.

But Mann, seeing Manning flying at him, had to adjust his shot. The ball rolled around the rim—and off. Manning grabbed the rebound and was immediately fouled. Only one second was left. The Jayhawks were celebrating as Manning went to the line. "Hey," Manning commanded sternly, "calm down. It's not over yet."

They calmed down. But it was over. Manning made both shots, then intercepted the last Murray inbounds pass. Kansas had survived, 61–58. In the last forty seconds, Manning had hit the winning basket, helped out on the crucial defensive play, grabbed the rebound, made the free throws, and intercepted the final pass.

Remarkably, Kansas was in the final sixteen. "That's not my goal," Manning said softly. "I've been to the final sixteen before. There's still more to do."

18
AND THEN
THERE WERE SIXTEEN

March 24. . . Birmingham, Alabama

The term Sweet Sixteen is a relatively new one in the sports vernacular, coined partly to grant glory to more teams at the end of each college basketball season, but also used in recognition of the fact that reaching the NCAA round of sixteen is not nearly as easy as it once was.

Until the 1975 expansion of the tournament, seven conference champions were seeded right into the round of sixteen without having to play a game. Nowadays, with sixty-four teams in the field, it takes two victories to reach the sixteens. Often getting those two victories is not so easy.

The 1988 tournament was a perfect example of how difficult it is. None of the 1987 Final Four made it back as far as the sixteens. Providence didn't make the tournament: Indiana was gone in round one; Syracuse and Nevada–Las Vegas were gone in round two. In fact, only five of the Sweet Sixteen of 1987 made it back in 1988: North Carolina, Iowa, Kansas, Oklahoma, and Duke. To go one step further, only three of those five—North Carolina, Kansas, and Duke—had gotten to this point three years running.

And, of those three only North Carolina, with a remarkable eight-year string, had been this far more than three straight times. Looking at that last stat, one might conclude that Dean Smith was in the most successful coaching slump in history.

So, where once there had been just a Final Four there was now also a Great Eight and a Sweet Sixteen. No doubt the Thrilling Thirty-two and Special Sixty-four aren't far behind. Nonetheless, to be among the last sixteen in a race that 291 started is no small achievement.

Four of the Sweet Sixteen were genuine surprises. Only in the West, where Arizona, Iowa, Michigan, and North Carolina had all advanced with ease, was there no need for any glass-slipper purchases.

In the East, there were two Cinderella types, Richmond and Rhode Island. The Spiders had followed up their "nonupset" of Indiana by beating Georgia Tech. In a way, this victory was even more surprising because the Yellow Jackets had lost to the Spiders in the regular season. But Richmond played another near-perfect game and sent Bobby Cremins home with his third straight NCAA disappointment. (That loss and a couple of recruiting defeats sent Cremins on a junior-college shopping spree. By April, he'd signed three JC transfers—and had basketball people wondering what direction the one-time boy wonder was heading in with his program.)

Rhode Island, after beating Missouri, had turned around and shocked Syracuse, building a big first-half lead, then hanging on for dear life. Syracuse's season ended when Earl Duncan's three-point shot, which would have tied the game, spun out at the buzzer. The four-year battle between Boeheim and center Rony Seikaly had finally ended. Each was delighted to be rid of the other, even though the relationship had been beneficial to both. Two weeks after his shot failed to drop, Earl Duncan announced he was dropping out of Syracuse to transfer.

In the Midwest, the surprise entry was Vanderbilt. C. M. Newton, at fifty-eight, is someone everyone in coaching respects and almost no one outside of coaching has ever heard of. Newton built the program at Alabama in the late 1960s and early 1970s, recruiting black players long before it was in vogue and making basketball something more than filler time between football seasons in Bear Bryant country.

He had now done a similar rebuilding job at Vanderbilt, taking high school players wanted by few other coaches and making them into standout college players. "C. M. hasn't got any high school All-Americans on that team," Don DeVoe commented, "but they sure play like they are." Now they had played their way into the Sweet Sixteen.

And then there was Villanova. The Wildcats, to the amazement of everyone but themselves, were in Birmingham along with the power-houses: Oklahoma, Louisville, and their round-of-sixteen opponent, Kentucky. Their 66–63 victory over Illinois in the Thrilling Thirty-two was, in many ways, a microcosm of their season. Realistically, there was no way to pull this one off. But they found a way.

This was not your average upset. Late in the first half, Doug West went down hard, hit his head and suffered a concussion. It was not a serious go-to-the-hospital concussion but it was apparent, after West tried to come back in the second half, that he was woozy and couldn't play. With West, beating Illinois would have been a major undertaking. Without him, it looked impossible.

This, of course, is where Pat Enright comes in. If anyone specialized in the impossible, it was Enright. His presence on the team was impossible to begin with—he *had* been cut twice and graduated once—but there he was. When West went down, Enright knew he was going to play more than just a run-in, run-out role. His reaction? Was he cool, ready to go, just dying for his chance?

"I was scared to death," he said. "I sat there and looked around and there were seventeen thousand people in the place [including his parents and brother] and now I'm going to play a role, some kind of role in this game. I thought to myself, 'Oh God, Pat, what have you gotten yourself into now?' "

But when the time came and Enright was in the game, his mind went blank. The crowd, the situation, the quality of the opponent, all went out of his head. The Wildcats were rallying from 14 points down, Illinois was missing free throws all over the place (the Illini only made 10 of 23 for the game), and Enright was out there instead of their best shooter when his team had to have points—and quickly.

He took one shot and missed badly. "Concentrate, stupid!" he told himself. Fear was replaced by anger—with himself. Mark Plansky and Tom Greis were leading the rally, but they needed help. A Plansky bucket cut the Illinois lead to 61–59 with a minute to go. The Illini missed at the other end and here came the Wildcats. The ball swung to Enright and this time he just did what he had been doing for years in practice, alone in his yard in the summer, on the schoolyard: He caught the ball, squared up and shot from outside the three-point line. *Swish!* Villanova led 62–61 with thirty seconds left. But Illinois came right back and scored to lead 63–62.

This time, the Wildcats went into the other corner to Plansky. He head-faked and drew a foul with four seconds left. "I knew Mark would make at least one," Enright said. "But I was scared if he only made one and we went into overtime we'd be in trouble with me in and Doug not in. I was praying he'd make 'em both."

Plansky made 'em both. Another Illinois miss, one last foul and, amazingly, Villanova, down 14 with less than four minutes left, was in the Sweet Sixteen. "All the years I've watched and coached basketball, that was as fine an effort as I've ever seen," Massimino said, drained but overjoyed. "I told the kids they had to earn this and today they certainly did."

Later, when he looked back and thought about Enright's role in the victory, Massimino just shook his head and said, "Can you believe that little schmuck is a hero?"

Kentucky was next. Wildcats versus Wildcats. This was exactly the kind of matchup Massimino craved. Not only was his team an under-dog, it was facing a team so arrogant it did not believe it could lose. One of the first questions Massimino faced in Birmingham was, "How does it feel to have the chance to play a school with Kentucky's great tradition?"

Massimino's answer was brief: "We're not exactly chopped liver."

To Kentucky and its fans, that is about what Villanova was. The local papers were full of stories wondering whether Kentucky would play Oklahoma or Louisville in the regional final.

In truth, Kentucky was not a great team. It had won a close race for the Southeastern Conference title in a year when the SEC was not nearly as strong as it had been in recent years. The Wildcats were talented—they always are—but they weren't overwhelming. The back-court was superb, with underrated senior Ed Davender and The Boy King, Rex Chapman. But Rob Lock was hardly frightening at center. Winston Bennett was solid and experienced but not scary at power forward. And Eric Manuel was a major talent, but still only a freshman. The bench was good but Coach Eddie Sutton hadn't used it all that much during the year.

Villanova's coaches looked at all the tapes, then showed them to the players. By Wednesday everyone was in agreement. "We play our game," Enright said, "we definitely beat these guys."

The coaches felt the same way. Oklahoma scared the hell out of them, but Kentucky didn't. Steve Lappas, who had been assigned to look at the Oklahoma tapes, kept walking out of his office groaning after watching the Sooners. "If we beat them," he told John Olive, "it's a bigger upset than when we beat Georgetown in '85. They're at least as talented—and now there's a shot clock and a three-point line."

Olive understood. "Lapp, we need to beat them just once. If we played them a hundred times could we beat them once?"

Lappas thought for a moment. "Maybe" was the best he could finally come up with.

There were no such thoughts concerning Kentucky. Respect, yes; fear, no. Either way, Massimino was having a great time. The national media—the 'Neers—were back. How did Rollie do it, everyone wanted to know. Rollie reveled in it, talked about the extended family of his team, the great kids, the graduation rate (100 percent) of his seniors. They told him he was a genius—and he certainly wasn't going to contradict them. But when someone asked him the secret of his success, he smiled and told the truth: "Good players."

As his team practiced on Wednesday, Massimino stood on the floor, looking around at the empty arena. "Hard to believe we're back here again," he said. "Hard to believe it was three years ago. We've gone 360 degrees in three years and touched every degree on the way around."

Game day was hot, the temperature approaching 80 degrees. The players gathered for pregame meal shortly after two o'clock. They would eat steak. Massimino would eat nothing. "I went out to Church's Fried Chicken a little while ago," he said. "When I'm nervous, I get hungry and I can't wait."

Father Bernard Lazor was there to say the mass. Lazor has been the team's chaplain for twelve years; he'd been through all the ups and downs with Massimino. Today, he had assigned a reading to Rollie, so when the coach walked to the front, he was handed a Bible to read from.

"Father," Massimino said, "this isn't what you wanted me to read."

Lazor checked. "I'm on the wrong page," he said, turning it.

"What's-a-matter, Father," Massimino asked, "you nervous?" The giggles were hardly suppressed.

Before he ended the mass, Lazor talked to the players about keeping things in perspective. "Remember where we were a year ago, fellas," he said. "All we wanted was to get the season over with. We've had a lot of glory and a lot of fun this week. But let's not forget the pain we went through last year. The embarrassment and the humiliation. Whatever happens tonight, we've all come a long way from there. There's no pressure in this, just fun."

If the players were feeling any pressure, they sure didn't show it. While Enright started the talent show, Massimino sat reading a registered letter he had received from a Kentucky fan. The letter was three pages long. In essence, it said, 'Don't bother showing up.'

"Listen to this," Massimino said to his coaches, reading softly. "The guy says, 'You're in SEC country now and when you walk on the court you're going to see how we can intimidate officials here in SEC land. You're in with the big boys now.' " Massimino was laughing when he reached the last line. It said, "Just remember one thing: Mules can't outrun Secretariat and when it comes to college hoops, we are Secretariat."

It was, of course, unsigned. Someone suggested Massimino read it to the players. He shook his head. "Nope," he said, "there's no need."

By now, the players were into their rendition of "Under the Boardwalk." Only they had rewritten the song in honor of Paul Vrind, the redshirt freshman from Holland. Now, the lyric was, "Under Paul's Nose." That was followed by a Massimino-led version of "Kansas City."

One thing was certain, the mules were here to have a good time. One also suspects that there wasn't any singing at Kentucky's pregame meal.

The game was as close to perfect as a basketball game can be. Chapman was fabulous, making just about every shot imaginable, including a running one-hander on the baseline that he shot directly over the seven-foot-two-inch Greis. He did the impossible—actually living up to his press clippings, and finished with 29 points.

But the Boy King's court could not keep up with the chopped liver mule team from Philadelphia. They played as if they were putting together a textbook on how to play tournament basketball. Wilson did a terrific job containing Davender, who on most nights was Kentucky's most important player.

Everyone contributed. West, fully recovered from his concussion, led the way with 20 points. All five starters were in double figures. Gary Massey came off the bench to play excellent defense. The Wildcats took control late in the first half, going on a 14–3 binge during the last five minutes. Plansky hit two three-pointers, and West hit a pair of

jumpers. The half ended with West cleanly stripping Davender as he
went up for a buzzer-beating jumper, and Villanova had a 43–32 lead.

There was little Massimino could say to his team. "You are an
amazing team," he said simply. "Just keep it up."

The Big Bad Blue was in trouble. No doubt they would come back,
though, and they did, led by Chapman. His jumper over Greis made
it 55–48. Then Manuel, one-for-six in the first half, hit a three-pointer
to cut it to 57–51. A moment later, with the lead still six, referee Paul
Housman badly missed a call, taking away a West dunk and calling
him for a charge. Replays showed the contact coming well after
the shot *and* that the foul should have been on Lock. Massimino
went wild.

But the players stayed calm. Plansky and Kenny Wilson hit buckets
and then, after a Chapman three, Wilson answered with a three of his
own. Kentucky just couldn't get close. Every time they made a move,
Villanova had an answer. "Nothing seemed to bother them," Sutton
said. "They just didn't make any mistakes."

The last nervous moment came after Chapman had stolen a pass and
cut the lead to 72–67 with 3:10 left. Massimino called time to make
sure his team took care of the ball and got a good shot. The shot clock
was at three when Plansky caught a pass in the post, a bit further out
than he wanted to be. He turned and shot from ten feet, banking the
ball in just before the buzzer. "I called bank in the air," he kidded later.
Bank or no bank, that was the game.

The final was 80–74 but it could have been worse. Kentucky never
got within five. The mules had outrun Secretariat and made it look
easy. When the buzzer sounded, Chapman stood at center court, hands
on his head, clearly in shock that his team had actually lost. Plansky,
the only survivor of the '85 championship team, stood holding the ball
high in the air as the clock ran out.

"They called that team a Cinderella team," he said. "There were
three first-round draft choices on that team. *This* is what you call a
Cinderella team."

Cinderella was now one step from the big ball in Kansas City. But
the last obstacle was Oklahoma, and it would take a one-in-a-hundred
game (at least) to beat the Sooners. After the assistants watched Oklahoma beat Louisville, they knew the task was formidable. "We played
a perfect game tonight," Olive said. "We'll have to play better on
Saturday."

True enough. But the very fact that they were playing on Saturday, with the rest of the Big East and 283 other teams sitting at home, was in itself not exactly chopped liver.

March 25. . . Pontiac, Michigan

The NCAA picks some very strange places to stage this basketball tournament, but it is hard to think of one stranger than the Pontiac Silverdome.

To begin with, the Silverdome is in the middle of nowhere. It is somewhere outside of Detroit but no one is quite sure where. Is there, in fact, a Pontiac? People wonder. The building itself is a giant white whale. For basketball games, a huge blue curtain is pulled down along the middle of the football field to give the place more intimacy. It's a very effective strategy, making the place about as intimate as Red Square must be on May Day.

The four teams gathered here for the Midwest Regional didn't really care about those details. Without question, Purdue, as the No. 1 seed, came as the top-heavy favorite. But Kansas was beginning to suspect that something was going on, something that would lead to something good. And as Purdue's Gene Keady would later point out, "No team coached by Lon Kruger is going to be scared of anything."

Kruger was the young Kansas State coach who had taken the Wildcats from the depths of an 11–20 record to the Sweet Sixteen in two quick years, thanks in great measure to Mitch Richmond, his swingman with the butt so wide it brought back memories of Mark Aguirre. Kansas State was Purdue's opponent.

The opener here matched Kansas and Vanderbilt, the two teams that had squeaked to victories the previous Sunday in Lincoln. Larry Brown respected Vanderbilt but, as he had said to his coaches the previous week, matching up with the Commodores would be a lot easier than matching up with Pittsburgh would have been.

By now, Kansas was playing great defense. Since the moving of Kevin Pritchard to point guard and the insertion of Jeff Gueldner into the lineup, the Jayhawks had become an aggressive, overplaying, attacking defensive team. "If we called zone at this stage," Brown said, "I think the kids would rebel."

Actually, the rebellious types were gone. Brown had kicked junior

college guard Otis Livingston and freshman center Mike Masucci off
the team before the tournament began for assorted and varying offenses. That meant that, in all, six players who had been part of the
team on October 15 were no longer playing.

But Danny Manning was playing—and as long as he was on the
court, Kansas had a chance to compete against anybody. The reticence
to dominate and to lead that Brown had been fighting for four years
was now a thing of the past. Manning understood that, if his team was
to win, there were things that had to be done that only he could do.
He understood that the other players looked up to him and that he had
to lead not just by example but with words. Sometimes he had to shout
and sometimes he had to cajole. It didn't delight him to do these things
but losing would have delighted him even less.

Manning wanted to be certain that his teammates didn't come into
the regional satisfied, simply happy that they had gotten this far. While
everyone else went around saying, "We're just glad to be here," Manning's message was simple: "We're here so we can get to Kansas City."
He started the Vanderbilt game by swishing a three-point shot and his
teammates just followed him from there.

"That's probably the first time he's ever taken a three-point shot
without getting yelled at," Brown said later. "He just had that look in
his eye."

The look didn't go away. He produced 25 first-half points, taking
Kansas to a 41–29 lead, and in the second half the Commodores never
got within 9. Kansas won it easily, 77–64. Manning finished with 38
points. When Ed Manning looked at the stat sheet, he did a double
take. "He shot 16-for-29," the father yelled. "I can't believe my boy
took 29 shots in a game. I will have to get on him about that."

Everyone's mood was jubilant. Hardly surprising. "It's hard to believe that it was only six weeks ago we were lining up an NIT home
game," Alvin Gentry marveled. "Now, we actually have a shot at the
Final Four."

They had a *great* shot at the Final Four. As they sat watching the
second game, the Kansas coaches were openly and unabashedly rooting
for Kansas State. Part of this was personal. They knew the K–State
coaches and liked them. But part of it was pragmatic. Matchups again.
Kansas knew it could beat Kansas State—it had already done so once—
but it didn't know if it could beat Purdue.

Early on, it didn't look as if anybody could beat Purdue. The Boilermakers flashed to a 10–0 lead before the Wildcats knew what had hit them. These two teams had played in late December and the result had been a 101–72 rout by Purdue. Now, it looked like a rerun might be in the offing.

But this Kansas State was different from that December team. It was smarter, it was more mature, and it played the game at a much slower pace. Patiently, the Wildcats came back. Coach Lon Kruger's appearance was best described once by a reporter who wrote that "he has the bearing of a young Republican congressman." But underneath Kruger was as intense a competitor as anyone in the business. At halftime, Purdue's margin was 43–34.

"It wasn't like we were blowing them out," Troy Lewis said. "But we were comfortable. All year we had been a team that came out in the second half and took over games. It was like we used the first twenty minutes as a warmup."

But this time K–State turned the tables. Before anybody could say, 'Look out, Boilers,' Kruger's team had screeched to a 12–1 start, William Scott's two straight three-pointers giving them a 46–44 lead before a shell-shocked Keady could call time with 16:53 left in the game.

"Runs are part of basketball," Keady said later. "Teams had made 'em on us before. But when I called that time-out, when the kids came into the huddle, I saw doubt in their eyes. I knew then this was going to be a long night."

Keady's instinct was right. All year long, it had been so easy for the Boilermakers. They hadn't put any pressure on themselves to win the Big Ten because they had seen it only as being preparation for March. They had rolled through, then in their first two tournament games they had never really been in trouble.

Now, though, they were up against a team bursting with confidence, a solid, well-coached team that would not self-destruct. The game seesawed for seven minutes until it reached 54–54. Then Richmond hit a three-pointer to make it 57–54. Fred McCoy posted to make it 59–54 and Buster Glover hit a baseline jumper to make it 61–54. Purdue looked flustered.

"All of a sudden it seemed like they were making everything," Lewis said later. "But there was still so much time left. We just had to stay calm, run the offense and take good shots." Lewis took one, a three-pointer that cut the lead to 61–57 with 8:20—an eternity—still left to play.

Then came one of those shots that makes a team wonder if someone is out to get them. Closely guarded, Richmond threw up a three-pointer from beyond the top of the key. The shot was way too strong, so strong that it hit the glass and banked in. "I thought then," Richmond said, "this one is ours."

When Melvin McCants bobbled a pass a moment later and Richmond hit a leap-and-lean jumper over Todd Mitchell to make it 66–57, it certainly looked that way. But Purdue was too good and too experienced to just roll over and die. Lewis, the coolest man on the court at this stage, hit two free throws. From the bench, the coaches were screaming, "Patience, patience," because there were still five minutes left. Ron Meyer missed for K–State and Everette Stephens made the kind of play that makes pro scouts drool, taking one giant step down the lane and laying the ball in as he was fouled. The free throw cut the margin to 66–62. There was still 4:34 left.

They traded baskets, then Lewis got his hand on a Scott jumper. Purdue had a chance to cut the lead to two. Lewis found Mitchell inside. He went to the basket—and missed. He went over everybody, rebounded and was fouled going back up. Two shots. Mitchell, an almost 80-percent foul shooter, could cut the lead to two.

Stephens and Lewis, watching their friend line up to shoot, had the same thought: "Lots of time, Todd. Make these and we're okay."

Back in January, at Indiana, with a chance to put the Hoosiers away, Mitchell had gone to the line to shoot one-and-one with fifteen seconds left. He had missed. After that game, when someone had pointed out to him that he had played well in spite of the miss, Mitchell had shaken his head and said softly, "Good players play well, great players win games."

He stepped to the foul line, looked at the rim and shot. It was off left—*way* off. A brick. Mitchell shook his head, wiped his brow and stepped back. He took the ball again, aimed and shot. Off right—and short. Another brick. K–State rebounded and called time to set up its spread offense. As Mitchell ran to the bench, his plaintive cry could be heard clearly several rows back: *"Shit!"*

Good players play well, great players win games.

Shocking as the misses were, the game wasn't over. Meyer hit one free throw to make it 69–64 but Stephens drilled a three-pointer to make it 69–67 with 1:30 left. After a time-out by each team, K–State ran the clock to fifty-eight seconds before Purdue fouled Charles

Bledsoe. It was one-and-one. He missed. Purdue now had a chance to tie or take the lead. Keady wanted no miscommunications.

He called time with forty-four seconds left. The first time Purdue tried to inbound, it couldn't and another time-out was called. The second time, the ball came in to Stephens. The play called was "40." Lewis, after throwing the ball inbounds, stepped in on the baseline as McCants came over to screen for him. But Bledsoe made a quick switch onto him and Lewis threw the ball back out to Stephens.

Now, Mitchell came across the lane and moved into the low post on the right side. Stephens dribbled toward him. But just as he released a pass to him, Mitchell cut away, thinking he was covered, looking to set a screen. Stephens's pass went right to the shocked Bledsoe, who was only too happy to catch the ball and wait to be fouled with twenty-seven seconds left. But, with a chance to ice the game, Bledsoe could only make the first free throw. It was 70–67. Mitchell rebounded the second. A three-point shot could tie.

Stephens quickly called "Santa Clara," a play designed to get a three-point shot, preferably for him or for Lewis. On the play, McCants screens for Stephens while Mitchell screens for Lewis. If Stephens isn't open, he can pass to Lewis. But Stephens never had a chance to make a decision. As he began to dribble left into position, the ball somehow hit his leg. It was a fluke, a once-in-a-lifetime nightmare. Coming around Mitchell's screen, Lewis saw the ball hit Stephens's leg and begin to roll toward the sideline.

Horrified, his first reaction was to scream: *"Everette!"* Then, he and Stephens both dove after the ball futilely. It rolled out of bounds with nineteen seconds left. Now, Purdue was all but done. Steve Henson hit two free throws to make it 72–67 with seventeen seconds to go. Stephens—too late—hit a three-pointer with nine seconds left. Purdue was out of time-outs. Richmond was fouled with three ticks left. He only made one but Stephens's desperation shot from center court was too late—and way off the mark anyway. Kansas State–73, Purdue–70. Final.

This was not the way it was supposed to end for Lewis, Mitchell, and Stephens. Not so soon and not this way. They had won twenty-nine games but the last loss was the one they would remember. In the locker room, Lewis found himself filled with anger. Stephens, the calmest of the three seniors, was telling everyone it had been a great year anyway. Lewis wasn't buying it. As he walked around the room, too angry to talk to anyone, Lewis suddenly spotted Keady, who, in the immediate aftermath of the loss, had told the team how proud he was of their season. The coach was sitting by himself in a corner.

Suddenly, all the fights and arguments over the years seemed trivial. All Lewis could think of was how hard Keady had worked to make him, Mitchell, and Stephens into good players. "I wanted to just go over and hug him and tell him it was okay," Lewis said. "I argued with him and got mad at him so much. I was really mad at him at the start of the year but you know what, he was right about almost everything. Losing didn't change that and I wanted to tell him all that."

But when Lewis started to open his mouth, he started to choke up. He would have to tell Keady how he felt later. The postmortems were typical. It was not until two days later that Lewis could bring himself to ask Mitchell what had happened on the free throws.

"How'd you miss 'em?" he asked softly.

"I don't know," Mitchell answered. "I just don't know. I felt good, felt fine and then I just missed."

Lewis took the loss the hardest of the three seniors, at least partly because he believed because his future as a pro was the most questionable. "It might have been my last game," he said. "Who knows? Everyone kept telling me it wasn't that big a thing, that I'm just twenty-one and I still have my whole life in front of me and in the grand scheme of things basketball isn't that important.

"I understand all that and I know my whole life is ahead of me. But let's be real. For most of my life, basketball has been *it*. Nothing else has been as important. I haven't spent as much time on anything else I've ever done. You can't just walk away from something like that and say it was no big deal. It hurts. It hurts a lot and I'm not exactly sure when it will stop hurting."

Two days after the loss, the three seniors attended their last team meeting. Lewis was the last of them to speak. He didn't have any great messages except for one thing he wanted to say to the juniors. "Start out next year right away showing people that it's your team. And when Coach Keady tells you something's right, believe him, because he knows what he's talking about. And remember to enjoy it. Because before you know it, it will be over."

Lewis, Mitchell, and Stephens then left their former teammates with their coach. The Final Four would begin in four days. But for them, all too soon, it was over.

March 26. . . East Rutherford, New Jersey

As those final tortured seconds were ticking away for Purdue, another session of that popular show, "Late Night with Billy King," was being convened. These sessions, held in the hotel room shared by King and Kevin Strickland, had become a regular part of Duke's pregame routine.

Shortly after Coach Mike Krzyzewski finished his night-before-a-game team meeting, King, Strickland, Quin Snyder, and Danny Ferry would convene to watch a movie or talk about the game or talk about girls or talk about whatever was on their minds.

Tonight's special guest on "Late Night" was Ala Abdelnaby, the talented 6–10 sophomore who could be so good and so bad, sometimes within the same game. All four of the regulars wanted to take a shot at Abdelnaby—verbally. Since Snyder's emergence as not just the team's point guard but its offensive leader, he had joined the other three as the team's leadership. King and Strickland were the captains, but the four of them together were the ruling junta.

In fourteen hours, the Blue Devils would be playing Temple for the Eastern Regional championship. The Owls were the No. 1 seed in the East and the No. 1 ranked team in the country. There was no doubt that Duke would have to play its best game of the season to pull the upset. But they were going to play the game without John Smith, the 6–7 junior who was the first forward off the bench. On Thursday, during the 73–72 victory over Rhode Island, Smith had taken a charge late in the first half. He had already contributed 11 points at that stage and when he took the charge he was so pumped up that he jumped up and slammed his fist into the stanchion under the basket.

Even though the padding softened the blow, Smith broke a bone in his hand. He would not play against Temple. That meant Abdelnaby would have to play a significant role, especially if Robert Brickey got into foul trouble.

Abdelnaby's talent was unquestioned. His potential had never been more apparent than in the ACC semifinal, when he had come in to score 12 vital points in just nine minutes. But he was also immature. To the ruling junta, Abdelnaby was a playful little brother who hadn't quite figured out what life was all about. He made mistakes, got into trouble, drove the coaches to distraction, and made it impossible for anyone to stay mad at him for very long.

He was, in short, the team flake. But the time for flakiness was long since past. "Ala," King said, speaking for the group, "you have got to come in ready to play tomorrow. No fooling around. No silly mistakes. We really need you in this game. This isn't fool-around time anymore. This is for the Final Four."

Getting to this no-fool-around time hadn't been easy. After watching Rhode Island beat Syracuse, the Blue Devils had fully expected a battle with the Rams, a talented, confident team on a roll. Duke had opened a nine-point lead early, but had blown all but one point of it, leading only 37–36 at halftime. Krzyzewski wasn't happy at intermission. Strickland had played one of his languid halves, acting as if this were November, not March. "Goddamn it, Kevin, when are you going to stop this shit?!" Krzyzewski yelled.

The second half was a struggle. Owens and Garrick were so tough to stop that Krzyzewski played a few possessions of zone, something he hated doing. King had his hands full with Garrick, but he felt responsible for Strickland too. Midway through the half as Strickland went to the foul line, King walked up behind him and hissed, "Goddamn it, Kevin, if you don't get going, this is going to be our last game. And if it is, I'm going to kill you!"

Whether that threat registered with Strickland or not, he finally shook loose for a couple of key jumpers. Ferry got open inside and Snyder, who had become Mr. Clutch, also hit. And, when Rhode Island was rallying in the last minute, Brickey stepped forward and made four straight free throws to deny the Rams a chance to catch up.

The victory put the Blue Devils into the final against Temple. Since becoming No. 1 in the rankings in February, the Owls had been virtually unstoppable. They had won that classic game from Villanova, then had embarrassed North Carolina in Chapel Hill. They rolled through the Atlantic 10 Tournament—beating Rhode Island in the final—and won their first three NCAA games with ease, beating Lehigh, Georgetown, and Richmond. The Spiders' dream tournament had ended emphatically when the Owls beat them, 69–47.

The key matchups in the final were Billy King versus Temple's cerebral freshman Mark Macon, and Kevin Strickland versus Mike Vreeswyk, the Owls' designated three-point shooter. Strickland had always been known for his offense. In this game, his defense would be crucial.

The game could not have started any worse than it did for Duke.

Vreeswyk opened the scoring with an open three-pointer. Ferry threw a pass away. Brickey missed a dunk. The Blue Devils were zero-for-five before they made a basket. They were down 9–4 when Krzyzewski drew a technical trying to tell Larry Lembo that he and his partners didn't know what walking was. It was 17–7 when Macon hit a soft jumper with 10:02 left.

Abdelnaby came in for Brickey. Duke's 6–5 sophomore was having serious trouble with Temple's 6–8 Tim Perry. Brickey is such a wonderful jumper that he almost never gets his shot blocked. Perry was blocking it. "Robert had a problem," Krzyzewski said later. "He was trying to shoot and Perry was playing catch. He would catch Robert's shots and throw them back to him."

Krzyzewski needed Abdelnaby's size against Perry. He also needed some offense. Strickland, Ferry, and Greg Koubek began to supply some. Abdelnaby went to the boards with Perry and drew two fouls from him. When Strickland hit two straight jumpers, the Blue Devils were within 19–17. Temple opened the lead to seven again but Strickland hit once more just before halftime to cut the margin to 28–25.

Krzyzewski's message at halftime was simple. "You played terribly for ten minutes and you're still right in the game. You *know* now that you can beat this team. Now, go do it."

Defense had kept Duke in the game. Macon was 4-for-16; Vreeswyk 2-for-6. Could King and Strickland keep that up? Could the Blue Devils find some offense? Yes and yes. After a three-point play by Perry started the half, Duke took over the game. Ironically, King's offense started it. He rolled to the basket for a short pop that made it 31–27. Ferry hit and King followed a Strickland miss to tie the score for the first time. Then Strickland, on a switch play, blocked a Macon jumper. Enter Snyder. He knocked in a three-pointer to make it 34–31. Strickland hit again. The run was 11–0.

Duke wasn't finished. A jumper by rarely used Derrick Brantley made it 40–35. Snyder hit two free throws. Macon, with King in his face, threw his *seventh* air ball of the game. Strickland hit a three. Perry threw a bad pass. Strickland hit another three, this one falling down as the shot clock ran out. Ferry hit a jumper. It was 50–35. Coach John Chaney called time. It was too late. "When Strickland hit that second three-pointer, that was the one that killed us," Chaney said. "You play good defense for forty-five seconds and then a guy hits one from the boondocks."

Duke's defense was the story of this game. By the time the befuddled Macon was through, he had gone 6-for-29. Strickland had held Vreeswyk to 2-for-12. The two Duke seniors, neither one ever really a star, had starred. Especially King. This was his day. Ferry was voted the MVP after scoring 20 points, but a strong case could have been made for King. When he took Macon out of the game, he had taken Temple out of the game. The Owls just couldn't adjust. The final was 63–53, the last two points coming when King giddily tapped the ball over his head to Strickland, who laid the ball in at the buzzer.

The ruling junta took turns hugging while Krzyzewski dashed across the court to where his wife, Mickie, and his daughters, Deborah and Lindy, were sitting. This was no small thing for Duke. Two Final Fours in three years—with different players in the key roles—was the mark of a program that was going to be a factor for a long time to come.

For King, the feeling was almost indescribable. He had spoken back in February about collecting memories during this season because he expected to be in the real world next year. Now, he had not only captained an ACC champion and a Final Four team, but in doing so had put together a string of defensive performances that would be remembered for years to come.

During a two-week, six-game stretch King had guarded Vinny Del Negro, Jeff Lebo, Kato Armstrong, Tom Garrick, and last but not least, Mark Macon. Only against Boston University in the first round of the tournament had he not faced a player with a big-time scoring reputation. The five sharpshooters had shot a combined 30-for-95, topped by Macon's 6-for-29 against King.

King is not a sentimental person by nature. But as he and his teammates were cutting the nets down, he knew this was one time when he wanted a souvenir. "Let me finish," he said, grabbing the scissors. With that, he clipped the last two strands, put the net around his neck and walked off. Another keepsake to show the children in the years to come.

While the Blue Devils were celebrating, Villanova was trying to pull off one more miracle—and coming remarkably close.

The Wildcats knew they couldn't possibly run with Oklahoma. They knew they had to get the game at a slow pace, take a long time whenever they had the ball, and hope that the Sooners would give in to impatience and make mistakes.

For almost thirty minutes, the strategy worked. Oklahoma was frustrated at every turn as Wilson, West, Plansky, and Massey handled the ball almost flawlessly against the Sooner press. But this was an Oklahoma team that did not give in easily. Its press was one of attrition. If it didn't get you early, it was probably going to get you late. A 14–2 run by the Sooners turned an eight-point deficit into a four-point lead.

Still, the Wildcats hung in. With less than four minutes left, Massey went to the foul line for a one-and-one. Oklahoma was leading 59–54. If he made both, the margin would only be three points. But Massey missed, Harvey Grant sneaked behind the defense for a dunk, and suddenly the lead was seven. Villanova had to foul. The Sooners made their free throws and the Wildcats ran out of gas. The final was 78–59, deceptive because it had been anybody's game until those last four minutes.

"You only get this close only so many times," Massimino said. "That makes it disappointing. But how can I possibly have asked for any more than this team gave me? They were great, from day one to the last day. They gave me everything they had to give."

And the little coach had given everything he had to give. Remember: In adversity, the true guy comes out.

March 27 . . . Seattle, Washington

Steve Kerr was worried. Arizona was in the West Regional Final but it had been too easy. Cornell had been a walkover, but that was expected. Seton Hall had been a rout. That was a surprise. Iowa's press, which had seemed so tough to handle in Iowa City in December, had been a breeze. No one had come within 20 points of the Wildcats and they were one step from the Final Four. Only North Carolina stood in their way.

That was why Kerr couldn't sleep. "I kept tossing and turning, having completely different ideas about the game. One minute I would wake up and say, 'Jeez, Dean Smith has lost three straight regional finals, maybe this is his turn.' Then, I would say, 'Yeah, but Ranzino Smith's the only senior, they're all back next year.' I just kept going back and forth in my mind all night.

"All I wanted to do really was get on the court and play the damn game. That's the hardest thing about the tournament. You play for two hours and then it seems like you wait forever before you play again. All you can think about is the game coming up. It drives you crazy."

Standing on the court in the empty Kingdome ninety minutes before tip-off, he was not his usual, joking self. "It's almost like I can't believe we're here, not in the sense of the team being good enough but in the sense of how quickly it's gotten here. I mean, this is it. We win, we go. Everything we've worked for since October happens. We lose and—boom—just like that the whole thing is over.

"I woke up this morning and I started thinking about the game and I actually found myself praying, saying, 'Please, God, let us win.' I've never done that before in my life. But then I can't remember ever wanting something so much in my life."

While Kerr was talking, the giant screen in the Kingdome was showing the Kansas–Kansas State Midwest final. Kansas had taken control and Kerr, being the student of the game that he was, couldn't help but notice.

"Kansas is playing unreal defense," he said admiringly. "But I can't believe the luck they've gotten with the draw. Every time they're about to play somebody really good, they get upset. First N.C. State, then Pittsburgh, then Purdue. It's almost like a destiny thing with them."

It was indeed almost like a "destiny thing" for the Jayhawks. Larry Brown had felt inklings in that direction in Lincoln and now they were coming in loud and clear in Pontiac. Every button he pressed was correct. After the Jayhawks had lost in the Big Eight Tournament to Kansas State, Brown had been furious with Scooter Barry, who had played horribly in point guard Pritchard's place.

"If I ever try to put that little sucker in a game again when it matters, stop me," he had told his assistants in the immediate aftermath. Today, against K–State, when Jeff Gueldner missed two easy shots early, Brown yanked him and put Barry in the game so quickly the assistants never had a chance to stop him. Barry responded with the game of his life: 15 points, 5 rebounds, and 3 assists in 25 minutes. That, combined with Manning's 20 points, Milt Newton's 18, and the suffocating Kansas defense (Mitch Richmond was held to 11 points, 24 less than he had scored in the teams' last meeting) was enough to put the Jayhawks in Kansas City.

"Well," Kerr said as the final minutes of the Kansas game wound down, "that makes three. Now the question is, who will be number four?"

It was a good question. North Carolina had been playing well. The Tar Heels had bounced back from the Duke loss in the ACC Tournament to beat North Texas State easily in the first round. They had then routed a Loyola–Marymount team that was getting all sorts of attention because of its tremendous scoring, then had shut down Gary Grant in the round of sixteen en route to beating Michigan. Now, for the third time in four years, they were one step from the Final Four.

"But we're hurt," Smith insisted before the game. "Jeff [Lebo] is sore and I'm not even sure [Steve] Bucknall can play." Bucknall would play. People don't take the day off because they're "sore"—not with a Final Four spot at stake. Smith, ever stubborn, bet a reporter a dollar that Bucknall wouldn't play. When Bucknall was introduced as a starter, Smith took a dollar out of his pocket and waved it. It was a bet he was more than willing to lose.

By the time Kerr was introduced, his stomach was churning. "It was the first time I ever caught myself thinking in terms of, 'This could be my last game,' " he said later. "It sort of unnerved me for a minute."

The butterflies slowly began to fade once the game started. Both teams were tentative early. Arizona had an early 5–0 lead, but Carolina came right back to go up 7–6. The first half was a cautious one, each team afraid to be the aggressor for fear of making critical mistakes. Kerr, after missing his first shot, made two straight three-pointers midway through the half.

The Wildcats were playing zone, laying back to deny the inside to the Tar Heels' J. R. Reid and Scott Williams. As a result, North Carolina was taking close to forty-five seconds on almost every possession. The slow pace of the game, combined with what was at stake, made the crowd feel as if it were in a dentist's chair. Everyone kept squirming uncomfortably, hoping the waiting would end soon.

The half ended badly for Kerr and Arizona. A Ranzino Smith three-pointer with forty-five seconds left put Carolina up 27–26. Arizona came down and set up for a final shot. But, to the amazement of everyone, Kerr threw as poor a pass as he had thrown all season, tossing the ball right to Carolina's Rick Fox. As Fox broke away for a lay-up, Kerr seemed to compound the error by intentionally fouling him.

The Tar Heels, instead of getting two points out of the mistake, had a chance to get as many as five—the two free throws plus the ensuing possession. Instead, Fox only made one of the free throws and King Rice's jumper was long at the buzzer, so the halftime lead for Carolina was only 28–26.

Lute Olson was not a happy man during intermission. He didn't feel his team had been aggressive enough. To combat that problem, he decided to switch to a man-to-man defense to shake his team out of its lethargy. Tom Tolbert, in particular, had struggled. Olson asked him a simple question: "Do you want to go to Kansas City?" Tolbert didn't have to answer.

Both teams picked up the pace as the second half began, sensing that the time for playing chess games was past. Sean Elliott and Craig McMillan quickly hit three-pointers for Arizona, while Scott Williams hit twice inside for Carolina. Kerr stole a pass and fed McMillan for a dunk. Arizona led 34–32.

The game stayed tight. Tolbert put Arizona on top with a circus shot, an over-the-head flip that went into the basket just as Reid crashed into him. Reid answered that seconds later and Carolina led 44–43. But then Kerr hit a three-pointer and Tolbert produced another spectacular move, driving under the basket and reversing the ball up and in as he was fouled. The free throw made it 49–44.

Kerr fouled Scott Williams—"Oh my God, no! That was no foul!" he screamed in frustration—but Williams missed the first free throw. Then Reid stepped into the lane as Williams was shooting the second. On the bench, Smith looked a little shell-shocked. His team was unraveling and he knew it. Tolbert hit inside again. Reid dunked to make it 51–46 with 9:20 left but that was the last field goal for the Tar Heels until a Fox fifteen-footer with 1:45 left.

By that time, Arizona had put the game out of reach. Tolbert and Elliott had taken command, leading the Wildcats on a 13–4 run, giving them a 64–50 lead. Just as it had done against Duke, Carolina had fallen apart on offense during the last ten minutes. Nothing would fall for any of the Tar Heels. As the lead mounted, Kerr began to realize that he was, at last, going to the Final Four. When the buzzer sounded and Arizona had won, 70–52, Kerr felt as if a giant weight had come off his shoulders.

"I can't even remember how many times I fantasized going to the Final Four," he said. "It was just an unreal feeling, looking up at the scoreboard and knowing we had it. I couldn't believe Carolina fell apart the way it did. You just don't expect that from them. We expected the game to go right to the end but they just didn't seem to have anything left. It was really kind of shocking."

There were more shocks left for Kerr. As he was being guided toward the CBS camera for the postgame interview, the on-site producer, Roy Hamilton, who had played at UCLA when Kerr was a ballboy there, whispered to him, "When you go on the air, Steve, do us a favor and say, 'We're going to Kansas City!'"

CBS, it seems, not only pays for the NCAA Tournament and determines when the games will be played, it now also feels it must script the postgame interviews. Kerr shrugged. "What is this," he wanted to know, "a Disneyland commercial?"

But Hamilton had been a friend since boyhood. Kerr delivered the line. When the interview was over, CBS's Brent Musberger asked Kerr how his mother would hear about the game. "I guess I'll give her a call," Kerr said.

"If you'd like," Musberger said, "you're welcome to use the phone in our truck to call."

Kerr thought this was a generous offer and would save him quite a few dollars on a phone call to Egypt. "That would be great," he told Musberger.

"We'd love to put a camera on you while you make the call," Musberger said.

Kerr was stunned. And embarrassed. "Calling my mother is kind of a private thing," he said politely. "I guess I'll just do it later."

It was later that Kerr learned CBS had been told by the NCAA that Kerr could make the call from the truck as long as he later reimbursed the network for the call. So Kerr would not even have saved any money by accepting the CBS offer. As always, the NCAA was right on the case in a matter that should have meant absolutely nothing.

By the time Kerr was finished with all the interviews, he was exhausted. It had been a grueling game, one surprisingly full of trash talk back and forth. Kerr had not expected this from North Carolina. In fact, afterwards, Bucknall had claimed that if he had been playing on two good legs, Elliott would not have scored 24 points. When he heard this comment, Elliott laughed.

"At least," he said, thinking back to December, "Billy King took it like a man."

Now, Billy King was in the Final Four. So was Elliott—and Kerr. Two hundred and eighty-seven teams were done. Four were left and, as the people at CBS would tell you again and again, they were all going to Kansas City.

19
FINALLY,
THE FINAL FOUR

March 30–April 5. . . Kansas City

Once upon a time, fifty years ago, when the NCAA Tournament was played for the very first time, a total of eight teams participated and four of them came to Kansas City to decide the championship. Oregon State won that first tournament and it has never again been so quiet in Kansas City.

Now, the Final Four ranks with the World Series and the Super Bowl among the great annual events in American sports. It is covered by several thousand members of the media, it dominates whatever town it is played in for an entire week, and it is a major television event around the country.

When the NCAA awarded the 1988 Final Four to Kansas City, it did so with tradition and nostalgia in mind. Kansas City had hosted nine of the first twenty-five Final Fours; since this was to be the fiftieth anniversary of the tournament, it would be a nice touch to return there.

All well and good. It would be wonderful if all Final Fours could be played in basketball gyms like Kemper Arena. Basketball is an intimate sport and when it is played in domes, it loses intimacy, especially for those fans sitting miles and miles from courtside. But the future of the Final Four is, without question, in domes. In 1990, the Final Four will be played in Denver's twenty thousand-seat McNichols Arena. It is unlikely to be played in a real basketball arena any time after that.

So, in more ways than one, this Final Four was a tribute to the past—very shortly this kind of Final Four will be a thing of the past. With only 16,200 seats for sale in the arena, scalpers were asking—and getting—close to $2,000 a ticket.

The Final Four is much more than three basketball games. It is a week-long convention of the entire sport. The National Association of Basketball Coaches actually holds its annual convention during the week. The rest of the college basketball world has its own less-formal convention at the same time. Nobody skips the Final Four. A lot of people come for the week with absolutely no chance of getting in to see the games. They come to see the people.

Until 1973, the national championship game was played on Saturday afternoon. In fact, until 1969, the Final Four was, basically, a twenty-four-hour affair. Two games were played Friday night and one game was played Saturday night. By Sunday morning, everyone had gone home.

In 1969, when NBC–TV first took over the television contract, the semifinals were moved up to Thursday night and the final was played Saturday afternoon. Back then, NBC only televised *one* semifinal nationally. Four years later, the format was changed again. The semifinals were moved to Saturday afternoon and the final was pushed back to Monday night so it could be televised in prime time. In that first prime-time final, Bill Walton hit 21 of 22 shots for UCLA as most of America watched open-mouthed. From there, the tournament simply got bigger and bigger and bigger.

Its growth is difficult to measure, but consider this: In 1986, when Syracuse hosted the first and second rounds of the East Regional, it had more requests for press credentials than the NCAA received for the Final Four in Atlanta in 1977.

Now, the Final Four is a week-long social occasion, beginning for many people on Wednesday and not ending until the following Tuesday. There are more parties than anyone can keep track of, even more rumors than there are parties, an extraordinary number of hotel-lobby arguments and, just by the way, these three basketball games. It is, in short, a celebration of a greatly flawed but truly great sport by the people who have flawed it and made it great.

To begin at the beginning in 1988 . . .

The city is just beginning to fill up when the first bombshell of the week hits. Word comes out of Los Angeles that, to almost no one's surprise, Walt Hazzard has been fired at UCLA. The Bruins have just finished a 16–14 season marked by shoddy play, embarrassing losses at home, and constant battles between Hazzard and almost everyone around the program.

Everyone knows Larry Brown wants the job. But he is tied up right now with the small matter of preparing Kansas to play Duke in the first semifinal on Saturday. On Wednesday evening, the story breaks: Jim Valvano is going to be the UCLA coach.

The main perpetrator of this story is Dick Vitale of ESPN. On Wednesday evening Vitale goes on the air with a story that says Valvano has been offered the job and is likely to take it before the weekend is over. In the lobby of the coaches' hotel, the word spreads like wildfire. In the coaching world, this is what is known as a domino job. If Valvano moves to UCLA, it starts a series of dominoes: N.C. State will hire a head coach from somewhere to replace Valvano. Rumors are starting already: Gary Williams of Ohio State? Jeff Mullins of UNC–Charlotte? Lefty Driesell? (Did someone say Lefty Driesell????) Yes, someone said Lefty Driesell.

Moments after "breaking" the story, Vitale appears in the lobby, clearly delighted with himself. "It's done, baby, it's over, I just broke the story, we went with a bulletin," Vitale says. "Jimmy V. is goin' to UCLA. He's gone. It's a done deal." Vitale is taking bets he is so sure. "Dinner, baby, you name the place," he says. "Anyplace."

It is tough getting angry at Vitale even when he is as full of himself as he is right now. He is a genuinely nice person who loves basketball and can't quite believe what a celebrity he has become in recent years as a TV analyst. He says he won't reveal his sources on this story but he's locked in and he's got it right. Standing right behind Vitale is Sonny Vaccaro, the maven of Nike shoes who is tight with all the coaches who are paid by Nike to wear their equipment. Vitale is a Nike man. So is Jim Valvano. Vaccaro is also betting Valvano is going to UCLA. Any guesses as to who Vitale's source might be?

"This is unreal," Virginia Assistant Coach Dave Odom says. "If Valvano goes, who knows how many jobs could open up?"

By now, the lobby is crowded. Most of the coaches arrive on Wednesday because their annual golf tournament is on Thursday morning. Usually, Wednesday is warmup night. Everyone arrives, has dinner, and takes things easy. No wild nights—yet. But the Valvano rumor has energized everyone. The lobby is alive.

In one corner, Bill Foster and Dick Stewart are sitting, fending off questioners. Foster, the Northwestern coach, coached Valvano at Rutgers. They remain close friends. "If he takes the job I'm going with him and sit on the bench and keep track of the time-outs," Foster says. "I'm old enough to do that job. They can just call me Father Time."

Stewart, who also played for Foster, is Valvano's top assistant. "I don't know anything," he says over and over again. "I wish I did. Jimmy's coming in tomorrow and I'll talk to him then."

Jim Boeheim joins the conversation. A year ago, Boeheim was still working during this week. Now, he will coach the annual coaches' all-star game on Thursday night. His opponent in that game will be Jerry Tarkanian of Nevada–Las Vegas. Boeheim is not very happy with Tarkanian at the moment. Recently, Boeheim's star recruit, Billy Owens, has qualified to play as a freshman by improving his SAT score from 590 to 730. Tarkanian thinks Owens's improvement is miraculous—too miraculous—and he has said so, implying that someone took the test for Owens.

"I don't see anyone questioning Alonzo Mourning," Boeheim says. "His score went up a lot more than Billy's." But Alonzo Mourning is a Georgetown recruit. Basketball people will privately question John Thompson—but never publicly. Thompson is the Olympic coach. He is tied closely to Dean Smith and Dave Gavitt. He is too powerful to take on publicly. So it is Boeheim who gets ripped. "All I know is Billy studied like hell in that SAT course before he took the test again," Boeheim says.

Foster and Stewart nod politely. More coaches drift over. "What about Lefty?" asks Joe Harrington of Long Beach State, a former Driesell assistant. "Is he going to James Madison or not?"

"Nothing's final," Driesell keeps insisting. "It's up to the lawyers. I ain't sayin' nothin' beyond that."

The coaches agreed that Lefty would go to James Madison. But what if Valvano went to UCLA, would State want to hire Lefty? And who would James Madison hire then? On and on it went. . . .

Across town, in the lobby of the press hotel, the Valvano rumor was spreading rapidly. "I don't believe it," said Billy Packer of CBS. "He may be talking to them, but I guarantee you nothing is final yet. It's just too fast."

By now, Vitale, having worked his way through the coaches' lobby, was in the press lobby. It was late, though, almost 2 A.M., and Vitale had talked about the story so much even he seemed to be getting tired. Finally, he looked up from a rare silence and said, "So what do you think, will Jimmy take the job?"

That seemed a perfect time to end the opening evening. Four hours after insisting that Valvano *was* UCLA's new coach, Vitale was asking if he would take the job. It could only happen at the Final Four.

DAY TWO: THURSDAY

This is the day when the four teams get to town. The team that will travel the shortest distance, Kansas, will be the last to arrive. The Jayhawks will bus the forty miles from Lawrence after a late afternoon practice in time to see the coaches' all-star game. They also must wait until their bus driver arrives. The ever-superstitious Brown has flown his bus driver from Pontiac in for the weekend. This is a first: the bus driver flying in while the team busses in.

No one is happier to get to Kansas City than Steve Kerr. The three days since the victory in Seattle have been exhausting. After the team flew back to Tucson on Sunday—a trip highlighted by Bobbi Olson dancing in the aisle of the team bus—they were taken straight to McKale Center. There, more than thirteen thousand people awaited their arrival.

"When we walked in, the place just went crazy," Kerr said. "I think I knew, at least for a minute, what it feels like to be a rock star. It was just unbelievable."

Each member of the team had spoken, Kerr going last of course. He had to wait for the "Steeeeeve Kerrrrrrr" chants to die. When he finally got quiet, he played the rock star bit to the hilt. "Hi," he said, "my name is Steve Kerr."

The party at McKale was followed by a party at Kerr's, a wild and wet one. Kerr's last memory of the evening was joining about thirty other fully-clad people in the complex's swimming pool.

He had finally reached his mother—without a CBS camera present—that evening. She already knew of the outcome, having listened on Armed Forces Radio, and was making plans to fly to Kansas City. In fact, the arrangements were already made. Ann Kerr was still a member of the board of American University in Beirut. One of her fellow board members was the president of Royal Jordanian Airlines. As a courtesy, whenever he could, he flew his friend Ann Kerr for free on his airline. Ann and John Kerr would fly first class from Amman, Jordan, on Royal Jordanian Airlines. They would be in Kansas City on Saturday morning.

The next three days after the Sunday victory party were a blur to Kerr. He was forced to have his roommate screen all his phone calls because the phone never stopped ringing. There were dozens of interviews to do with a whole new crew of reporters wanting to hear the whole Steve Kerr story all over again. The mail was piling up so fast Kerr couldn't keep track of it.

"I just want to get to Kansas City and play," he said. "Practice is about the only escape I have right now."

Arizona's practices were simple. The reserves, the so-called 'Gumbys,' were mimicking Oklahoma's offense every day in practice. There wasn't very much to it: three players out and two in. One day, the Gumbys called ten different plays in a row and ran the same play every time. That was what Oklahoma did. Stopping it was the problem.

Arizona arrived in Kansas City late Thursday. Kerr had only been in his hotel room for a few minutes when one of Arizona's assistant athletic directors asked to see him. The NCAA had called. Apparently, the ever-vigilant ones had spotted an item in the paper noting that Ann and John Kerr would be flown to the U.S. courtesy of Royal Jordanian Airlines.

According to the NCAA, if the Kerrs were getting their free airline tickets because Steve Kerr was a basketball player, this might be a violation of the extra benefits rule. Of course, the free tickets had absolutely *nothing* to do with Kerr playing basketball.

This was remarkable. The NCAA couldn't even begin to police the real cheating in college basketball. In 1985, the Lexington *Herald Leader* had produced a Pulitzer Prize-winning series of stories in which twenty-six former Kentucky players admitted—on the record—that they had received payoffs while at Kentucky. Almost thirty months later, the NCAA had reported the findings of its Kentucky investigation: *nothing.* Kentucky, it said, had not done a good job undertaking its own investigation of the matter. This comment was a little bit like Richard Nixon saying that Ronald Reagan's administration had been rife with corruption.

The NCAA almost never caught the big-time cheaters. Its member schools had little *interest* in catching the big-time cheaters. Why mess with a goose that is laying a golden egg? The NCAA investigative staff was woefully undermanned, and any suggestion that maybe a tiny percentage of the $55.1 million CBS was annually paying the NCAA for the rights to the basketball tournament should go to enforcement was laughed off. What would happen if the enforcement staff was increased from 25 to 250 by an influx of, say, $5 million to its annual budget? What would happen is that cheaters might get caught. Few people really wanted that.

Kentucky was an important part of the TV package. No one wanted it on probation or ineligible for the tournament. The same was true of any other big-name school. So the NCAA cracked down on schools like Marist and Cleveland State and called Steve Kerr in to explain why his mother was flying free to see him play in the biggest game of his life.

Kerr, of course, was flabbergasted when the "extra benefits" question was raised. He explained the situation and walked out of the room wondering what the NCAA people did with their spare time.

The only arrival more heralded than that of the four teams was the arrival of Valvano. He and his wife Pam arrive at midafternoon and walk into the coaches' lobby to find a cordon of media waiting for them. Valvano is playing it cool. "There is an appropriate time to comment and an inappropriate time," he says. "When the time is appropriate, I will certainly comment."

Each time the question is asked in a different way, Valvano pulls an imaginary string on his neck and repeats his little speech. Somehow, though, the word is out. He is flying to Los Angeles in the morning, will meet with UCLA people on Friday and Saturday, look at possible places to live and then fly back to Kansas City Sunday. Sunday evening he is guest-hosting Bob Costas's weekly radio show on NBC.

Valvano is amazed that people know this. But he is saying no more. He goes off to do a taping with Al McGuire at a studio on the other side of town. McGuire does an annual show for NBC on Final Four Sunday and Valvano is always part of the show. The taping finished,

Valvano is handed a bourbon in a plastic glass, then gets in a car to go back to the hotel. Driving along he spots a sign: "Welcome to Westwood."

It is a section of Kansas City. But Valvano is thrown. "Holy shit, is that an omen or what?" he yells. UCLA, of course, is in the Westwood section of Los Angeles.

Valvano is genuinely interested in this job. And, he has already met with UCLA Chancellor Charles Young and Athletic Director Peter Dalis earlier in the week. "I was in San Diego for a speech and they asked me to stop in L.A. on the way back," he says. "They wanted me to check into the hotel there under an assumed name. I said, 'Fine, how about Biff?' They undoubtedly thought I was crazy right away."

Valvano met with Young and Dalis for three hours. He and Young hit it off. Part of Valvano wanted the job. UCLA was still, after all, UCLA. He was very happy at N.C. State but there was only one UCLA. And, living near Hollywood intrigued him. He had taped a TV pilot the previous summer and enjoyed the experience. One could almost see Valvano fantasizing himself as Carson's Monday night stand-in. "Heeeeeeeere's Jimmy!"

But there were problems. For one, Valvano's middle daughter, sixteen-year-old Jamie, didn't want to leave Raleigh. She was happy, she had a boyfriend, and she considered it home. "She told me, 'Dad, I am a southerner,' " Valvano said. "If she can't handle it, I don't go. I just can't do it."

There was also a buyout clause in Valvano's new contract. If he left, he had to pay State a lot of money—close to half a million dollars. Even for Valvano, that was a lot of money. And yet, the idea of coaching in Pauley Pavilion excited him. "I wish," he said quietly, "this had happened two years from now."

Vitale would lose his dinner bet. The deal was far from done.

Two major events took place that night. One was the fiftieth anniversary dinner for the NCAA Tournament. To say that it was filled with luminaries was a vast understatement. Every coach who had ever won a national championship was invited. Most came.

The room was filled with members of the Hall of Fame. The largest ovation of the night was reserved for John Wooden, the man who had won ten national titles and made UCLA such a tough job that five men had come and gone since he had retired in 1975. At seventy-five, Wooden still looked like he could coach the Bruins. Maybe he should have been offered the job.

While the history of the Final Four was being relived, the coaches' all-star game was taking place in the building that had hosted nine Final Fours, the old Memorial Auditorium. It was fifty-two years old now, an ancient barn of a building with ten thousand seats but still a good place to watch a game.

Larry Brown brought his team in to watch to a huge ovation from the many Kansas fans in the crowd. Danny Manning and the rest of the Jayhawks happily munched on popcorn while the twenty-four senior all-stars ran up and down the court. Neither Boeheim nor Tarkanian made any attempt to coach, they just let the players play. David Rivers was the MVP, a nicer final memory than the opening-round loss to SMU and Kato Armstrong.

Troy Lewis was one of the all-stars. Six days after Purdue's loss, he still hadn't recovered. "Every time I walk on the street and I see that building that has the huge copy of the draw on it, I get sick," he said. "I keep thinking, 'How can we not be here?'"

Gene Keady, watching the game, was going through the same thing. "Every time I turn around, someone comes up to me and says, 'Gee, Gene, we thought you'd be playing here,'" he said. "Well, dammit, I thought we'd be here too. This is kind of hard to take."

John Thompson, the Olympic coach, was at the game, scouting. This made perfect sense. At his side was his academic coordinator, Mary Fenlon. This made no sense. Thompson and Fenlon had worked together since Thompson became Georgetown's coach in 1972. They were, without question, basketball's oddest couple.

Thompson is 6–10 and black; Fenlon is perhaps 5–4 and white. She is an ex-nun, a squat, wide woman who considers the Georgetown players her surrogate children. She calls them all "Honey," and all but snarls at anyone, especially members of the media, who get too close to them. If you want to incur Thompson's wrath, say something bad about Fenlon.

One rarely sees Thompson without Fenlon. Not just at games but in Las Vegas when he flies out there for fights or on scouting trips like this one. No one in college basketball thinks for a second that there is anything more between Thompson and Fenlon than a strong professional relationship and a warm friendship, but her omnipresence in his life baffles everyone.

"It is the strangest relationship in sports since Fritz Peterson and Mike Kekich," Keith Drum, the national college basketball writer for UPI once said. Peterson and Kekich were New York Yankee pitchers who swapped families in the early '70s.

Thompson watches the game with Sonny Vaccaro. Thompson is Nike's highest-paid coach, a pal of Vaccaro's, and was no doubt aided in the recruitment of Alonzo Mourning by Vaccaro's "friendship" with Mourning. That "friendship" included supplying Mourning's team with Nikes and being in town the week before Mourning chose his college. Vaccaro claims this was coincidence.

The coaches' lobby is hopping after the dinner and the all-star game. Some of the coaches are going out on the town, others are looking for rumors. Tonight's rumor du jour is a dandy: Rollie Massimino (who is skipping the convention to play golf in Florida) is going to the Miami Heat as coach of that NBA expansion team and Bob Staak, the Wake Forest coach, will take his place at Villanova.

"I love that one," Staak says. "Spread it, will you?"

Joey Meyer, the DePaul coach, and his wife Barbara are standing near the elevators. "You never miss anything standing here," Meyer says.

Virginia Coach Terry Holland comes by. He has been besieged by people who want to know if his old boss, Driesell, is going to James Madison. He insists he knows nothing. Someone suggests to Holland that if Driesell goes to JMU he should help him out by agreeing to play at James Madison. "No way," Holland says, grinning. "I like him, but I don't want him to beat me."

Valvano, back from the NCAA dinner, whisks through the lobby, Pam on his arm, pulling on his imaginary string. He will fly to Los Angeles in the morning. By the time he arrives, there will actually be basketball at this Final Four. The teams will be practicing in Kemper Arena.

DAY THREE: FRIDAY

This is the day when everyone starts to get serious. The teams have finished celebrating their victories in the regionals and are thinking about Saturday's games. The coaches actually move out of the hotel lobby and begin to hold meetings as part of their convention. The media gets a chance to interview someone other than each other. And scalping prices skyrocket.

The weather has not been cooperating so far; the parking lots at Kemper Arena are mud-caked as cars begin piling into them at around noon. The four one-hour practices begin at 1 P.M. and, with admission free and on a first-come-first-serve basis, the building will be jammed. None of the teams is going to do anything very sophisticated during the public workout, but this is a chance for those not privileged enough to buy tickets to see the players up close and sort of personal.

If there was any doubt about who the favorite son is in this tournament, it was erased when Duke walked out onto the floor to begin the first workout. As soon as the Blue Devils emerged from the tunnel, the boos started. Duke was not only Kansas's opponent the next day, it was the team that had beaten the Jayhawks the last time the two had reached the Final Four in 1986.

"Has to be the first time in history a team got booed for walking on the floor to practice," Danny Ferry quipped.

Practice is not exactly what Mike Krzyzewski had in mind. Robert Brickey has had an allergic reaction to penicillin and is too sick to practice. He should be fine by Saturday but it is not a good sign.

There's more: When Mickie Krzyzewski tries to get on the floor to give her husband a message, she is stopped by a policeman. Showing identification as a coach's wife does her no good. The cop isn't budging. She has to go off in search of help. Later in the day, Bobbi Olson will be unable to get into the building for a while during Arizona's practice because the doors have been shut by the fire marshals.

The Blue Devils are getting very superstitious. King is now wearing a good luck tie that he started wearing during the ACC Tournament and, since the ruling junta watched a movie the night before the semifinals in East Rutherford, it will watch a movie tonight.

"We're going to watch *The Terminator*," Quin Snyder says. "That should get us ready."

If there is one thing the NCAA can do efficiently, it is run a basketball tournament. Everything is planned and organized down to the minute. When Duke leaves the floor at 2 P.M., Krzyzewski and three of his players are quickly whisked into the interview room. Kansas takes the floor at 2—to a standing ovation—and will be there until 3 when Arizona (which will arrive at 2:30 for interviews) will take its turn on the floor.

Dave Cawood, one of the NCAA's assistant executive directors, is in charge of this operation. Each year he brings in eight sports information directors from around the country to help him run the tournament. Each of the eight is equipped with a walkie-talkie and a code name. Cawood is Big Daddy. Roger Valdiserri, the longtime Notre Dame SID, is Double Dome—the references being to the golden dome and Valdiserri's. Rick Brewer of North Carolina is, predictably, Tar Heel. David Housel of Auburn is War Eagle. And so on.

If you listen you will hear things like, "Tar Heel, this is War Eagle, I've got the Jayhawks en route to the interview room." Tar Heel, who is the interview moderator, will then announce that Larry Brown and his players are on their way to the interview room so the press can begin scrambling for seats.

The PA announcer at the Final Four for the last thirteen years has been Frank Fallon, a professor of radio and TV journalism at Southern Methodist. Cawood knows Fallon from his days at SMU and brought him in to do the PA in 1976 when the tournament was in the Philadelphia Spectrum. The NCAA was concerned that the legendary Dave Zinkoff, one of the most colorful PA men ever, might be a little wild for its oh-so-proper tournament. So Cawood brought Fallon in.

It is a move that can hardly be criticized. Fallon has the perfect PA voice. When he says on Monday night, "Ladies and gentlemen, welcome to the game that will decide the national championship," it sends chills down your spine.

Rick Brewer, the North Carolina SID, has become another staple of the Final Four. He more or less fell into the job of interview-room moderator six years ago, and has retained it because most media members would riot in protest if he were replaced. Part of this is Brewer's ability to keep the interviews moving when writers are fighting deadlines. Another part is his succinct way of repeating the questions. Because the Final Four interview room is so large, questions must be repeated for everyone to hear.

Beyond that, though, is Brewer's sense of humor. It isn't really a

Final Four until Brewer gets off a one-liner. In 1986, when someone asked Krzyzewski what the best thing about coaching at Duke was, Brewer interjected, "Well, it is only eight miles from Chapel Hill."

Today, when Billy Tubbs comments that Brewer sounds like Ed McMahon, Brewer answers, "That's why I have this job. That and the fact that I never have anything better to do at this time of year."

It has been six years since Carolina reached the Final Four. No one is more aware of that than the listening media. When Brewer finishes the last interview, someone hands him a phone and says, "It's Dean [Smith] and he sounds angry."

"Tell him I'm busy," Brewer answers, tongue still firmly in cheek.

For the press, this is a good Final Four. Duke and Arizona are full of "good talkers": Kansas has the father-son angle of the Mannings; Oklahoma has the renegade coach in Billy Tubbs, and, of course, there is Kerr. At an event like the Final Four, many of the credentialed reporters are columnists who have seen about three basketball games all year. Each is convinced that his column on Kerr or Tubbs will be the first one written on the subject.

Tubbs is certainly cooperating with those doing columns on him for Saturday. When someone asks him about the uncanny resemblance between his voice and Jack Nicholson's, Tubbs shrugs. "I just go along with that stuff because it makes Jack feel good. If he can get a little pub out of it, that's just great."

Tubbs does most of the talking for his players. The Sooners—with the notable exception of Stacey King—are not a team full of great interviews. Their attitude toward the media was perhaps best summed up when Harvey Grant was asked to appear as a guest on an Oklahoma City TV show during the regionals. When Grant arrived, in a limousine sent for him, to do the interview, the show's producer gave him a shirt with the show's logo on it.

Grant looked at the shirt and said to the producer, "Yo man, you got a cap?" Grant is happy today. He is wearing a CBS cap. CBS always has caps.

The loosest of the four teams appears to be Arizona. The Wildcats spend a lot of their locker room time staging their own version of Wrestlemania; when someone asks them in the interview room about Final Four nerves, Kerr grabs the microphone and pretends his hand is shaking so much he can't hold it still.

Olson isn't quite so loose. He is still upset about a flap in the Seattle papers the previous week that came about when Kerr, clearly joking, said, "We haven't got any respect for North Carolina." Sometimes, Kerr's sense of humor goes over people's heads. "Sometimes," Olson says, "I wonder about the ethics of journalists."

Sitting in the curtained-off runway area next to the interview podium, waiting to go on, Danny Manning hisses, "Tell 'em, coach!" His mood is jocular too. Starting up the steps to the podium, he pretends to trip. "No headlines," he says, "I'm okay."

There are never any headlines on Friday. If the NCAA was paid one dollar for each time a player or coach said, "We're just glad to be here," it wouldn't need the money it gets from CBS. That is always Friday's theme.

One group that is truly glad to be here are the officials. This year, thirty-six officials worked the four regionals—nine at each site. From those thirty-six, nine and one alternate were selected for the Final Four. Who they are is a closely guarded secret, largely because the NCAA worries that bettors will be given some kind of edge if they know who is officiating a game.

That may be so. But since the officials are not given their assignments until 10 A.M. Saturday morning, knowing which nine are in town won't do a bettor much good. Joe Forte is one of the final nine for the fifth time in seven years. But he will not know until Saturday if he will work his second straight final.

Friday evening is another night for parties. The NCAA throws one in the Memorial Auditorium and it draws a crowd. If there is one thing coaches and the media have in common, it is an inability to turn down a freebie.

Lefty Driesell has arrived in town and everyone has one question for him: Are you going to James Madison? "No comment," Lefty says to everyone. Lefty has given out so many "no comments" that his son, Chuck, who will be his No. 1 assistant if he takes the job, sidles over to a reporter and says, "What's the word, is the Lefthander taking the job?"

Tonight's rumor du jour has Gene Keady leaving Purdue to take the job at Texas. Keady has always said that the only thing he doesn't like at Purdue is the weather, and the weather in Austin is certainly warmer than in West Lafayette. "Some of my friends say it's a pretty good job," Keady says. Clearly, he is intrigued.

The Valvanos are in Los Angeles and everyone is waiting to see what the outcome of that meeting will be. "You watch," Larry Brown tells friends, "one way or the other, no one has that job locked up yet." Brown is still very interested in UCLA. Now, word leaks out that UCLA is very interested in Mike Krzyzewski.

But Krzyzewski is not that interested in UCLA. When the school called him earlier in the season, he said he wouldn't talk to them until after his season was over. Fine, said UCLA, we'll call you then, what's your home number?

"You can reach me," Krzyzewski answered, "at my office."

The argument in the press lobby tonight is about the three-point shot. Ed Steitz, the secretary of the rules committee, who has been the most vocal defender of the ridiculously close shot, is being hounded by several people who think the shot stinks. "People love it," Steitz keeps insisting.

The Division 1 coaches don't love it. Earlier in the day, they voted almost unanimously in favor of moving the line back. But the Division 2 and Division 3 coaches were almost as unanimous in saying it should stay where it is. "Are you people saying," asked Iowa State's Johnny Orr, "that you think the damn line should be in the same place where high school kids and girls are shooting it from?"

That is what they are saying. At 2 A.M. Steitz is still saying it. It must be almost time to play basketball, mustn't it?

DAY FOUR: SATURDAY

The new TV contract between CBS and the NCAA calls for the Saturday doubleheader to begin at 5:30 P.M. eastern time. That is 4:30—or to be precise as to actual game time, 4:42, in Kansas City. That makes for a lot of waiting for everyone on Saturday.

The first formal meeting of the day takes place at the Kansas City Club, which is where the officials are being housed for the weekend. At 10 A.M. they meet with Hank Nichols to learn their game assignments. Nichols has been the NCAA's supervisor of officials for two years. A professor at Villanova, he is one of the most highly respected officials in the history of the game and the creation of this job for him has been applauded by everyone.

Technically, the basketball committee selects the officials and makes the assignments. But only Nichols saw all four regionals last week. His recommendations are, in all likelihood, going to be followed.

Politics plays a role in these selections. As has been the case in recent years with teams, there is a preponderance of good officials in the East. The fact that seven of the nine officials here are from east of the Mississippi—five from the ACC/Big East—is evidence of that. But the West Coast must be represented, especially with a Pac–10 team in the Final Four for the first time in eight years. That is why Booker Turner, a nice man who is well past his peak as a referee, is among the nine men in the room.

It also has something to do with Forte not making the final. In fact, of the three men who worked the '87 final, Forte is the only one back in the Final Four. Nichols announces the assignments, in order. "Game one: Booker Turner, Larry Lembo, Jim Burr." The three nod, each of them disappointed. Everyone wants the final.

"Game two," Nichols continues: "Paul Housman, Joe Forte, Luis Grillo."

Forte's heart sinks. "The first thing you think is, 'Aah shit,' " he admitted later. "It's a competitive thing. The first thing you feel is as if you lost a game. We would all like to work the final."

The three officials chosen to work the final are Tim (Barney Rubble) Higgins, Ed Hightower, and John Clougherty. Forte is delighted for Higgins and for Clougherty, both good friends. But he also knows that Clougherty's selection for the final may influence ABA–USA's decision on which referee will represent the U.S. at the Olympics. Unofficially, the two finalists for the assignment are Forte and Clougherty.

Later that morning, the NCAA does something nice. At a brunch thrown for the media as part of the fiftieth anniversary celebration, NCAA executive director Dick Schultz presents a plaque of appreciation to Marvin (Skeeter) Francis. Skeeter Francis is the assistant commissioner of the ACC. Each year he runs the ACC Tournament and each Final Four he helps run the press operation. He is one of those rare people who is liked and respected by everyone he comes in contact with. Francis never sees himself as being important, yet he is invaluable.

Even as the brunch is ending, word is starting to make the rounds that Valvano has pulled out of the UCLA job. This is a surprise because most people expected him to wait until after the Final Four to make a move one way or the other. But in Los Angeles, Valvano is telling people he will stay at State. Speculation immediately swings to Larry Brown, who would be delighted to give UCLA his home phone number.

Kansas is a grim group when it arrives at Kemper Arena. Many teams come to the Final Four wanting to win but—as they all like to say—so happy to be involved that they show up on Saturday almost giddy just to be taking part. This is not true of the Jayhawks. They feel they owe Duke one (at least) and, playing so close to home, they feel this is now their tournament to win.

"Danny hasn't smiled once all week," Assistant Coach R. C. Buford says. "He feels like we're on a mission now and he isn't going to relax until we've got it done."

By contrast, Duke is loose—maybe too loose. The Blue Devils have oozed confidence all week. They believe that, having beaten Kansas in Lawrence, there is no reason not to beat them again. What they haven't counted on is how much Kansas has improved in the six weeks since that game.

King, having shut down Mark Macon a week ago, has no reason to believe he will have any serious trouble with Milt Newton. Snyder is convinced he can make life miserable for Kevin Pritchard at the point. The concern, of course, is Manning. But he will be double-teamed most of the time and, even though he scored 31 points in Lawrence, the Blue Devils won the game. Why should today be any different?

It is different because Kansas is primed for the tip-off and Duke is not. On the opening possession of the game, Ferry misses a wide-open lay-up. The team's exchange turnovers before King fouls Chris Piper inside, and he opens the scoring with two free throws for a 2–0 Kansas lead.

No big deal. Except that Manning steals the ball and feeds Newton, who promptly hits a three-pointer. Then Manning steals the ball again and, a moment later, takes a feed from Pritchard and scores to make it 7–0. Quickly, Duke turns tight. Ferry and Strickland miss. Krzyzewski goes to the bench looking for help. Manning scores again. Phil Henderson misses and Newton hits another three-pointer. Snyder forces a pass inside and Manning makes his third steal, flipping the ball upcourt to Newton for a breakaway lay-up.

The game is less than five minutes old and Duke is down two touchdowns, 14–0. Abdelnaby finally breaks the shutout with a hook shot at 15:12. But the Blue Devils are in a hole they will never dig out from.

"As long as I live I'll never figure out what happened there," King said later. "I know we were ready to play. We were prepared. Kansas just came out *so* ready. They surprised us a little and we reacted by panicking with some of our shot selections." What Kansas had done was out-Duke Duke. The Jayhawks had thrown a Duke-style, overplaying, hawking man-to-man defense at the Blue Devils and had caught them off guard. They had shown flashes of this in the game in Lawrence but had not been able to sustain it. This time, they did. Even after Duke scored, the carnage continued. The lead built to 24–6 when Piper drove through the entire Duke defense for a lay-up. At that point, even Krzyzewski was shell-shocked. "I was thinking that if this kept up we were going to get beat 82–20," he said. "We just couldn't do anything right." Ever so slowly, the Blue Devils began to work their way into the game. Greg Koubek, the talented freshman who had been inconsistent with his shooting, hit a three-pointer to give everyone a boost. Strickland hit a drive and Brickey dunked. Snyder, whose first two shots would not have hit the water if thrown from a boat, hit a fourteen-footer. Ferry, who had missed four straight shots, made a pair of free throws. That cut the margin to 11, and that was where it was at halftime, 38–27. Everyone's sentiment was the same: Duke was lucky to be so close. That was certainly the feeling in the Duke locker room. King reminded everyone of their good start in the second half of the Temple game. "We do that and we'll be back in it in no time," he said. Kansas was thinking the same thing. Duke had come from behind to beat them—though not nearly as far behind—in '86 and in the game in Lawrence. No one wanted a repeat performance. "Start out playing the same kind of defense we showed in the first half and we'll be fine," Brown told them. "Danny, stay aggressive." Manning already had 15 points and 3 steals. He couldn't get much more aggressive than he had been. Newton had 14 points, a stat that staggered King. "I didn't give him enough respect," he said. "I didn't think he could do that to me."

By accident, King may have explained Duke's problem in this game. Because this group had always had success against Kansas, one way or the other, it had no reason to believe that this game would be any different. In a sense, this helped with a large deficit to overcome because no one was giving up. But it was also probably the reason for the deficit.

They say the tone for a game is always set in the first five minutes of the second half. That was certainly the case in this game. Once again, it took Duke almost five minutes to find a field goal. Snyder's free throw was their only point in the first 4:30. In the meantime, the Jayhawks were scoring 8 points and the lead built back up to 18 at 46–28. And now, there wasn't plenty of time left to come back.

And yet, Duke almost found a way. Ironically, it was King's fourth foul with 14:06 left that started Duke's turnaround. He had to come out of the game. Greg Koubek replaced him, King walking to the bench mumbling obscenities, something he almost never did. "I don't usually talk to myself during a game," he said. "But this game, I did."

Down 16, Duke rallied. Ferry scored 6 quick points and Koubek popped a jumper. The margin was down to 8. Manning hit a hook shot to stop the run, but Koubek bombed for 3 to cut the lead to 51–44. King came back and took a pretty pass from Ferry for his first and last field goal of the game. That made it 51–46 with 9:26 still left. An eternity. For the first time all afternoon, the Jayhawks looked a bit apprehensive.

"Come on," Manning yelled at his teammates, "settle down!"

The next five possessions probably decided this game. Pritchard missed a jumper and Duke came down with a chance to cut the lead again. But Strickland took a bad shot, an air ball that was woefully short. "Think, Kevin, think!" King yelled at his roommate.

Kansas's turn. Manning drove—and missed, a rare occurrence. Again, Duke had a chance. This time, Strickland took a good shot, a lined-up three-pointer. The ball went in the basket, seemed ready to drop through and then spun out. The ball was so far down that the Duke bench had come to its feet, thinking the lead was down to two.

If Strickland's shot had dropped, Brown would almost certainly have called time-out. The lead would have been two with almost eight minutes still left. Instead, Kansas raced back the other way and Newton fed Piper for a lay-up. That built the margin back to 53–46. Manning and Ferry exchanged baskets and then Booker Turner made the one key call in the ball game, taking a basket away from Koubek on a player control foul.

That lost basket and Strickland's in-and-out were awfully significant when Strickland dunked off a Snyder feed and Ferry stole a pass and dunked. That made it 55–52 with 4:17 left. Duke could have been leading. Instead, Pritchard came up with a circus shot, a short bank as he was falling down trying to draw a foul with five seconds left on the shot clock.

Duke cut the lead to three once more on a Snyder jumper with 2:27 left, but then Manning came up with the game's key rebound, grabbing a Pritchard miss and scoring to up the lead to five with 2:09 to go. Duke never got that close again. The Jayhawks then made five of six free throws during the next ninety seconds while the Blue Devils were making two of four and Manning was blocking a Ferry shot.

In the last minute, desperate for points, Krzyzewski had to take King out. This was not the ending King had envisioned. He sat on the floor in front of the bench, his eyes averted as the final seconds of his career ticked away. Newton had scored 20 points. "The gunslinger got shot down," King would say of himself in the aftermath.

It ended, 66–59. Manning was hugging Archie Marshall when the buzzer sounded, wanting him to be a part of this. King, a towel around his neck, had his eyes on the floor when he felt an arm around his neck. It was Ed Manning, who had recruited him four years ago. King was fighting tears. Ed Manning just put his arm around him and walked him off the floor.

"Finally," Danny Manning said to Alvin Gentry. "We finally got them."

Indeed they had. Now, there was one more team still to get.

Most people expected Arizona–Oklahoma to decide the title. Both had been No. 1 seeds and won their regionals. Both had been in the top five for the entire second half of the season.

No one was more ready to play than Kerr. As the teams warmed up, Kerr felt tingly as he looked around him. "I thought about all the times I had watched the Final Four and now here I was playing in it," he said. "Everything had gone perfect getting ready for the game. Coach Olson never gave us any speeches about the Final Four, he just talked about what we were going to have to do to beat Oklahoma."

Kerr had seen his mother and brother briefly at the hotel after they had arrived and had come over to the arena with his teammates during the first game. As he warmed up, his shot felt great. "Everything was going in," he said. "I felt the same way Friday practicing in front of all those people. I really thought I was ready to have a good game. I was watching Tom [Tolbert] and Sean [Elliott] and they weren't making a thing. I remember thinking, 'I hope these guys aren't tight.' "

Kerr laughed at the irony in those words. "As it turned out, I was the one who stunk the joint out."

It didn't start out that way for Kerr or Arizona. Quickly, the Wildcats led 9–2, handling the Oklahoma press with ease. But the Sooners, especially guards Mookie Blaylock and Ricky Grace, kept forcing the tempo. If they didn't steal the ball, they forced Arizona into a quickened pace, and that was not what the Wildcats wanted. A bank shot by Stacey King and a steal by Blaylock put the Sooners up 16–13.

Then, with the score 22–19, Oklahoma made one of its patented runs. Dave Sieger hit a three-pointer to push the lead to six. Harvey Grant hit two free throws and Andre Wiley hit a follow. Grant then hit a jumper. In two minutes, Oklahoma had pushed the lead to 31–19. Kerr finally hit a three-pointer to end the drought but a Grace three and a Terrence Mullins three upped the lead to 39–25 before two Elliott free throws made it 39–27—a score startlingly similar to the first game—at the half.

Elliott had 12 points and Anthony Cook seven but Tolbert, Craig McMillan, and Kerr were a combined 3-for-12 (Kerr, 1-for-6) and that wasn't going to get it done. Oklahoma's 20–14 margin on the boards hurt too. There were no hysterics from Olson at halftime. He had a veteran team that knew what had to be done.

Sure enough, the Wildcats came back. Coming off the bench, Jud Buechler provided a big boost with two quick buckets, one off a pretty feed from Kerr. King hit a free throw but Elliott made a spectacular coast-to-coast move, finishing with a jarring dunk. That made it 51–48 and there was still 12:50 left. "Right there we should have really been able to take it to them," Kerr said later. "But we just didn't give Sean enough help." The lead fluctuated between nine and four, Elliott cutting it to 58–54 with 8:08 left with another strong move inside. Grant and Blaylock both scored, but Elliott bombed a three to make it 62–57. Single-handedly he was keeping Arizona in the game.

If I could have just hit one three," Kerr lamented. "Just one." Actually, he hit one, but it came after the Sooners had put together a 10–2 burst that widened the margin back to 72–59. By then, just three minutes were left. Try though they might, the Wildcats couldn't get closer than 8 during those last three minutes. The final was 86–78.

Oklahoma had too many weapons. Grant and King each finished with 21 points, Grace had 13 and 8 assists, Wiley came off the bench to score 11, and Blaylock had 7 points and 6 assists.

Elliott had 31 for Arizona in a performance worth remembering, and Cook had 16. But Kerr finished 2-for-13, his worst shooting day of the season at the worst possible time. "I felt sick," he said. "The only person to blame for that loss is me. I didn't choke, but I'm a shooter and I had a bad day shooting. I'm convinced that if I had shot well, we would have won. Sean had a great game, everyone else had an average game, and I had a horrible game. It was simple as that."

It wasn't anywhere near that simple. Kerr had shot poorly but that was not the entire story. Oklahoma had just been the better team. Kerr didn't buy it. "My mother could have stayed in Cairo and seen better basketball," he said.

As disappointed as Kerr was by the loss, he came away from Kansas City with one indelible memory. Back in the locker room, Olson quietly told his players how proud he was of them and the season they had had, winning thirty-five games. He told them that they could have done better but that there was no shame in losing to Oklahoma. Then, as the players and coaches all moved to the middle of the room to put their hands into a final huddle, Olson grabbed Anthony Cook, hugged him and started to cry.

"A lot of us had our heads down, maybe crying just a little before that happened," Kerr said. "But when Coach Olson did that, we all just started hugging each other and crying. Everyone broke down completely. It sounds so corny but it was just an unbelievable feeling of love we all had for one another right then. I mean, everybody was crying, just kind of hanging on to one another for a while. It wasn't so much that we had lost, but that it was over, that we would never be together like this again and we knew that we had all gone through something together that was incredibly special.

"I hate the fact that we lost that game. But I'll never forget what it was like in that locker room with the guys the rest of my life. It was something really, really special. I don't think any of us had ever seen Coach Olson like that. No one in the room was ashamed to cry. It was the right thing to do."

For Olson, this was an emotional evening. A few minutes later, standing in the hallway, Olson was asked to talk about Kerr's career.

It was then, for the first time, that it occurred to Olson that Kerr's career was, in fact, over. "In the five years I've known him," Olson said, "I wouldn't change one thing." He choked up as he spoke and his eyes glistened.

Inside, as Kerr sat on a training table talking quietly about the game, someone informed him of what Olson had just said. Kerr grinned wistfully when he heard the last line. "I'd change one thing," he said. "Today."

DAY FIVE: SUNDAY

This is always the quiet day at the Final Four. Already, some people have headed for home: fans of the two losing teams Saturday who sell their Monday tickets and get out of town. Some of the coaches also sell their tickets and head back to the recruiting trails.

Only two teams are left now and, with the media hordes surrounding them, they are asked most of the intimate details of their lives. In 1987, during the massive Sunday press conference, Indiana's Steve Alford had been asked to describe his four years with Bob Knight. Glancing to his left where Knight sat, Alford, without cracking a smile, said: "I've made it this far, I'm not going to blow it now."

He didn't say another word. No one blamed him. Today, the columnists were off in pursuit of Archie Marshall, the martyred inspiration for what had now become a legitimate miracle team. The Jayhawks were one step from a national championship less than a month after most people, including themselves, had written them off.

Now, they were playing Oklahoma—again. This was the first time since 1976 (Indiana–Michigan) and only the second time in NCAA history that two teams from the same conference were meeting for the national championship. This wasn't bad for what was basically a football conference. It was especially interesting for Oklahoma. The basketball team playing for the national title was such big news in Norman that football coach Barry Switzer had called off a day of spring football practice. Now *that* was news.

"I talked to Barry this morning," Billy Tubbs said. "He told me if we win the toss we should kick and take the wind."

To say that Tubbs was enjoying all this attention was a bit like saying Oklahoma was, is, and always will be a football school. He charmed the media, telling funny stories, flirting outrageously with a female TV reporter from Kansas City—"Would you like a private interview?" he said when she tried to ask a question—and reeling off one-liners.

Still, it was Rick Brewer who got off the best line of the day. When a reporter asked Tubbs if he thought that perhaps God was on Kansas's side, Tubbs answered by saying, "What's his number?"

Without missing a beat, Brewer said, "Twenty-three," identifying the number Michael Jordan had worn at North Carolina and was now wearing for the Chicago Bulls.

When it was time for Tubbs to leave, he seemed disappointed. "I'll talk some more," he said before someone pointed out it was time to go to practice. Off he went.

Down the hall, Steve Kerr was receiving an award from the U.S. Basketball Writer's Association, its annual "Most Courageous" award. The reasons he was the recipient were obvious. He arrived for the ceremony with his mother and two brothers, John and Andrew, with him.

Saturday had been a difficult night for the Kerrs. Steve had been inconsolable after the loss and had sulked all through dinner. To him, this made perfect sense. He had just lost the biggest game of his life and had played lousy to boot. But mothers are mothers. Ann Kerr thought Steve should pick his spirits up. After all, it had been a great season.

"She just couldn't understand," Steve said later. "I mean, she's only seen a few of the games I've played in college so she couldn't understand how much it meant to me. My whole life was geared to this one thing for so many years and now it was over. She started getting pissed off at me and I started getting pissed at her for being pissed."

Everyone was tired. Later, up in the room, Steve dozed off for a while. When he woke up, he heard his mother crying softly. It had all kicked in for Ann Kerr. "She really did understand finally how disappointed I was," Steve said. "But I also think she started thinking about how proud my dad would have been if he had been there to see the game."

Mother and son hugged, sharing their losses together for a moment. From that point on, the Kerrs were back to being themselves. "He's still pouting a little," Ann Kerr said at the awards ceremony.

It turned out that this was the highlight of the day for those who were there. Olson spoke briefly, repeating his words of Saturday. Once again, his eyes glistened as he spoke. When it was Kerr's turn, he started—as always—with a joke.

"This is really a great plaque," he said, turning it over in his hands. "But since Coors sponsors this award, I was wondering, since my eligibility is used up, if maybe I could have a couple of cases instead?"

No doubt he could. Kerr turned serious. "I guess I won this award because of all the things I've been through. But the reason I've been able to get through these things is really pretty simple. I have the best family in the world and the best teammates a guy could have . . ."

Kerr stopped. On the word *teammates,* a large lump had formed in his throat and he couldn't go on. He paused for a full minute, fighting to regain control. "When I said *teammates,*" he said later, "I realized that they weren't my teammates anymore. That it was over. It really kicked in on me right there."

Kerr regained his composure. When he finished he wasn't the only one crying. "I'm glad he was emotional," Ann Kerr said. "He should be that way." Looking at her son, still so unhappy about Saturday, she shook her head. "I feel like it's ten years ago and he's back on the pitcher's mound being a poor loser again."

Mothers are always going to be mothers.

The coaches held their annual banquet that night, a monstrous affair in perhaps the longest ballroom in the history of ballrooms. There were ninety-seven people on the dais. When emcee Curt Gowdy introduced the Final Four coaches, he stumbled a bit while pronouncing Krzyzew-ski (pronounced Sheshefski). "I have a little trouble with that name of yours, Mike," Gowdy said.

"That's okay," Krzyzewski answered, "I have trouble with Gowdy."

The dinner tends to be among the longest affairs in the history of mankind. Everyone who has ever coached a game, it seems, is intro-duced. The highlight of the dinner is the introduction of Jud Heath-cote of Michigan State as the new president of the NABC. Heathcote is genuinely funny. Tonight, his victim is Michigan Coach Bill Frieder.

"When Bill was a boy," Heathcote says, "he climbed an ugly tree and fell down and hit every branch on the way down." And, "Bill had a charisma transplant but his body rejected it."

The best speech of the evening is given by Henry Iba, the immortal Oklahoma A & M coach, the grand old man of coaching at age eighty-three. In accepting his award—he gets a different one just about every year—Iba says, "I'm happy to get this award from you coaches—my best friends."

End of speech.

At the press hotel, one of the more remarkable upsets in Final Four history is taking place. Many writers have abandoned the media hospitality room, where the booze is free, for the hotel bar, where it is not. The reason is Jennifer Sturpin.

Every once in a while, the Final Four uncovers a new star. This year, it will not be Milt Newton or Mookie Blaylock. Jennifer Sturpin is twenty-four, a recent graduate of the University of Missouri–Rolla, where her father is a physics professor. She is just under six feet tall with long blond hair and legs that can literally mesmerize. She is a singer in a group called Lupé, which is playing in the bar, and her presence—not to mention her legs—has drawn the attention of the nation's media.

Many of them are sitting in the front row. In the back, the officials not working the final are having a drink with Hank Nichols. They have their wives with them, which explains why they are sitting in back.

Nonetheless, the writers can't resist. A note is sent to the officials' table. "We're trying to get you a table up front since we know you guys have trouble seeing." The officials laugh, Jennifer keeps singing, and the writers keep looking.

Back at the coaches' hotel, the rumor du jour has a blue plate special: The appetizer, that Lute Olson is being wooed by UCLA, is no big deal. The entree, though, is a doozy: Lefty Driesell, in his first act as coach at James Madison, hires Sharr Mustaf as his assistant coach and in the process wins the recruiting battle for Jerrod Mustaf. This ranks as one of the all-time rumors. Clearly, the end is near.

DAY SIX : MONDAY

Two sports collided here today. On the last day of the college basketball season, major league baseball opened its 1988 season. While Kansas and Oklahoma were sitting in their hotel rooms—across the street from one another—waiting anxiously for their 8:12 P.M. tip-off, the Kansas City Royals and Toronto Blue Jays were opening their seasons on a glorious spring day. George Bell hit three home runs for the Blue Jays. But he would not be the biggest star in town on this day.

The U.S. Basketball Writers held their annual meeting in the morning. Normally, the USBWA meeting is about as exciting as, well, watching a bunch of writers sit around and talk. But this year the meeting was special. The reason was Katha Quinn.

Katha Quinn is the sports information director at St. John's. She is funny, blunt, and brash, qualities that serve her in good stead in dealing with reporters day in and day out. In December of 1986, Katha Quinn wasn't feeling very well. She went into the hospital for some tests. The test showed cancer of the liver. One morning Katha Quinn was a young woman in her early thirties, the next she was a cancer patient locked into a fight for her life.

The cancer frightened Quinn, hurt her, knocked her down over and over. But each time she got up, dusted herself off, and came back. She never stopped working. If she knew she needed a chemotherapy session, she would schedule it so as not to miss an important St. John's game. That summer, she ran the press venue at the Pan American games in Indianapolis. During the '87–88 season, she was at almost every St. John's game, bugging Lou Carnesecca to get his butt into the interview room, pushing players to talk to reporters and, generally speaking, being Katha.

All too often in life, people confuse people who are victims with people who are courageous. Katha Quinn was certainly a victim. But having been victimized, she had shown remarkable courage. The USBWA wanted to recognize her for her courage. When incoming President Malcolm Moran introduced her, everyone expected some emotion. Perhaps Katha Quinn would choke up a little, cry a little in saying thank you.

She didn't cry once. As it turned out, she was the only person in the room who didn't. Her voice clear and firm, Katha Quinn looked at the 120 people in the room and said this:

"When they told me I had cancer, I knew I was in for the fight of my life. And I knew I was going into a fight with an opponent that didn't fight fair. So I knew I would have to not fight fair myself. So, I brought to this fight not only my family but three different groups to help me. First, I brought the SIDs in the Big East and around the country and all of you guys, the writers. God only knows what you writers have done to me over the years. You've made me lose sleep, you've chased me all over town looking for players or for Coach and you've wreaked havoc on my social life. But now, when I really needed you, you were there, every step of the way.

"After that, I brought my coach to the fight." She stopped to look at Lou Carnesecca, sitting a few feet away. "My coach has worked me so hard I wondered if I'd ever get sleep. He's been there all the time, pushing, demanding, and loving, and I don't know what I would do without him.

"And finally, I brought the players. The very same players who make me crazy by missing interviews, who say they'll call someone and don't, who get me called in the middle of the night. I love every one of them. And, when Shelton Jones walked across the floor to me after the Holiday Festival final, handed me the game ball and said, 'Kid, this one was for you,' well, you'll never hear me say one bad word about any of them again.

"So when I go into the hospital now for another chemotherapy session and the doctors and nurses say to me, 'Katha, what keeps you going through all this?' I just look at them and tell them about my three groups. I tell them, 'One more game, one more season, one more Final Four.' That's what keeps me going. So don't any of you let me down. I know you won't because I've got a lot of fighting left in me."

Her voice quavered only on the words *Final Four.* By then hardly anyone noticed because there wasn't a dry eye in the house. Danny Manning would be voted the Most Outstanding Player of the Final Four that night. But no one was better at the Final Four than Katha Quinn.

Among the 16,392 in Kemper Arena that night there were two groups who undoubtedly would have preferred being elsewhere. The NCAA provides tickets and very good seats to the semifinal losers, a nice gesture that both teams would probably just as soon live without.

Steve Kerr didn't want to go to the game. He had been up until six in the morning, drinking with the Duke ruling junta, the players sharing the pain of their losses together. "The only guys in the world who could absolutely understand the way we felt were the Duke guys," Kerr said. "To be one step away from playing for it all but not getting there. No one but them knew how we felt."

They had drowned their sorrows together and then, the following day, each had followed his instincts: Kerr, jock all the way, went to the baseball game. The Dukies, whose team motto should have been "Do you take Visa?" went shopping. "I got a great pair of shorts," Billy King said.

Kerr was in shorts for the final, as were many of his teammates. Duke showed up in jackets and ties. Neither group was dressed the way it wanted to be, though. No one had a number on.

For Kansas, it had been a long day. Brown wanted everything to be as normal as possible in a situation where normal was impossible. He had told his players that he honestly believed they could handle Oklahoma's press, having seen it twice already. "Just go out and play the way you've played for thirty-seven games and you'll be just fine," Brown said. "You aren't here on any fluke. You're here because you're damn good."

Brown's major concern was keeping Manning out of foul trouble. He was certain that Stacey King would go right at Manning. That made perfect sense. "Danny," he said, "King can score 25 or 30 points and we can still win the game. But we can't win if you're on the bench."

Manning nodded. In truth, there wasn't much he needed to be told at this point. He knew that Kansas was in the final because he had stepped forward and become a dominant player in the tournament—he was averaging 26.4 points and 9 rebounds a game—and that to win this last game, he would have to be dominant again.

The coaches expected Manning to be brilliant. They thought the key to the game was Pritchard. He had the quickness and the athletic ability to handle the Oklahoma press as long as he played on instinct and didn't think too much. It was strange. A national championship was at stake and the most crucial thing for a coaching staff was convincing a player *not* to think.

As the teams were introduced, everyone in the building felt the tingles that are part of a national championship game. It had been 172 days since Manning had sung his awful rendition of "My Girl." Now, he was getting ready to play The Game, and there were 289 other teams wishing they could be where Kansas and Oklahoma were.

It wasn't just the players who felt the tingles. Everyone in the building felt it. The officials had butterflies too. Tim Higgins, waiting to throw the ball up to start the game, stood bouncing the ball so hard it seemed possible he would put a hole in the floor.

The beginning was not encouraging for Kansas. Six seconds into the game, Blaylock hit a jumper. Nine seconds later, working against the press, Pritchard traveled. One could almost hear Brown thinking, "Don't think!"

But the Jayhawks settled down quickly. Manning hit a jumper and then a baby hook, letting the Sooners know he had definitely come to play. Then Pritchard made two good plays, hitting a pull-up jumper and feeding Newton for a lay-up. It was 8–4 Kansas.

Tubbs, hyper in his first national championship game, was all over the officials. John Clougherty, not hyper in his second, walked over and said quietly, "Billy, just calm down." Tubbs did.

The first twenty minutes of this game belong in a time capsule somewhere. Basketball just didn't get much better than this. Kansas was not the least bit intimidated by Oklahoma's press. Rather than pull the ball out at center court after breaking it, the Jayhawks went right to the basket. Since Oklahoma was doing the same thing on every possession, the pace was torrid.

There were omens early on. Newton, trapped by the Oklahoma defense, threw up a reverse prayer and it dropped. Clint Normore, the converted football player, threw up a three-point shot as the forty-five-second clock was running out—and it swished. Keith Harris, zero-for-four against Duke, tossed up a hook as soon as he came into the game and it went in. Lincoln Minor, a forgotten man for the last month, came off the bench (because Brown had to play a lot of people due to the pace) and made a quick steal and two free throws.

Still, nothing was easy for Kansas. Manning picked up his second foul trying to block a King jumper with 10:26 left and had to come out for three minutes. The Jayhawks were making every shot they looked at, but also were turning the ball over. That explained why, with 7:16 left, they had hit 17 of 20 shots from the field but only led 36–35.

On the bench, even though his team was playing wonderfully, Brown was petrified. "We can't play with them like this," he kept saying to his assistants. But the shots were there, they had to be taken and they were dropping. Two straight OU steals gave the Sooners a 39–36 lead, the second a thunderous one by King off a bad Scooter Barry pass. That made 13 turnovers for Kansas. Would the wheels come off?

No. Manning hit a hook shot and Minor made his steal. Dave Sieger, having a remarkable first half with six three-pointers in eight attempts, hit another one. But Newton answered that to make it 43–42. Sieger hit again, Minor tied it. Sieger hit one more and Newton answered. Back and forth they went, quicker, it seemed, than a Ping-Pong ball.

Manning then made the play of the half, stealing the ball from Sieger, driving across the lane on King and flipping the ball in over him as he was going down. Normally impassive, Manning was shaking his fist after that one and Kemper was rocking. That made it 50–48 before Ricky Grace tied it once more. Manning missed a three-pointer at the buzzer and walked off with his hands clasped on the back of his head, angry with himself. He had 14 points and 8 rebounds. It was 50–50. Twenty minutes to decide a championship.

If the players weren't exhausted, everyone else was. The game was reminiscent of Villanova–Georgetown in 1985 when the Wildcats had shot 79 percent to pull one of the great upsets in history. Kansas had shot 71 percent in the first half—and was even.

"We have to slow them down some, guys, you know that," Brown told his players. "If the break is there, I want you to take it, but be prepared to run some time in our halfcourt offense."

They understood. There wasn't much more for Brown to say. They had heard it all. "Twenty minutes," he said simply. "We just need one more great half."

To Manning, that meant him. "If you lose, it's because the best player doesn't play well enough," he said. "I had lost us some games during the year. Now it was down to this. It was my job to make sure we got what we came for."

Once again, the start was not encouraging. After Harvey Grant had hit a jumper to put OU up 52–50, Manning was called for his third foul, a charge, only twenty-five seconds into the half. He would stay in, though. He had to.

The third foul wasn't going to deter Manning. He put Kansas ahead with a rebound basket and hit a double-pump scoop inside to make it 58–54. By now, Oklahoma had dropped its press to a halfcourt trap on most possessions. Kansas went cold briefly. Grace hit a three-pointer and Sieger hit one more. That gave Oklahoma the lead, 61–60.

Blaylock stole the ball from Barry for a lay-up and Sieger stole it from Pritchard. He missed, but King rebounded and scored. It was 65–60 and Kansas looked frazzled. Strangely, though, the game was right where the Jayhawks wanted it. By dropping the press, Tubbs was playing into Brown's hands. Kansas didn't want the racehorse pace that Oklahoma loved. Now, the game was being played at a walk.

Piper hit a jumper to break the Kansas drought and Manning beat the defense with a shoulder dip and roll. He was fouled and tied the game at 65 with 11:33 left. They seesawed to 71 each. Pritchard hit a jumper to make it 73–71 and then Manning stuffed King. Television took a time-out with 4:26 to play. In the huddle, Brown was screaming.

"Look at the clock," he said. "We've got 'em now if we just keep playing like this. They haven't been through this before. We have. Okay?"

Okay. Down came the Jayhawks with a chance to go up by four. Manning took the ball on the right side, drove the middle, found his right hand up against a body, put the ball in his left hand and hit a short hook. It was the shot of the tournament. Kansas led 75–71.

Grace missed. Manning—who else?—rebounded. Piper hit a jumper as the shot clock buzzer went off with 3:05 left. It was 77–71 and, suddenly, it was the Jayhawks' championship to win or lose. Oklahoma didn't quit. Grace cut the lead to 78–75 with fifty-eight seconds still on the clock. Piper tried to inbound to Pritchard. But Blaylock was too quick. He stole the ball and flipped to Grace, wide open for a three-pointer to tie. No good. Manning rebounded and was fouled. He had just missed twice, proving he was human and a little too pumped. Now, still quivering, he missed the free throw. A Blaylock jumper cut the margin to 78–77 with forty seconds left.

Oklahoma called time to set up the press once again. The Sooners were a tired team. Tubbs, who had used his bench effectively all year, had not used it at all in the second half. This was as strange as his decision to drop the press. Brown had gambled, subbing the entire game, and now it had paid off. His team was fresher at the end.

Kansas got the ball inbounds and up the court. The Jayhawks spread the floor and, with the shot clock off, the Sooners had to chase. Finally, with Tubbs screaming at them to foul, Blaylock fouled Scooter Barry. This had not been Barry's best game. He had missed a lay-up, made a bad turnover, and committed a silly foul. But if there is one thing Rick Barry's son can do it is shoot free throws.

There were sixteen seconds left. Tubbs called time to let Barry think about it. When he walked back to the line, Barry was itching to get the ball. He practically snatched it out of Clougherty's hands. The first shot swished. It was 79–77. But the second one was short. Manning and King scrambled after it. One more time, Manning was a tad quicker. He picked up the ball, just as King piled into him. Now the clock was at fourteen seconds.

Throughout this sequence, Ed Manning never moved. He was frozen on the bench, almost afraid to move for fear he might change what was happening on the court. "All I was thinking," he said later, "is 'When is this game going to end?' It just seemed to go on forever."

The end was near. Manning stepped to the line, taking deep breaths to make sure he didn't get overexcited. "Sometimes at the end of a game when he's a little tired he forgets to bend his knees on the foul line," Ed Manning said. "During the last time-out I just reminded him."

Danny Manning remembered. He bent his knees and pushed the shot up. It hit nothing but net. Again, he bent his knees and shot. Again, it was a swish. Kansas led 81–77. Grace raced downcourt and, with Kansas not wanting to foul, quickly hit a lay-up to make it 81–79. Seven seconds were left and Oklahoma used its last time-out.

Piper would inbound again. In his mind, he could still see Blaylock stealing the pass fifty-one seconds and several of Ed Manning's lifetimes ago. When no one flashed open immediately, he called time quickly to avoid a five-second call. Oklahoma was one steal from getting back in the game. Kansas was one pass and two free throws away from finishing it. This time, Brown made certain the ball would get to Manning, ordering a screen for him as he came to meet Piper's pass.

Piper threw the pass, a half-lob, and Manning jumped to catch it. Grant, a half-step behind, fouled him quickly. With five seconds left, the national championship was in Danny Manning's hands. Oklahoma was out of time-outs. If Manning made both shots, even if the Sooners scored, they would be helpless. The clock would run out.

Manning knew all this. "It's over," he told himself. "It's over." Ed Manning, several years older than he had been nine clock seconds earlier, folded his hands as his son walked up to shoot. Brown took off his glasses, wiped his brow, and put them back on. In the stands, Darnelle Manning said a silent prayer for her son.

Kemper Arena, except for the far corner where the Oklahoma fans were trying to make noise, was almost quiet. Everyone was standing. Manning dribbled, looked up and shot. The ball hit the top of the front rim, slid over it—while Ed Manning's heart stopped beating for a split second—and dropped through. It was 82–79. Now, it came down to the last shot of Danny Manning's college career. This was exactly the way he wanted it, the way he had always dreamed it. Like every kid who had ever held a basketball in his hands, Danny Manning had played this scene out thousands of times. *Make this shot and win the national championship. . . .*

This time, Manning didn't need the rim. It was 83–79. The celebration began as Grace threw up one final shot. Manning, playing right to the buzzer, grabbed the rebound and turned around, the ball in his hands as if to say, "Is there anything else I need to do?"

There was nothing. Except jump for joy, fall into Piper's arms and go find his mother. "If Danny plays basketball for twenty years in the NBA and wins ten titles, he'll never feel like he felt that night," Ed Manning would say. "All I could think of was how close he came to leaving and how sad it would have been if we had missed out on this."

It was a poetic ending to a superb basketball game, one worthy of the setting and the stakes. Kansas had achieved one of the most dramatic victories in tournament history, not just on this final night but throughout the nineteen days. They had come a long, long way from taking the court in Lincoln, wondering if they could beat Xavier.

"If we had lost in the first round it wouldn't have shocked me," Brown said. "But right from the beginning it seemed like one of those destiny things, starting with Xavier getting booed because of what they said about Lincoln and us all of a sudden being like a home team. Then all the upsets and us getting to play our last three games against teams that had beaten us before."

It had fallen into place for the Jayhawks. But their victory had little to do with luck. It had to do with grit and perseverance and an extraordinary coaching job by Brown. It had to do with Manning becoming what his coach and father had always pushed him to be, *the* best player. On the final night he had 31 points and 18 rebounds in a memorable performance. Four years after the beginning, he and Brown could part friends, knowing it had all been worth it for both of them.

"You play for him, there are going to be times you want to kill the guy," Manning said later. "But there is no question about his coaching ability. He's the best."

And now Manning was the best, a part of history. The 1988 NCAA Tournament would be known forevermore as "Manning's tournament."

The parties on the last night are generally quiet. Everyone is tired and a lot of people have early planes to catch. The Kansas fans were the exception, of course, staying up well into the night to celebrate. Brown retreated to his room to contemplate his future, changing his mind about whether to go to UCLA or stay at Kansas several times before dawn.

In the press hotel, they showed a replay of the game. It was closing in on 3 A.M. when Manning grabbed the last rebound one more time. Outside, Dick Vitale still wasn't tired. As the screen flickered off, his voice could be heard very clearly.

"So, who is Number One preseason? Illinois? How about Duke? . . ."

The basketball season was officially over. Only 194 days were left until October 15th.

EPILOGUE

The weeks following the end of the 1987–88 college basketball season were almost as hectic as the Final Four. Almost every day, or so it seemed, a new story of major import to the sport broke.

It started two days after the Kansas victory when Lefty Driesell made it official: He was coming back to coaching. He signed a five-year contract at James Madison and hired his son, Chuck, as one of his assistants. "My wife thinks I'm crazy doing this," he said a few days later. "I had a great setup at Maryland and now I gotta go out and get players and work all kinds of crazy hours again."

He smiled. "I couldn't be happier."

There was little doubt of that. The day after Driesell was formally introduced as coach, Miami Coach Bill Foster, an old Driesell friend, was awakened at 6:30 in the morning. It was—you guessed it—the Lefthander. "I need players," Driesell said. "Is there anybody left out there who's any good?"

Lefty was truly back.

There were other changes. Shortly after the Final Four, much to his surprise, Rick Barnes got a phone call. Would he be interested in interviewing for the Providence job? Certainly, Barnes was interested in interviewing. He didn't figure he had any chance of getting the job but there was nothing to be lost by interviewing for a Big East job after just one year as a head coach.

"I never really thought of it as anything but a formality," he said. "I thought someone had thrown out my name and they had a list of like ten people and I was on that list. But then, a couple days after my interview they called me back and asked if I would come up and meet with the president. That was when I said, 'Whoa, this is getting serious.' "

It was serious. Barnes left his second meeting with the Providence people convinced he was going to be offered the job. He had mixed emotions about the situation. On the one hand, this was the Big East, one of *the* prestige leagues in America. On the other hand, he felt a sense of commitment to George Mason and to his boss, Jack Kvancz. "I went to George Mason with the idea of really moving the program into the big time. After this season there was no doubt in my mind that we were going to get it done. There was definitely part of me that wanted to stay and do it."

But Barnes is a pragmatist. Even Kvancz, who desperately wanted him to stay, told him that if the job was offered he had to take it. After his meeting with the president, Barnes got a phone call from Rick Pitino, who had left Providence a year earlier to become the New York Knicks coach. "Do you want this job?" said Pitino, who was working informally as a consultant for Providence. "You have to be prepared to say yes if they make you an offer."

Barnes understood. He talked to his wife, Candy. If this happened it would mean four moves in four years: George Mason to Alabama, Alabama to Ohio State, Ohio State to George Mason, and George Mason to Providence. Tough under any circumstances. With two very young children, even tougher. Candy Barnes understood. This was something her husband had to do.

The offer came on a Wednesday night. Two days later, Barnes was introduced as the new coach. Providence billed him as a southern version of Pitino. He was the same age—thirty-three—that Pitino had been when he took the job and he was enthusiastic and boyish just like Pitino. But Barnes knew that to expect a Final Four team in two years, which was what Pitino had produced, was unrealistic. And yet, in Providence, they often expect miracles. Barnes figured his getting the job was pretty close to being miraculous. Producing the kind of team people were going to expect would be at least as miraculous.

. . .

Jim Valvano stayed at N.C. State. But Charles Shackleford did not. After initially saying that he would return to State for his senior year, Shackleford changed his mind. Given that Shackleford was not exactly a candidate for a Rhodes Scholarship, there was some thinking that he didn't have very much choice about returning. This had happened in 1986 when Chris Washburn had initially announced his intention to return only to learn at the end of the semester that he could not do so. But that wasn't the case with Shackleford. *If* he had gone to summer school he could have returned. He chose not to. Three summers was enough for him.

Shackleford's leaving was a blow to Valvano, although not a fatal one by any means. With Shackleford back, State would have had two potential first-round draft picks playing inside—Shackleford and Chucky Brown—two outstanding sophomore guards in Chris Corchiani and Rodney Monroe, and great depth. Now, defenses would be able to concentrate on Brown inside. Instead of being a top ten team— at least—State would now be a good, solid, not great, team.

In truth, though, this didn't break Valvano's heart. Working with Shackleford had never been easy and he had enough confidence in his coaching ability to believe he would still put a very strong team on the floor. And then there was still the question of motivation. Valvano had been at State eight years. His interest in UCLA was a reflection of his never-ending search for a new challenge. He had won ACC championships and a national championship and had won twenty or more games in six of his eight years at State. He would win more than twenty games, no doubt, again in 1989. But so what?

In late April, on the road to make yet another $8,000 speech, Valvano woke up in the middle of the night pouring sweat, his chest pounding. As it turned out, he was just overtired. But it was enough of a scare to convince him to cancel most of his May speaking schedule and take some time out to go to the beach with his family. At age forty-two, Jim Valvano was rich, famous, and confused.

Larry Brown was not all that different from Valvano. If Kansas had lost the national championship game to Oklahoma, Brown would have been the coach at UCLA before the week was out. It was, without question, the job he wanted. But with all the celebrating that was going on in Lawrence, Brown just couldn't bring himself to say, in effect, "It's been great, thanks for the memories and the Mannings and we'll see you." Instead, after reaching a verbal agreement with UCLA, he changed his mind and told a packed press conference in Allen Field House that he was staying.

No one was more shocked to hear this news than Ed Manning. He had assumed almost since the last strand of net had been cut in Kansas City that Brown would be moving to Los Angeles and he would be going with him. "When he said, 'I'm staying at Kansas,' I almost fell over," Manning said. "I thought the deal was done."

If UCLA had been willing to wait a week, it would have had Brown. But having been publicly rejected in one form or another by Valvano and Mike Krzyzewski, UCLA wanted to get the announcement done and introduce the new coach right away. Brown simply couldn't deal with that. "It was a no-win situation," he said when it was over.

In truth, it was a no-lose situation. If he stayed at Kansas, Brown would be staying in a place where he had been a hero *before* the national championship. Now, with the banner that would hang in Allen Field House, his future there was assured. Sure, Manning would be gone, but with the national title in his portfolio, Brown's chances of recruiting top players would be increased greatly. If he had gone to UCLA, there would have been a major rebuilding job to do (if you can rebuild anywhere, it is at UCLA). Either way, Brown was in a good situation.

Naturally, he saw it the other way. Either way, he was missing out on something. It may be that coaches simply have to think there is something else out there for them to do or they can't go on. In leading Kansas to the national title, Brown had done a coaching job that would be talked about for decades. It was something to savor and enjoy. He did just that—for two months. Then the San Antonio Spurs waved huge dollars at him—$3.5 million for five years—and Brown was packing again, searching once more for that elusive perfect job.

As for Danny Manning, his NCAA performance erased any doubt about his being the No. 1 pick in the draft. Some had wondered if he didn't have a small dose of Ralph Sampson Disease—amazing talent, but no heart—but after the NCAAs, that question was answered forever. Manning spent a good part of April running around the country collecting awards. He was gracious and patient and acted as if each award was the most important thing that had ever happened to him. But by the time he collected the final award in New York on April 20, he sighed and said, "I'm glad this is the last one."

He had done everything he wanted to now. He would get his degree in May, he had won the national championship and proven he was as good as they had said he was in high school. He had stepped forward as the leader when he had to and at the same time had never been separated from his teammates by his ability. He had fought often with Brown, thought terrible things about him, and was delighted to look ahead and not see him in his future. But the two men parted friends, each understanding what the other had done for him.

"Without Coach Brown, I wouldn't be the player I am today," Manning said.

"Without Danny, I wouldn't ever have coached a national championship team," Brown said.

Enough said.

When Paul Evans walked out of the locker room in Lincoln after Pittsburgh's loss to Vanderbilt, he knew that Charles Smith and Demetrius Gore would not be back. He also knew there was a possibility that Jerome Lane would also not be back, that he would skip his senior year to turn pro. He did exactly that.

That specter did not frighten Evans, even though he knew that was an awful lot of talent to lose in one year. Smith, Gore, and Lane were the last of Pitt's old guard, products of the Roy Chipman regime. Chipman had recruited lots of talent, but it had been spoiled, undisciplined talent.

Even with the Big Three gone, Evans believed he had the program on the right track. He loved the four freshmen who had played extensively in '88 and felt that they would form the nucleus of teams he could coach to the next level in the future. In Evans's first two years, Pitt had won forty-nine games, a Big East regular season title, and been to two NCAA Tournaments. Those were impressive numbers. But Evans wanted more. He had come to Pitt because he believed he could win a national championship there. With Bobby Martin, Sean Miller, Darelle Porter, and Jason Matthews, he thought he had the kind of cornerstone class that would lead to a Final Four in the near future.

It had not been an easy year for Evans, though. The feud with

Massimino, the run-in with Thompson, and his new image were not comfortable for him. At Navy, his relationship with the media had been excellent. After Smith and Gore mouthed off in Lincoln, saying that Evans had been guilty of not telling them to foul on the last play of regulation, Evans blamed the media for goading them into their comments. This was not an encouraging sign. Evans is an extremely talented coach—even Massimino would concede that—but he needed to find a lower key to work in, one that would be less confrontational and more like the Evans who had coached for six years at Navy and won games and friends all at the same time.

Pitt would be a young team in 1988–89 with much lower expectations than the previous season. That would mean less attention and less pressure for at least one season. That might be exactly what Evans and his program needed.

Things were much more sanguine at Villanova than they were at Pitt. Massimino and his program had come through their crisis and emerged as strong, if not stronger, than ever. In 1987, the record had been 15–16, there had been no NCAA Tournament, and two recruits, Bobby Martin and Delano DeShields, had backed out of verbal commitments—Martin to go to Pitt, DeShields to play baseball. There had also been the Gary McLain fiasco. In 1988, the record had been 24–13, the team had reached the NCAA Final Eight, and a good recruiting class was on the way, with only Mark Plansky and Pat Enright—yes, at last—not returning for 1989.

Massimino, who had felt tarnished and dirtied by the McLain incident, was back at the top of his profession. Once again, people were marveling at how he had gotten the job done with a team that didn't seem to be that talented. "But the thing is," he said, "these kids had talent and heart. If you have that combination, you can't go wrong."

If you have the right leadership. There was no doubt after 1988—if there had ever been any—about Rollie Massimino's ability to lead.

The feud with Evans was, of course, not over. There was still bitterness between the two men but perhaps most of it had been spent in the confrontations of the past season. They had finally managed to execute a postgame handshake after Villanova's 72–69 victory in the Big East semifinals and, simple as that sounded, it was a sign of progress. Maybe the future would produce more progress. Then again, basketball being basketball, maybe not.

After losing to Florida in the Southeast Conference Tournament, Tennessee was invited to play in the NIT. Much to their surprise, the Volunteers were sent on the road to play, at Middle Tennessee. This was about as tough a first-round game as Tennessee could face. Not only was Middle Tennessee at least as talented as they were, but it was a team that wanted nothing more than to beat the Vols who were, after all, the big and powerful state school.

Middle Tennessee did just that, leaving Tennessee with a 16–13 record for the season. It was not a season to treasure by any means, but it was the season Don DeVoe needed. Doug Dickey had told him, "Show me progress," after his second straight losing season in 1987, and DeVoe had done that. Tennessee had finished sixth in a league that sent five teams to the NCAA Tournament, it had a winning record, and it upset Kentucky and Florida late in the season. That was enough to get DeVoe a two-year extension on his contract, leaving him with three years in all. He would have preferred a three-year extension, but under the circumstances, two was just fine.

"This will give us a chance to get the program back where it should be," DeVoe said. "We should have a strong senior class next year. And with Tennessee having such a strong high school senior class, we should be able to put together the nucleus of a team that will take us back where we were a few years ago."

DeVoe had been rehired for two reasons: One, even with the loss of Elvin Brown because of the shoplifting incident and Rickey Clark because of his hand injury, Tennessee had hung in and played well enough to beat good teams late in the season. But beyond that, DeVoe had run the Tennessee program with class for ten years. In a league known for scandals more than schooling, this was no small thing. Doug Dickey had proven that in a sport where many people believed that cheating *does* pay, at least occasionally, doing things the right way can also pay off. It was a message college basketball needed to be sent more often.

Gary Williams's Ohio State team, after not getting an NCAA bid, went all the way to the NIT final, losing in the championship game to Connecticut. That meant a record for the season of 20–13, which was a lot better than Williams had realistically hoped for at the beginning of practice in October.

In fact, ironically enough, the record was identical to Williams's first year at Ohio State, although that season had ended in the second round of the NCAA Tournament (and, as a result, was more impressive). But what was really important was that Williams had hung on until the cavalry arrived. In October, he would have six new players in uniform— the two Proposition 48 freshmen of '87–88 and the future Ohio State class of 1992, one he believed would be great. The only down note was that point guard Mark Baker did not meet Proposition 48 and would sit down his freshman year.

As always, having coached a team without much talent to more victories than had been predicted, Williams's name kept popping up in connection with other jobs. Rutgers was interested at one point but, even though the money might be huge, Williams wanted to stay and coach the players he had recruited. The Charlotte Hornets, an NBA expansion team, called. This was flattering, but Williams felt the same way about not leaving. He also knew that he probably was not emotionally equipped to handle losing sixty games a year, which was inevitable coaching a new team in the NBA. Kansas, after Brown's resignation, also called. Williams was tempted once more, but once more stayed put.

Williams would stay at Ohio State and he would spend the summer looking forward to coaching his new players, but also thinking about James Jackson, the "A-men," senior-to-be guard. He knew that in two years he had put together most of the pieces of the puzzle to bring Ohio State back to prominence. The 1988–89 season would be a first step in that direction. But once again, recruiting would be vital. Sign James Jackson in the fall and the winter would probably seem easy. Williams knew that better than anyone.

"When I came here, people wondered if I could recruit," he said. "I think I've shown them so far that I can. But the key is to put the whole package together. Get the players who can play the way you want to coach, then put them on the floor and really be able to go after people. That's what I want. I want to go out on the floor against *anybody* and feel like my team can really get after people and win the game. We're getting close to that, but there's still a lot of work to do to get it done."

If work was the key, there wasn't much doubt that Gary Williams would get it done.

For Todd Mitchell, Troy Lewis, and Everette Stephens, the doing had ended for them that night in Pontiac against Kansas State. For them, there would be many happy memories of Purdue. Lewis and Mitchell would graduate on time, Stephens a semester behind. When they played their last home game against Minnesota, Mitchell had told the crowd, "I really wasn't sure if Purdue was the right place when I first came here. I've been through a lot of ups and downs, we all have. But if there's one thing I'm sure of, it's that I made the right choice, no matter what happens the rest of the way."

The rest of the way had not turned out the way the three seniors had hoped. They had finished their Purdue careers with a record of 96–26. Included in that were two Big Ten titles and four NCAA bids. But their record in NCAA play had been 3–4. No trips to the Final Four; in fact, no trips beyond the Sweet Sixteen.

"I think years from now when we all get together, we'll remember all the good things and the good times first and foremost," Lewis said. "There's no question we had a great four years and we did a lot of great things that we should be proud of. But it will always bother me a little that we never put it all together in March. That's what this season was all about. We said it all along, we didn't make any bones about it, so there's no use making excuses for it now. It's funny, for all the fighting we did with Coach Keady I think the thing I regret the most is that we let him down."

Keady didn't really feel that way. "It's disappointing as hell, because we all worked so hard to get to the Final Four," he said. "But I don't have any regrets about those seniors. All they've ever done is bring us compliments. Anyone who has ever dealt with them has always come back to me and told me what class young men they were. I know we lost a ball game we wanted like hell to win. But no one will ever be able to tell me that Troy Lewis, Todd Mitchell, and Everette Stephens aren't winners."

Case closed.

Billy King's last game was also a disappointment. It should be remembered that 99 percent of the seniors who play college basketball lose their last game—unless they play for a team so poor it cannot make postseason play and they happen to win their last game in an abysmal regular season. Ninety-six teams were good enough to make postseason play in 1988. Only two—Kansas in the NCAAs and Connecticut in the NIT—won their last games.

Nonetheless, King was baffled by his team's poor performance against Kansas in the Final Four. He had been so convinced the team was ready to play, then the Blue Devils had come out flat and fallen too far behind to catch up. King had wanted for *his* team, the one he and Kevin Strickland captained, to surpass the great team of 1986 that had played for the national championship. The only way to do that would have been to win it all. The Blue Devils had come pretty close, going 28–7 and winning the ACC title and the East Regional.

"It feels kind of funny to realize it's all over, but I think I would have felt that way if we had won," he said. "I knew all year that this was it and I think I played that way. I hope I get a shot to go to an NBA camp [King did get a last-minute invitation to the Olympic trials but was cut early] but I really don't expect to be playing ball next year. I've taken the approach all year that this was it for me as a basketball player. Where there's an ending, there's a beginning. I'm looking forward to whatever I begin next year."

With his degree in political science, his articulate manner, and his personality, King had job offers even before the season was over. He had chances to coach, to go into radio and television, or to teach. He was lucky because he never saw basketball as a be-all and an end-all. "It's just something that I love," he said. "I'll never stop loving it—but I've always known that I can live without it."

He would never have to live completely without it, though. Even after he stopped playing, Billy King would always have the tapes of his games against David Rivers and Mark Macon. And, he would have plenty of stories to tell his children.

While Billy King was coming to the end, Jerrod Mustaf was coming to the beginning. In March, after he had led DeMatha to the D.C. City Title and a 27–3 record, he surprised no one by announcing he would attend the University of Maryland.

The word had been out on the coaching grapevine since December that Mustaf would play for Maryland. He had narrowed his choices back then to Georgia Tech, Howard, and Maryland. He had never taken an official visit to Georgia Tech and, since he had made it clear that he wanted to play for a team that had a chance to be a national championship contender, he wasn't going to Howard. That left Maryland.

One wondered how much this was Jerrod's decision and how much it was his father's. Sharr Mustaf clearly wanted his son to play for a black coach. He defended Bob Wade often even when it appeared there was no defense for Wade. At one point, shortly before Jerrod announced his choice, Sharr Mustaf said, "We have to support people like Bob Wade in the black community. We have so few role models that when we get one, we have to do everything we can to help them and build them up."

There was absolutely nothing wrong with Jerrod Mustaf selecting Maryland. But he had selected Maryland without using three of his official visits; without ever leaving the Washington area for a visit, and in spite of the fact that the Maryland program was clearly in turmoil. Two days before Steve Hood announced he was transferring, Sharr Mustaf, who was friends with Hood's father, said he didn't believe Hood would leave. "Bob Hood's too smart for that," he said. "He knows that Steve hasn't worked hard enough to get more playing time."

Apparently Bob Hood *wasn't* that smart, because Steve Hood transferred to James Madison to play for the man who had originally recruited him at Maryland, Lefty Driesell. That made five players who had left the program in Wade's two years at Maryland. His claim was that they were all Driesell recruits who were malcontents. One month later, Brian Williams, the 6–10 center from California—who had been Wade's key recruit—a cornerstone player, announced he was leaving. Wade, naturally, blamed the media.

But he had Jerrod Mustaf. Exactly who had made that decision was unclear. Or perhaps it was quite clear. "I want him to go to Maryland," Sharr Mustaf said just before Jerrod announced his decision. "But I think he's leaning towards Georgia Tech." If so, it didn't stay that way for long.

Mustaf was not the only one faced with a decision in the spring time. In April, shortly after the college season had ended, the NBA announced it would use three referees at games next season rather than two. One of the first college officials contacted by the league was Joe Forte.

The offer was intriguing to Forte. His dream, as far back as the early 1970s when he first began officiating, had been to work in the NBA. Turning down a chance to work during the 1976 strike had been heartbreaking for him. Now, he had a chance to move up to the NBA at a time when he could honestly say he had done everything there was to do on the college level. His whistle, the Fox40, was selling well enough that he had quit his job in Atlanta to work on it full time.

Part of Forte hated to leave the college game. He had been in five Final Fours in seven years and was always going to draw top assignments. He was still young enough at 42 that if he stayed in college basketball he would no doubt break all the records for Final Four appearances and end up in the college basketball Hall of Fame.

But the NBA meant less work—an average of three games a week as opposed to five or six—and more money. Forte earned about $32,000 during the 1987–88 college season working more than 80 games. In the NBA, the starting salary was closer to $38,000 and someone like Forte would no doubt make more than that. It was tempting.

Forte thought it over, talked to his wife and two children about it and to other officials who had been approached. He talked to his ACC supervisor Fred Barakat. "I told him what Dean Smith tells his players who are thinking of leaving early for the NBA draft," Barakat said. "If the money is there and you think you're ready, leave school. There's no question Joe was ready for this."

That was the bottom line, really. Forte was ready and he wanted a new challenge. He didn't know it that afternoon, but Arizona–Oklahoma was his last college basketball game. There was, however, one last bonus for his college years: Forte was chosen to represent the United States at the Olympics in Seoul. A nice way to climax eleven gratifying years.

David Robinson and Kevin Houston were both a year removed from college. Robinson's future was clear: Play for the Olympic team, finish his commitment to the Navy, and go on to play for the San Antonio Spurs for the small sum of $26 million. That didn't begin to count the endorsements he was piling up even while he was twiddling his thumbs waiting for a chance to play.

Kevin Houston's future was much less clear. But in April, he got what he had been hoping and wishing for ever since he graduated from

West Point: an invitation to the Olympic trials. Public relations was
part of his invitation. So many people had been angered when Houston
was passed over for the Pan American trials the year before that ABA–
USA knew it would be a crucial mistake to leave Houston out again.

Houston didn't care about the reason for his invitation. All he had
wanted was a chance and now he had it. "Whatever happens, I'll go
down swinging," he said. "I've worked as hard for this as I've ever
worked in my life and if I don't make it, it will just be because there
were other guys better than me. I can live with that. I can walk away
and say, 'Kevin, you were good, you did the best you could but you
weren't quite good enough.' At least I won't always wonder what would
have happened if I had the chance. Now, I'll have the chance. That's
all I've ever asked for."

Houston's invitation ended the wondering, but it started the work.
Knowing he was going to the trials, he picked up his practice time,
working for hours and hours on his shot, knowing his ability as a
three-point shooter represented his best chance to make the twelve-
man team out of the eighty-plus players who would be at the trials.

"This is my final chapter as a basketball player," he said. "Anything
after this will be just for laughs or to stay in shape or for the memories.
I knew when I finished college that with the five-year Army commitment my chances to play in the NBA were almost none. This is the
way I want to go out, taking a shot at playing for my country overseas.
Whatever happens, I'll have no regrets." Houston was an early cut. But
he had his chance. It was all he had ever asked.

One year after he left N.C. State, Walker Lambiotte had no regrets
either. His first season at Northwestern had often been frustrating. He
had almost frozen to death more than once and he hadn't been able
to help a 7–21 team that badly needed help. But he was through all
of that, his grades were good, and he knew he was an almost certain
starter for 1988–89.

"In some ways I expected it to be tougher than it was," he said. "I
like the school, I like the people, I feel like I fit in with the players and
I really like the coaches. I've really got nothing to complain about. All
I can say is, I can't wait for October fifteenth."

That was a sentiment Lambiotte shared with many people. October
15 would bring many new questions and, already, the NCAA had

another scandal to deal with. A package mailed from Kentucky Assistant Coach Dwain Casey to a recruit in California, Chris Mills, had been accidentally opened in transit and $1,000 in cash had fallen out. Kentucky, of course, claimed it had no idea how the money got in the package. It put out all sorts of statements, somehow involving an office secretary, implying that the courier company might be guilty somehow, and implying that a frame-up might have taken place.

A representative of the courier company may have responded best to all of Kentucky's various excuses when he said, "If you believe that, then you believe in Santa Claus and the Easter Bunny."

Of course, two months earlier the NCAA had proven that it *did* believe in Santa Claus and the Easter Bunny—and maybe the Wizard of Oz, too—when it had let Kentucky off the hook in the aftermath of the Lexington *Herald–Leader* stories detailing payoffs to at least twenty-six Kentucky players. Now, the NCAA was faced with Kentucky being caught once again red-handed and, naturally, denying, denying, denying.

What would it do? Rex Chapman, the Boy King, decided not to wait for an answer. On May 13th, he announced he was passing up his last two years of eligibility to turn pro. Chapman insisted the Mills investigation had nothing to do with his decision. If you believe in that then you believe in Santa Claus and . . . you know the rest.

Steve Kerr would also turn pro in 1988. His college career had not ended the way he dreamed or imagined. In a perfect world, Kerr would have finished his college career by hitting the winning shot for Arizona in the national championship game. But instead, he had shot horrendously in the national semifinals and Arizona had lost to Oklahoma.

"I will always blame myself for us losing that game," Kerr said. "People keep coming up to me and saying it wasn't my fault but I really don't believe that. I really think and I always will that if I had shot well we would have won that game. What people don't understand is I can live with it. It will always bother me a little bit but that's all. I didn't choke or anything, I just had a bad shooting day. I'm a shooter and my shot was off at the worst possible time.

"Because of what's happened to me in my life, I'm not going to brood for that long about a college basketball game, even the most important one of my life. Was I down? Absolutely. Pissed off? You bet.

But done in? No way. I've bounced back from losses a whole lot bigger than that one."

Which is, of course, the point. Losing a game always matters—up to a certain point. But in a larger sense, Arizona's loss to Oklahoma didn't matter at all. Nothing could ever change what the Wildcats in general and Kerr in particular had accomplished. Quite literally, Kerr and his teammates had reached into an entire city's soul and brought out everything that was good in people. They had made themselves part of Tucson and Tucson part of them.

That was never more evident than the day the team returned home. At the airport, the Wildcats were greeted by a huge throng and were escorted quickly to convertibles—one for each player—for a parade through downtown. They lined the streets of Tucson to cheer for this team because one loss couldn't wipe out the feeling people had for them. "It was pretty amazing," Kerr said. "But when we got to the football stadium, that's when I really couldn't believe it."

There were thirty thousand people in the football stadium, sitting in sweltering ninety-degree heat, waiting to welcome the team back. Then, and only then, did Kerr really understand the depth of feeling people had for him and for his team. "They didn't just care when we won, they cared, period," he said. "What we had done mattered to them and one disappointment didn't change it. It's really hard to put into words the way I felt when I looked up and saw all those people waiting for us."

Kerr told the people that and he also told them that he was thinking of trying out for quarterback on the football team in the fall because he liked the way cheering sounded in the football stadium. As he spoke, looking at the McKale Center—which is adjacent to the football stadium—Kerr knew the feeling he had standing there was one he would remember long after he had stopped playing basketball.

All season, he had said over and over again, "I want to enjoy every minute of this because I know it will never be like this the rest of my life."

He was right. What makes college basketball different from the pro game is that no one plays more than four years. The names and faces always change. No one ever signs an extension on their contract because when your time is up, that's it, you move on. Some move on to play more basketball, most do not. But all of them have memories, and the best of them *provide* memories.

In that same perfect world where Steve Kerr wins the national championship, he is what college basketball is all about. Unfortunately, in real life college basketball is, all too often, cash stuffed in the mail and a governing body that believes in the Easter Bunny. It is about broken dreams and coaches who make promises they can't and won't keep.

But the game not only survives, it prospers. It does so because of Billy King and because of Danny Manning and because of the Purdue seniors. And others like them. And because of Steve Kerr. Perhaps no one in the long history of college basketball went through more during a college career and refused, time and again, to allow himself to be beaten. He dealt with rejection before he ever played a college game and then the unspeakable tragedy of his father's assassination, the heartbreak of his knee injury, and the sickness at Arizona State. Never once did Steve Kerr feel sorry for himself. More remarkably, he never let anyone else feel sorry for him. He made college basketball better by being a part of it. He was special, so the game he played was special too.

He became a hero in Tucson not because of the way he played, but because of the way he lived. Always, the people of Tucson wanted to give Steve Kerr something. Always, he gave back. In the end, the trade they made was a fair one: Tucson gave its heart to Steve Kerr. And he gave his heart to Tucson. In the process, Steve Kerr made everyone who came to know his story smile. He also made them laugh. And cry.

His team lost its last basketball game. But no one has ever defeated Steve Kerr.

ACKNOWLEDGMENTS

I am beginning to think, now that I am a veteran of two books, that the most difficult thing to do in writing one is make certain you thank all the people without whom you could not have finished the project.

To begin at the beginning, this book would not have happened without my editor at Villard, Peter Gethers, and my agent Esther (Sally UConn) Newberg. They were the first ones to believe this concept could work and they were the ones who bolstered me throughout the writing process.

Once again, the powers-that-be at *The Washington Post* were patient and helpful in giving me the time I needed to run around the country and do the reporting. Executive Editor Ben Bradlee and Assistant Managing Editor Bob Woodward were the two men responsible for this and I am forever grateful to them for their understanding. I would also like to thank Managing Editor Leonard Downie, Sports Editor George Solomon, his assistants, Leonard Shapiro, Sandy Bailey, and O. D. Wilson. Special thanks at the paper go to people like Kevin Coughlin, Elizabeth Cale, David Levine, and Ben Gieser, who took care of a million details I could not have done without. I would also be remiss if I did not give an extra thank-you to Joyce Manglass, who arranged every airplane, every hotel, and every car, and let me cry on her shoulder throughout.

Then there are friends and family, too numerous to list, but I'll try anyway. These are the people who put up with more than any friend should ask: Keith and Barbie Drum, Juan Williams, Dick (Hoops) Weiss, Michael Wilbon, Steve and Lexie Barr, Dave Kindred, Ken Denlinger, Bob and Anne DeStefano, David Maraniss, Jackson Diehl, Ray Ratto, Tom and Linda Mickle, Tony Kornheiser, John Caccese, John Hewig, Sandy Genelius, Lesley Visser, Bud and Mary Lou Collins, Pete Alfano, Susan Kerr, Norbert (noted sports authority) Doyle, Richard Justice, Sally Jenkins, Donald Huff, Larry Meyer, Martin Weil, Gene Bachinski, Bill Gildea, Mark Asher, Rich Pearson, Rick Brewer, Jeff Neuman, Lenis Edwards, and Jack Ketcham. My family can never receive enough thanks. My mother and father are always there when I need anything and my sister Margaret and my brother Bobby are everything an older brother could ask for and more.

Last, but certainly not least, are the people who made this book: the players and coaches who gave remarkable amounts of time and understanding to what I was trying to do. The coaches: Rick Barnes, Larry Brown, Don DeVoe, Paul Evans, Rollie Massimino, Jim Valvano, Gary Williams, and Dale Brown. And the players: Kevin Houston; Steve Kerr; Billy King; Walker Lambiotte; Troy Lewis–Todd Mitchell–Everette Stephens; Danny Manning and his parents, Ed and Darnelle Manning; David Robinson. Also the high school recruits: Jerrod Mustaf, his father Sharr Mustaf, and DeMatha Coach Morgan Wootten; Chris Jent; Eric Riley; Keith Tower, and their families.

At each school, there were others whose help was invaluable, including countless sports information directors and their staffs. A few stood out because of the extra time they gave me when I needed it: Mark Adams at Purdue; Butch Henry and Tom Duddleston at Arizona; Doug Vance at Kansas, a heroic figure if there has ever been one; Craig Miller at Villanova; and George Mason Athletic Director Jack Kvancz.

Believe it or not, there are many others who should be thanked, including Bob Knight. After all, *A Season on the Brink* led to *A Season Inside*. No one understands that better than I do.

JOHN FEINSTEIN spent eleven years with *The Washington Post.* His first book, *A Season on the Brink,* spent twenty-five weeks on *The New York Times* best seller list, fourteen of those weeks at No. 1. He has also written for *Sport, The Sporting News, Inside Sports,* and is currently a special contributor to *Sports Illustrated.* His stories have appeared in five editions of *Best Sports Stories,* and he has won nine U.S. Basketball Writers awards. He is a 1977 graduate of Duke University, which he attended during the only four seasons in which the school finished last in the ACC in basketball.

Mr. Feinstein lives in Bethesda, Maryland, and Shelter Island, New York, with his wife, Mary Clare.